THE LONDON
UNITED TRAMWAYS

Volume One, Origins to 1912

Car No. 336 with another standing at the temporary terminus outside the 'Duke of Wellington' public house at New Malden, before the opening of the extension to Raynes Park. (Photo: LUT)

Cover Picture –
A procession of four cars standing outside Garrick's Villa led by No. 51 on a festive occasion, probably the August 1905 "tea party" in the Villa grounds for the wives and children of LUT staff. (Courtesy: John Sheaf)

The London United Tramways

Volume One, Origins to 1912

by

C. S. SMEETON

Published in London by

THE LIGHT RAIL TRANSIT ASSOCIATION
13A The Precinct, Broxbourne, Herts. EN10 7HY
in association with
THE TRAMWAY AND LIGHT RAILWAY SOCIETY

1994

Printed by W. J. Ray & Co. Ltd., Warewell Street
Walsall, West Midlands WS1 2HQ.

CONTENTS

MAPS

FOREWORD

by G L Gundry

I have been invited to write an introductory note about the London United Electric Tramways, to give them their full title, generally shortened to London United. My chief qualifications for the task is that these were the first trams I ever saw or rode on. I travelled on the LUT to and from school twice daily each way for some years, so I knew the system well and almost grew up with it. I should, perhaps, add that I really only knew a part of it, the lines which later formed the basis of the trolleybus scheme in 1931.There were many other parts of the LUT which I only knew of by hearsay or from the large coloured metal maps that were displayed at busy stops and on tramway offices and buildings.

The LUT was a large system, extending far beyond the boundaries of London and its suburbs. Uxbridge was a country town with a market, separated from built-up areas by large stretches of open country. Even so, the plans were for an even larger network, and the ultimate target was Maidenhead, which is not even in the former London Transport area! Other towns that were to be served included Staines, Sunbury, Esher and Epsom. Nearly all these proposed routes were extensions of existing ones in the neighbourhood of Kingston-on-Thames, and the depot at Fulwell would have housed the cars for the extensions. Indeed, in the literal sense it did so, for the cars were bought to meet future requirements and were far in excess of daily needs.

All these far-reaching projects were the work of one man, the guiding genius of this and some other tramays, Sir James Clifton Robinson. He was an enthusiast for electric trams when many of the authorities in London regarded the electric tram as something to be fought tooth and nail. Sir Clifton gave London its first electric street trams, which commenced operation in 1901 from Shepherds Bush and Hammersmith to Ealing, Southall and Kew Bridge. He had to pay the penalty of the pioneer everywhere in overcoming prejudice and opposition, and even had to go to the extent of issuing his own free newspaper to influence local opinion and explain the advantages of the new form of transport.

In those early days, all the cars were open-topped except the last forty cars bought, type T, which were top-covered with open balconies, These opened the routes in Kingston, but soon withdrew elsewhere. After a while, top covers were added to many of the other cars but without any glazed windows at the sides, the openings being closed by spring blinds which could be pulled down when it rained. The habit of youthful schoolboy passengers (including the present writer) of running them up and down continuously, shortened their lives and after these blinds were written off some windows were glazed but others were left to let in the elements.

In the early days the cars were quite luxurious inside. They had cushions and curtains, in contrast to most London trams which had wooden seats downstairs as well as up. The blue cars which ran in Kingston had blue cushions with a red flower pattern, while the red cars which ran from Shepherds Bush and Hammersmith to Hounslow and Hampton Court had red cushions with a blue or black pattern. The white cars – the original cars in the Ealing and Southall area – had cushions and curtains of golden russet. Later in life the cushions disappeared, leaving woven rattan seating, of the type once used on the Tubes and the District Railway. It was better than wood, but not so comfortable or attractive as the cushions. The white colour scheme was later discarded, and in the 1920s the red livery became standard for all LUT cars.

Another development about the same time was the introduction of conductorless cars for one-man working. The first of these, No 341, was a four-wheel car, a rebuild of one of the Metropolitan Electric company's cars used for the Alexandra Palace routes. The car ran experimentally in Kingston, closely shadowed by the next car on the service, while passengers fumbled for money, paid their fares, got their change and so on. Later one route, the Boston Road line from Brentford to Hanwell, was worked exclusively by one-man cars. The additional cars used here were LUT double-deckers cut down to single deck and provided with rear exit operated by a treadle plate in the floor. The only time I rode in one of these cars, a passenger boarded with a large crate which he dropped heavily on the plate for the other direction of running. Brakes went on, circuit breakers blew, and there was general excitement while the driver asked him to move it!

Very little was done in the way of modernising the fleet, except for the last forty, Nos 301 to 340, of the top-covered T type. These had the so-called "Pullman" seating with transverse seats on the lower deck, as well as higher-speed motors and magnetic track brakes. A few earlier cars were rebuilt on similar lines, with balconies to the top decks, while others just had new motors. But the big fleet of trams bought to serve the future extensions, were never all needed and in consequence the fleet dwindled; some cars were broken up, and others were sold to three other tramways, Walthamstow, Erith and Blackpool. By the time London Transport took over, the LUT had only 156 cars in all out of the original 340.

One plan which seemed promising was to upgrade much of the long Uxbridge route to reserved track, with fast running, making use of the new Feltham cars, an advanced design of large double-decker evolved by the Metropolitan. However, traffic did not develop enough, and the idea was abandoned. It would not have been difficult, as in places a new road had been made on another formation, leaving the old road with the trams which could easily have been converted to reservation.

The last major service development was the through running of LCC cars from the Embankment, via Wimbledon, to Kingston and Hampton Court. This service ran on Saturday afternoons and Sundays only, in summer only. The big LCC cars were far faster than the ancient Y and Z cars that were working the LUT part of the route, although they could not give of their best – there just weren't enough volts in the LUT wires for the 120 hp LCC cars, which were noticeably livelier on their own metals. The service was, however, a success and a boon to the public, but it was ended in 1931 when the routes in Kingston were changed to trolleybuses.

It is interesting to speculate on the course of transport history if the motor bus had not developed as it did, and if the local authorities in the area had awoken earlier to the benefits of public transport instead of opposing it. The tramway empire imagined by Sir Clifton Robinson might have become a reality, with blue (or red) trams in Maidenhead or even beyond. Whatever the outcome, the London United Electric Tramways made a very big contribution to the development of the areas they served, and the traffic they handled at Bank Holidays and similar times of pressure would have been unthinkable with the small motor buses of the pre-1920 era. The LUT should be remembered with gratitude for all the benefits it brought to the population it served.

G.L. Gundry

INTRODUCTION

The London United Tramways, genenally referred to in this book as the LUT, was the first electric street tramway system in the greater London area to be worked from a fixed power source. Earlier essays in electric traction had involved battery-driven cars, which proved to be uneconomic, or of operation on private land, exemplified by a short-lived line of 1898-99 in the grounds of Alexandra Palace. By the turn of the century, experience in British provincial cities had shown that under almost all conditions the overhead trolley system was the most reliable and economic method of transmitting electric power to a moving tramcar, and this system was adopted throughout the areas in Middlesex and Surrey which the LUT aimed to serve.

Aquisition of the decrepit horse tramways of the West Metropolitan Tramways Co. by the new London United Tramways Ltd., in 1894 marked a turning point in the provision of public transport facilities in the London area. The White family of Bristol, who became the owners of the old system, and James Clifton Robinson, the Engineer and Managing Director of the new company, who together had earlier begun electrification of the Bristol tramways, rehabilitated the existing WMT lines as a temporary measure pending their electrification and extension. Owing to opposition by the London County Council and the Authorities responsible for the geomagnetic observatory at Kew, the first LUT electric trams were prevented from leaving their depots for nearly a year. There then followed sereral years of expansion, as the LUT electric lines were extended to Uxbridge, Hounslow, Hampton Court, Kingston and Wimbledon, far beyond the limits of the former horse tramways. Even so, the full scheme was never implemented.

Publication of the work was postponed a few years ago when it was learned that hitherto unknown material from records of the White family, the London United Tramways and James Clifton Robinson had become available to researchers. The results are included in this history. The chapters which describe these events are arranged in geographical sequence, followed by specialist material on rolling stock and fixed installations. This volume therefore, contains much information previously unseen, especially between the years 1893 and 1910.

The second volume, taking the story from 1913 to 1933 will deal with the Great War period, relations between the LUT and the London County Council, financial matters, routes and services, tickets and fares, depots and works, remotoring and rehabilitation of the track and rolling stock, the trolleybuses and the new "Feltham" cars of 1931. Chapters on road and rail competition, proposed rebuilding schemes and sections dealing with works cars, staff conditions, author's acknowledgements, biographies covering the post-war period and bibliography will complete the history.

In its presentation, this book follows closely the scheme proposed by Mr. J.H. Price for my earlier books on the Metropolitan Electric Tramways. Owing to ill-health, Mr. Price was unable to complete his work as production editor for this volume, and Mr. E.R Oakley has kindly undertaken to continue with this. I am most grateful to both.

This work does not supersede the earlier book on the same subject by Mr. Geoffrey Wilson, having been compiled largely from sources which have become available to researchers only during the last twenty years. A high proportion of its content represents these new discoveries, and the story that emerges is complex but fascinating.

Cyril S. Smeeton,

Ambergate, Spring 1994.

ABBREVIATIONS IN THE TEXT

ac	alternating current
BET	The British Electric Traction Company Ltd.
BoT	Board of Trade
BTH	The British Thomson-Houston Company Ltd.
BWEC	The British Westinghouse Electric & Mfg. Co. Ltd.
CLR	Central London Railway
dc	direct current
ft	feet (units of length)
GE	The General Electric Company, Schenectady, USA
GEC	The General Electric Company Ltd., Witton, Birmingham
GWR	Great Western Railway
hp	horse-power
in	inches (units of length)
ITC	Imperial Tramways Company Ltd.
lb	pounds (units of weight)
lb^2	pounds per square inch
lb/yard	pounds per yard
LCC	London County Council
LER	London Electric Railway
LGOC	London General Omnibus Company Ltd.
LPTB	London Passenger Transport Board
LRTJ	Light Railway & Tramway Journal
£sd	pounds, shillings and pence (UK currency to February 1971)
LSWR	London and South Western Railway
LTAC*	London & Home Counties Traffic Advisory Committee
LTE	London Transport Executive
LUER	London United Electric Railways
LUT	London United Tramways Ltd.
MBC	Metropolitan Borough Council
MBW	Metropolitan Board of Works
MCC	Middlesex County Council
MDR	Metropolitan District Railway
MIEE	Member of the Institution of Electrical Engineers
mile/h	miles per hour
MTOC	The Metropolitan Tramways & Omnibus Company Ltd.
NMT	The North Metropolitan Tramways Company
RE	Royal Engineers
SCC	Surrey County Council
SESB	Southall, Ealing & Shepherds Bush Tram Railway Company Ltd.
SMET	The South Metropolitan Electric Tramways & Lighting Co. Ltd.
T&RW	Tramway & Railway World
UCC§	The Union Construction & Finance Co. Ltd.
UDC	Urban District Council
UEC	United Electric Car Company Ltd.
UERL	Underground Electric Railways of London Ltd.
WMT	West Metropolitan Tramways Company
yd	yards (units of length)

* The London Traffic Advisory Committee appointed by the Minister of Transport was re-titled London and Home Counties Traffic Advisory Committee on 1 January 1925

§ Union Construction Company; name changed 4 February 1929

CHAPTER ONE

THE SOUTHALL, EALING & SHEPHERDS BUSH TRAM RAILWAY CO. LTD.

Numerous attempts to establish tramways in West London and its environs were made from the year 1865. Some companies obtained powers which were not exercised, owing mainly to inability to raise capital, and some schemes failed either to obtain powers or capital, while one promoter obtained powers and actually constructed part of an authorised line, which, however, was never completed or put to any use.

The forerunner of all tramway operation in the area which became the preserve of the London United Tramways was the Southall, Ealing and Shepherds Bush Tram Railway Company, which was incorporated under the Companies Acts on 12 May 1870 with authorised share capital of £25,000 in one pound Ordinary Shares. Some initial capital was subscribed by local residents and businessmen, mainly in the Acton area by the Spring of 1871, and the remainder was offered to the public in a prospectus issued on 22 April. The directors were Lord William Lennox (Chairman); Alexander B. Brown, FRAS; T.A. Masey, FRGS and Matthew Newman. Lord William Lennox was a son of the Duke of Richmond and Gordon. The Secretary was J.W. Thomas and the Engineer George S. Billington. Billington was a member of an old Acton family of businessmen, where his memorial was, until redevelopment in later years, a street named Billington Place. The company's registered office was initially at 1, Circus Place, Finsbury Circus, London, EC and was transferred to another address following a change of Secretary in 1874. Of the £25,000 authorised share capital £4,659 had been subscribed by 31 December 1871.

The main object for which the company was incorporated was the construction and working of a tramway between the centre of Southall and the West London Railway Company's station at Shepherds Bush, wholly in the county of Middlesex (the county of London having not then come into existence). The route was through Hanwell, Ealing and Acton and the distance between the two termini was 6.912 miles. The plans deposited in Parliament on 30 November 1870 show that the line would commence at a point midway between the Black Horse and Red Lion public house in High Street, Southall and continue to Shepherds Bush as single line but with one loop, in Acton Vale, where the Old Tollgate is shown on the plans as lying in the centre of the road with the line forming the loop on either side. The Tollgate was situated immediately facing the end of the present-day Bromyard Avenue. It was stated in the company's prospectus that an "on and off" system of rails would be used in the construction of the line, which presumably means that cars on the single line could without too much difficulty leave and regain the track by use of a rail ramp when it became necessary to pass a car travelling in the opposite direction.

At this time there were extensive market gardens and nurseries along the route beyond Acton and the company stated that special wagons with wheels which could be used either on the rails or the ordinary road surface would be provided for transport of the growers' produce. The company's promoters had held preliminary discussions with the London Street Tramways Company on interchange traffic over that company's intended line between Marble Arch and Shepherds Bush, but this traffic did not materialise following the failure of the London Street company to obtain the necessary powers.

Passenger services along Uxbridge Road, and indeed on most other roads radiating from London were at this time sparse and the population of the outer suburbs was increasing. In 1867 there was a half-hourly bus service between Acton and London Bridge, the same from Acton to Ealing and twice daily each way to Hanwell, Southall and Uxbridge. These services started from the White Hart Inn at the top of Acton Hill. From the North London Railway station at Acton there was a half-hourly service to the City and buses left Shepherds Bush for the City at 15 minute intervals. The Great Western Railway ran more or less parallel with the Uxbridge Road but its services were infrequent and some of the stations were placed at some distance from populated areas.

From the end of the first quarter of the nineteenth century a movement of the population from central London had begun and this gathered momentum with corresponding increases in the suburbs. It was foreseen that increased, and improved methods of public transport for these new suburban populations would become necessary as, in the main, the new residents in the areas continued to have their workplaces in the central area.

The first shareholders' meeting of the new Southall, Ealing & Shepherds Bush Tram Railway Company took place in October 1870 at which it was stated that the directors had experienced difficulty with their first share placing. George Billington had almost completed his survey of the proposed line and the directors expected "co-operation from the Bank to Notting Hill Company" (The London Street Tramways), which at the time was seeking powers for an extensive network of lines mainly in the areas north of the Thames. The cost of constructing the first section of the SESB from Shepherds Bush to Ealing was estimated at £3,000 and Billington's report indicated that few difficulties would be encountered during the construction work.

The passing of the 1870 Tramways Act resulted in a large crop of applications for powers all over the country, and on the same day that the SESB deposited their plans with the Board of Trade a competing scheme was submitted by the West London Tramways Company, covering the part of the SESB scheme from Shepherds Bush along the Uxbridge Road to the Hammersmith – Acton boundary at Askew Road. At this time the road authority for the parish of Hammersmith was the Fulham Board of Works and on 1 March 1871 this body considered the rival schemes in their area. The Works Committee resolved to approve the SESB scheme if the West London Tramways Company's application for a Provisional Order did not succeed. The latter company did in fact obtain an Order for part of their scheme, which did not include the Uxbridge Road section and consequently the SESB scheme was approved by the FBW.

The SESB Provisional Order was granted by the Board of Trade in 1871 following the consents of the local authorities. The Order was submitted to Parliament for inclusion in a Tramways Orders Confirmation Bill. This Bill was suspended at the start of its passage through Parliament pending resolution of matters arising from the 1870 general tramways Act. Three Metropolitan Tramways Acts of 1869, which were the first to authorise tramways in the Metropolis and were regarded by the overall body for London, the Metropolitan Board of Works, as "experimental" were superseded by amended Acts in 1870. The SESB line was affected by the suspension of the Confirmation Bill because that part of it which lay between the Shepherds Bush terminus and the parish boundary of Hammersmith with Acton lay within the Metropolitan area, and the Metropolitan Board of Works did not wish to approve any tramways in its area additional to the three "experimental" lines until it was proved that tramways were a satisfactory form of transport, although the three amended Acts were not opposed. Following settlement of various matters brought up in Parliament the Confirmation Bill resumed its passage through both Houses and the Order was confirmed in the Metropolitan Tramways Orders Confirmation Act (No. 2) 1873 which received the Royal Assent on 7 July.

Having thus obtained their powers the company took steps to increase their capital and on 5 September 1873 an Extraordinary General Meeting of the shareholders approved a proposal by the directors to double the authorised share capital with an offer of 25,000 new Ordinary shares, confirmed by a further meeting on 2 October. At this meeting the directors' fees were fixed at £300 per annum and the registered office was transferred to Victoria Buildings, Queen Victoria Street, EC.

As soon as the powers were obtained the company sought tenders for construction of the line. The successful bidder was Reid Brothers, a large and well-established firm of public works contractors of Wharf Road, City Road, London, EC. Their tender of £5,500 per mile to construct the line from end to end was accepted and work began at the Shepherds Bush end on 16 December 1873. Reid Brothers' tender was stated to be the lowest price at which any Metropolitan tramway contract had so far been let. The first section was built from Shepherds Bush West London Railway station to a point 900ft east of the Hammersmith – Acton parish boundary at Askew Crescent, near the Princess Victoria public house, a distance of 1.125 miles, consisting of a single line with three passing loops.

Difficulties with the construction came at an early stage. On 18 March 1874 The Fulham Board of Works reminded the company that the margins outside the rails should be 18in wide and paved in granite setts, the space between the rails in hardwood blocks and the rails level with the road surface. On 25 March the FBW repeated their requirements, but their requests were ignored and the work continued. With construction as far as the Princess Victoria public house completed a Board of Trade inspection was arranged to take place on 22 May 1874 by Maj. Gen. Charles Scrope Hutchinson. On arrival at Shepherds Bush Gen. Hutchinson found that no cars had been delivered and he made a second visit on 29 May.

On this visit he found serious faults in the construction. The work had been started without plans having been submitted to and approved by the Board of Trade. The paving was unacceptable, as it extended only to 4in outside the rails instead of the mandatory 18in. The concrete base measured a mere 2in thickness against the minimum requirement of 4in. Gen. Hutchinson told the company's

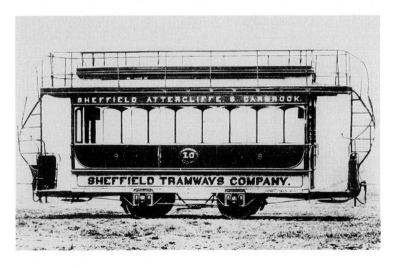

The Southall, Ealing & Shepherds Bush Tram Railway Co. Ltd, began operations on 1 June 1874 with two double-deck cars. They were possibly built by George Starbuck of Birkenhead to the same design as this 1874 Starbuck car for Sheffield.
(Courtesy: Tramway Museum Society)

11

representatives that until the faults were rectified he could not recommend the Board of Trade to issue a certificate of fitness for public use.

Notwithstanding the General's strictures the company opened the line for public service, between Askew Crescent and Shepherds Bush on Monday, 1 June 1874, using two cars. A formal opening ceremony took place on that day at the Princess Victoria public house at Askew Crescent. Two days later, on 3 June the event was celebrated at a luncheon given by the directors at the Princess Victoria at which the Chairman, Lord William Lennox presided. He said that the next section, to Southall, was expected to be opened in March or April, 1875. The guests were mostly local dignitaries and business people, and among them was Charles Light, who had been involved with early horse tramways in America. Lord William Lennox described the cars to be used on the line as "light, commodious and ornamental" and said they would run "at short intervals up to midnight". As it was stated that first and second accommodation was available, presumably the cars, of which there were two, were double-decked and probably built by the Starbuck Company of Birkenhead. Despite exhaustive research no drawing or other illustration of these cars has come to light.

The line was horsed by the London General Omnibus Company, an agreement for the hire of horses and harness was concluded on 29 May 1874, and the depot and stables was on a site now partially occupied by Shepherds Bush Public Library, at 7 Uxbridge Road. In 1874 this site, which was then owned by the Homage Jury of the Manor of Fulham and the Ecclesiastical Comissioners, was rented to a number of occupiers and some were sub-tenants. The site, then unnumbered, was described in the rate books as "land, buildings and stables" and is situated on the south side of Uxbridge Road east of the Hammersmith & City line of the Metropolitan Railway.

The constructional details of the tramway are interesting: continuous longitudinal baulks of fir timber were laid in cast-iron chairs of box form at 5ft intervals, which were in turn spiked to transverse sleepers. The rails, weighing 54lb/yard were made with an extended shoulder on each side which fitted over the rebated edges of the longitudinal sleepers, which were spiked to the chairs with dog-spikes, except at rail joints where there were two spikes each side. Slotted tie-bars held the rails to gauge, which was 4ft 8½in. The space between the rails was paved with wood blocks with a four inch margin of setts outside the rails, which, as noted earlier was contrary to Board of Trade regulations.

On 11 June 1874 Gen. Hutchinson reported to the Board of Trade on his inspection of the line on 29 May. On hearing of the defects and that the line had been opened, the Board, on the same day, ordered the company to cease working the tramway and to comply with the Inspector's requirements. This request was ignored and on 25 June the Board again ordered the company to cease illegal working of the line, adding a warning that the Attorney General was considering taking court proceedings to enforce their demands. On 3 June Gen. Hutchinson was instructed to carry out a further inspection which he did on 2 July. Earlier, on 17 June, the Board of Trade had reinforced their demand with the threat of an injunction against the company in the Court of Chancery. Gen. Hutchinson, reporting on his 2 July visit said that the defects still remained unrectified and the trams were continuing to run. George Billington, the Engineer, on being confronted with this, said that the company had not received notice of an impending inspection or an injunction against the company in the Court of Chancery. The Board of Trade insisted that the latter had been sent on 17 June but the company ignored this.

The Board of Trade officers discussed the position and it was mentioned that the company's secretary, J.W. Thomas, was also secretary of the Great Yarmouth Tramways Company, owned by the East Anglian Tramways Company, and which the latter was attempting to sell without the sanction of the Board. The Board's officers considered that Thomas was "not so satisfactory as is desirable" and the outcome was that the Board yet again demanded, in forthright terms, that the

Southall, Ealing & Shepherds Bush Tram Railway Co.
(4' 8½" gauge)

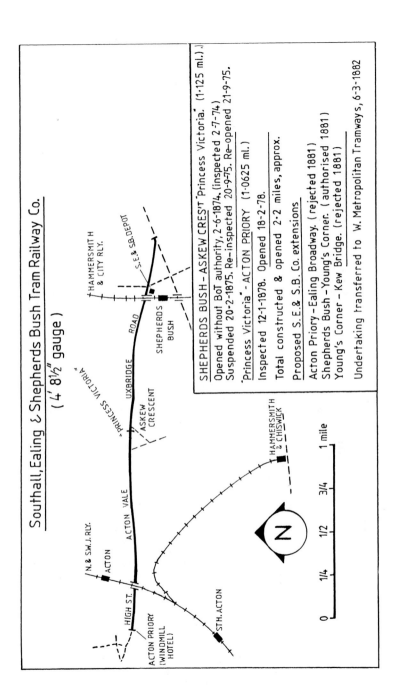

HAMMERSMITH & CITY RLY.

S.E. & S.B.DEPOT

UXBRIDGE ROAD

"PRINCESS VICTORIA"

SHEPHERDS BUSH

ASKEW CRESCENT

HAMMERSMITH & CHISWICK

ACTON VALE

N. & S.W.J. RLY.

ACTON

HIGH ST.

ACTON PRIORY (WINDMILL HOTEL)

STH.ACTON

N

0   ¼   ½   ¾   1 mile

SHEPHERDS BUSH — ASKEW CRES'T "Princess Victoria." (1·125 ml.).

Opened without BoT authority, 2-6-1874, (inspected 2-7-74.)
Suspended 20-2-1875. Re-inspected 20-9-75. Re-opened 21-9-75.

"Princess Victoria" — ACTON PRIORY (1·0625 ml.)

Inspected 12-1-1878. Opened 18-2-78.

Total constructed & opened 2·2 miles, approx.

Proposed S.E. & S.B. Co. extensions

Acton Priory — Ealing Broadway. (rejected 1881)
Shepherds Bush — Young's Corner. (authorised 1881)
Young's Corner — Kew Bridge. (rejected 1881)

Undertaking transferred to W. Metropolitan Tramways, 6-3-1882

13

remedial work on the SESB track be carried out without delay and operation of the trams ceased. Failing compliance with these demands the Board would activate the injunction against the company. Once again the Board's demands went unheeded and still the cars continued to run.

By 1 August 1874 Thomas, now *persona non grata* at the Board of Trade, had been replaced as Secretary by Henry Kendrick and the registered office of the company had been transferred to 24, Gresham Street, London, EC. A new development was taking place, and on 3 November Kendrick wrote to the Board of Trade saying that a petition for compulsory winding-up of the company had been presented in the Court of Chancery on 4 October by James and Robert Nicol Reid, who had constructed the line but had not been paid for their work. The Court duly made a winding-up order on 7 November and on 3 December an Official Liquidator, James Cooper, was appointed. On the same day an order was made for the sale of the undertaking and an auction was arranged, which took place on 16 April 1875. Meanwhile, the trams had ceased to run on 23 February. The auctioneers. Frank Lewis & Kemp, failed to raise a bid for the property, which consisted of the tramway, the two cars and the company's Parliamentary powers. The auction particulars stated that "the two cars can be seen at the company's premises in Uxbridge Road, Shepherds Bush".

The auction having failed to attract a buyer, the undertaking remained in the hands of the Liquidator. He evidently considered that the line, if completed as far as its authorised terminus, had a greater potential value than in its then incomplete form, and on 26 April 1875 Henry Harris, the Liquidator's solicitor, told the Board of Trade that the Liquidator had entered into a provisional contract with Reid Brothers for them to purchase the undertaking. Reids had undertaken to carry out the remedial work on the track, which would take up to three months, and would require an extension of time to complete the work, the powers for the line being due to expire on 7 July. As an interim measure the Board of Trade on 1 June, granted an extension for one month from 7 July.

Meanwhile Reid Brothers were carrying out the necessary work to rectify faults in the existing work and an inspection was requested on 13 July. Gen. Hutchinson visited the line on 22 July but declined to pass it for traffic as there were still paving defects and the rail edges were sharp. Fulham Board of Works had complained about the paving, and more work was done. On 20 September Gen. Hutchinson once more visited the line, and following a minute inspection he reported "… I find it in fair order … a certificate can be issued". On 21 September 1875 a certificate of fitness was issued under the signature of Henry G. Calcraft covering "the completed portion of the line" i e. from Shepherds Bush to Askew Crescent. The trams re-entered service on the same day, operation of the line was leased to Charles Courtney Cramp for an annual rent of £600 and horses continued to be supplied by the London General Omnibus Company.

At the same time as the extension of time to complete the work on the existing line was granted, the Official Liquidator asked for an extension of time to continue the line on to Southall from Askew Crescent. The Board of Trade sought the views of the local authorities and a public meeting was held in the Acton Assembly Rooms on 5 July 1875. There had been opposition to the line being taken through Acton, mainly on the grounds of the narrowness of the High Street. After a stormy meeting a proposal to support an extension of time to complete the work was agreed.

Gen. Hutchinson conducted an inquiry into the application at the Acton Local Board offices on 29 July. It was stated in evidence that the existing line had been used by over a thousand passengers per day and that Reid Brothers were prepared to complete the line. They had been approved as purchasers of the undertaking on 29 April. £19,000 had been spent on the line so far built and Reids were prepared to carry out the rest of the work for £5,500 per mile. Up to the time the line had closed, on 23 February 1875, working expenses had amounted to £27 and income £40 per week. One objection was that the rails as laid projected above the road surface. The meeting lasted from 11am until 5pm and the views expressed were generally unfavourable to the application.

The *Acton Gazette* on 7 August 1875 carried a leading article in favour of taking the line through the town, and on 11 August Gen. Hutchinson reported on the inquiry to the officers of the Board of Trade. He pointed out that the Liquidator had at the time no power to sell the undertaking to Reid Brothers, and Acton Local Board had objected to the proposal on the grounds of the narrowness of the High Street and "the additional railway accommodation provided in Acton". Hutchinson suggested that subject to the satisfactory completion of a further section of the line as far as Priory Road (then the carriage drive to Acton Priory and now Acton Lane) a further extension of time might be considered, to take the line on to Southall. An alternative suggestion was to grant an extension of time until 31 March 1876 to complete the line as far as Acton and to obtain an Abandonment Order for the rest of the route.

The Board of Trade officers conferred at length and on 19 September 1875 agreed that it would not be advisable to grant any extension of time. There had been powerful opposition to the application – among those objecting had been Baron Lionel de Rothschild, many other influential residents, the Rector of Ealing and the Ealing, Hanwell and Southall Local Boards. The legal difficulty was that an extension of time could be granted only to the promoters, i.e., the Southall, Ealing and Shepherds Bush Tram Railway Company Ltd., and not a purchaser of their undertaking. The tramway would have to be open for six months before it could be sold – "and the tramway means the entire authorised line and not a mere section of it". A number of Acton residents were in favour of the application and had submitted a petition in that vein to the Board of Trade on 29 July.

In the period up to the recommencement of services on 21 September 1875 legal matters of some complexity had occupied the minds of the various parties involved in settling the company's affairs. In the interim the undertaking was in the hands of Reid Brothers on behalf of the Official Liquidator, who was at the time not empowered to sell it for the legal reasons mentioned in an earlier paragraph.

Having failed to obtain extensions of time to complete the then-authorised line to Southall, Reids sought entirely new powers to extend from the Princess Victoria public house through Acton Vale and into High Street, Acton to a point there 25 yards west of the carriage drive to Acton Priory, a distance of 1.062 miles and a little short of the bottle-neck further along the High Street. On 26 October 1875 a deputation of Acton businessmen met Acton Local Board to ascertain if the Board would object to the scheme proposed by Reids. They pointed out that the line as far as the Princess Victoria was now in use with very fair results. Reids deposited plans at the Board of Trade indicating that a double line would be laid throughout. The Local Board had declined to agree with a proposal on behalf of local residents to take the line right through the town on account of the restricted width of the High Street west of the Priory carriage drive. Acton, or Berrymead, Priory was a historic mansion formerly the home of the Duke of Kingston, Lord Lytton and many other notables, and it gave way many years ago to municipal buildings, a bakery and other developments.

The full text of the Shepherds Bush and Priory Road Acton Tramway Order 1876 was published in the *Acton Gazette* on 1 April. The deposited plans show a double line throughout from the Princess Victoria at Askew Crescent, where an end-on connection was made with the existing line. Like the legislation for the first line the Order contained extensive provisions for the carriage of goods and livestock with comprehensive tables of charges for different classes and weights. The principle of first and second class passenger accommodation was retained, with fares being fixed at 3d and 2d respectively for the full journey between Shepherds Bush and Acton. Special workmen's cars were specified, to run not later than 7am or earlier than 6pm at a fare of 1d for the full journey.

The Board of Trade, having heard the comments of the Local Board and other interested parties submitted the Provisional Order to Parliament and it was duly confirmed in the Tramways Orders Confirmation (Bristol, &c.) Act 1876, which received the Royal Assent on 24 July.

The winding-up of the Southall Ealing & Shepherds Bush Tram Railway Company delayed construction of the extension, and during this period the Reids had indicated their interest in purchasing the undertaking then still in the hands of the Official Liquidator. Charles Courtney Cramp, operating the line, was working under the sanction of the Liquidator, who had been appointed by the Court on 3 March 1875. It was at this time that the Reids abandoned their claim for £2,000 owed by the SESB and offered £1,500 for the undertaking. This offer was accepted on 26 April and confirmed by an Order of the Master of the Rolls three days later. Consent of the Board of Trade to the sale was delayed for the reasons mentioned in a previous paragraph and was finally given on 27 November 1877, followed by the approval of the Court of Chancery on 11 January 1878. The final conveyance of the undertaking to Reid Brothers took place on 25 January, the cash consideration being £1,250 which did not include the extension into Acton as Reids had carried out this work on their own account.

During this final phase Reid Brothers were completing construction of the new section and on 8 January 1878 they advised the Board of Trade that the line was ready for inspection. Gen. Hutchinson visited Acton on 12 January and found the new work in good order. The paving was mainly in granite setts and a few defects were being rectified. He approved the line for public service and the necessary certificate was signed by Henry G. Calcraft on 17 January. The line opened for public service on 18 February 1878, giving a continuous end to end mileage of 2.218 miles. Details of the rolling stock are sparse, but it is recorded that two cars originally in service had been increased to three at the time the new section opened. By 1879 four cars were operating.

The passenger service from the opening of the extension was half-hourly, the first car leaving the Windmill public house near the Acton terminus at 7.30am and continuing until 11.30pm. Reid Brothers sought consent from Acton Local Board to erect a depot on land which now forms part of Acton Park, on the north side of Acton Vale and close to the North London railway line. At their meeting on 26 February 1878 the Board refused consent "because it would mean laying tramlines across the footpath".

A local omnibus proprietor, Bollin, operated an hourly service between Acton and Ealing and from 20 May 1878 this was increased to half-hourly and extended east from the centre of Acton to the Windmill, where the trams were met.

The final liquidation of the Southall, Ealing & Shepherds Bush Tram Railway Company Ltd. took place on 28 April 1881 and the company was dissolved on 4 May 1883.

Some of those concerned in the SESB formed the London County Tramway Company Ltd. which proposed to continue the line from Southall to Uxbridge and to construct other local routes. None of this was realised.

Other Tramway Activities of Reid Brothers

The Reid Brothers having obtained the powers and constructed the extension into Acton, which was running regularly and producing reasonable traffic, were in 1880 considering extensions in two directions, in and around the Hammersmith area and westward from the new Acton terminus. Consequently, on 16 November 1880 they deposited plans with the local authorities for an extension of the line at Acton Priory through the town to Ealing Common and on to a terminus at the Ealing Broadway cross-roads, where the Broadway, Spring Bridge Road and High Street met. This line would be 1.918 miles long, mainly single track, but was not constructed owing to opposition by Ealing Local Board.

Shortly afterwards, on 20 November 1880 plans were deposited for another, and more extensive scheme. This provided for a line to commence at the Shepherds Bush terminus and to pass along Goldhawk Road to Young's Corner, a distance of

1.537 miles of mixed double and single track, and to continue westward from Young's Corner through Chiswick to Kew Bridge, terminating on the north side of the bridge outside the Star and Garter Hotel. This section totalled 1.903 miles of mixed double and single track. The Engineer for both these schemes was Joseph Kincaid.

In the event only the Shepherds Bush – Young's Corner line was authorised, by the Shepherds Bush and Hammersmith Tramways Order 1881 confirmed in the Tramways Orders Confirmation (No. 3) Act which received the Royal Assent on 11 August 1881. The line was, however, not constructed by Reid Brothers as they had meanwhile decided to dispose of their tramway interests to a new syndicate which was formed by a company promoter, Henry Osborne O'Hagan, as related in the next chapter, covering the formation and operations of the West Metropolitan Tramways Company.

In Chancery—In the Matter of the Companies Acts 1862 and 1867,

AND

In the Matter of the Southall, Ealing, and Shepherd's Bush Tram Railway Company (Limited).

The Particulars and Conditions of Sale

OF ALL

THE RIGHT AND INTEREST

OF THE

Southall, Ealing, and Shepherd's Bush Tram Railway Company (Limited),

IN THE

SOUTHALL,

EALING, AND SHEPHERD'S BUSH

TRAM RAILWAY,

WITH ALL

The Rails, Plates, Sleepers, and Two Tramway Cars ;

Which will be Sold by Auction, by

Mr. FRANK LEWIS,

(Of the Firm of FRANK LEWIS & KEMP)

The person appointed by the Master of the Rolls, to whose Court the winding up of the Matter is attached,

AT THE MART, TOKENHOUSE YARD, CITY,

On Friday, April 16th, 1875,

At One for Two o'clock precisely, in One Lot.

H. HARRIS,

SOLICITOR,

34A, MOORGATE STREET, E. C.

H. KIMSHEAD's Steam Printing Works, Kennington, S.E.

The announcement of the unsuccessful S.E. & S.B. auction of 16 April 1875.

CHAPTER TWO

THE WEST METROPOLITAN TRAMWAYS

This title was borne by no fewer than three companies from 1878, two of them incorporated as joint stock limited companies under the Companies Acts. The third, a successor of the second was incorporated as a statutory company by an Act of Parliament in 1882.

The first of these was incorporated with limited liability on 14 November 1878 with nominal share capital of £100,000 in ten-pound Ordinary shares. Several distinguished names figure in the list of subscribers, they were Sir Wilford Brett, Chairman of the Sheffield Tramways Company; William Barfoot, Chairman of the Leicester Tramways Company; C.E. Davison, a director of the Wolverhampton Tramways Company; Francis Heseltine, a director of the Swansea Tramways Company; Alexander Wood, Chairman of the Edinburgh Street Tramways Company; Clement Stretton, Lord Mayor of Leicester and William Mousley, a public works contractor. The Engineers were the firm of Nimmo & McNay and the registered office was at 3 King Street, Cheapside in the City of London.

On 14 November 1878 plans were deposited for the 1879 Parliamentary Session for tramways in Maida Vale, Regents Park, Camden Town and Paddington. This scheme, covering 6.381 miles of mainly double line consisted of a main route from Marble Arch to Brondesbury North London Railway station along Edgware Road and Maida Vale from which another route branched into St. John's Wood Road and continued through Regents Park by way of Prince Albert Road and Park Street to High Street, Camden Town where a junction with the London Street Tramways was planned. Another branch led from Edgware Road into Harrow Road and Bishops Bridge Road as far as Porchester Road, and a little further to the south-east another line left Edgware Road to continue along Praed Street and Eastbourne Terrace to join the line in Bishops Bridge Road. There was much opposition to tramway schemes in these throughfares and this scheme did not proceed.

On 21 November 1878 another scheme was produced and plans deposited for the 1879 Session, covering a double line tramway from Young's Corner at the Hammersmith – Chiswick boundary through High Road, Chiswick and Turnham Green to Kew Bridge; a single line with passing loops from Young's Corner in the opposite direction along King Street, Hammersmith into Hammersmith Broadway and round into Beadon Road and The Grove, returning to King Street via The Grove. From Barnes London and South Western Railway station a line was projected via Rocks Lane and Castelnau to the Red Lion Hotel in Barnes and across Hammersmith Bridge to meet the proposed line in the Broadway. Another line was proposed to start from the existing tramway at Shepherds Bush and traverse Goldhawk Road to meet the King Street line at Young's Corner, with a link north into The Grove to meet the proposed tramway in Goldhawk Road, totalling 7.171 miles. The Engineer for this scheme was Joseph Kincaid. Objections by local interests ensured the withdrawal of the scheme and the company was wound up following a shareholders' meeting on 8 September 1879, the final liquidation taking place on 28 November.

After the sale of the Shepherds Bush and Acton tramway to Reid Brothers in 1878 numerous attempts were made to establish tramways in West London and earlier, from 1865 there had been abortive attempts to gain powers, of which none came to fruition except that of the Brentford & Isleworth Tramways Company, which succeeded in obtaining powers and constructed part of its authorised mileage, but was unable to complete its scheme or operate a service owing to financial difficulties.

The second West Metropolitan Tramways Company was incorporated under the Companies Act on 12 August 1881 with authorised share capital of £100,000 in £10 Ordinary shares. The stated objects of the company were the establishment and operation of tramways in Middlesex and Surrey. The first directors were John Beattie, Chairman of the North Staffordshire Tramways Company; C.E. Davison, a director of the South Staffordshire Steam Tramways Company; Major Luke Bishop, a director of the Stockton & Darlington Steam Tramways Company and Arthur Handyside, a director of the Manchester, Bury, Rochdale & Oldham Steam Tramways Company. Beattie was Chairman and Davison was a subscriber to the first West Metropolitan company. The Secretary was Thomas Jervis and the registered office was at 28 Cheapside, EC. The Engineer was Joseph Kincaid.

The origins of the new West Metropolitan Tramways Company lay in the decision by Reid Brothers to sell the Shepherds Bush and Acton tramway and their powers for the Shepherds Bush and Hammersmith (Goldhawk Road) tramway which they had just obtained but had not constructed. The moving spirit in the formation of the WMT was Henry Osborne O'Hagan (1853-1930), a company promoter who was about to become active in tramway promotion schemes and was in partnership with Major Luke Bishop, a director of the new West Metropolitan company. O'Hagan was at this time promoting steam tramways in Staffordshire and buying up early horse tramways and introducing steam traction. John Beattie, Major Bishop and C.E. Davison were associates of O'Hagan in these early steam tramway promotions, and O'Hagan's formation of the new West Metropolitan Tramways Company was one of the earliest of his tramway promotions.

The Reid Brothers, having obtained a Provisional Order for the Goldhawk Road tramway had decided to dispose of their tramway interests in November 1880. The ultimate owners of the undertaking were to be the West Metropolitan Tramways Company but the sale was through an intermediary, Charles Phillips, owner of a contracting business, Charles Phillips & Co. Phillips undertook this commission for an agreed fee of £3,000 and paid a £650 deposit, the purchase price being £23,000, and when the sale was completed he was repaid the £650 he had paid as a deposit. These arrangements were negotiated by O'Hagan and the final conveyance from Phillips to the West Metropolitan Tramways Company Ltd. took place on 6 March 1882, the properties involved being the Shepherds Bush – Acton tramway, the powers for the line and the powers for the as-yet unbuilt Goldhawk Road tramway with the lease of the depot. Horses, rolling stock and plant were not included and were the subject of a separate transaction. A return made in 1880 indicates that four cars and 41 horses were either owned, or in use, and that Charles Courtney Cramp leased the line for operation at £600 per annum.

On 6 March 1882 an extraordinary general meeting of the WMT shareholders approved a motion from the Chairman to submit a Bill conferring Parliamentary status upon the company and to empower the company to acquire existing tramways and construct new ones. The position of the Acton tramway was questioned at this meeting; owing to confusion about the affairs of the former Southall, Ealing & Shepherds Bush Tram Railway Company at least one shareholder believed that the West Metropolitan company was being acquired by the SESB company rather than *vice versa*. The advisability of seeking Parliamentary status was questioned and numerous points were clarified by the solicitor. The solicitor, Walter Webb, was with difficulty able to convince some shareholders that the WMT had gained possession of the SESB undertaking. The meeting was told that the directors had not pressed completion of the SESB purchase during the winter and had preferred instead to press forward construction of the Goldhawk Road tramway. They had seen no advantage in completing the Acton purchase until the spring, when traffic prospects would be better. As it happened, the transaction was to take place at mid-day on that day, 6 March, the Goldhawk Road line was shortly to open and all would be to the advantage of the

WMT. The purchase of working stock, construction of stables and other facilities had also made it an advantage to delay completion of the Acton purchase until the Goldhawk Road line was ready and open for traffic. The Chairman, John Beattie, put the motion to the meeting, it was carried unanimously and a further extraordinary general meeting confirmed the resolution on 25 March.

The powers of the Shepherds Bush and Hammersmith Tramways Order passed to the WMT on 6 March with the Acton tramway, the Board of Trade having agreed to the sale but not without misgivings, although they saw no alternative to the arrangements. Discussions among the Board's officers had continued at length and previous unsatisfactory dealings with the SESB clearly weighed heavily upon their minds.

The Goldhawk Road tramway was constructed by a local firm, Stevens & Alldred, working on behalf of Henry Osborne O'Hagan. The Engineer, Joseph Kincaid, had submitted plans to the Board of Trade on 26 August 1881. 50lb/yard rails were keyed to cast-iron chairs spaced at 3ft intervals, the chairs being set in 6in of concrete. The rails were laid in 24ft lengths. The Board of Trade inspector, Maj. Gen. C.S. Hutchinson, asked for angle plates to be fitted to hold the chairs and rails to gauge because no tie-bars had been fitted. Dummy points of chilled iron were to be fitted at turn-outs; with no moveable blades reliance was placed upon a continuous groove on the left hand side at a turn-out with the opposite side of the point having no guide.

Construction of the line was completed by 11 March 1882, and Gen. Hutchinson inspected it on 18 March. He found the work satisfactory and recommended the line should be certified for public use and the certificate was signed on 20 March. Meanwhile, Gen. Hutchinson had given verbal sanction for the line to open and public service commenced later on 18 March. The transfer of the Acton tramway to the WMT having been effected on 6 March, the service of trams ceased on that day until 11 March whilst completion of formalities was carried out.

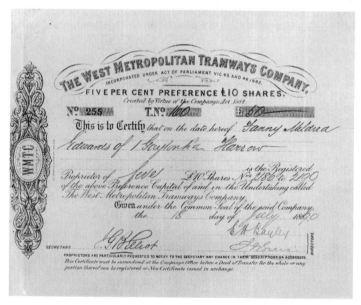

A Preference Share Certificate issued on behalf of the statutory West Metropolitan Tramways Company, and dated 18 July 1890.

On 10 November 1881 the WMT submitted a Bill for the 1882 Parliamentary Session seeking powers to construct a tramway extending from Richmond LSWR station along Kew Road, Richmond to Kew Bridge across the Thames into Kew Bridge Road, Brentford and along High Road, Chiswick to meet the authorised Goldhawk Road tramway and continue past Young's Corner along King Street, Hammersmith into the Broadway and Beadon Road, Glenthorne Road and Studland Street back to King Street forming a loop. The Kew Bridge Commissioners refused consent to cross the narrow eighteenth-century bridge and the line across the bridge was struck out. As a consequence the line on the Surrey side of the river was isolated from its counterpart on the Middlesex side despite several attempts to make the crossing after the bridge was rebuilt in 1903.

The rest of the mileage sought, amounting to 5.007 miles of single and double line was sanctioned. Widenings were stipulated in Glenthorne and Beadon Roads, and the company was debarred from constructing the section in Richmond between its terminus 120 yards from the centre of the bridge and the Selwyn Fountain at the junction of Kew and Mortlake Roads, without the consent of the London and South Western Railway Company. The Act sanctioning these extensions received the Royal Assent on 10 August 1882. It contained specifications for construction of the lines in the areas of the Fulham Board of Works (Hammersmith), the Chiswick Improvements Commissioners, Brentford Local Board and Richmond Select Vestry. These bodies required the use of 50lb/yard Bessemer steel rails fixed by wrought-iron wedges 3ft apart on cast-iron supports 10in wide at the base to give continuous support to the paving setts either side of the rails, and the track to be laid upon a 6in bed of concrete.

During this time, in June 1882 Henry Osborne O'Hagan formed the company through which he conducted his tramway promotions and construction schemes. The City of London Contract Corporation was registered with capital of £300,000 and was formed to acquire the contracting firm of Charles Phillips & Company. O'Hagan was Chairman and his fellow directors who remained unchanged for eight years were Sir William Magnay, Bt., Major Luke Bishop and Rear-Admiral Brookes, CB. Charles Phillips was instrumental in the sale of the Southall, Ealing & Shepherds Bush undertaking to the WMT and Luke Bishop, with John Beattie and others were directors of some of the companies promoted by O'Hagan in Staffordshire and Lancashire.

One of the provisions of the WMT 1882 Act was the dissolution of the WMT limited company and its incorporation as as a statutory company, and another stipulated that all officers and servants of the 1881 company were to retain their respective offices and posts "until they resign or their tenure is otherwise terminated". The new Act increased the authorised share capital of the company to £130,000 in £10 shares and gave borrowing powers up to £32,500 but specifically did not allow the company to issue debenture stock.

Construction of the tramways authorised in the 1882 Act commenced on 12 October 1882 with the section from Young's Corner to Kew Bridge and despite exceptionally bad weather causing stoppages of work the section was almost completed by 2 December.

A trial run over this section took place on 7 December and meanwhile work had started on the line from the south side of Kew Bridge to Richmond. On 16 December Gen. Hutchinson inspected the Young's Corner – Kew Bridge (north side) section and on finding the line "well laid" he recommended the issue of the certificate of fitness which was signed at the Board of Trade on 19 December. The line opened for public service later on 16 December with the approval of Gen. Hutchinson. With the Shepherds Bush – Young's Corner tramway there was now a continuous line from Shepherds Bush to Kew Bridge of 3.354 miles.

The construction of all the WMT lines was carried out by a local public works contractor, Stevens & Alldred, working on behalf of Henry Osborne O'Hagan's company, the City of London Contract Corporation Ltd.

21

The WMT had entered into a contract with the Corporation on 17 August 1882 to construct the Young's Corner – Kew Bridge and the Kew Bridge – Richmond lines, and to provide the stabling and accommodation at Richmond and Chiswick depots, together with the Parliamentary expenses of the 1882 Act, for a total of £61,525. This figure did not include the costs of building the Goldhawk Road tramway or the later line east from Young's Corner to Hammersmith Broadway, which were the subject of separate arrangements with the contractors.

The next line in the 1882 Act to be completed was the Kew Road tramway. The intention of the WMT was to make the terminus of this line at the entrance to Richmond LSWR station. When the Bill was before Parliament the only opposition was from the railway company, and the WMT directors were induced to insert a clause in the Bill which precluded the company from taking the line further than the Selwyn Fountain at the junction of Kew and Lower Mortlake Roads, some 150 yards north of the station, without the consent of the LSWR. The LSWR thereupon withdrew their opposition and the Bill passed as an unopposed measure. The LSWR declined to give their consent to continue the line as far as the station unless the WMT undertook never to go beyond that point. The directors refused to give this undertaking because their ultimate objective was Hampton Court, and matters stood at a deadlock.

Construction of the tramway commenced in December 1882 and on 10 February 1883 it was reported that the work was nearing completion. The single line and loops was 1.531 miles in length and one of the passing loops, at the Cumberland Gate of the Royal Botanic Gardens, Kew was the subject of a complaint to the Board of Trade by Sir Joseph Hooker, the Director of the Gardens. He wanted the loop moved 30 yards to the south; at first the WMT acceded to the request, but when it transpired that the loop had already been laid they withdrew their agreement to move the loop. They pointed out that their plans had been approved by Parliament, but nevertheless the Board of Trade had passed a copy of Sir Joseph's letter to the company "for their observations". Evidently the company felt finally that it might be politic to defer to the Director's wishes, and the Secretary told the Board of Trade on 22 January that the matter would have "the immediate attention of the directors."

Two double-deck cars of the company at the Kew Green terminus of the horse tramway to Richmond. The top deck seating was of 'knifeboard' pattern.

(Courtesy: London Borough of Richmond Library)

22

Gen. Hutchinson inspected the line on 10 March 1883 and noted that the loop complained of had been laid as authorised. One other loop had been made fifteen yards too long, the roadway adjacent to the rails had been poorly reinstated and the method of construction varied in some details to that laid down in the Act. Gen. Hutchinson suggested a method of operating at Cumberland Gate which might be acceptable to Sir Joseph Hooker, which the WMT undertook to institute accordingly. It was agreed that cars would not stop on "as much of the passing loop as lies between points respectively 33 yards and 49 yards from the South end of the passing place". In a letter to the Board of Trade dated 6 April 1883 Hooker indicated that he was not satisfied with the proposed arrangements, saying that he was "concerned that carriages for the nobility and gentry – and others – would be impeded by not being able to wait outside the gate", and said that the loop should be moved to another place on the line. Evidently the parties were later able to agree on procedure at the Cumberland Gate loop as the Board of Trade issued their certificate of fitness on 13 April and traffic commenced on 17 April,

The cars which commenced service at mid-day on 17 April 1883 were furnished with red velvet seat cushions and riding was described as "comfortable if not luxurious". The pair-horse cars ran every fifteen minutes in each direction and the fare for the full journey from end to end was 2d, but it was suggested that it would later be reduced to one penny.

The depot serving this always-isolated line was situated at the Richmond end of the line, at No. 125, Kew Road; it was held initially on a 21 years lease from Christrnas 1882 at an annual rent of £75 and stabling and equipment were installed as part of the WMT contract with the City of London Contract Corporation. The cars were overhauled at Chiswick Depot, being hauled across Kew Bridge on their flanges, probably under a dispensation from the Kew Bridge Commissioners. This procedure continued throughout the length of the line's existence.

The opening of the Kew Road line was marked by a dinner given by William Stevens, of Stevens & Alldred who had built the line as sub-contractors to the City of London Contract Corporation. Stevens presided, and the directors of the WMT, members of Richmond Select Vestry, the Chiswick Improvements Commissioners and Fulham Board of Works attended, with Henry Osborne O'Hagan, Sir William Magnay, a director of the City of London Contract Corporation, the WMT Manager, F.J. Farrell and many others. The hope was expressed that the opposition of the LSWR to the extension of the line to Richmond station would soon be withdrawn, various toasts were proposed and drunk, and among those thus honoured were O'Hagan and the Richmond Select Vestry. The function ended on a note of goodwill and expressions of faith in the future of the West Metropolitan Tramways Company.

Notwithstanding the atmosphere of goodwill at the dinner, Richmond Select Vestry persisted in complaining about the condition of the roadway and as agreement between the company and the Vestry could not be reached the Board of Trade appointed Captain Douglas Galton, RE to arbitrate in the dispute, which was finally amicably resolved.

Yet another dispute between the WMT and Richmond Select Vestry arose over the position of the terminus in Richmond. Owing to the intransigence of the LSWR the line had been laid only as far as the Selwyn Fountain at the junction of Kew Road and Lower Mortlake Road. The WMT wished to continue it closer to the station, or at least as far as Church Road. The Vestry would not agree to this and Joseph Kincaid, the Engineer said the company would extend the track without a loop at the end of the line. This was done, and the additional 150 yards of single track was laid as far as Church Road. The Vestry protested that the new terminus would be a danger to other road users and Gen. Hutchinson inspected the new section on 9 July. Gen. Hutchinson upheld Richmond Vestry's complaint and suggested that the cars should be reversed a few yards short of the new terminal, close to St. John's Church. Following agreement between the parties on this point the Board of Trade issued their certificate for the short extension on 17 July 1883.

The last line in the 1882 Act, between Young's Corner and Hammersmith Broadway brought the Kew Bridge line directly into Hammersmith via King Street. This consisted of a double line from Young's Corner for 0.415 miles eastward along King Street as far as Studland Street and continuing into Studland Street, Glenthorne Road, Beadon Road and The Broadway back into King Street as a single line as far as Studland Street, forming a loop measuring 1.20 miles in extent. This new line gave a total of 1.616 miles of route giving a direct connection from central Hammersmith to Kew Bridge, where the Richmond cars were reached by crossing Kew Bridge on foot. At first omnibuses were provided to cross the bridge but this service was short-lived.

The WMT and Fulham Board of Works did not at first agree about widenings specified in the company's Act. These were in Beadon Road and Glenthorne Road but by 2 May 1883 the Clerk of the Board of Works reported that the WMT had paid £4,500 in settlement of the Board's requirements and construction of the extension had commenced. Another difficulty was the widening of the railway

28421 Kew. Road & Entrance to Gardens.

Upper: By horse tram between Kew and Richmond. Northbound car No. 45, in brown and yellow livery, is seen at the Cumberland Gate entrance to Kew Gardens.
Lower: Car No. 27, in blue and cream livery, is not far from Richmond terminus.
(Commercial views: The Photochrome Co. & C.F. Barker. Courtesy: J.H. Price)

24

bridge in Beadon Road. The railway companies agreed to the works involved after initial delays, and construction of the track was completed by 14 July 1883, when Gen. Hutchinson carried out the Board of Trade inspection. He passed the line for public service and the cars commenced working over the new section later in that afternoon, although part of the work at Beadon Road railway bridge remained to be completed, and the certificate of fitness was delayed until 27 July pending final agreement on the rights of the railway companies. The opening of the lines in Hammersmith marked the completion of the authorised WMT system, although some doublings and minor alterations took place from time to time. The total extent of the system amounted to 8.737 miles of route.

Although the WMT system was destined not to expand further, the company had ambitions for a greatly enlarged network, and in November 1882 a Bill was deposited in Parliament for the 1883 Session seeking powers for 8.554 miles of new routes. One was to start at the existing Shepherds Bush terminus to continue the line eastward along Holland Park Avenue for just under a mile to Notting Hill Gate, and another was to leave the Uxbridge Road tramway and link it with the line in Goldhawk Road by way of the west side of Shepherds Bush Green (The Lawn) and cross Goldhawk Road to join the line in Hammersmith Broadway via Shepherds Bush Road and Brook Green Road, and to cross the Broadway to reach the north side of Hammersmith Bridge by way of Hammersmith Bridge Road. The lines in Beadon Road and King Street were planned to continue into the Broadway and along Hammersmith Road as far as Russell Road and into Russell Road as far as the present Kensington Olympia station (then named Addison Road).

From Hammersmith another proposed line diverged south at North End Road to Walham Green and into Fulham Road, reaching King's Road, Chelsea via Holmead Road and turning into Beaufort Street, along Cheyne Walk and Chelsea Embankment, to leave the Embankment at Westmoreland Street and proceed via Lupus Street, Gloucester Street and Churton Street to terminate in Vauxhall Bridge Road on the east side of Victoria station. At Queen's Road (now Royal Hospital Road) a line left the Embankment to proceed via Queen's Road and Pimlico Road to Buckingham Palace Road to a terminus on the west side of Victoria Station opposite Lower Belgrave Street. These proposals included a request for running powers over the London Tramways Company's line in Vauxhall Bridge Road to Victoria station and there was also a proposal to extend the authorised tramway in Richmond to George Street, a little under a quarter of a mile further into the centre of the town.

The proposals met with implacable opposition over almost the whole of the routes from frontagers and local authorities, especially the wealthy Chelsea and Westminster districts, where residents considered they had no need of tramways, which they thought would damage local amenities. As a preliminary measure these lines were removed from the draft Bill, leaving only the extension from Hammersmith Broadway to Walham Green via North End Road and the short branch to Addison Road station. At the first shareholders' general meeting of the new statutory company on 16 February 1883 the solicitor, Walter Webb, said that there was much opposition to the Bill in many of the districts and it would be inadvisable to press forward in the present climate of opinion. The company had only recently overcome difficulties in reaching Hammersmith Broadway and they had the goodwill of Fulham Board of Works. It was felt that prevailing adverse opinion might spread to Hammersmith, and friendly opinion in the Fulham Board of Works had suggested that the company should not press in the current Session for consents which might be strongly opposed. The directors continued to regard extensions in the easterly and south-westerly directions as essential to the well-being of the company. The solicitor said there was every reason to believe that opinion in 1884 would be favourable and the consents would be easily obtained. The meeting endorsed the withdrawal of the whole of the 1883 Bill.

At the half-yearly shareholders meeting on 31 August 1883 Maj. Luke Bishop presided and reported on progress. All the authorised share and debenture capital amounting respectively to £130,000 and £32,500 had been allotted and a five per

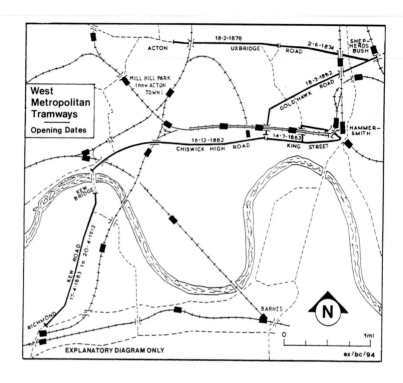

West
Metropolitan
Tramways

Opening Dates

EXPLANATORY DIAGRAM ONLY

ex/bc/94

cent per annum dividend would be paid for the half-year to 30 June. Maj. Bishop said that 176,336 car miles were run in the half-year and 867,194 passengers carried. Average receipts per mile were 11d and expenditure 7.95d per mile. All the authorised lines were open and on the Richmond and central Hammersmith lines £5,000 had been taken between 30 June and 30 August. The new depot at Chiswick was in the course of construction which would reduce the wear and tear on the rolling stock.

On 16 November 1883 further plans were deposited for the 1884 Session. This scheme covered most of the routes in the abortive 1883 Bill, with several additions. Outside the Metropolitan area powers were sought only to double the single line sections on the Young's Corner – Kew Bridge line. The line linking the Uxbridge Road tramway with Hammersmith Broadway via the west side of Shepherds Bush Green, Shepherds Bush Road and Brook Green Road was included in the Bill as was the extension from the Broadway along Hammersmith Road, but only as far as the west side of Russell Road. The line from Hammersmith Road via North End Road through Walham Green was included, but to continue only as far as Chelsea Barracks via Pimlico Road and Buckingham Palace Road to the west side of Victoria station. This route also diverged slightly from the 1883 scheme, in that it was planned to reach Cheyne Walk from King's Road via Dartrey Road instead of Beaufort Street. Another tramway was proposed to start from Fulham Road at Walham Green and continue south-west along Fulham Road and High Street, Fulham as far as Church Street (now Church Gate) near the north side of Putney Bridge, and a continuation of the tramway in Beadon Road, Hammersmith was projected through Queen Caroline Street, Fulham Palace Road, Crown Road, Munster Road and Dawes Road to join the Chelsea and Putney Bridge lines at

26

Walham Green. From the proposed tramway in Hammersmith Road a line was projected into Edith Road through Queen Caroline Street, Fulham Palace Road, Crown Road, Munster Road and Dawes Road to join the Chelsea and Putney Bridge lines at Walham Green.

In north Hammersmith, at Shepherds Bush a tramway was proposed to continue from the existing terminus at Uxbridge Road West London Railway station into Norland Road and Latimer Road to Bramley Road, thence along Lancaster Road to Ladbroke Grove, along Cornwall Road to Porchester Road and across the bridge over the Great Western Railway at Royal Oak station to Harrow Road. From Ladbroke Crescent the line in Ladbroke Road was projected through Ladbroke Grove to Harrow Road, Kensal Green, turning west for 132 yards as far as Wellington Road. From this point the line continued east along Harrow Road for 1.60 miles as far as Blomfield Crescent, near the present Westbourne Terrace and a short distance from the Lock Hospital and the Grand Junction Canal bridge. This extensive scheme amounted to 13.32 miles of double and single track.

The Bill contained clauses for extensive widenings and other works. Chief among these were widenings in North End Road as far as Cumberland Crescent and of Cheyne Walk by making an embankment on the Thames foreshore at Beaufort Street. Clauses were inserted in the Bill to enable the Metropolitan Board of Works, Fulham Board of Works and Chelsea Vestry to enter into contracts for widening North End Road and to construct and maintain the proposed embankment. The Bill sought powers to raise new capital of £280,000 and borrowing powers up to £70,000. The company anticipated completing the scheme within three years and the Bill proposed that construction of the tramways should be to the same standards as the lines already built.

Despite the earlier hopes of the WMT Board that the scheme might be more favourably received in 1884, opposition to the lines in the Chelsea and Fulham area remained implacable. Sir Joseph Bazalgette, the Metropolitan Board of Works Engineer told the MBW that the line in Cheyne Walk would cross the approach to the new Battersea Bridge at a right angle and would interfere with the raising and forming of the approach to the bridge when built. He also said that the line along the Chelsea Embankment would spoil the roadway and damage new buildings and general amenities there, and he recommended that the MBW should refuse their consent to the Bill. Chelsea Vestry refused to consent to the line from Pimlico Road to Ebury Bridge and asked the MBW to join them in this refusal. Moreover, the Vestry approached the other authorities affected by the scheme to form a unified opposition. Paddington Vestry resolved to oppose the scheme but Chelsea Vestry consented to the part of the scheme in Harrow Road. At this time a detached part of Chelsea lay in the Harrow Road area, which was later transferred to the Kensington authority. The opposition ensured the withdrawal of the tramway provisions from the Bill. During the Bill's passage through Parliament the financial clauses were modified to authorise the company to raise additional capital of up to £40,000 in Ordinary or Preference shares and to borrow on mortgage up to £10,000, the sums asked for in the Bill having been scaled down as a result of the withdrawal of the tramway proposals. The Bill was passed as the West Metropolitan Tramways Act 1884 and received the Royal Assent on 3 July.

From 1884 the company went into a period of retrenchment. Favourable traffic receipts in 1883 were not maintained in 1884 and the falling-off of traffic in that year had shown that the company was vulnerable to bad weather and other adverse factors, and plans for further development were shelved. From 1 October 1885 the Shepherds Bush – Kew Bridge cars were cut back to Young's Corner and through tickets issued from Shepherds Bush to Kew Bridge by way of cars from Hammersmith. At the same time a fare reduction came into force, the 2d fare between Shepherds Bush and Young's Corner being reduced to 1d. Maj. Bishop, presiding at an adjourned half-yearly shareholders' meeting on 26 October 1885 said that if the reduction was successful similar reductions would be made on other parts of the system.

Details of shareholders' meetings for 1884 and 1885 are sparse. The August 1885 half-yearly meeting, details of which were not reported, was adjourned until 26 October, and only the fare reduction was reported. Evidently a further meeting was held subsequent to this, and on 26 December 1885 the Railway Times briefly reported that E.H.Bayley, Chairman of the London Road Car Co. Ltd. and W.W. Duncan had been elected as directors of the WMT and Bayley appointed as Chairman. The directorate was now Duncan, Bayley, Luke Bishop and Arthur Handyside. It is evident that the shareholders were dissatisfied with the management of the company and had been successful in making radical changes. Of Henry Osborne O'Hagan's original nominees, only two remained on the board, Bishop and Handyside.

Edward Hodson Bayley, Chairman of the London Road Car Company, whose omnibus fleet was second in size only to that of the London General Omnibus Company, was also a director of some provincial tramways companies and owned a large specialist vehicle building firm manufacturing fire appliances and omnibuses, which later developed an extensive trade in motor versions of such vehicles. He was also Liberal Member of Parliament for West Camberwell. W.W. Duncan, a stockbroker, had interests in tramway companies in various parts of the country and published the trade directory, Duncan's Tramway Manual.

On 2 January 1886 Duncan published a prospectus inviting tenders for 2,957 ten-pound 5% Preference shares at a minimum tender price of £9 per share. The Ordinary share capital at this time consisted of £140,000 in £10 shares. The new capital had been authorised in the 1884 Act and the prospectus said that it was required to provide new cars, horses and other equipment and additional depot accommodation. The prospectus stated that two depots were in use, at Richmond and Shepherds Bush but did not mention Chiswick Depot, which may not have been completed at this time. 224 horses, 30 trams and six omnibuses were in stock and the tram fleet was to be "immediately increased". Additional passing loops were to be constructed.

Duncan strongly recommended the new issue in his stockbroking circular, saying that there was much scope for improvement and expansion of the WMT undertaking and he said that with a little patience investors would have every reason to be satisfied with their investment. The circular said that the contractors (the City of London Contract Corporation) took payment for their work in the Preference shares and the shares not so appropriated were offered as a sound and desirable security.

By 1 April 1886 the Traffic Manager, F.J. Farrell had announced a further reduction of fares. The one penny fares introduced earlier were extended to most, if not the whole, of the system and services were improved. Details were not given but it appears that 2d fares had been largely, if not completely, abolished, except on Sundays.

Plans to connect the lines in Hammersmith with the Uxbridge Road tramway via Askew Road had been submitted by earlier promoters, without success, and on 11 November 1886 plans and a proposed Bill were submitted for an "Acton and Hammersmith Tramways" scheme. The intended Bill sought powers to construct the line from the Askew Arms in Uxbridge Road through Askew Road, across Goldhawk Road and into Paddenswick Road and Dalling Road to meet the existing West Metropolitan tramway in Glenthorne Road. At the Uxbridge Road end a south to west junction was planned at the Askew Arms. From Hammersmith Broadway a line was proposed to continue along Hammersmith Road as far as Avonmore Road, close to Addison Road station and a short branch was planned from the Broadway into Bridge Road as far as the Ship public house close to the river bank. The scheme involved a total of 2.160 miles.

This proposal had provisions for the incorporation of the Acton & Hammersmith Tramways Company as a statutory undertaking, the first directors of which were to be Charles Courtney Cramp "and four others to be nominated by him". Cramp was a member of Hammersmith Vestry and a shareholder in the

WMT. Share capital, if authorised, was to be £40,000 in ten-pound shares. Provisions were sought to enable the WMT to subscribe to the capital of the new company and for the new company to amalgamate with or acquire the WMT. Powers were also sought to enable the WMT to lease portions of the proposed company's lines and operate them. The WMT directors took steps to protect the WMT's interests against this hostile move and the Bill was opposed in Parliament at a cost of £804 and did not proceed. If the Bill had succeeded a disaffected group of shareholders, led by John Willis, would have been in a position to gain control of the WMT.

In 1887 the WMT obtained a Provisional Order from the Board of Trade to allow the use of mechanical or electrical power other than steam, which was confirmed in the Tramways Provisional Orders Confirmation (No. 1) Act of 2 August 1887. F.J. Farrell the traffic manager who had been appointed at the inception of the company was succeeded in 1887 by Thomas Boyce Goodyer, whose tenure in that office was short, being followed in October that year by J.H. Gaynor. 1887 ended with expressions by shareholders of dissatisfaction with the management of the company; while receipts had been reasonable a body of opinion held the view that there had been policy shortcomings for which the directors were held responsible.

The half-yearly shareholders' meeting on 17 February 1888 was a stormy one; the directors explained Charles Courtney Cramp's attempt to gain a hold on the WMT in his 1887 Bill. Bayley said that had Cramp succeeded the WMT would have suffered annual losses of £1,000. He also said that the six omnibuses owned since the inception of the company, which had lain idle ever since, had been disposed of for £79. The Golden Jubilee celebrations of 1887, general trade depression and unfavourable weather had caused traffic losses to places like Kew Gardens. Nevertheless a dividend of 1½% per annum on the Ordinary and 5% on the Preference shares was declared.

At this meeting the disaffected group of shareholders who had supported Cramp's Bill attempted to obtain control of the company. John Willis was a persistent critic and he proposed the replacement of the director retiring by rotation, W.W. Duncan, by W.J. Carruthers Wain. Wain was prominent in tramway promotions in various parts of the country, being at one time Chairman of the Croydon Tramways Company and of the famous London department store, Swan & Edgar. Wain failed to be elected and Duncan retained his seat by 4,334 votes to Wain's 257. A move to reduce the directors' fees and to appoint fresh auditors was similarly defeated. There was, however, much general criticism of the handling of financial matters, including the fact that at the start of operations the company had paid £3,000 for a ten years' lease of Shepherds Bush Depot. The Engineer, Arthur Ramsden, CE recommended doubling the line between Hammersmith and Kew Bridge and the adoption of electric traction to compete successfully with the railways running parallel with much of the WMT routes. The place of J.Webber on the board of directors was taken by J.W.Greig, a director of the North Metropolitan Tramways Company and a number of others.

The August 1888 half-yearly meeting heard another story of indifferent receipts, little changed from the previous half-year. After operating expenses, debenture interest and income tax £919 remained from gross receipts of £12,382 which the directors proposed to carry forward. Competition from the "General" and London Road Car omnibuses was severe and the trams were handicapped by being unable to cross Kew Bridge to make a direct route from Hammersmith to Richmond. The auditors advised the directors to reduce the capital to bring it more in line with the assets. The capital at this time was £140,358 in Ordinary and £29,570 in 5% Preference shares with debentures to the value of £32,500. After a lengthy and acrimonious discussion the directors' report and the accounts were adopted as was a proposal to approve a 5% per annum dividend for the Preference shareholders. Payment of this was deferred pending clarification of demands by the local authorities for extensive track repairs.

On 9 February 1889 John Willis' circularised his fellow shareholders in an attempt to secure the election to the Board of Thomas Boyce Goodyer, the erstwhile traffic manager, and thus gain control for the dissidents. Bayley's position as Chairman was compromised by his being Chairman also of the London Road Car Company, whose omnibuses were in direct competition with the WMT trams in Hammersmith. At the half-yearly meeting on 15 February 1889 Bayley came under fierce attack from all sides. The directors reported a slight increase in traffic receipts for 1888 and dividends on 5% on the Preference and 2% on the Ordinary shares were declared. Referring to the competition, Bayley said it had been intense – "the Road Car Company put fifty cars against us on the Hammersmith line and the London General Omnibus Company put on fifty more vehicles in competition with the trams".

At this meeting it transpired that several shareholders' names had been appended to John Willis' circular without their knowledge or consent, and these told the Chairman that they wished to dissociate themselves from the circular and its contents. Bayley was heavily criticised in the circular, his management of the company's affairs condemned as inept and he was called upon to resign. Notwithstanding that there had been much general criticism of Bayley most of the shareholders closed ranks behind him and the report and accounts were adopted. Bayley, the retiring director, was re-elected and remained as Chairman. Willis, having failed to get Goodyer elected to the Board, returned to the attack, saying *inter alia* that "Bayley had done repairs for the company", presumably irregularly. Willis' tactics in issuing his circular were described as unscrupulous and he later withdrew, but he had succeeded in undermining the confidence of the shareholders in Bayley's and the other directors' management of the company. It was evidently the intention of Willis and his associates to get Goodyer elected to the Board and appointed as Chairman. From this time Thomas Jervis was replaced as Secretary by J.G.B. Elliott, who was also secretary of the Harrow Road and Paddington Tramways Company.

Following the general meeting a special meeting approved the text of a Bill which had been deposited for the 1889 Session of Parliament seeking powers to construct additional tramways and to increase the company's capital. The Bill contained clauses for a number of lines which had featured in the 1883 and 1884 Bills. A major new route would extend the tramway in Acton through the town and Ealing to a terminus at Boston Road, Hanwell. In the Notting Hill area it was proposed to revive the attempt to extend the line at Shepherds Bush terminus into Norland Road, Latimer Road, Bramley Road and along Ladbroke Grove into Cornwall Road, Westbourne Park Villas and along Porchester Road as far as Bishop's Road. At Gloucester Terrace a single line was planned to diverge into Pickering Place (now Westbourne Park Terrace) to terminate there north of the intersection with Westbourne Grove.

The lines sought in Cramp's 1887 Bill to link the Uxbridge Road and Hammersmith lines via Askew Road and the connecting lines in Hammersmith were included in this measure, and there was provision for doubling some of the track in King Street, Hammersmith and the track in Chiswick, from Young's Corner west along High Road to the boundary with Brentford at Clarence Road, a little short of Kew Bridge. The Shepherds Bush – Acton tramway, dating from 1874 and 1878 was in an extremely poor condition and had long been the subject of complaints by the Hammersmith and Acton local authorities, which had demanded complete reconstruction of the track with double lines and new paving along the whole route. The Bill provided for the reconstruction of the Uxbridge Road track from Shepherds Bush terminus as double line throughout as far as Birkbeck Road, Acton, just west of the North London Railway bridge across Acton Vale. No part of this work on the Hammersmith portion of the line was to be undertaken until the roadway had been widened to allow 9ft 6in clearance between the outer rails and the kerb to the satisfaction of the new London County Council which replaced the Metropolitan Board of Works in 1889. The Hammersmith section extended from Shepherds Bush terminus to the Acton boundary at the Askew Arms public house.

Widenings were planned in parts of the narrow Acton High Street, and powers were sought to allow the purchase of up to five acres of land for the use of the undertaking. An important clause covered the use of electrical or mechanical power; the 1887 Order authorised the use of mechanical or electrical power but not steam. The new Bill removed the prohibition of steam haulage and allowed the introduction of electric power, wire rope or cable haulage with the consent of the Board of Trade and the local authorities for a period of up to seven years after passing the Bill.

The directors had discussed the reduction of the company's share capital, and this had provoked some of the dissension among shareholders. The 1889 Bill sought a reduction of the Ordinary share capital from £140,430 to £56,172, reducing the ten-pound shares to four pounds. At the same time additional capital was proposed of, if required, up to £150,000 in ten-pound 5% Preference shares, together with borrowing powers up to one quarter of the half-paid up capital. Provision for the appointment of a receiver was envisaged and mortgagees of the company would be empowered to do this to enforce payment of interest or capital for sums of not less than £10,000. No new debentures would be created and power was sought to redeem existing debentures within two years of passing the Bill.

This large Bill was the WMT's last Parliamentary essay of significance. The extension from Acton to Hanwell was disallowed on objections from Ealing Local Board and earlier objections to the extensions from Shepherds Bush in the Notting Hill direction were upheld. The doublings in Hammersmith and Chiswick were authorised together with the reconstruction and doubling of the Uxbridge Road line. An important clause postponed the purchase powers of the London County Council until 14 years after passing the Bill, which received the Royal Assent on 26 August 1889. The Bill had asked for the LCC purchase powers to be postponed for twenty-one years but this was opposed on behalf of the LCC.

At the half-yearly shareholders' meeting on 29 August 1889 Bayley reported increased receipts and after providing for payment of dividend on the Preference shares for the past half-year a balance of £1,640 remained. At the previous half-yearly meeting the dividends had been declared and Acton Local Board had immediately obtained a Writ of Mandamus in the High Court to compel the WMT to reconstruct the tramway between the Askew Arms and Birkbeck Road. The solicitor had accordingly advised the directors to withhold payment of the dividends and Bayley said immediate steps would be taken to raise the newly-authorised capital *so that the dividends may be paid.* It emerged that while profits had increased over the previous two years the company had been paying dividends out of capital for a considerable time. The Acton tramway was in a parlous state and the rest of the system little better, especially in Hammersmith. Heavy expenditure was necessary to make up arrears of maintenance of both track and rolling stock and this could not be postponed further. Hammersmith Vestry was pressing for extensive repairs which could no longer be deferred. This emerged at the general meeting on 22 August 1890 when Bayley said that negotiations had been taking place with the Lineff Electric Traction and Lighting Syndicate Ltd. for electrification of the Uxbridge Road route. Successful trials had been carried out but the negotiations had failed. In response to demands by the Willis faction of shareholders for payment of the Preference dividends, the auditor told the meeting that a large sum must be voted for the reconstruction of the Acton line and he asked the directors to bear in mind that this sum should be retained for the purpose. If this were not done he would not consent to sign the accounts.

Further discussion on electric traction ensued and one shareholder, who had accompanied members of Hammersmith Vestry at the Lineff trials at Chiswick Depot spoke very favourably of the success of the experiment. It was hoped that terms could be agreed with another company for the electrification of the system. The directorate of the company was now Bayley, Duncan and Greig.

Before closing the meeting Bayley said that he hoped that in a year hence the directors would be able to distribute the accumulated dividends. At this time J.H.

Gaynor was the traffic manager and later in the year he was succeeded by Richard Robert Fairbairn, who was to remain in that post throughout the remainder of the life of the company.

The Board of Trade was receiving increasing complaints from the local authorities about the condition of the track and paving. The rolling stock was also the subject of adverse comments. The poor state of the track accelerated the deterioration of the car bodies and running speeds became so low that on many sections the cars were able to travel at little faster than walking pace. The stock of horses was likewise becoming decrepit and many were in need of replacement, this becoming another factor in slowing down the service and increasing costs.

As a result of the complaints by the local authorities the Board of Trade deputed Gen. Hutchinson to inspect and report upon the Acton and Hammersmith tracks, and Hammersmith Vestry asked that the matter should be taken up with the company. Hutchinson carried out his inspection on 12 March 1891 and said that he had found the Goldhawk Road tramway "in fair order". Only single-horse cars were in use and the line was suitable for such light traffic. He said he could not see his way clear to compel the company to relay the track in heavy girder rail but noted that there were plans to electrify the system. Hutchinson was less definite about the Acton line, in view of the fact that in November 1890 113 residents in Uxbridge Road, Shepherds Bush had petitioned Hammersmith Vestry, calling attention to "the disgraceful state of the tramway in Uxbridge Road". Hutchinson made the point that the Vestry's portion of the paving was no better than that on the tramway. Acton Local Board wanted not only complete reconstruction but also demanded that the level of the tramway be raised throughout. An old sewer in the town was due for replacement and the Local Board said that the tramway would have to be taken out to carry out the essential work.

These matters were discussed at the half-yearly shareholders' meeting on 20 March 1891. Receipts had again increased but maintenance costs were heavy. Bayley accused the local authorities of allowing their portion of the roads to fall into disrepair and force the general traffic onto the tramway area, rapidly wearing

Between 1882 and 1894 the Goldhawk Road service was worked by Falcon single-deck one-horse cars. This view of No. 10, at The Lawn, Shepherds Bush, can be dated as being between c1891/4 by the name of the Manager, R.R. Fairbairn, shown on the rocker panel.
(Courtesy: London Borough of Hammersmith & Fulham Libraries)

it out at the company's expense. The directors felt able to recommend dividends on the Ordinary shares and the Preferences; however, they were unable to recommend their distribution in view of the heavy reconstruction costs now imminent. They proposed to reconstruct the Shepherds Bush – Acton and Young's Corner – Kew Bridge tramways as double lines, paying the contractors partly in shares and partly in debentures. Bayley insisted that the time for "cobbling up" the old track was past and had arrived for the authorised reconstruction to be put in hand.

Some shareholders suggested that the accumulated dividends should be at once distributed in the form of Preference shares; the directors preferred that the money should be treated as a loan from revenue to capital. Bayley stressed the importance of not allowing the reconstruction powers of the 1889 Act to lapse, saying that if the works in the Act had not been completed by August 1891 the company faced a very bleak future. The Bill to extend the powers was deposited in November 1890 and was about to pass through Parliament. The powers of the 1889 Act were due to lapse on 26 August 1891 and the new Bill, in addition to seeking the extension of time, also sought to vary the terms of the 1889 Act to the extent that the reconstruction of the track in Acton as a double line should be carried out as such, as far as Birkbeck Grove, instead of Birkbeck Road. This came about on account of the North London Railway bridge across Acton Vale, then an old brick arch which was very narrow, and it had been found that the track beneath it could be constructed only as a single line. As a result, the 1891 Bill sought authority to reconstruct as a double line only as far as the east side of the bridge, near Birkbeck Grove. A two-year extension had been requested but the 1889 powers were extended for twelve months only from the date of passing the Act and the powers relating to electrical or mechanical power were extended by seven years from 21 July 1891 when the Act received the Royal Assent. Experiments with electric traction in 1888 and 1890 are described in Appendix 2.

The company's lease of the depot premises in Uxbridge Road, Shepherds Bush was due to expire in 1892 and the site was required for the new Shepherds Bush Public Library, which opened in 1896. The WMT secured a lease on a monthly tenancy of premises a short distance away at 43a Goldhawk Road; these premises were situated to the rear of buildings fronting Goldhawk Road and were approached by a narrow entry between them. The company submitted plans for a rail access to the premises in the Summer of 1892 and Hammersmith Vestry granted permission to lay the necessary track on 11 August 1892. The depot was leased from W.J. Apperley at £41.0s.4d per month and the WMT's successor company, the London United Tramways vacated the premises at the end of the term in September 1902. The directorate of the company at 1891 remained as Bayley, Duncan and Greig.

From 1891 reports of the company's activities are sparse. Tram services continued unchanged but there were frequent stoppages on all routes owing to rapidly deteriorating track and rolling stock, notwithstanding that receipts had been improving. The high costs of patching-up the worn-out track and paving swallowed up large sums and the withheld dividends, which had been invested in Government securities were still held pending reconstruction of the Acton and Kew Bridge routes. Work commenced during the early Summer of 1893 on relaying the Young's Corner – Kew Bridge section. The work had been completed by 31 August 1893 when Bayley told the shareholders that the work had been carried out on advantageous terms and that accumulated dividends now amounted to £13,974. The shareholders resolved that this sum should be spent on reconstruction and regarded as a loan from revenue to capital.

The powers of the 1891 Act for reconstruction of the Uxbridge Road tramway were restricted to twelve months and had expired on 26 August 1892. Plans were therefore made for the 1893 Session to renew the powers for this reconstruction together with the reconstruction of the Goldhawk Road tramway, between Shepherds Bush and Young's Corner, as a double line throughout. The Uxbridge Road scheme of reconstruction in the 1891 Act as double track from Shepherds Bush to the east side of the North London Railway bridge in Acton Vale was amended by the 1893 Bill to continue as a double line beneath the bridge from Birkbeck Road to Priory Road, now renamed Acton Lane, the terminus of the Reid Brothers line of 1878. From this point to Oldham's Terrace 0.116 miles of single line intervened, and from Oldham's Terrace to a new terminus east of The Steyne the extension was planned as 0.269 miles of double line.

The extension west from Priory Road was rejected on objections by Acton Local Board and the reconstruction as double line reverted to Birkbeck Grove as in the 1891 Act. The reconstruction of the Goldhawk Road tramway was also rejected and the Act which received the Royal Assent on 9 June 1893 granted an extension until 26 August 1895 for the Uxbridge Road reconstruction. Stringent guidelines were laid down covering the methods to be used for reconstructing the part of the Uxbridge Road tramway within Hammersmith (from Shepherds Bush terminus to the Askew Arms). These called for the use of 88lb/yard Bessemer steel girder rails 6in deep with a 6in flange and 1in groove, the joints to be fishplates of Bessemer steel 17in long by 3½in wide and ½in thick. Rails were to be held to gauge with flat iron tie bars, points to be of best cast crucible steel and crossings fabricated from the rails with bed plates and angle pieces supporting all special work. A concrete base to a depth of 6in was also specified. Wood paving between the rails and 18in from the outer rails was to be of the best quality blocks jointed with pitch, creosote oil and fine shingle. There was provision for Hammersmith Vestry to come to an agreement with the WMT to pave the whole width of the road and maintain it subject to agreement with the company on the costs of maintaining the tramway area. This provision was not applied to the Acton portion of the line, west from the Askew Arms.

Shareholders' meetings during 1892 were not reported, but there was a change in the directorate when W.W. Duncan, who had been a director from 1886 was replaced by Alfred Love, who was also a director of the Harrow Road and Paddington Tramways Company. A shareholders' meeting on 31 August 1893, with Bayley presiding presented a confused picture. Traffic had increased over the previous two years and a profit of £1,956 in the past year justified a dividend of 5% on both classes of shares. The £13,974 in accumulated dividends were invested in Government securities, and in 1892 the shareholders had agreed that this sum should be expended on doubling the Young's Corner – Kew Bridge tramway. The work had been carried out on advantageous terms and as a result traffic had increased and·maintenance costs were reduced from £3,000 per annum in a recent half-year to £700. At this point Bayley said "... the property of the company is in a most excellent condition. The stables, buildings and granary are all in first rate order and our stud of horses is second to none...". However, he said that the accumulated dividends would have to remain as a loan from revenue to capital "pending adjustment of the capital account". The shareholders were now up in arms and Bayley was the target of fierce criticism after he had told the meeting that the debenture holders had obtained the appointment of a receiver and manager.

On 25 May 1893 the directors had circularised the shareholders saying that the company's assets stood at £102,000 and average annual net profits were £4,200. The outstanding debenture stock was £32,500 and some of the stockholders had agreed to renew their investment, leaving a shortfall of £10,000. Bayley asked the shareholders to raise this sum. They did not respond and Bayley and his colleagues were attacked in forthright terms and payment of the outstanding dividends was demanded. Bayley had shortly before this been in dispute with his colleagues on the London Road Car Company board and had been removed from the chairmanship after accusations of improper dealings. It became clear that the WMT directors were out of control of the situation, and although the report and accounts were approved at this meeting it was the last at which Bayley officiated as Chairman.

The receiver appointed by the High Court Chancery Division on behalf of the debenture holders was George White, a wealthy Bristol stockbroker with extensive business interests throughout the West Country. He was Chairman of the Bristol Tramways & Carriage Company and had interests in several other tramway undertakings. He and a number of his Bristol associates owned debenture stock in the WMT and their patience with Bayley's management style had run out. The proceedings started on 9 August 1893 before Mr. Justice North when Alderman John Bartlett and Henry Gale Gardner "for themselves and others" applied for the appointment of a receiver and manager for the West Metropolitan Tramways Company. Bartlett was a director of the Gloucester Tramways Company and Gardner a wholesale grocer in Bristol; both were business associates of George White. Evidence was given that payments to the debenture holders including principal and interest amounting to £34,079 were overdue. The judge held that the debenture holders had power to appoint a receiver and manager; appointment of a manager meant that the company could continue to function whereas appointment of a receiver and manager meant that the company would have to be wound up.

After legal submissions the judge said he would appoint a receiver and manager; the company appealed on 10 August and ultimately an Order was made by consent dismissing the appeal. On 24 August the Court made the Order appointing George White receiver and manager of the company. Following this judgement the Court found on 11 November that the debenture holders were entitled to a charge upon the company and on 5 April John Bartlett applied to the Court on behalf of the debenture holders for an Order for the sale of the WMT undertaking. The application was not opposed and Mr. Justice North, after disposing of legal points raised by Counsel, made an order for sale subject to the consent of the Board of Trade. Counsel for the debenture holders asked that the sale should take place out of Court and the judge ruled that if a reasonable offer was obtained it could be brought before a Judge in Chambers for his approval.

As soon as White was appointed receiver he set about the task of making the WMT saleable as a going concern. He had referred to the Court a proposal that he should promote a Bill for the 1894 Session in the name of the company to sanction a rearrangement of the company's capital and to double part of the track in Hammersmith and make additional loops. The WMT directors, who should have approved promotion of the Bill delayed consideration of it until it was too late for submission for the 1894 Session. The text of the Bill had been submitted to the road authorities and the proposal for additional loops in King Street, Hammersmith resulted in objections by the large number of street traders who had from very early times set up stalls in King Street. They feared that if the line was doubled they would no longer be allowed to trade from the pitches allocated to them by Hammersmith Vestry. The traders petitioned the Vestry and the London County Council against the proposals and the LCC Highways Committee discussed the matter on 4 February 1894. They deprecated the position but noted that the Vestry had power to consent to the proposals. The Committee pointed out that the formation of the loops and double track giving less than 9ft 6in clearance between the kerb and outer rails "may be prevented by giving notice to the company under section 7 of the company's Act of 1882". This would have been the case but in the event the Bill was not presented in Parliament owing to the failure to make the necessary deposit in November 1893.

George White and the WMT directors were at loggerheads, the directors accusing him of acting unfairly against them. Following the 31 August 1893 shareholders' meeting a further meeting took place at an unrecorded date prior to 8 February 1894 at which Bayley was replaced as a director by Edwin H. Sloper and as Chairman by Alfred Love. The directorate now consisted of Love, Greig and Sloper. Sloper was a financial agent with directorships of a number of small British and foreign railway companies. It transpired that Love and another WMT director were assisting in the promotion of a Bill by the dormant West London Tramways Company, which had originally been formed in 1890. This company deposited plans in November 1893 for the 1894 Session seeking powers for, yet again, the Askew Road link between Hammersmith and the Uxbridge Road line, an extension of the line in Acton from the Acton Lane terminus to the centre of the town at Mill Hill Grove and from Hammersmith Broadway eastward to William Street (since renamed Russell Road) opposite the Olympia Exhibition Hall.

The shares in this dormant company had changed hands in 1893 and the company's file at 12 February 1894 indicates that Charles Courtney Cramp (a WMT shareholder) had become the largest shareholder and was the engineer to the scheme. Two directors of the Harrow Road & Paddington Tramways Company, Alfred Love (Chairman of the WMT) and William Peacop had purchased shares at 31 December 1893. White condemned this scheme which he said had the objective of obtaining running powers over the WMT system. It was an injurious attack upon the WMT undertaking and if successful would reduce its selling value and the chance of raising new capital would disappear. The West London Tramways Chairman had said he was willing for the WMT to acquire the powers in the Bill on payment of Parliamentary expenses. White said that to gain consent of Hammersmith Vestry for the short piece of line to Olympia the promoters had undertaken to construct the "cross-country" (Askew Road) line which, said White, could not possibly pay.

Already bad feeling between the WMT directors and White worsened as a result of this and White wrote to them on 8 February 1894 pointing out that he was unable to resist the demands of the Hammersmith and Acton authorities for immediate reconstruction of the lines, which had been postponed so many times and for which so many promises had been broken. He pointed out that some 200 rails were split, the rest worn through and the paving setts, used and re-used many times, were worn out. He would be unable to defend any actions the authorities might take and said that the state of the lines was "such that at any moment serious accidents may happen".

White had opened negotiations with Hammersmith Vestry which had resolved to lend the company the money for wood paving in their district, some £8,000, and had been able to obtain better terms than the company envisaged when the 1893 Act was passed. The cost of reconstructing the lines in Hammersmith and the new double line in Acton would amount to between £12,000 and £15,000. The traffic manager, Richard Robert Fairbairn, had drawn White's attention to the state of the cars. Of a total of 45 (32 large and 13 small) the Police would refuse to relicense more than ten of the small cars. Eleven cars were scrap and should be broken up and replaced with new ones. Ten more required extensive reconstruction at a cost of £80 each and the remainder could be overhauled at the cost of £40 each. White thought Fairbairn's estimate was the minimum expenditure required, and to enable the work to be done some £1,000 was required for machinery as none existed at Chiswick Depot. Fairbairn's estimate for work on rolling stock amounted to £4,500 and £1,500 was needed for horses for the Summer traffic. These could be foregone but at the expense of curtailing the car services and the resulting revenue.

White went on to say that within two months the cars' use would be prohibited by the Police and the services suspended. If funds for doubling the Uxbridge Road track could not be found the money necessary to reconstruct the old single track would have to be immediately raised as the two authorities would execute the work themselves or take proceedings to compel the company to do it. White asked the directors to at once provide the necessary funds or, if they were unable to, to allow him to do so by creating a first charge for the money, or finally, if they so preferred, to arrange a sale of the undertaking before the impending perils came to a head. He warned the directors that it was for them and the shareholders to take prompt action to protect their own interests, otherwise the debenture holders would act to secure a realisation. He would report the directors' decision to the debenture holders later in the month.

On 24 February 1894 the WMT Secretary, J.G.B. Elliott replied formally to White, saying that lack of capital prevented the directors from carrying out the works. The late WMT board had made arrangements to purchase new cars in June 1893 and but for the appointment of the receiver the cars would have been delivered and working. He also said that the West London Tramways Bill had been promoted some years earlier (in 1890) but the new board was not committed to the scheme and would probably not proceed with it. Elliott complained that the WMT directors had received no assistance from White and they took exception to his proposal to extend the line at Hammersmith to Olympia and his acting without the consent or knowledge of the company. Elliott went on to complain that the company's books and other documents had been removed to Bristol and the WMT staff had been ordered not to furnish the directors with information. This meant that the shareholders could not be given details of White's proposal in the 1894 Bill to over-ride the Preference and Ordinary capital of the company. The directors were resigned to the debenture holders losing part of their money and the total loss of the Ordinary and Preference share capital.

White replied to Elliott on 2 March pointing out that management failures and the directors' withholding from the shareholders the disgraceful condition of the cars, quoting Fairbairn's report to the directors on 1 January 1892 in which it was stated that "the rolling stock and buildings are in a thorough state of repair" and on 1 January 1893, "the rolling stock and buildings have been well maintained". White said that since his appointment he had been trying to negotiate with the Hammersmith and Acton local authorities postponement of their impending legal action on the permanent way, but without success as they were taking out court summonses on 6 March. White reminded Elliott that the directors had opposed his proposals to re-organise the company's capital to finance the necessary works and the proposed Bill to effect his proposals had failed. White concluded by condemning the directors' actions in forthright terms and said that their reply to his previous letter left him with no alternative except to leave the debenture holders to act to protect their interests. He had done everything in his power for the shareholders but the debenture holders' interests were paramount.

White accordingly asked the Court to approve a sale of the company's assets, consent for which was given by a Judge in Chambers. The sale was thereupon approved by the Board of Trade. The firm of Edwin Fox & Bousfield was instructed to submit the undertaking to auction as a going concern. The assets listed in the sale catalogue consisted of the powers of the company under the Acts of 1873, 1876, 1881, 1882, 1884, 1887, 1889, 1891 and 1893; the tramways in Uxbridge Road between Shepherds Bush and Priory Road, Acton; the Goldhawk Road tramway; the Young's Corner – Kew Bridge tramway; the Kew – Richmond tramway and the tramways in Central Hammersmith between Young's Corner and the Broadway with the loop line. Buildings offered consisted of Richmond Depot held on a 21 years lease from Christmas 1882 at an annual rent of £75; Chiswick Depot held on a 60 years lease from Midsummer 1883 at an annual rent of £225; Shepherds Bush Depot held for ten years from September 1892 at a monthly rent of £41.0s.4d. Chiswick Depot could accommodate 140-170 horses and 20 cars; Richmond Depot had space for 30 horses and a yard to hold 6 cars and Shepherds Bush Depot accommodated 61 horses and the yard had space for seven pair-horse cars. Rolling stock consisted of 33 pair-horse and single-horse cars with fifteen new pair-horse cars on order from Geo. F. Milnes & Co. of Birkenhead.

The auction took place at the London Auction Mart on 13 June 1894 and the auctioneer failed to receive a bid. The undertaking was thereupon purchased privately on 6 August by August Krauss, a public works contractor of Bristol, who acted as an agent for the Imperial Tramways Company Ltd. of which George White was Managing Director. Krauss paid £30,000 for the undertaking and the property was reconveyed on 20 August to a newly-formed company, the London United Tramways Limited, the Chairman of which was George White. The West Metropolitan Tramways Company's debenture holders recovered their assets but the Preference and Ordinary shareholders' investments were lost. The WMT trams had stopped running on 6 March and a new chapter was about to commence in the story of tramways in West London.

CHAPTER THREE

THE LONDON UNITED TRAMWAYS 1894-1900

Following the collapse of the West Metropolitan Tramways Company and the failure of the auction of the company's assets to attract a buyer at the sale on 13 June 1894, some far-reaching moves took place behind the scenes, involving George White, the Receiver and Manager of the WMT, August Krauss, a director of the City of York Tramways Company and a public works contractor of Bristol, and James Clifton Robinson, the last bringing to the London scene a name which was to become one of the best-known, if not the best known personality in British tramway history.

On 19 July 1894 a new company, the London United Tramways was incorporated under the Companies Acts, with authorised share capital of £50,000, half in Ordinary and half in 4% Preference shares, all of £10 each. The first subscribers were August Krauss; Hugh G. Doggett, a solicitor; Henry Gale Gardner, a director of the City of Gloucester Tramways Company; Joseph Kincaid, Chairman of the Gloucester Tramways Company and the Engineer to the first LUT scheme; William Butler, Chairman of the Bristol Tramways and Carriage Company; Alderman John Bartlett and James Clifton Robinson, a civil engineer and Managing Director of the Imperial Tramways Company Ltd. The company's registered office was initially at 19, Clare Street, Bristol and by 31 January 1895 had been transferred to Clare Street House, 28, Clare Street, Bristol. The first directors were George White (Chairman); James Clifton Robinson (Managing Director); Samual White; William George Verdon Smith; Edward Everard, a printer and publisher and Hugh C. Godfray, a solicitor associated with a number of other tramway undertakings. James Clifton Robinson was Secretary and the new company was largely financed by the White family and the Imperial Tramways Company also had a large shareholding. All of these initial subscribers and directors were business associates of George White in various ways. George White

Sir George White   Sir Clifton Robinson

had a controlling interest in the Imperial Tramways Company. At first the firm of Kincaid Waller & Manville acted as consulting engineers and by 31 January 1895 the office of company secretary had passed to Samuel White, brother of George White.

On 21 August 1894 the company entered into a contract with August Krauss. Krauss, acting as nominee for George White and the new company had bought the assets of the West Metropolitan Tramways Company from the Court of Chancery, which had held the assets on behalf of George White, the West Metropolitan Company's receiver. These assets are described at the end of Chapter 2. Krauss had submitted to the Court an offer of £30,000 for the assets, and on being advised that this sum satisfied the West Metropolitan debenture holders' claim, the Court sanctioned the sale of the West Metropolitan Tramways undertaking to the London United Tramways Ltd. The undertaking was duly conveyed to the LUT by an indenture dated 20 August 1894 for the sum of £30,000. The Board of Trade approved the transaction on 10 October.

Under the terms of the contract Krauss undertook to reconstruct the tramway between Shepherds Bush and Acton as laid down in the West Metropolitan Act of 1889. This tramway had been the subject of lengthy disputes between the West Metropolitan company and the Hammersmith and Acton local authorities, which had obtained court orders to compel its reconstruction. The powers for this work had been extended from time to time and no further delay in executing the work would be countenanced. In addition to this work Krauss undertook to build offices and stores in High Road, Chiswick at the entrance to the depot and to generally refurbish the depot at Richmond both of which were inadequate for the requirements of a satisfactory tramway service.

There was a clause in this agreement which indicates that the LUT might not proceed with the reconstruction of the Acton line or, if the work had already commenced, it might be stopped, the rails taken up, the road restored and any part of the existing tramway removed or damaged in the course of the work reinstated. The contract also stipulated that the contractor should supply not less than fifty suitable horses, forty double sets of harness and "all such other articles and things

LUT car No. 54, designed by J.C. Robinson, was one of ten built in 1896 at the new workshop of the company at Chiswick.   (Source Unknown)

as in the opinion of the Engineers shall be required in order to completely equip the tramways depots works and establishments of the company and put the undertaking of the company into a proper condition as required for a well organised and properly equipped tramway undertaking". The agreed contract price for these works was £49,930, to be paid by the issue of £25,000 in paid-up 4% Preference shares in the company and £24,930 in paid-up Ordinary shares, by instalments starting with £10,000 within three months of the date of the contract and further payments as and when the Engineers might certify from time to time.

George White and Clifton Robinson were determined at the outset to electrify on the overhead trolley system the old WMT lines and future extensions. This, however, was to be fraught with difficulties, the chief obstacles to this being the London County Council and the authorities responsible for the Geomagnetic Observatory at Kew. On a local level Hammersmith Vestry had been won over by Robinson, who had taken the Vestry Surveyor, H. Mair to France to view the recently-installed overhead trolley tramway at Le Havre. Robinson had formally asked for sanction for overhead working on the Shepherds Bush – Acton line on 31 October 1894 and the visit was promptly arranged. Mair reported favourably upon the Le Havre system to the Works Committee on 12 November and on 14 November he reported to a full meeting of the Vestry, recommending them to consent to electrification of the Hammersmith lines on the overhead system. The vote in favour was unanimous and members hoped that the London County Council "would give their rapid consent" for electrification.

Earlier, on 11 July 1894 August Krauss had met the Works Committee, saying that he was contracted to spend £25,000 to reconstruct the Uxbridge Road tramway as a double line. Work would start early in 1895 and the line would be ready for traffic on 1 May. Meanwhile he would do his utmost to keep the existing track in a fair state of repair. The Vestry had complained to the Board of Trade about the state of the Hammersmith tracks, as had Acton Urban District Council, and Gen. Hutchinson carried out an inspection in company with George Hopkins, Engineer to the North Metropolitan Tramways Company. Hutchinson reported to the Board of Trade and the Vestry on 28 July, saying that a large amount of remedial work had been carried out, and while the line was not dangerous "the rails were not of any use". Hopkins concurred with this view and pointed out to the Board that the whole Uxbridge Road line from Shepherds Bush to Acton was about to be reconstructed "in accordance with the (West Metropolitan) 1889 Act".

Immediately after taking possession of the West Metropolitan lines the LUT had tackled the arrears of maintenance on all the lines. By September 1894 the Acton line had been returned to a reasonable working condition and urgent repair work was being commenced in Hammersmith and on the line to Kew Bridge. The Kew Bridge – Richmond tramway was also taken in hand, and some repair work was done in Goldhawk Road. Much of the rolling stock was incapable of refurbishment to the requirements of the Police and was scrapped out of hand, including four of the cars working on the Kew Road line. The West Metropolitan company had, shortly before the appointment of George White as receiver, ordered fifteen new pair-horse cars from Geo. F. Milnes & Co. of Birkenhead; these were forty-six seaters, twenty in the saloon and 26 on the upper deck. The new cars were supplemented by a number of the old cars which had been taken in hand at Chiswick Depot and renovated to acceptable standards.

The facilities at Chiswick Depot for maintenance of the cars were minimal and part of Krauss' contract covered the extension of the buildings there and installation of machinery to cope with overhaul work and construction of new vehicles. As soon as this work had been carried out the company embarked upon the construction of a number of cars to Robinson's designs, which were described as among the best horse-drawn trams in the country, boasting excellent seating, interior finish and lighting, with easily-negotiable staircases and wearing smart and decorative liveries. Platform and other operating staff were provided with well-cut blue uniforms, in contrast to the rough and ready appearance of the men on the old company's cars.

Hammersmith Vestry Works Committee met on 23 January 1895 and discussed the London County Council's attitude to electrification. The LUT representative at the meeting said that the moment the company received approval for electric traction in Uxbridge Road they would reduce fares on Sundays and public holidays over the whole system. If, however, the LCC did not consent to electric traction the company would reconstruct the line for horse traction. Charles Courtney Cramp who, it will be recalled, operated the 1874 Uxbridge Road tramway on behalf of its then owners, was a member of the Vestry and was taking an active part in promoting the LUT electric traction proposals. He moved that a clause be inserted in an agreement with the LUT under which the LUT would agree to proceed with the reconstruction of the Uxbridge Road tramway within fourteen days of receiving a decision either way on electrification. This was resolved and the Vestry consented to the draft Provisional Order.

The LCC continued with its refusal to sanction electric traction and on 6 March 1895 the company advised the Vestry that reconstruction had started in King Street, Hammersmith and Uxbridge Road on 4 March, with King Street to be completed within six weeks and Uxbridge Road in thirteen weeks. King Street had been paved in setts and at first it was agreed that setts would be used in the reconstruction. However the company and both the Acton and Hammersmith authorities came to agreements to pave in hardwood blocks. Some initial work had been done in setts but this was halted and the setts laid replaced with wood paving. Hammersmith Vestry repaved the rest of King Street and Uxbridge Road with wood blocks at the same time as the LUT was reconstructing the track and Acton UDC followed a similar pattern. Thus a consistent standard of construction was achieved throughout. George Wimpey & Co. carried out the paving in both thoroughfares. The Vestry had undertaken to reimburse the LUT part of the cost of repaving the tramway area in wood blocks under the terms of the West Metropolitan Tramways Act of 1893.

The negotiations with Acton UDC on the company's proposals in the 1895 Provisional Order were protracted and initially acrimonious. Local residents and business interests at the outset expressed support for the company's proposals, while the UDC, doubtless with memories of earlier dealings with the erstwhile West Metropolitan Tramways Company, declined to approve the LUT proposal to extend the existing tramway through the town to the top of Acton Hill, where it was proposed to erect a new depot at a cost estimated between £3,000 and £4,000. The extension sought was a little more than half a mile in length and was described in the Order as commencing on the east side of the North London Railway bridge across Acton Vale, at Birkbeck Grove. The West Metropolitan Act of 1889 empowered the company to reconstruct the Uxbridge Road tramway as far as Birkbeck Road, west of the bridge. A later WMT Act of 1891 extended the time to complete this work by one year to 26 August 1892 and at the same time amended the termination of the line at the Acton end to Birkbeck Grove, which was east of the bridge. No reason was adduced in the Act for this alteration of the terminal point from the west side of the bridge to the east side, but it may have been due to the possibility that track below the bridge might have to be single instead of the double line authorised in 1889. The original brick arch did not allow space for a double line, and even after the bridge was reconstructed the track beneath the bridge remained an interlacing to the end of tramway operation.

The 1895 Provisional Order authorised the extension to the top of Acton Hill, 0.602 miles, of which 0.407 miles was single and 0.195 miles double line. Neither Birkbeck Grove or Birkbeck Road were terminal points of the original authorised tramways in Acton, the 1878 extension from the Princess Victoria at Askew Crescent having terminated at the present-day Acton Lane, some 150 yards west of Birkbeck Road.

Acton UDC declined at the outset to approve the LUT application to take the line to the top of Acton Hill, despite local interests being largely in favour of the extension. Consequently a number of influential residents and businessmen formed a committee in support of the company's proposals, and at their inaugural meeting in the Acton Assembly Rooms on 15 January 1895 the committee unanimously approved the details of the LUT application of 22 October 1894 and asked the UDC to consent to the application at once, to allow the construction work to be commenced at the earliest possible moment. A copy of the resolution was sent to the council, and at the same time the newly-formed Tramways Extension Committee drew up a petition to the Board of Trade in favour of the scheme, to which 1,300 signatures were appended.

A further meeting of the committee was held at the George and Dragon Hotel on 18 January 1895 at which Clifton Robinson was present. He told the meeting that he had attended a meeting of the Urban District Council, and placed before them the position of the company. The council considered that insufficient inducement had been offered to them to consent to the application. When the West Metropolitan Tramways obtained their 1889 Act for reconstruction of their lines, Hammersmith Vestry was empowered to ask for wood paving in the whole of the tramway area in their district, and it was agreed that at the same time as the WMT reconstructed the tracks and paved the tramway areas in wood blocks, the Vestry would similarly and simultaneously pave the rest of the roadway in King Street, which was then paved in granite setts from kerb to kerb. Acton Council, on the other hand, and Brentford Council, had asked for granite sett paving in the tramway area in their districts, and the powers of the 1889 Act in respect of the Uxbridge Road tramway, which were extended in the 1893 Act until 26 August 1895 still carried the obligation, now vested in the LUT, to pave the Acton section in granite setts.

Robinson told the meeting that at the time the WMT 1889 Act was passing through Parliament, the Acton district surveyor had distinctly requested granite sett paving on the Acton part of the Uxbridge Road tramway. This requirement was incorporated in the 1889 Act and placed a statutory obligation upon the LUT to use granite setts on the tramway area in any future reconstruction, which could only be altered by agreement between the parties. The condition of the line when the company came into possession of it, called for complete reconstruction and expenditure of some £30,000 was envisaged. The work would have started earlier if the question of electric traction had not intervened. Hammersmith Vestry had given cordial support for electrification in their district but Acton UDC, when approached on the subject, did not commit themselves. Meanwhile, the London County Council flatly refused their consent for electric traction in Hammersmith, thus nullifying Hammersmith Vestry's readily-given consent, and the Middlesex County Council was also threatening to veto electric traction on the county's roads. The LUT was therefore, for the time being, unable to pursue the matter of electric traction and would proceed with the necessary works to reconstruct the lines for horse traction.

On 11 October 1894 the LUT had received a letter from Acton UDC asking on what terms the company would abandon the use of granite setts and lay wood paving in the tramway area along the whole of the line about to be reconstructed. Robinson said he had told the UDC that the company would be able to incur the expense of wood paving in the event of sanction being given by the local authorities for electric traction on the Acton tramway, and the consent of the council to the construction of the half- mile extension to the top of Acton Hill. Electric traction being ruled out for the foreseeable future by the action of the London County Council meant that the extra expense of laying wood blocks in Acton could not be justified. Robinson said he had offered to abolish double fares on Sundays and Bank Holidays, to run workmen's fares on early mornings and late evenings at half fares and to introduce scholars' fares and season tickets. The council refused to move from their position and no progress was made.

At a meeting of the council on 26 February 1895 Joseph Kincaid of the firm of Kincaid, Waller & Manville, consulting engineers to the LUT, attended on the company's behalf and pressed for a decision. The company offered the council £1,000 as a contribution towards the cost of widening the narrow High Street, which was refused. Robinson told the Committee that with electric traction the company could have met the additional costs of wood paving with equanimity. He pointed out that the difference between electric traction and horse traction costs was 50% of gross revenue for electric traction against 90% for horse traction. There would also be an increase in paving costs of between £4,000 and £5,000 for wood paving and maintenance costs would be enormous. Maintenance costs of a granite-paved tramway were about £50 per mile per annum but with wood paving patching and tinkering never ceased. Robinson pointed out that the existing terminus near the North London Railway bridge was not the natural terminus and that the company had met some objections to a double line through the town by amending the plans suitably. The company proposed to build a depot at the top of Acton Hill, their men would live in the town and increase the town's trade.

Members of the Committee expressed approval of the scheme and resolved to send a further deputation to the council to press the urgency of their acceptance, without delay, of the company's terms, believing that the proposed extension of the tramways "would be conducive to the best interests of trade, and beneficial to the whole of the inhabitants".

Following this meeting, Robinson consulted his co-directors and they agreed to offer, in lieu of the cash payment of £1,000 to pave the whole of the existing tramway and the extension to Acton Hill with hardwood blocks if the council consented to the Acton Hill extension and agreed to contribute £100 per annum towards the maintenance of the track paving. They pointed out that Hammersmith Vestry had agreed to pay the company £150 a year towards the costs of maintaining the shorter wood-paved track in King Street.

In February 1895 Middlesex County Council proposed to follow the London County Council's example to veto the use of electric traction in their county. It was reported that this could be the last straw for the LUT and lead to the abandonment of the Acton Hill extension. The Acton newspapers strongly urged Acton UDC to accept the company's offer to wood pave the line in consideration of the £100 annual maintenance contribution. In March the company made a further offer, to forego this contribution, and at last the council agreed, in principle only, to consent to the Acton Hill extension and a draft agreement was being prepared by the council's clerk.

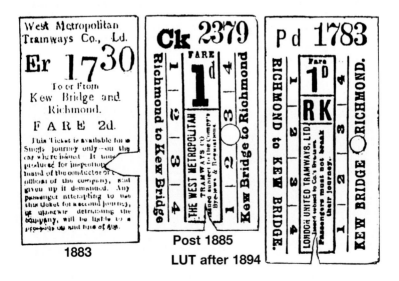

A selection of tickets used by the WMT and LUT before electrification.

Early in May, Middlesex County Council asked Acton UDC if they had consented to the grant of the company's Provisional Order, and the council's Clerk was instructed to "reply in the affirmative". After further discussion the council agreed to the use of wood blocks in lieu of the granite sett paving but resolved to insist upon the company paying the legal costs of the council's opposition.

With these difficulties cleared the major obstacle to the realisation of the company's plans, the county councils' vetos on electric traction remained to be surmounted. The LUT directors turned their attention for the time being to the construction and reconstruction (for horse traction) authorised in the 1895 Provisional Order, which had meanwhile been confirmed in the Tramways Confirmation Act (No. 1) 1895, which received the Royal Assent on 6 July 1895.

Before the part of the Uxbridge Road line which lay in Hammersmith between Shepherds Bush terminus and the Askew Arms could be reconstructed as a double line replacing the single track with eight loops the road had to be widened at several points to the satisfaction of the London County Council and Hammersmith Vestry. These works commenced on 4 March 1895, in both Uxbridge Road and King Street, Hammersmith, the work in Uxbridge Road to be completed within 13 weeks and that in King Street in six weeks. Work went on apace and reached Birkbeck Grove, in Acton, from whence the existing line was reconstructed and extended under the 1895 Provisional Order to the top of Acton Hill as authorised. When completed the line from the county and district boundary at the Askew Arms consisted of double track from that point to Birkbeck Grove, east of the North London Railway bridge and single track with five loops westward from Birkbeck Grove, all these loops being west of the bridge. The total of reconstructed and new route consisted of 3.116 miles of which 0.407 miles was single track wholly in Acton and the remainder double.

The work carried out in King Street, Hammersmith consisted of replacing four short single track sections as loops, between Rivercourt Road and The Grove. The company's Order authorised five loops, but one, at a spot near the present Nigel Playfair Avenue (then named Waterloo Street) was, by agreement with the Vestry, not constructed. The other authorised work in Hammersmith consisted of a short connecting single line in The Grove (now renamed Hammersmith Grove) between Beadon Road and King Street to form a relief line to allow cars to reverse short of the busy junction at the Broadway, King Street and Beadon Road at busy times. The loops in King Street were authorised to ease congestion along the stretch between Studland Street and The Grove where street traders had acquired rights to set up stalls along the roadway and had objected to the laying of a double line throughout King Street on the grounds that these rights would be imperilled if a double line was laid.

The 1895 extension through High Street, Acton was laid as single track with passing places, also shown on the plan overleaf. (Courtesy: Acton Library)

44

The work in Acton and Hammersmith was completed by mid-August 1895 and was inspected for the Board of Trade by Major F.A. Marindin on 30 August. His report dated 31 August stated that he had found the work satisfactory, paving over all the new work being in hardwood blocks. Part of the earliest work had been paved with granite setts but the local authorities had come to agreements with the company and the setts at first laid were replaced with wood blocks, and some small part of the paving remained to be completed at the time of the inspection. Maj. Marindin recommended the Board of Trade to issue a certificate of fitness for public use, which was signed and despatched to Clifton Robinson on 6 September. In view of the earlier difficulties over paving he made a further inspection of the paving on 15 January 1896, and finding the work completed he reported briefly on 16 January that all work was satisfactory "and presents an excellent appearance".

The *Acton and Chiswick Gazette* reported on 7 September 1895 on the opening of the line from Shepherds Bush to the new terminus at the top of Acton Hill. The trams had started running from Shepherds Bush to the top of Acton Hill on Saturday 31 August The whole of the cars working on the Uxbridge Road route were newly-delivered from Geo. F. Milnes & Co. of Birkenhead and the construction work and paving on Uxbridge Road and in Hammersmith were carried out on behalf of August Krauss by George Wimpey & Co. of Hammersmith. New harness and other fittings had been supplied by Krauss with fifty new horses. The company was running workmen's cars from Acton Hill to Shepherds Bush from 5am until 8am at one penny for the complete journey with similar return cars at late afternoons and evenings. To celebrate the re-opening of the Uxbridge Road line and the extension to Acton Hill Robinson fulfilled his promise to abolish double fares on Sundays and Bank Holidays, and this welcome alteration was applied to the rest of the system. The LUT was in the process of acquiring a three-quarter acre site at the top of Acton Hill on the south side of Uxbridge Road, and spacious stables and a car shed were about to be erected on the site. For the time being the depot and stables in Goldhawk Road provided accommodation for the Uxbridge Road services.

Plans deposited with the Board of Trade showed six-inch deep girder rails of 88lb/yard and heavy concrete foundations for the track. The Acton and Chiswick Gazette referred to rails of 92½lb/yard – "the heaviest rails used on any tramway system in the world". There is conflicting evidence on this point, as a report on the LUT system prepared in 1909 by J.G. White & Co. Ltd. states that the rails on the Acton and Kew Bridge lines had been laid in 80lb/yard rails. The fact that both these sections had to be relaid in 1908 and 1904 respectively in 100lb/yard and 92½lb/yard rails indicates that the lighter weight of rail had been used for both the 1893 reconstruction of the Kew Bridge line by the WMT and the 1895 Uxbridge Road reconstruction, notwithstanding the requirement in the 1893 and 1895 legislation for 88lb/yard rails.

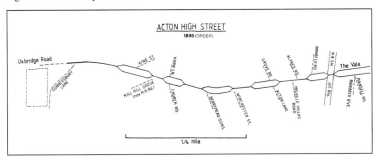

A plan of the tracks laid through High Street, Acton, showing the single track sections with passing loops. With electrification, the single sections were replaced with interlaced track, but subsequently mostly doubled.

The new offices of the company, built in 1896 at Chiswick, on the north side of the High Road. Part of the depot building can also be seen. (Photo: LUT)

In consideration of the reconstruction in Hammersmith the London County Council postponed their power to purchase the lines there from 1903 to July, 1909. Notwithstanding the LCC's oft-repeated declaration of their intention to own all tramways in the county, the LUT started looking ahead to extend their lines into Central London at the same time as they prepared to make further attempts to obtain the consent of the LCC to use electric traction in Hammersmith.

During this time the depot at Chiswick had been extended under the terms of August Krauss' contract with the company. A new office building in classical style was erected at the west corner of the entrance, car sheds enlarged and a machine shop built to enable repairs to rolling stock and other work to be carried out. There had previously been virtually no facilities for this work and doubtless this accounted for the decrepit state of the WMT company's rolling stock and other equipment at the time the LUT came into possession of the system. The installation of a large new Tangye gas engine enabled machinery to be driven from overhead shafting, not only for repairs to the cars but also machinery for cutting, grinding and mixing the various substances which went up to make up the feed for the horses.

The new depot at Acton went into use in March 1896, allowing a considerable reduction of dead mileage between Shepherds Bush and Acton. It was a handsome brick building with stone ornaments, with stabling on the west side and a seven-track car shed, with offices and stores and a house for the depot superintendent on the east side.

The company was not disposed to embark upon further large schemes with the question of electric traction unresolved. This problem was two-fold, the first part being the continued refusal of the London County Council to consent to electric operation in Hammersmith, while the other difficulty was centred upon the Geomagnetic Observatory at Kew, whose proximity to the intended electric lines was to be the subject of prolonged argument between the LUT and the scientific institutions over the effect of the tramways' earth returns on the instruments at the Observatory.

Earlier refusals by the LCC to approve electric traction resulted in the LUT abandoning, for the time being, any further attempt to gain their consent. However, neither the LUT or Hammersmith Vestry allowed the matter to rest for long. One move on the part of Hammersmith Vestry was to accept an offer by the British Westinghouse Electric & Manufacturing Company to inspect a model electric tramcar. The Vestry Works Committee viewed the model at the Westinghouse offices at 32, Victoria Street, Westminster on 3 October 1895, but the Vestry's archives do not record any further action on their part. In February 1896 the LCC Parliamentary Committee discussed a proposed LUT Provisional Order seeking exemption from the London Overhead Wires Act of 1891 and authority for the LUT, with LCC consent, to use overhead electric traction. The LCC had twice in 1895 refused consent and this time their Highways Committee had once more recommended the Parliamentary Committee to refuse consent which, they in turn duly recommended the county council should do.

The rehabilitation of the horse tramways in Hammersmith and Acton was but a stepping-stone towards the ultimate goal of George White and Clifton Robinson, notwithstanding the as-yet unbending attitude of the LCC to electric traction. Their goal remained the electrification of the existing lines and the extension of the line at Acton through Ealing and on to Uxbridge and even beyond. The route along Uxbridge Road was developing fast; Ealing was already a large and important town and Hanwell becoming built up as a residential suburb, into which there was a steady influx of people from the more crowded areas of inner west London, while Southall, at the time a small, self-contained market town at some remove from its eastern and western neighbours, had much scope for industrial development which followed in the wake of the trams. Beyond Southall the small townships of Hayes and Hillingdon had ample scope for development, while Uxbridge, the county town of Middlesex, was an important centre containing some large hotels, some industrial development related mainly to agriculture at the time, and was a favoured resort for West Londoners at week-ends and holiday times, the attractions being the nearby river and many inns.

The existing terminus at Kew Bridge was being considered for extension through Brentford and Isleworth to Hounslow and beyond, and plans were mooted to carry the line at Isleworth, when built, through to Twickenham and on to Hampton Court, thence across the Thames to reach the important town of Kingston, a Royal Borough and the county town of Surrey. From Kingston it was

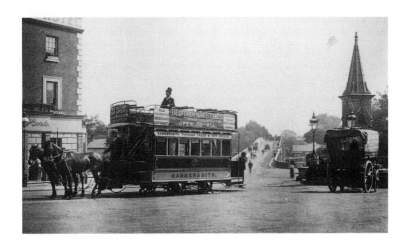

Looking towards the narrow 18th century Kew Bridge, this c1896 view shows car No. 7, one of 15 supplied by G.F. Milnes in 1894. The top deck passenger may have been celebrating at the nearby 'Star & Garter' hotel.   (Brentford & Chiswick Times)

intended to extend eastward through Malden and Wimbledon to Tooting, at which point the yet-to-be electrified lines of the London County Council might be met with the hope of mutual running powers allowing the future London United electric trams to reach Central London.

The Kew Road tramway, which was a mainly single line between the south side of Kew Bridge and Richmond was isolated from the main route through Chiswick and Brentford on account of the condition of the bridge, which was a narrow, eighteenth-century structure with steeply graded approaches unsuitable for any type of tramway, was also a candidate for electrification and, once the bridge was rebuilt, linking the Chiswick and Hounslow route with Richmond and beyond through Barnes and across Hammersmith Bridge to Hammersmith Broadway. Alternative proposals for the Kew – Richmond line at this early stage were for a route from the south side of Kew Bridge through Sandycombe Road, Manor Road and Queen's Road to Richmond Hill and on to Kingston via Petersham and Ham.

The first London United Tramways Bill was submitted to Parliament in November 1897 and sought powers to electrify the lines already in operation, to construct extensions to these and to construct additional lines, the total mileage of new construction being a little over 9.25 miles, almost the whole of which was intended as double line. The line terminating at Kew Bridge was to be taken through Brentford to The Bell at Hounslow. From Acton Hill, at which point the new depot had been built in 1895/6, the Uxbridge Road line was to continue through Ealing as far as the River Brent at Hanwell. A new cross-country route was proposed to link the main road through Brentford with the proposed line in Uxbridge Road at Hanwell, starting in High Street, Brentford and passing along Half Acre, Boston Road and Lower Boston Road to join the intended line in High Street, Hanwell 75 yards east of the bridge across the River Brent. The Bill also sought powers to construct generating stations on land adjacent to the depots at Acton and Chiswick and to purchase up to five acres of land for the purposes of the undertaking but not for use as generating stations.

The main opposition to the Bill came from Ealing Urban District Council. Ealing, the self-styled "Queen of the Suburbs" (for which honour it vied with Richmond) was already a high-class town containing many large residences standing in extensive gardens, with well-kept parks and was an excellent shopping centre, as well as the home of a large number of influential people who, being largely carriage owners, were opposed to the extensions of tramways through their town. Clifton Robinson realised at the outset that it would require a determined effort to overcome the powerful local opposition, and with council elections due to take place in the spring of 1898 he commenced publication of a newspaper, the *Ealing Election News,* which ran for seven issues between 16 February and 30 March 1898. A companion paper, the *Chiswick Electric Tramway News,* ran for five issues, from 16 February to 5 April. Both papers contained forthright pro-tram articles by Robinson, with powerful propaganda on behalf of the pro-tramway candidates. An article in the Chiswick paper on future electric rolling stock told its readers that "in summer awnings will protect the 'outsides' from the heat of the sun". Robinson received great encouragement in his endeavours from the proprietors of the *Middlesex County Times* and the *Ealing Gazette* and other local newspapers, King & Hutchings, who doubtless provided Robinson with professional assistance with his publicity machine.

Chiswick did not prove so intractable as Ealing, where the anti-tram party had won the local council elections by a small majority, Ealing UDC refused to consent to the line in their district, which was struck out of the Bill. The extension from Kew Bridge to Hounslow, the new Brentford – Hanwell line and the proposals for the generating stations and acquisition of lands were authorised, the Bill receiving the Royal Assent on 12 August 1898.

The merits of different forms of electric traction had loomed large in the arguments for and against in the 1898 Bill; Ealing UDC had been horror-struck at the idea of the overhead trolley system. The question of electric traction was

THE CHISWICK
ELECTRIC
Tramways News.

| No. 1. | SATURDAY, MAR. 5, 1898. | PRICE ONE PENNY. |

The masthead from one of J.Clifton Robinson's propaganda newspapers.

touched upon in the 1898 Bill. At the instance of the Royal Society and the scientific committee responsible for the Kew Geomagnetic Observatory provisions were inserted on behalf of the Observatory which called for a fully insulated return with special cabling and for representatives of the Commissioners of the Office of Works to have the right, if they suspected that the company's earth returns and insulation was producing a magnetic field likely to affect the Kew instruments, to inspect the company's equipment and if thought necessary, to require the company to take such steps as thought desirable to prevent the production of such magnetic fields. The LUT was also required to furnish the Commissioners with particulars of the methods of insulation proposed to be adopted and the distances between conductors carrying the current to and from the cars. Details of the lengthy negotiations on this subject and their effect upon the company's operations are given in Chapter 4.

Acton UDC, mindful of the company's submission in 1895 that the costs of electric traction were considerably lower than those of horse traction, gained a clause whereby, on the day that electric trams commenced running through the district no journey from Shepherds Bush terminus to any part of the parish of Acton should be charged at more than one penny.

Concurrently with the passage of the 1898 Bill through Parliament an application was lodged with the Light Railway Commissioners for an Order under the 1896 Light Railways Act. The sponsors of this Act envisaged that it would facilitate the promotion of railways in sparsely-populated rural areas to link poorly-served districts between main lines, and assist the agricultural community to convey their produce and supplies more cheaply and expeditiously than by main line railways or by roundabout routes over indifferent roads. The exact nature of a "light railway" was not defined in the Act, and Clifton Robinson saw in this omission a cheaper and faster way of obtaining powers than by the Parliamentary process. There were other advantages in so proceeding, among them a reduction of the local authority rate demands, which were a considerable expense to tramway undertakings. There were some disadvantages in the procedure, but on balance there were numerous advantages and following Robinson's example a large number of undertakings obtained powers under the Act for what were in everything but name, street tramways.

The LUT application of May 1898 was for an Order covering nearly twelve miles of which 7.25 miles would extend from Hanwell, Southall, Hayes and Hillingdon to Uxbridge and consist largely of single track and passing loops, entirely within the county of Middlesex, commencing at the termination of the proposed extension of the line from Acton at Hanwell. The other line in the application, in the county of Surrey, 4.875 miles of single and double line commenced at the south side of Kew Bridge and passed along Sandycombe Road, Manor Road and Queen's Road and on to Richmond Hill and Kingston via Petersham and Ham, with a bridge to avoid crossing the LSWR on the level at Manor Road.

The Light Railway Commissioners held an inquiry into the application at Southall Town Hall on 29 June 1898. Residents and local authorities along the Uxbridge route expressed themselves in favour of the scheme and placed few difficulties in the way of the company. The inquiry into the Surrey application was held on 12 May 1899 at Twickenham. Richmond Tradesmens Association voted almost unanimously in favour of the scheme but local residents and many councillors objected strongly on the grounds that the trams "would bring in hordes of undesirables from the East End of London". The council could, moreover, purchase the Kew Road tramway in 1903 under the terms of the 1870 Tramways Act, and they saw this as grounds for the rejection of the scheme, The Surrey application was withdrawn in the face of this opposition, but the Commissioners approved the Middlesex lines and the Board of Trade confirmed the Order on 2 February 1899.

The problem of Ealing remained, Clifton Robinson embarked upon a policy of winning over local opinion for a second attempt to obtain the consent of Ealing UDC for the line through the town. This was to prove successful.

In 1898 and 1899 the battle with the London County Council continued, with the LUT and their ally Hammersmith Vestry deadlocked against the opposition of the LCC while the Kew Observatory authorities persisted in their demands for fully insulated earth returns and special regulations for the use of electric traction. Notwithstanding these continuing difficulties George White and Clifton Robinson pressed on with their plans, chief of which at this time was the design and construction of the generating station on a site adjacent to Chiswick Depot and powers for which were granted in the 1898 Act, Details of power generation and distribution will be found in Chapter 15.

Prior to the passing of the 1898 Act the LCC and LUT had attempted to resolve differences over electric traction. On 27 January 1898 the LCC Highways Committee discussed negotiations with the company on a suggestion that the LCC might construct, or purchase when constructed, proposed lines in Hammersmith and lease them to the company for operation. This matter was postponed and deferred again at a later meeting on 8 February. The Committee adjourned and on 15 February the Committee finally adopted the proposal from which the leasing provision had been deleted.

The matter was raised later, on 5 July 1898 when the LCC Parliamentary Committee were advised that the Select Committee of the House of Commons, which had been discussing the 1898 LUT Bill, had expressed the hope that in view of the congested London streets making the speedy introduction of electric traction necessary, "they earnestly trusted that arrangements would be made by the LCC with the LUT by which the benefits of electric traction can be secured to the public". From this Robinson seized the initiative when, on 27 September he wrote to the LCC asking for sanction to use overhead trolley electric traction on the lines in Uxbridge Road, Goldhawk Road and King Street, Hammersmith. Robinson said the LUT would be prepared to hand over to the LCC, free of charge, after 6 July 1909 the whole property in feeder cables, main cables and other equipment in the streets plus the poles and overhead wires, thus leaving the question of ultimate purchase of the Hammersmith tramways by the LCC wholly unprejudiced. Robinson also offered to remove the poles and other equipment at any time during the currency of the term on receiving one year's notice from the LCC to do so, and would adopt any other form of traction the LCC might find practical and superior to the overhead system. Should the LCC later construct tramways to connect with the LUT system the company would, if required by the Board of Trade, adopt on its lines such method of mechanical haulage as the LCC might adopt for its connecting lines.

The LCC Highways Committee discussed this and reported to the County Council on 6 October 1898. The Committee said they were still of the opinion that the overhead system was unsuitable in crowded districts "but as the LUT is prepared to make concessions which might be of considerable benefit to the County Council, the Council might, in the circumstances, give consent to the LUT for the use of electric traction on the overhead system, but only on the line between the Askew Arms and Shepherds Bush, the company to give a written undertaking to use conduit electric traction or horse haulage on the other two sections (Goldhawk Road and King Street). This motion was debated at length, withdrawn and amended to approve the use of overhead on condition that the company also reconstruct for conduit working the Goldhawk Road and King Street lines. The Committee chairman said that consent to the use of overhead on the Uxbridge Road section "would be a useful trial to assess the advantages or otherwise of conduit traction."

At about this time Robinson visited a number of tramway systems in Europe, where he viewed various forms of electric traction in operation. An undated report to the LUT directors gave details of a surface contact line in Paris worked on the Claret-Vuillemier principle; a surface contact system at Monaco based on the designs of the General Electric Company of Schenectady, USA, together with open conduit systems in use in Berlin, Brussels and Budapest. He reported in detail on the Paris and Monaco systems, and singled out a mixed overhead and open-conduit system in Paris of some 3.25 miles between Place Bastille and Charenton, two portions of which were conduit operated and at which changes from the one mode to the other were quickly and easily accomplished. He put this system forward as one which could be offered to the LCC as an alternative to a surface contact system which he had seen on an experimental line and strongly favoured in the event of the LCC refusing to countenance any system other than open conduit.

The surface contact system put forward by Robinson had been developed by Professor Silvanus P. Thompson and Miles Walker, an electrical engineer. A single track had been laid on land near Willesden Junction station on which a four-wheel double-deck converted horse tram was used to demonstrate the system. The car used is reported to have had a capacity of sixty persons, and as almost invariably was the case with surface contact systems, carried a heavily magnetised skate slung beneath the body which was of sufficient length to be always in contact with one stud, from which current at 500 volts dc was collected and conveyed via the skate to the controllers and thence to the motors.

A disadvantage common to almost all types of surface contact systems was the risk of a stud remaining live after the passage of a car, thus creating a danger to horses or any person coming into contact with it. The Thompson-Walker system was claimed to virtually eliminate this risk and in addition the contact studs were arranged electrically to blow a fuse should a leakage to the stud occur. The use of oil within the plug box was intended to eliminate the common fault of the mechanism in the box sticking and causing a stud to remain live after the car had passed. A battery carried on the car provided initial starting current, and the controller was so arranged that in the event of the car encountering dead studs current could be drawn from the battery to carry the car over the dead section without loss of traction. Changes from stud to trolley and vice versa could be quickly and easily accomplished.

The costs of construction of this system at £8,600 to £9,500 per mile of single line compared favourably with £11,400 per mile for an open conduit system and £8,200 to £9,000 per mile for overhead construction. These figures were submitted by the system's inventors at a trial during October 1898 at which the technical Press was present, but at this date no practical operating line was under construction.

It was this system which Robinson submitted to the LUT directors as a viable alternative to the open conduit system then being insisted upon by the LCC. There is no record of the directors' views on the report and the exact date of its submission to them is not recorded, but it was subsequent to May 1899.

The LCC resolved to adopt the Highways Committee's motion of 6 October on 18 October 1898, on the terms of Robinson's letter of 27 September. However, matters took a turn in favour of the LUT when the LCC's resolution on the use of conduit became known to the residents and business interests of Goldhawk Road. The whole thoroughfare had been reconstructed and widened in 1898 by Hammersmith Vestry and at the same time the LUT had rebuilt the single line

KEW BRIDGE TERMINI

Upper: An animated scene at Kew Bridge terminus, as two cars, by now operated by the LUT, are being prepared for their return journeys to Hammersmith, Kew Bridge L&SW Railway Station is in the background, next door to the 'Dining Rooms'. (Courtesy: E.C. Dawes)

Lower: Car No. 22, smartly turned out in LUT livery, is seen on the south side of Kew Bridge at the terminus of the isolated line to Richmond. Despite repeated attempts, the company was never able to connect the two lines together. (E.R. Oakley collection)

tramway as a double line throughout in "heavy girder rails". £20,000 had been spent on repaving in wood blocks and moreover the tramway had been equipped, except for the conductors, for overhead trolley operation. Concern was expressed that this new thoroughfare would be taken up for a second time in a matter of months for the extensive excavations necessary for laying conduits, and the Vestry and local residents combined to bring pressure upon the LCC to reconsider the matter.

The LCC Highways Committee reviewed the matter at some length on 9 May 1899 after the LUT had asked the county council to allow the use of overhead in Goldhawk Road, pointing out that the company had, at the request of Hammersmith Vestry, carried out reconstruction of the track as a double line and installed the equipment necessary for overhead traction. The Committee accepted the company's submission and voted to sanction the use of overhead in Goldhawk Road, again on the terms outlined in Robinson's offer of 27 September 1898. The Committee recommended the LCC to rescind the 18 October 1898 resolution and adopt the proposal accepted by them, adding a clause for the LCC to pay the "then value" of the tramway in King Street when the purchase date arose in July 1909. A decision was deferred, but on 16 May the resolution was adopted by the full council and it was resolved an agreement be drawn up.

This was not the end of the matter. On 13 June 1899 the LCC Highways Committee resolved to add "the lines in Beadon Road, Glenthorne Road and Studland Street to King Street and along part of The Grove between Beadon Road and King Street West" and "including the equipment for underground electric traction" to the resolution. The LUT Bill for 1899 was passing through Parliament at this time and as a result of these accords the LCC withdrew their opposition to this measure on 4 July, agreements in similar terms between the LUT and Hammersmith Vestry and the LUT and the LCC having been signed on 19 June and 2 July respectively. These agreements constituted the formal consents of the LCC and the Vestry to the use of electric traction by the LUT, specifying the use of overhead trolley traction in Uxbridge and Goldhawk Roads and underground conduit on the line between Young's Corner and Hammersmith Broadway and the loop line via Beadon Road, Glenthorne Road and Studland Street with the short connecting line between King Street and Beadon Road via The Grove. The agreement with the LCC also confirmed the terms of Robinson's offer to the LCC of 27 September 1898.

On 19 December 1899 the LCC considered their Highways Committee's report of 31 October. All the arrangements were confirmed, and a few minor conditions added, mainly regarding the fixing of wires to Hammersmith Vestry's lamp standards. The LUT was to supply detailed plans of wires, inspection chambers and other equipment to be placed in the streets. The "Bristol" pattern for side and centre poles was to be used and the company was to be asked to submit an amended design for the conduit equipment.

The LUT was now resigned to the inevitability of having to use conduit traction in central Hammersmith and had resolved, initially at least, to avoid the necessity for change-over arrangements between trolley and conduit and vice versa at Young's Corner by working the line in King Street and the loop separately. As, at this time, the use of double trolley overhead equipment was envisaged owing to the attitude adopted by the Kew Observatory authorities, it was clear that the working of through cars to Hammersmith Broadway would be attended by time-consuming changing over of the equipment.

During the latter part of 1899 the company was, however, still endeavouring to avoid the use of conduit anywhere on the system. A further report of the LCC Highways Committee was submitted to the LCC on 19 December. Frontagers in central Hammersmith and Hammersmith Vestry had made strong representations to the LCC about the dislocation of traffic which disturbance of the roads for laying conduits would entail. The LUT had given notice to the LCC of its intention to ask Parliament to amend the 1899 Act to allow overhead trolley traction throughout

LUT car No. 49 of Milnes' manufacture standing in High Road, Chiswick c1900, possibly while the horses were changed. The overhead wiring for the new electric cars, soon to come into service, can also be seen. (Tramway Museum Society)

Hammersmith. On 8 February 1900 the LCC was told that Hammersmith Vestry had approved the company's plans for the positions of poles and other equipment in Uxbridge and Goldhawk Roads. King Street was not mentioned in this report, and on 14 February it was reported that the LCC was to petition against the company's 1900 Bill.

The 1900 Bill contained proposals for new lines in the county of London and the LCC Parliamentary Committee recommended that consent to introduce the Bill should be refused under Standing Orders. There is no further mention in the records of the central Hammersmith lines except an earlier report, dated 1899 of Hammersmith Vestry's Joint Sub-Committee on electric traction. This report gave details of the overhead system and reported on the Sub-Committee's visits to view overhead trolley systems at Bristol and Dover. The report recommended approval of the overhead system and was critical of the LCC's insistence upon the use of conduit in central Hammersmith. It pointed out that the narrowness of King Street, combined with the necessity to move large numbers of pipes below the surface, would cause great inconvenience to shopkeepers and traffic if the road were taken up to install the conduit system. The Sub-Committee also pointed out that the District Railway ran beneath Beadon Road for some 127 yards, and there was only a depth of nine to twelve inches between the surface of the road and the top of the girders of the railway tunnel. This made it impossible to install conduits along that section.

The Sub-Committee recommended that for this and other reasons given in the report the Vestry should strongly press the LCC not to insist upon the use of the conduit system in King Street and the loop and to ask the LCC to use its utmost endeavours to agree with the LUT to substitute the overhead trolley system for the proposed conduit scheme. The report was signed by the Sub-Committee's Chairman, Charles Courtney Cramp, who it will be recalled had been associated from 1874 with tramways in west London. The company, having taken the issue to Parliament in their 1900 Bill obtained in the subsequent Act power to work the central Hammersmith lines on the overhead trolley system. The chief obstacle to the LUT's development plans now remained the Kew Observatory authorities' demands, then no closer to resolution. Notwithstanding this, work was put in hand to electrify the existing lines on the overhead system and preparations made for construction of the newly-authorised extensions.

By mid-1900 construction work on the extension from Kew Bridge to Hounslow and electrification of the existing lines was completed. The powers for the Hounslow section were due to expire on 12 August 1900 and on 26 July 1900 Robinson asked the Board of Trade to carry out the necessary inspection, pointing out that fresh powers would have to be sought if the line had not been sanctioned for service by that date. Robinson wrote again to the Board on 4 August and the inspection was arranged to take place on Saturday 11 August when it was carried out by Lt. Col. H.A.Yorke, RE. A horse tram was used for the inspection and the Colonel found that the new work was in excellent order and ready for public service. This applied only to the track, as although the electrical installation had been completed it was not yet connected to the generating station pending resolution of the Kew Observatory difficulties, and could not, therefore, be tested by the Board of Trade's electrical inspecting officer, A.P. Trotter. The Board of Trade's certificate of fitness was signed on the same day as the inspection took place, by F.J.S. Hopwood. The company did not wish to extend their horse tram operations and consequently the extension did not go into use until after the Kew impasse had been overcome and electrical regulations in respect of the section settled, on 6 July 1901.

The 1900 Bill received the Royal Assent on 6 August 1900 and in addition to provisions for just over seventeen new miles of new route, details of which will be found in the appropriate chapters in this book, the new Act authorised the use of the overhead trolley system throughout Hammersmith, the reconstruction as a double line throughout of the 1896 single line through Acton, an extension of time to complete the Boston Road tramway authorised in the 1898 Act and a connection at Hanwell at Upper Boston Road and Uxbridge Road.

One of the first electric cars to be put into service early in 1901 to replace the horse cars. It is complete with velvet curtains in the lower saloon. (E.R. Oakley collection)

CHAPTER FOUR

THE LUT VERSUS KEW OBSERVATORY

The Kew Geomagnetic Observatory, situated in the Old Deer Park, Richmond, immediately south of the Royal Botanic Gardens at Kew, was one of a number of Government scientific establishments carrying out studies into the effects of ground currents on recording instruments measuring terrestrial movements and other phenomena. This work was of especial importance to the Admiralty and consequently was regarded as being essential to the wellbeing of the realm. Much of the work of the Kew establishment was carried out by eminent scientists who were members of the Royal Society and following the establishment of the National Physical Laboratory in 1900 the Observatory became part of that organisation.

The first intimation of the Observatory's interest in the LUT electrification proposals came in letters to the Board of Trade in February 1898 from the Royal Society and the First Commissioner of Works, both expressing concern at the LUT electrification proposals in their 1898 bill. Both bodies feared that the work of the Observatory would be threatened by the electrification of the lines, and they asked the Board of Trade for their assistance in ensuring that their work should not be affected by the electrification proposals. The Board of Trade replied, offering both bodies all support in ensuring that their work should not be disturbed. The Commissioner of Works asked for protective clauses in the Bill and on 17 June was insisting upon the provision of an entirely insulated earth return on the electrified lines. On 8 September, H.F. Parshall, MInstCE, MIEE, consulting engineer to the LUT electrification scheme noted that the all-insulated earth return system was demanded in the Chiswick, Acton and Isleworth areas, and suggested to the Board of Trade that the three-wire system, with the inside wire neutral and outside wires at 1,000 volts should be adopted. This arrangement necessitated the use of two trolleypoles on each car.

The Company's 1898 Act, which received the Royal Assent on 12 August contained a clause which placed an obligation upon the LUT to provide insulated conductors along the whole of their line to the satisfaction of the Kew Observatory authorities, and gave them the right to test the insulation and conductivity of the company's installation if they had grounds to assume that the insulation was no longer to the stardard they considered desirable, and to call upon the company to forthwith rectify the matter.

The company began discussions with the Board of Trade in September, 1898 and the Kew committee of the Royal College of Science wrote to the Board on 5 December insisting upon the use of the conduit system on the LUT routes in the vicinity of the Observatory, which were the Kew Bridge – Hounslow and the projected Hampton Court lines, the nearest points on which to the Observatory were two thirds of a mile and half a mile respectively. In response to this, the LUT said that the changes from conduit to overhead and *vice versa* could take up to five minutes, and the Committee countered that no such delay was experienced on the conduit system in use in Washington. Argument and counter-argument continued until 18 April 1899 when H.F. Parshall wrote formally to the Board of Trade proposing the use of the three-wire twin-trolley system, which would involve four wires in the overhead, the fourth (neutral) wire being the two centre wires, connected every half-mile and earthed at the generating station. Robinson agreed to this arrangement in a letter to the Board of Trade on 2 May 1899. The Kew authorities were not satisfied with matters as they stood, and meanwhile the company's 1899 Bill was passing through Parliament with proposals seeking a relaxation of the Kew clause in the 1898 Act. This measure received the Royal Assent on 1 August and modified the electrical provisions of the 1898 Act to the extent that the Kew clause in that Act was repealed and a new clause permitted the use of insulated returns or uninsulated metallic returns of low resistance and, furthermore placed regulation of the use of electric traction firmly in the hands of the Board of Trade. This change was asked for by the LUT and was warmly welcomed by George White and Clifton Robinson.

In an endeavour to resolve differences between the parties the Board of Trade appointed a small "Expert Committee" in November, 1899, under the chairmanship of A.P. Trotter, the Board's electrical adviser. The Kew authorities continued to object to the LUT proposals and George White had become impatient at the delays which threatened to undermine the financial wellbeing of the LUT. A meeting on 15 November had made little progress and the only concrete result was that A.P. Trotter said that modifications to the feeder cables could be defined for the future by Board of Trade regulation. There were differences of opinion on the advisability of working the twin-trolley system on 500 or 1,000 volts, H.F. Parshall having revised his earlier support for the higher voltage on the grounds of cost. Trotter reported on the proposals as they stood on 21 February 1900. The Kew requirement had meanwhile been altered and was delineated as a fully-insulated return system on any tramway within two miles radius of the Observatory, which was the line between Chiswick and Hounslow and the yet to be built line between Isleworth and Hampton Court, as well as the existing horse tramway between Kew and Richmond, which it was planned to electrify.

At this time Clifton Robinson put up a strong case against the adoption of the twin-trolley system. He pointed out the difficulties of maintaining satisfactory insulation with wires of different potential crossing each other, and the danger from a heavy fall of snow placing excessive strains on the double-wire overhead installation. Reversing cars with twin-trolley poles would increase operational difficulties and serious results could arise at junctions if both trolleys did not take the right direction. In addition heavier poles and suspension equipment was necessary and in the event of a serious dewirement the risk of injury and damage was greatly increased by the adoption of the twin-trolley system. Robinson also pointed out that some serious accidents had taken place on the twin-trolley system in Cincinnati.

Double trolley operation at Cincinnati, Ohio, where an all-insulated electrical supply was enforced by law to prevent possible electrolytic problems arising on underground pipes and telephone cables.   (J.H. Price collection)

By March 1900 electrification of the Shepherds Bush – Acton and Hammersmith – Kew Bridge lines and construction of the line from Kew Bridge to Hounslow was almost complete, on the earth-return single trolley pole system. On 13 March Robinson pressed the Board of Trade to apply their standard electrical regulations to the operations of the LUT. He pointed out the amount of time wasted in prolonged arguments, said the whole installation was at a standstill and asked for an early decision. Matters continued to drag on and he again wrote to the Board, on 30 June saying that some £500,000 continued to lie idle and called upon the Board to sanction the use of the lines in conformity with the plans deposited.

The Board of Trade, for their part had been trying for nearly a year to secure a settlement of the problem and by October 1900 matters still remained deadlocked. George White, whose patience had almost run out, called upon the Board of Trade to bring the parties together and on 31 October a conference took place at the Board's offices in Whitehall Gardens, Westminster, presided over by Sir Courtenay Boyle, KCB, the Permanent Secretary. He was accompanied by three senior officers, Sir Thomas Blomefield, F.J.S. Hopwood and A.P. Trotter. The representatives of Kew Observatory and other Government scientific departments were the Astronomer Royal (Dr. W.H.M. Christie), Professors Rucker, Ayrton and Perry, with Dr. R.T. Glazebrook, Director of the National Physical Laboratory with direct responsibility for Kew Observatory, Rear Admiral Sir W.J.L. Wharton, KCB and Lt. Col. E. Raban, RE representing the Admiralty. The tramway and railway interests were represented by George White, Clifton Robinson, H.F. Parshall and Samuel White (LUT) with seven others representing the London electric railway companies and the Ilford and Barking municipal tramway undertakings.

The meeting heard that in July 1900 Dr. Glazebrook had calculated the extent of possible disturbance to the Kew instruments if a scheme put forward by the LUT for special cables and feeders was adopted. Glazebrook was unable to state definitely if the scheme would have the desired result. The main features of the proposal were that the line should consist of one-mile isolated sections, fed and boosted so that no point on any one section of rail within two miles of the Observatory should differ in potential by more than 0.2 volts from the earth potential in its vicinity. Further than two miles distant a difference of one volt was suggested. These figures had been accepted by H.F. Parshall. On 8 August Glazebrook sent further calculations to Parshall, who prepared another scheme. Glazebrook's calculations necessitated considerable alterations to Parshall's scheme and Parshall's estimate of the costs showed that special work and additional cables would amount to a very large sum. Glazebrook wrote to the LUT on 7 September saying that the additional scheme would "in all probability" be sufficient to protect the Observatory.

Trotter told the meeting that Glazebrook had said that "several new tramways were proposed in the neighbourhood of Kew, and that these would cause disturbances unless dealt with in the manner suggested for the present lines". These were the projected Hampton Court lines, and Trotter remarked that "the general result is that we are deadlocked". The position was that the Observatory authorities could not predict with certainty the efficacy of the proposed scheme, and the engineer members of the committee protested that the expenditure would be quite unreasonable in view of the fact that it might be useless.

Sir Courtenay Boyle asked if the Observatory members still wished the Board of Trade to make regulations for the protection of their instruments (at Kew and Greenwich) and Professor Rucker, one of their representatives replied in the affirmative. Rucker went on to say that the scheme put forward by the LUT was for the overhead trolley earth return system, whereas the Observatories had originally wanted an all-insulated scheme, but had been disposed to accept later schemes put forward by the LUT. Parshall commented in reply to Rucker that while Glazebrook had accepted part of the latest LUT scheme, he had made reservations regarding the Baber Bridge extension of the Hounslow route, which would involve the company in several thousand pounds' additional expenditure. Since then the lines had been completed as far as possible to test the practicability of the proposed scheme. Trials had shown that currents circulating in the lines from outside sources *even before the lines were put into operation* caused a difference of potential at certain times of 0.8 volts, or four times greater than the level accepted at the time as necessary for the protection of Kew Observatory. Such regulations would debar the use of rails in the ground at all, quite apart from electrical working.

Parshall said he had placed a magnetometer near the Observatory and passed a current of 80 amperes into the line and back through the rails to observe the effect. The effect on the instrument was negligible and the current of 80 amperes was about 100 times greater than that shown on the plans for the scheme. These readings and others described by Parshall indicated that the liability of Kew Observatory to effects from the tramway had been grossly over-estimated. Existing currents circulating from unknown sources and totally unconnected with the tramways exceeded the requirements of the proposed regulations, and this was before the LUT made use of their own rails as a return circuit. Parshall said he would advise the LUT of the impracticability of arranging their lines to conform to the regulations proposed by Glazebrook. Some £40,000 expenditure would be necessary to conform to Glazebrook's proposals outside the two-mile radius plus £25,000 to cover his other requirements.

At this point Sir Courtenay Boyle said that he hoped the Expert Committee would have been ready to come forward with an agreement. He pointed out that the companies had great claims to the consideration of the Board of Trade, and that they had an immense amount of capital locked up and were unable to meet the demands of their public.

George White said that the matter had become "a London United Tramways question", whereas in truth all the electrical undertakings proposed or recently authorised were affected. He said that in addition to the sums of £40,000 and £25,000 already mentioned, some £100,000 might be necessary to comply with all the technicalities involved. One effect of Glazebrook's proposals would be to cut the number of cars the LUT could work on their system by 50 per cent. In operation the cars would have to be spaced evenly apart over the system and it would be impossible to work the intensive service called for on the routes to such places as Hampton Court at holiday times. The newly-opened Central London Railway (the "Twopenny Tube") was thought to be a source of electrical disturbance. White posed the question "if disturbance was assumed to emanate from the Central London Railway could it be seriously suggested that that undertaking should divide its lines into numerous sections?" If this was so the traffic equipment would have to be severely curtailed. The London electric railways would have to be governed by strict timetables framed, not to suit public

KEW OBSERVATORY

A nineteenth century engraving of the Kew Geomagnetic Observatory.
(From Strand Magazine)

requirements but to keep to scientific restrictions to comply with the demands of Kew. White went on to say that if it was a matter of reasonable expenditure the LUT would endeavour to meet the Observatory's requirements, but during correspondence prior to the meeting White learned that Glazebrook had suggested that, so far as he could see, the only practical solution of the difficulty was the removal of the magnetic instruments from Kew to a more suitable site distant from the electrical disturbances emanating from the installations of large urban areas.

Glazebrook interposed here, saying that he had not made that suggestion, but White said that Glazebrook *had* put forward the suggestion, in writing, that removal of the instruments might have to be considered. Sir Courtenay Boyle accepted from this that the suggestion might have to be considered, and White pressed home his advantage, asking if it would be advisable to lose no more time discussing scientific problems impossible to solve from a commercial point of view, but to devote the time to finding means to move the instruments from Kew and locating them elsewhere. He said that there was no certainty that the proposed remedies would prove effectual, and it was asking too much to expect a single company like the LUT to undertake huge expenditure and submit to all the attendant complications and restrictions reducing ability to serve the public, and placing the company in an unprofitable position, all to maintain some instruments at a location from which, even according to the scientists, they may have to be moved, in which event all this expense would be wasted. The LUT had tackled the problem in September, 1898 when they approached the Board of Trade electrical department, and had kept the matter forward until November 1899, since when the Expert Committee had been dealing with it. The LUT had offered the Board of Trade the facilities of their associated undertaking at Stockton for test purposes and the Board's report on this had been produced on 1 May. The LUT had spent some £500,000 to date on their undertaking, which would be increased to £850,000 in the coming months, all lying practically idle; "we ought not to be penalized on behalf of the whole electrical industry of London".

White concluded by saying that the local authorities were now impatient over the delays in the commencement of electric tramway services, and urged the Board of Trade to allow electric trams to commence working under the Board's standard electrical regulations, and he undertook to carry out any modification necessary in the Board's view following operational experience.

Sir Courtenay Boyle referred to his own position and that of the Board of Trade, saying it was extremely difficult for him or the Board to suggest to the Kew authorities, who held the ground, that they should move their instruments at the cost of the State on account of certain commercial undertakings coming into their neighbourhood. White said that his company was prepared to contribute toward the cost of a removal, and he thought that other electrical undertakings in London represented at the meeting might be prepared to take similar steps. He asked if the "scientific gentlemen present" could indicate the probable cost and was ready to meet that in a most liberal spirit "as would certainly exceed our share of the sin, if it is a sin, that is involved".

The meeting continued for some time following White's remarks, and the "scientific gentlemen" proceeded to make various points. Professor Perry questioned Parshall's estimates: Kew had said from the beginning that they wanted an insulated return "which would give us perfect protection", and that was their position. Clifton Robinson said it would be impracticable to carry out the four-wire system. With two trolleypoles, at one point on the system no fewer than thirteen wires would have to be strung, forming a complete network over the line. Considering the matter not altogether as an aesthetic question, the company had appealed to the Board of Trade on the grounds of safety to eliminate that proposition. The first idea, of 1,000 volts in the overhead was altogether impracticable and "Mr. Trotter himself would not be a party to a thousand volts being carried overhead, especially under low railway bridges". He went on to repeat that the universal practice of working tramways was required – the standard rules and regulations of the Board of Trade.

Boyle remarked here that Parliament was apparently not satisfied with the old regulations' protection of the observatories, otherwise it would not have passed the new observatory clause in the new (1899) Act. Robinson insisted that the 1899 Act was more reasonable than the 1898 Act, which was prohibitive from a commercial point of view and had been properly repealed. Professor Rucker stressed the national importance of the Kew activities. Work was undertaken for foreign governments and companies and the Observatory had a world-wide reputation for its high standards. The instrument-making industry was being lost to Germany – "if you crush it out a serious injury will be done not merely from a scientific point of view but also to a Government institution which is useful for some of the purposes of trade".

Much scientific data was bandied between the opposing sides, and the Astronomer Royal brought Greenwich Observatory into the discussion. The magnetic registers there were of vital importance "and afforded material for interesting observations as to the connection between terrestrial magnetism and sun-spots". These registers had been disturbed since the construction of the City and South London Railway, and "if tramways were brought within 700 yards of Greenwich Observatory the register will be ruined completely and 60 years' work brought to an end just when it was becoming of increased interest and value". Major Cardew referred to the conduit tramway in New York where despite insulation earth faults occurred with regular frequency. Admiral Wharton suggested that "there are means by which these electrical tramways can be worked without disturbing scientific observations", but did not describe them.

Sir Courtenay Boyle tried to find common ground between the parties. He asked George White if he could give the approximate cost of providing "a perfectly insulated return". Parshall said such a proposition had not been considered, and Boyle asked for an idea of the probable cost, whereupon Robinson said he did not think it was practicable. Professor Rucker repeated the question of the cost of an insulated return "throughout the system". Boyle by this time had lost patience and brusquely remarked, "if you cannot answer my question, then it must remain unanswered". White then said it was impossible to give a definite figure but it would be approximately £150,000, in addition to the items which appear for £80,000 under Board of Trade regulations.

The Kew side would not budge and neither would White and Robinson. Robinson said the suggested conditions were impossible. White then said that it had earlier been agreed that the lines to Kew Bridge and from Shepherds Bush to Acton were not so serious a difficulty. Beyond Kew (i.e. in the Hounslow direction and down to Hampton Court) was the main point at issue. The Kew and Acton lines were ready to work and White suggested that the company should be allowed to work to Kew Bridge and Acton outside the two-mile zone, under Board of Trade regulations, enabling the "scientific gentlemen" to observe the practical effect of the operations. Glazebrook continued to maintain that opening the two sections would have a disturbing effect on the instruments. Col. Raban said that insulated returns were in use in some towns and agreed they might not be practicable in suburban districts, but thought that Kew and Greenwich were not suburban. He asked if there was such a thing as perfect insulation, the cost of installing it, and if it had been in use elsewhere under similar conditions to the LUT system. Others had answered these questions earlier, and Robinson flatly said that he believed there was no such thing as a perfectly insulated earth return on any tramway in the country. Trotter pointed out that there were two ways of providing an insulated return: the Central London Railway, with third rail traction was one, and the London County Council proposed to use the conduit system for their electrified lines. But the installation of conduit on extensive suburban systems would involve a huge expenditure. Twin-trolley systems were in use in the USA but had been subject to many serious accidents.

Boyle put forward some ideas, saying that he would suggest to the Government scientific departments the possibility of removing the magnetic work from Kew and Greenwich. He said the departments could frame regulations and the tramway companies could also propose regulations to which they might be prepared to accede and the Committee should sit again to consider the recommendations. Another course would be for the Board of Trade to frame regulations, drafts to be sent to the two sides, and which would have to be approved by a higher authority than the permanent officers of the Board of Trade, i.e. Parliament. Yet another course would be for the committee to sit again to advise the Board if it could allow the LUT to open at least parts of their system at once. H. Montague

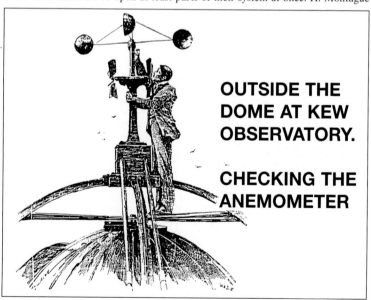

OUTSIDE THE DOME AT KEW OBSERVATORY.

CHECKING THE ANEMOMETER

An engraving of the anemometer being attended to at Kew Observatory.
(From Strand Magazine)

The London County Council line between Woolwich and Eltham, built in 1910, was equipped for double trolley wire working at the behest of the Astronomer Royal, who required an all-insulated supply to be provided for tramcars working within a three-mile radius of the Greenwich Observatory. This lasted until 1927.　　　　　　　(Commercial view)

Smith of the Charing Cross, Euston & Hampstead Railway Company, who had built the first experimental conduit tramway in Halifax, recommended this course. Sir Courtenay asked the meeting for a decision on whether the committee should meet to consider regulations proposed by the two sides, or that the Board should draft regulations.

White and others preferred that the Board should frame the regulations. White said, "we have been two years trying to hitch horses and we are still here. I think the Board of Trade should take the matter up". Without further comment Sir Courtenay Boyle said the Board of Trade would frame regulations and send them to the two sides. He said he was as anxious as those present to get a settlement, not only as it affected the LUT but all the other companies to which the Observatory Clause had applied. The "scientific gentlemen" continued a rearguard action on behalf of the observatories but Boyle concluded the proceedings by saying that the Board would frame the regulations as quickly as possible and send them to all parties in due course.

Meanwhile, with the repeal of the Observatories Clause in the 1898 Act allowing the LUT some relaxation of the onerous conditions in that clause the LUT had continued construction of the generating station at Chiswick and laid the cabling for the overhead trolley and earth return system between Shepherds Bush and Acton Depot, from Shepherds Bush and Hammersmith to Kew Bridge and the new extension to Hounslow. At a special meeting of the LUT directors on 24 November 1900 the gravity of the situation was discussed and on that day Samuel White wrote to the Board of Trade saying that the company wished to put the completed sections between Hammersmith and Kew Bridge, Shepherds Bush and Young's Corner and Shepherds Bush and Acton into service, and asked if the Board wished to carry out any tests or experiments on those sections. He placed the LUT engineers at the disposal of the Board and the Kew authorities in the matter. On 29 November A.P. Trotter advised the Board of Trade that a programme of tests had been agreed with R.T. Glazebrook.

During December 1900 some tests were carried out, when 40 amperes were passed into the line at Brentford, and some disturbance was recorded at the Observatory, which Glazebrook claimed had emanated from the LUT. Parshall pointed out that these disturbances took place and were recorded at times when the LUT tests were at a standstill, and had originated from electric railways. The Kew

Observatory Committee was still insistent upon regulating procedure and defining the exact nature of the tests to be carried out and incorporated in the Board of Trade regulations. At the request of the National Physical Laboratory these tests were carried out at night.

At this time it emerged that the Government had been considering the removal of the Kew instruments to Bushy Park, some three miles south of the Old Deer Park and where it would be surrounded on all sides by the projected Hampton Court Loop tramway, which would have been at no greater distance than two thirds of a mile from any part of the route. It was quickly realised that with the imminent large-scale development of electrical installations in the London suburban area this would not solve the problems of earth-borne interference. Glazebrook had given an estimate of between £70,000 and £100,000 as the cost of moving the instruments, which was at first taken to refer only to the Kew equipment; Glazebrook later admitted that the Greenwich instruments were included in the figures.

On 3 January 1901 the Director of the National Physical Laboratory wrote to the Board of Trade, saying that experiments had been carried out on the night of 31 December 1900. He said that no more than five cars should ever be on the line at once between Kew Bridge and Hounslow and tests should be done on that basis. Further tests should be carried out under conditions as near as possible to those expected in public service. Each individual car, up to a total of thirty, was to be tested by the National Physical Laboratory and to run for two hours.

The trial commenced at 12.30am on 22 February 1901 and Trotter reported to the Board of Trade on the same day. Serious disturbances to the Kew instruments had taken place and he flatly said that no practicable electrical regulations were possible. Glazebrook reported at length to the National Physical Laboratory. Thirty cars were run to simulate a two-minute service between Hammersmith and Kew Bridge. The first car left Chiswick Depot at 12.27am and the trial continued until 4.45am, when the first cars started to run in. It had been intended that the current should be supplied to the line at Turnham Green and Hammersmith and returned via the rails at Chiswick and Kew Bridge. Boosters intended to keep the potential at Kew Bridge and Chiswick in balance had not arrived from America, and to achieve the necessary balance a resistance was placed between the rails at

Testing the conductivity of a rail bond on the museum tramway at Crich, Derbyshire, on 16th May 1964, the first occasion on which the overhead was energised. Voltage drop on the line was negligible. (Courtesy: I.A. Yearsley)

Chiswick and the generating station equal to that between Kew Bridge and Chiswick. It was found that there was no connection with Kew Bridge and the connection could not be made until 4.25am, therefore until this time the whole current returned by way of the Chiswick connection. The total current rose to 300 amperes by 12.45am, part of this being supplied to the depot. At intervals varying readings were observed of between 300 and 600 amperes. Robinson started five cars at once from Kew Bridge, when the current registered reached 600 amperes. Voltage drops were recorded, at Hammersmith 2 volts and at Kew Bridge 2 to 3 volts, but readings of up to five volts were common. At 4.26am the connection to the rails was made at Kew Bridge when 250 amperes returned from there and 150 amperes from Chiswick. Various other tests were conducted and current curves supplied to the Board of Trade.

Glazebrook concluded his report by acknowledging the courtesy with which Robinson and his directors met his suggestions during the experiments and concluded, "I venture to suggest that they (the tests) will prove it will be impossible to devise practical rules for working lines nearer to Kew Observatory than the Kew Bridge – Hammersmith line without entirely destroying the value of the magnetic recording instruments, and that the only real solution of the difficulty lies in the removal of the magnetic recording instruments ... and I beg respectfully to urge upon the Board of Trade that they should put this view strongly before the London United Tramways Company". Glazebrook's report, dated 27 February 1901 was passed to the Board of Trade and from thence to the LUT. Trotter inspected the electrical installation on the lines in Hammersmith, the Goldhawk Road line and the line between Shepherds Bush and Acton Depot on 15 March and reported it was in excellent order.

Meanwhile, on 11 March matters were still at an impasse. George White, who had hoped that the electric trams would be able to start working in time for the forthcoming Easter holiday traffic, was despairing of reaching a settlement, and wrote to Sir Courtenay Boyle at the Board of Trade making an offer to contribute towards the cost of moving the Kew instruments. Earlier, Sir Francis Mowatt, Secretary to the Treasury, had written to White at the request of Boyle with an estimate of the costs of moving both the Kew and the Greenwich instruments. Mowatt referred to the strong objections to any move on the grounds of impairment of the value of continuous records, and gave a figure of between £15,000 and £20,000 to provide the necessary staff accommodation at a new location. The staff at the observatories carried out not only magnetic recording, but also standardisation research which was not affected by the electrical undertakings. The staff would have to be separated, with the standardisation staffs remaining at Kew and Greenwich. A third director would become necessary for the new site at a salary of £700 per annum, and other establishment costs were estimated at £800 per annum, representing a capital payment of £50,000, the two items buildings and staff, totalling between £65,000 and £70,000. The Admiralty had said these figures were too low, suggesting that a figure of £100,000 would be more appropriate.

White offered to pay £10,000 to move the Kew instruments to a temporary site pending construction of a new permanent establishment to embrace both Kew and Greenwich magnetic observatories. He would pay £3,000 for a new permanent building and provide an annual payment of £210, making a sum equal to £10,000 total capital value, the Treasury "and others" to provide the balance. He asked Sir Courtenay Boyle to use his good offices with the Treasury in stressing the urgency of opening the lines as soon as possible. On 25 March 1901 Boyle wrote to the Secretary to the Treasury, pointing out that it was very doubtful if any regulations could be made under the observatories clauses in the Acts, even if such regulations did require the use of insulated returns which could be relied upon to give full protection to the Kew instruments. The Board of Trade thought the time had come when His Majesty's Government should determine if the instruments at Kew or Greenwich, or both, should be moved, taking advantage of White's offer as a basis for ultimate financial contributions by other companies whose operations might make the removal necessary.

By 27 March 1901 White had almost given up hope of the lines opening by Easter, and he wrote to Boyle asking for reassurance. On 29 March the Treasury wrote to the Board of Trade concurring with the Board's view that the instruments should be moved. The Board was asked if White's offer of £10,000 was considered sufficient. The parties finally agreed the figure after the Treasury accepted it, and on 3 April the Board of Trade sanctioned the use of electric power on the lines in Hammersmith and outward from Hammersmith to Kew Bridge, together with the Goldhawk Road tramway and the line from Shepherds Bush to Acton Depot. Some final discussions were taking place on the extension from Kew Bridge to Hounslow.

The agreement between the Treasury and the LUT was signed by George White and Sir Francis Mowatt, for the Treasury, on 3 April. The horse trams ceased to run on that day and on the next day electric trams started to run from the inner London termini to Kew Bridge and Acton. Electrical regulations were drawn up by the Board of Trade and finally agreed between the parties by June 1901, when Sir Thomas Blomefield signed them on behalf of the Board. Meanwhile, the Treasury attempted to involve the Board of Trade in recovering the removal costs from other undertakings. On 29 June Sir Francis Mowatt wrote to Sir Courtenay Boyle saying that the Treasury did not commit themselves to "the precise course proposed" and "hoped the Board of Trade would co-operate in recovering the costs of moving the observatories from the undertakings making the removal necessary". They (the Treasury) would "readily fall in with suggestions by the Board of Trade to that end". This letter was studied by senior officers at the Board, who agreed that the matter was no concern of theirs and took no further action.

The Royal Society had sent a memorandum to the Board of Trade on 4 April 1901 conceding that as one of the LUT lines passed within two thirds of a mile of the Observatory the magnetic observations could not continue there and removal was the only possible course to take and a new observatory had to be established. On the same day the Treasury sent a similar letter to the Lord Chairman of Committees at the House of Lords. On 1 June the Board of Visitors of the Royal Observatory, Greenwich resolved that as interference by electric railways in Greenwich was not serious and the Astronomer Royal was satisfied with the London County Council's tramways scheme, they hoped that the Board of Trade's

THE ROYAL OBSERVATORY, GREENWICH PARK,
KENT

An early engraving of Flamsteed House, the original Greenwich Observatory building, then shown as being in the County of Kent. (Source unknown)

standard regulations would secure adequate protection for Greenwich and recommended that the work of removal should proceed. They were now convinced that terrestrial magnetism studies could only be carried out at a site free from all artificial magnetic disturbances.

The Treasury continued to press the Board of Trade to help them recover some of the Kew Oservatory removal costs from other electrical undertakings, and Sir Thomas Blomefield was pressed from time to time on the matter. The Kew Observatory Committee had been the moving spirits in demanding "perfect insulation" and had mobilised the leading scientific bodies of the day in their attempt to thwart the LUT electrification scheme. The Treasury was still trying to involve the Board of Trade in the Kew arrangements, and at 14 February 1902 they asked the Board to submit proposals of their own on the working of tramways other than under the Board's regulations. The Board of Trade however, had checked other tramways working on both conduit and overhead and no complaints, other than those from Kew, had been received, and moreover the Admiralty said they were happy with both conduit and overhead.

The Board's officers commented extensively on the Treasury's suggestions and were in agreement that they had no special proposals to make. Sir Herbert Jekyll commented on 7 March 1902 that Kew had been fighting a rearguard action with the tacit help and approval of the Treasury, and noted that the Office of Works were happy with arrangements for the Croydon, East Ham and Barking tramways. The Board agreed that they would do no more than tell the Treasury about the system of traction proposed to be adopted by the promoters of any of the undertakings within ten miles of Kew Observatory to which the Observatory clauses applied. The London United Tramways had single-handedly fought the battle for electric tramway development on economic lines in London, and the Kew instruments were finally removed to Eskdalemuir, Dumfriesshire.

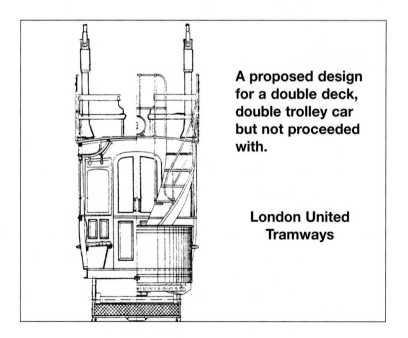

A proposed design for a double deck, double trolley car but not proceeded with.

London United Tramways

CHAPTER FIVE

ACTON, EALING AND SOUTHALL

The main road to the west from Central London at the Marble Arch passes through Bayswater, Notting Hill Gate and Holland Park for some two and a half miles before reaching Shepherds Bush where the line of the Southall, Ealing and Shepherds Bush Tram Railway Company commenced, to terminate ultimately near Acton Priory (or Acton Lane) in 1878, as related in Chapter 1. This main thoroughfare, the Uxbridge Road, was built up from Marble Arch with high-class property, then the homes of the nobility and gentry, as far as Shepherds Bush at which point a fairly abrupt change in the character of the neighbourhood, to middle-class and artisan residential areas took place. As the western extremity of the Shepherds Bush built-up area was reached about a mile to the west a further change to a semi-rural character became evident, with large tracts of undeveloped land flanking the road, interspersed with small groups of houses. Evidence of future development lay to the north of Uxbridge Road, at East Acton, where extensive brickfields were being established, and a little more than two miles west of Shepherds Bush the then-small town of Acton was reached.

Slightly more than one and a quarter miles beyond Acton was the centre of the larger town of Ealing. West of Acton the Uxbridge Road was, in the last quarter of the nineteenth century becoming built up with large properties, some in extensive grounds. Beyond Ealing Common, a large open space on either side of Uxbridge Road at the easterly approach to the town, the developing shopping and commercial centre of Ealing extended for a little over half a mile. Still further west the partially built-up area of West Ealing, where development was mainly of smaller suburban property, gave way to a sparsely developed stretch at the end of which lay the smaller settlement of Hanwell, where considerable development was taking place from about 1885 and large tracts of open space were already taken up by the City of Westminster and Kensington cemeteries occupying sites on opposite sides of the road. A further large site to the west was occupied by a mental hospital belonging to the Metropolitan Asylums Board and later, from 1889, the London County Council.

From Hanwell to Southall, a distance of approximately one mile, and today closely built up but with a number of sports grounds and other open spaces, the Uxbridge Road at the turn of the century was a quiet thoroughfare with small groups of dwellings interspersed with market gardens, with Southall the last settlement of any size until Uxbridge, the county town of Middlesex close to the Middlesex – Buckinghamshire county boundary is reached, twelve and a half miles from Shepherds Bush.

Horse buses were fairly frequent as far as Acton, becoming less frequent as the distance from central London widened. Ealing had reasonable local services but service intervals were wide and subject to the vagaries of weather and the effects of poor to indifferent road surfaces. There were local train services provided by the Great Western Railway but these were infrequent and the needs of an expanding population were beginning to make themselves felt.

The opening of the horse tramway between Shepherds Bush and Acton in 1874 and 1878 gave the promise of better services but the ambitious scheme of the promoters of this undertaking to reach Southall and continue to Uxbridge as recounted in Chapter 1 had failed to materialise. Their successors, the West Metropolitan Tramways Company, as described in Chapter 2, had failed to continue the line in Acton beyond the Priory, leaving the new London United Tramways to build a new depot west of the centre of Acton, to continue the line up to this point and ultimately to electrify and extend westward to reach Uxbridge.

On 4 April 1901, on the same day as the electrified line between Shepherds Bush and Kew Bridge and the lines in central Hammersmith opened, the electric cars started to run from Shepherds Bush along Uxbridge Road as far as the depot at the top of Acton Hill. These lines had been reconstructed between 1895 and 1898 for operation with horse trams. Following the removal of obstacles to electrification recounted elsewhere in this book an inspection of the electrified lines was carried out on behalf of the Board of Trade by Lt. Col. H.A.Yorke, RE on 30 March 1901. The Company's Act of 1900 had authorised the reconstruction of the line in Acton between Mansell Road, east of the North London Railway bridge, and Acton Priory and its extension beyond Priory Road through Acton and Ealing to Hanwell as a double line except a 40 yard section of single track between Gunnersbury Lane and Acton Depot and a short interlacing section in West Ealing. The distance between Mansell Road and a point immediately west of Acton Depot was 0.668 miles including the 40 yard length of single line near the depot.

The section from Mansell Road to the depot was a continuation of the line from Shepherds Bush, which the LUT had reconstructed as double track as far as Mansell Road in 1895 under the terms of the 1895 Provisional Order. At the time this Order was made the line in Acton still terminated at Priory Road, by then renamed Acton Lane. The Order authorised the half-mile extension from Priory Road to the depot as a single line with passing loops, of which there were four, at Acton Lane, Berrymead Gardens, Mill Hill Grove and Steyne Road, with another on the old line west from the North London Bridge at Birkbeck Road.

Under the terms of the 1900 Act, and arising from objections by traders in the High Street to double lines at certain points which did not allow 9ft 6in clearance between outer rails and the kerb, Acton UDC had agreed with the Company to the insertion of two additional interlacings to the four which had been shown on the deposited plans and approved earlier by the Council. The LUT relaid the section in 1901, using mainly the 80lb/yard rails of 1896, with the six interlacings of various lengths between the North London Railway bridge (beneath which the carriageway was 26ft wide) and Steyne Road, and the short single line section between Gunnersbury Lane and the depot.

Lt. Col. Yorke inspected the electrified line on 20 March 1901 and in his report to the Board of Trade dated 17 April he commented adversely on the fact that the two additional interlacings had not been shown on the plans deposited with the Board and said that he regretted the fact that the wording of the Act empowering

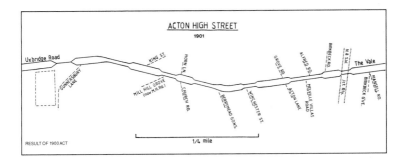

Plan of track as laid in High Street, Acton in 1901, showing interlaced sections.

a double line throughout had not been adhered to. He thought that the short interlacing sections were likely to lead to misunderstandings between the motormen of cars travelling in opposite directions and increase the risk of accidents. He said the Company should be asked to explain the reason for the deviation from the original deposited plans. He also commented upon the cars as described in Chapter 12.

Notwithstanding these reservations Col. Yorke did not feel justified in withholding the issue of a certificate of fitness for public use, subject to any comments the Board of Trade's electrical adviser, A.P. Trotter might wish to make on the electrical equipment of the line. He recommended the institution of speed limits for electrical working of the whole line, from Shepherds Bush terminus to Acton Depot: from Shepherds Bush terminus to Hetley Road, 8 mile/h; between Hetley Road and Mansell Road, Acton, 10 mile/h; between Mansell Road and Gunnersbury Lane, 8 mile/h and the single line between Gunnersbury Lane and 25 yards west of the Red Lion Public House, 4 mile/h. A short piece of double line, 40 yards in length had been laid beyond this point to give access to the depot but as it was not at this time to be used in public service it did not feature in the inspection. Compulsory stops were imposed in both directions before passing beneath the North London Railway bridge, in both directions at a stopping place proposed by the Company west of Grove Road and in both directions at a similar stopping place west of Horn Lane.

It was not possible to take a double line under the North London Railway bridge unless the abutments of the bridge were set back. To protect pedestrians metal railings were placed on the edge of the pavements on either side of the road to which were later added sheet metal panels. This situation remained throughout tramway operation in Acton.

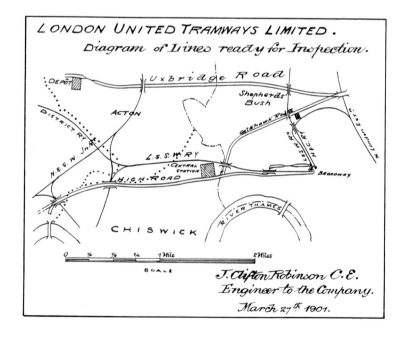

In his report Col. Yorke referred to the spacing between the tracks and width of the cars. He commented favourably on the high railings around the upper decks as likely to reduce the risk of accidents. The bodies of the cars were 6ft 10½in wide but the width across the upper decks was 7ft 3in, this dimension being a technical infringement of the Tramways Act of 1870. The 3ft spacing between the tracks thus allowed less than fifteen inches between passing cars. This spacing had existed in the past and in view of the height of the upper deck railings Col. Yorke did not recommend the Board to withhold their certificate on this account.

Col. Yorke's report was discussed in depth at all levels at the Board of Trade. It transpired that the LUT had not sought the views of the Board when negotiating with Acton Council to make the two additional interlacings in the High Street at Berrymead Gardens and Winchester Street. As a result the Board wrote to Robinson on 25 April 1901 asking him to consult the Board's officers before departing from plans deposited for future extensions. The Board also stressed the necessity for adhering to the prescribed overall width of future deliveries of cars. Robinson acknowledged all these points on 7 May and promised compliance with the Board's requirements for the future.

Final approval for electric operation had been delayed by the protracted negotiations between the Company and the Kew Observatory authorities, the Board of Trade and the Treasury which were not completed until 3 April 1901, as related in Chapter 4. Trotter sanctioned electrical working for all the electrified lines and the certificate of fitness for public service was signed by Sir Thomas Blomefield on 3 April, covering all the electrified lines except the line in Acton between Mansell Road and the Depot. Sanction for this section was withheld until 6 May pending receipt by the Board of Trade of Robinson's explanation of the agreement with Acton UDC and assurance of future compliance with the Board's requirements. Temporary sanction for working the section was, however granted, and electric trams commenced to work between Shepherds Bush and Acton Depot on 4 April 1901 at a fare of one penny for the full journey, from end to end.

Legislation for the route westward from Acton Depot was not easily obtained. In 1888 the West Metropolitan Tramways Company had sought powers to reach Hanwell via Ealing and the application was rejected. Ealing Local Board and their successor from 1894, the Ealing Urban District Council were unyielding in their opposition to this and later proposals and Hanwell Local Board was undecided. In November 1890 the WMT again gave notice of their intention to seek powers for the Acton – Hanwell route but Ealing Local Board maintained its opposition and the scheme was again withdrawn. A proposal by the West London Tramways Company for the Acton – Hanwell route was approved by Hanwell Local Board without dissent but once again opposition by Ealing Local Board ensured that the scheme did not proceed further. In October 1897 the British Electric Traction Company gave notice of its intention to apply for a Light Railway Order for the same route, this company wrote to the new Ealing Urban District Council explaining their proposal in detail but the UDC resolved to oppose the scheme, which did not proceed. Hanwell UDC voted similarly and also voted to ask the London General Omnibus Company and the Great Western Railway Company to provide improved services.

The earlier attempt by the LUT to obtain powers to extend beyond Acton in their 1898 Bill failed, as recounted in Chapter 3. At that time Ealing UDC were joined in their opposition by Middlesex County Council, who insisted that the main roads in the county should not be taken over by private interests. Ealing UDC, moreover, had debated the tramway question at length in May 1898 and had approved a motion to explore the possibility of providing omnibuses to serve the district or of providing its own electric tramway "with underground cables" (i.e. the conduit system). All this resulted in the defeat of the LUT's 1898 scheme.

Despite the powerful propaganda offensive mounted by Clifton Robinson, which included the publication of the *Ealing Election News* for seven issues between 16 February and 30 March 1898, opinion in Ealing which had polarized in the form of "pro-tram" and "anti-tram" parties, was able by the narrowest margin of one vote to secure the defeat of the Ealing proposals and as a result of this the Ealing – Hanwell clause was deleted from the Bill and the LUT concentrated upon expansion in other directions. Robinson had enlisted the aid of the Ealing publishing firm of King & Hutchings in the production of the *Ealing Election News* and other similar propaganda sheets and this firm lent the LUT active support through its chain of local newspapers which covered part of West Middlesex.

At the same time as the failed attempt to gain the Ealing powers was going through Parliament, Robinson and his associates had perceived hitherto unsuspected possibilities in the use of the 1896 Light Railways Act to obtain legislation for what amounted, in every respect but name, to street tramways. The Light Railways Act had been intended by its promoters to enable rural communities to obtain powers inexpensively, not only for passenger transport, but also for the carriage of goods and livestock, and to link up larger centres of population with farming and agricultural areas to their mutual advantage. Robinson had studied the Act and had seen that it offered a way to obtain powers for lines which passed through the districts of more than one local authority. One provision in the Act debarred consideration of a scheme which was wholly in the area of a single authority, but this was of little importance when set against the LUT proposals, which were all envisaged to pass through several districts.

To obtain powers under the Light Railways Act it was necessary to lodge application for a Draft Order with the Light Railway Commissioners in May or November. The three Commissioners, who were appointed by the Board of Trade as permanent officers, held local inquiries and if they considered that a case had been made out by the promoters they approved the application and passed it to the Board of Trade for consideration of technical and other details, requests for amendments by interested parties and if considered satisfactory, final confirmation by the Board. This procedure reduced the considerable costs and delays involved in promoting a Parliamentary Bill; though in some cases the Commissioners could decline to consider an application on the grounds that it was one for Parliament to decide. This could occur if powers previously sought in Parliament without success were subsequently sought under the Light Railways Act.

Car No. 31 was one of the first electric trams to reach Acton, when a service to and from Shepherds Bush commenced on 4 April 1901. Paper stickers served as destination indicators for the first few months of service. (Photo: LUT)

The Company's first attempt to obtain Light Railway powers was in 1898, for the line between Southall and Uxbridge and another from the south side of Kew Bridge to Kingston via Richmond, Petersham and Ham, reaching Richmond by a different route from the existing horse tramway via Kew Road. The Uxbridge line was sanctioned but the Kingston line was withdrawn owing to local opposition. Details of both these are outlined in the appropriate chapters. This led Robinson to make an attempt to get through Ealing with the aid of the Light Railways Act, but the Urban District Council was able to defeat this application by objecting that the Light Railway Commissioners were not in a position to overturn Parliament's rejection of the Ealing line in the 1898 Bill.

The company was now left with powers from Shepherds Bush to Acton and from Hanwell to Uxbridge, together with the line authorised in 1898 between Brentford and Hanwell by way of Boston Road. If necessary Uxbridge could be reached from Shepherds Bush and Hammersmith by using the Boston Road route thus by-passing Ealing, and plans were drawn up to put this into practice. Meanwhile, Robinson had been cultivating opinion in Ealing and neighbouring districts and had publicly stated that the Ealing gap would be closed. By 1899 Ealing was a quite large town which, in addition to a large majority of traditionalists who had no need of tramways and wished to retain a rural atmosphere, now had a growing population of people who had moved out from central London. This latter body of opinion was mainly settled in the areas west and south of the town, where development was of a greater density than in the older, central part of Ealing. Early in March 1898 a crowded meeting at the Victoria Hall had voted strongly in favour of local election candidates who were standing under the banner of "Electric Tramways, Incorporation and Progress".

From this date opinion in Ealing slowly became more favourable as Robinson continued to consolidate his position. The "old guard" did not give up the fight easily, however, and in November 1899 the Council again debated the tramways issue. The result of this was a motion passed in favour of applying to the Board of Trade for a Provisional Order authorising a tramway from the Acton boundary through Ealing as far as the Hanwell boundary, with a short branch from Uxbridge Road into Longfield Avenue in the centre of the town. This short length of line, 150 yards in length terminating 50 yards south of the bridge over the Great Western Railway was presumably intended as access to a depot site. The Town Hall was on the east corner of Longfield Avenue and to the rear was the municipal baths, there being a tract of council-owned land part of which could readily be available for the small depot needed for such a short route, 2.09 miles of standard gauge double line. The track in Longfield Avenue was shown as single line on the plans. This was clearly an attempt on the part of Ealing Council to block the company's impending new attempt to bridge the Ealing gap. The application for the Provisional Order was dated 15 November 1899.

During their battle with the LUT, Ealing had received the support of Middlesex County Council, who objected to tramway plans for the county roads on the grounds that the roads should not be allowed to fall into the hands of private companies; they also considered that the County Council's bridges would be endangered by the passage of trams. Middlesex also had other reasons for opposing the Bill: they were considering becoming a tramway authority in their own right and establishing a network of their own lines in the north of the County, where a number of proposals for powers by companies were under consideration. However, Parliament ruled that the County Council had no *locus standi* to oppose the LUT Bill and it was passed to a Select Committee of the House of Commons, but still had to pass the House of Lords. In consequence, the County Council withdrew its opposition to the LUT scheme and right at the end of 1899 Ealing withdrew its long-standing opposition and in February 1900 gave formal assent to the LUT 1900 Bill.

The 1900 Bill was an extensive one covering not only the Ealing and Hanwell part of the Uxbridge Road route, but also new tramways in Hounslow and a loop

Formal inauguration of electric services took place on 10th July 1901. Nos. 101-109 formed the ceremonial procession, part of which is seen awaiting departure from Shepherds Bush to travel to Ealing and Southall. (Photo: LUT)

line from Isleworth through Twickenham, Hampton, Hampton Court, Hampton Wick and Teddington back to Twickenham. The Uxbridge Road provision covered the line in Hanwell and Ealing, to commence at a junction with the Light Railway authorised in the 1898 Order at Hillside, High Street, Hanwell and pass eastward along High Street and the Broadway, Hanwell and into Ealing along Uxbridge Road, Broadway, The Mall, Uxbridge Road and into Acton at Birch Grove to meet the existing line at Acton Depot. The total distance of the line between Hanwell and Acton Depot was 2.988 miles, all double track except for 48 yards of interlacing line east of the Ealing – Hanwell boundary and 37 yards of single line near the entrance to Acton Depot.

Ealing UDC gave its formal consent to the Bill on 20 February 1900 and on the same day the Council and the LUT entered into an agreement, some of whose terms were onerous. One iniquitous provision was for reimbursement of the Council's costs of opposing earlier LUT schemes, up to £900, and a yearly payment of £500 in addition to general rates of between £400 and £500 per annum. Paving was to be of hardwood blocks, and the design of overhead equipment and poles had to be to the approval of the district surveyor. The traction poles were to be made available to the Council for lighting purposes. No journey wholly within Ealing was to cost more than one penny, and ordinary fares to be: Shepherds Bush – Acton, one penny; Acton (Railway Hotel) – Ealing, one penny; Railway Hotel – Hanwell, one penny. Workmen's cars to be run morning and evening and fares to be: Kasner's Corner, West Ealing – Shepherds Bush, one penny. The LUT also agreed with the Council that construction of the section between The Mall and Christ Church, in the centre of the town should be completed within fourteen days and the section westward to the Hanwell boundary in the shortest possible time. The provisions respecting fares were amended in the subsequent Act.

The 1900 Bill had passed through the House of Commons and on being passed to the House of Lords Middlesex County Council, having withdrawn their opposition in the Commons, again petitioned against the Bill in the Lords. This move was condemned in the *Middlesex County Times* on 12 May but the County Council persisted in their opposition throughout the remainder of the passage of the Bill. By 14 July the Bill was before a Select Committee of the House of Lords and by 21 July the MCC's opposition had been overcome. The *Middlesex County Times* on that day contained a leading article rejoicing in "the triumph of the tramways" and heavily criticised the obstructiveness of the MCC, castigating the majority party on that body as "the little knot of nor'-easters who rule the roost at the Westminster Guildhall" (the County Council's headquarters).

The 1900 Bill passed through the final stages by the end of July and received the Royal Assent on 6 August. However, Ealing UDC, despite having entered into an agreement with the company during the course of the 1900 Bill through Parliament, raised obstacles to the start of work on the line through the town. In November 1900 the Council refused to allow the work to start pending resolution of difficulties which had arisen regarding the responsibility for resiting mains, telephone and fire alarm cables along the route. This delay continued until 19 January 1901 when it was reported that the differences between the parties had been resolved and that construction in Ealing would begin shortly. Work had meanwhile started at the Hanwell boundary at the end of October 1900 in the Southall direction and on the section between Acton Depot and the Ealing boundary at Birch Grove.

In the central part of Ealing the Council had insisted on the use of highly ornate central traction poles, against the advice of both the LUT and the Board of Trade. The Board of Trade only sanctioned centre poles if the carriageway was sufficiently wide to allow their use, and that only reluctantly. These poles were also used by the Council for their street lighting. At the outer ends of Ealing, side poles and span wire construction was sanctioned, and over the rest of the route to Southall this latter type of construction was used, except for just under half a mile west of the bridge across the River Brent at the Hanwell – Southall boundary, as far as the Iron Bridge carrying the Great Western Railway across the road, where bracket arm suspension was used.

The Hanwell proposals in the 1900 Bill were not strongly opposed. Hanwell Urban District Council's share of the Uxbridge Road consisted solely of 0.615 miles of double line from the boundary with Ealing as far as the bridge across the River Brent, which formed the boundary with the Urban District of Southall. Of this distance a mere 130 yards was authorised in the 1898 Light Railway Order, which empowered the company to construct the line from that point westwards through Southall to Uxbridge. Up to that point, which was the junction between Uxbridge Road and Lower Boston Road the line was a tramway, part of the line from Acton Depot through Ealing. Hanwell UDC, with little more than half a mile of the track in their district in Uxbridge Road also had 1.09 miles of authorised line in Boston Road and Lower Boston Road and these sections were authorised in the 1900 Act. The tramway in Boston Road and Lower Boston Road, from Brentford was authorised in the 1898 Act throughout to the junction with the 1898 Light Railway Order line in Uxbridge Road, 17 yards west from Half Acre Road, Hanwell and some 110 yards east from the River Brent bridge, which formed the Hanwell – Southall boundary. The junction was from south to west as authorised, but when the Lower Boston Road line was built in 1906 an east to south junction was inserted which was not authorised by Act or Order but was nevertheless approved by the Board of Trade, the local authorities having raised no objection.

Hanwell UDC had heard Clifton Robinson's explanation of the LUT proposals for the district in February 1898 and had formally assented to the scheme in the 1898 Bill. Ealing UDC had tried to get Hanwell to join them in opposing the company's proposals, but without success. This had been crucial in view of the fact that to gain access to the Uxbridge Road route beyond Ealing the goodwill of the Hanwell authority was essential as the northward half of Boston Road lay in the Hanwell Urban District. The company and Hanwell UDC entered into an agreement on 20 February 1900 which provided for the company to pay an annual wayleave of £230 to the Council. The company also agreed that the paving in Uxbridge Road to within approximately 130 yards east of the Southall – Hanwell boundary should be in Jarrah wood blocks between the rails with granite setts in the 18in margins outside the rails. The 130 yards at the extreme western end of the

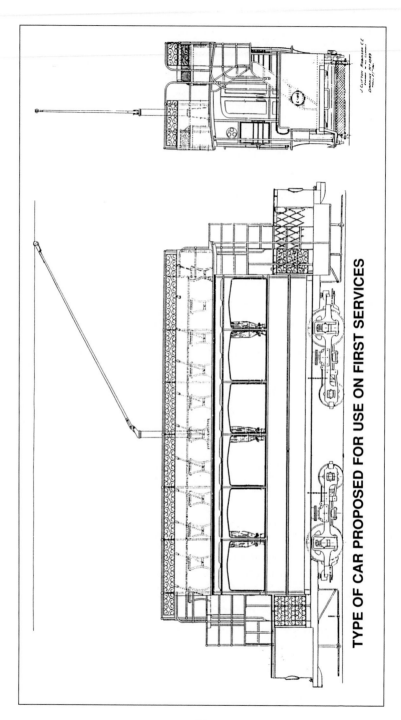

TYPE OF CAR PROPOSED FOR USE ON FIRST SERVICES

district, authorised by the 1898 Light Railway Order was paved in granite setts. In Boston Road and Lower Boston Road it was agreed that the paving should be in Jarrah wood blocks throughout.

The 1900 Act gave Hanwell UDC the right to use the company's traction poles for lighting purposes and placed upon the company an obligation to erect and maintain "a cluster electric light" to be supplied from the overhead in the Broadway at the junction with (Upper) Boston Road, a similar light opposite the Victoria public house in Boston Road and another in Uxbridge Road outside the Viaduct public house, to be kept lighted at all times when the cars were operating.

From the point in Hanwell 130 yards east of the Southall – Hanwell boundary through Southall, Hayes and Hillingdon to Uxbridge the line was authorised by the London United Tramways (Light Railways Extensions) Order 1898. Details of the acquisition of these powers are given in Chapter 7 covering the line from Southall to Uxbridge. West of Hanwell the local authorities welcomed the tramway proposals and the Order was gained with little difficulty. The removal of Ealing Council's long-standing objections at the end of 1899 had reduced the importance to the company of the Boston Road line and construction of this was deferred while work on the Uxbridge Road line was pressed forward, with the next priority being the Thames Valley route to Hampton Court and Kingston, sanctioned in the 1900 Act. Southall-Norwood Urban District Council had driven no hard bargains with the company. Whilst the Order had sanctioned granite sett paving between Hanwell and Uxbridge, the company had agreed to pave 0.320 miles in the centre of Southall with Jarrah wood blocks. Subject to this proviso to pave in wood and to the company allowing the Council the use of their traction poles for lighting and other purposes, the Council, which was attended on that day by George White and Clifton Robinson, agreed on 27 May 1898 to approve the company's application.

Construction between Acton Depot and Southall had been delayed by differences over responsibility for resiting gas and water mains and other underground installations. At the beginning of November 1900 the company broke the ground at Hanwell to commence laying the track to Southall, and this work went on apace until January 1901 when the differences with Ealing UDC were resolved and construction also started in their district At this time the difficulties with Kew Observatory and the Royal Society were still unresolved but the company had continued work on the new electric lines in the Uxbridge Road, which were sufficiently far from the Observatory. In any case the earth returns over the whole of the electrified and new electric lines were being fitted with special booster equipment imported from America, which H.F. Parshall, the company's consulting electrical engineer and Clifton Robinson were confident would eliminate earthborne disturbance to the Kew instruments.

By the time the line to Southall was ready for inspection by the Board of Trade the Kew Observatory difficulties had been resolved and electric trams had run to Acton Depot and Kew Bridge from 4 April 1901. Completion of the route as far as Southall marked a major milestone in the company's progress and on 2 July Lt. Col. H.A.Yorke RE inspected the line. The Colonel reported favourably on the trackwork on both sections and A.P. Trotter found the electrical installation in excellent order. The line through Ealing was double track throughout except for 48 yards of interlacing a little to the east of the boundary with Hanwell, and the track across the bridge over the Grand Junction Canal in Southall was laid as single line pending reconstruction of the bridge. Col. Yorke recommended speed limits of 10 mile/h from the end of the 1900 tramway at Hanwell to the boundary with Ealing; through the interlacing east of the Ealing boundary, 6 mile/h; from the interlacing to Hamilton Road, 8 mile/h and from Hamilton Road to Acton Depot, 10 mile/h. A compulsory stop was imposed before entering either end of the interlacing. On the Light Railway section from Hanwell to Southall Town Hall a 4 mile/h limit was imposed across the Brent Bridge at the Hanwell – Southall boundary pending a proposed widening of the bridge, with 10 mile/h between the bridge and the Red Lion Hotel in Southall and 6 mile/h from the Red Lion to the west end of the centre of Southall. From that point to the Southall district boundary the limit was 10

Car 208 descends Acton Hill, bound for Shepherds Bush c1903. The length of single track seen behind the car was later doubled.

(Courtesy: London Borough of Ealing Local History Library)

mile/h. A compulsory stop was called for between the corner of Lower Boston Road and Brent Bridge.

Col. Yorke commented upon the lifeguards on the new cars on this new section. These were fifty Milnes-built trams, Nos. 101-150, fitted with Wilson & Bennett lifeguards of all-metal construction, mainly steel rods and strong wire mesh. At the inspection a demonstration of the efficacy of this guard was given, in the yard of Hanwell Depot. At Clifton Robinson's suggestion, a member of the staff volunteered to undertake this duty and he was picked up safely by the guard, without injury, no fewer than thirteen times. Col. Yorke was suitably impressed and the manufacturers of the guard made use of the demonstration in their subsequent publicity material. The Colonel recommended the issue of the necessary certificate of fitness, and following final discussion of details at the Board of Trade the certificate was signed and issued on 13 August 1901, permission having been given for the line to be opened meanwhile.

This important extension from Acton to Southall gave the LUT a total of fifteen and a half miles of electric tramway route, nearly all of which was double track, but up to this time there had been no formal inauguration of the new electric system. The completion of the line through Ealing took place a short time before one of the most important events in the history of local government in Ealing and the county of Middlesex, the grant of a Charter of Incorporation as a municipal borough to the Urban District of Ealing, the first such charter to be granted in Middlesex. Clifton Robinson and George White were able to organise a grand formal opening of the LUT system to take place on Ealing's Charter Day, 10 July 1901. Moreover, Clifton Robinson, who had proved himself a master publicist, had so arranged matters that the LUT opening ceremony should become virtually a part of the town's own celebrations.

Long-standing differences between the LUT and Ealing UDC were largely cleared away with the passing of the 1900 Act and subsequent agreement of 20 February 1900. On Wednesday 10 July 1901 a procession of nine new tramcars, Nos. 101-150 class, resplendent in white livery picked out in blue, green and gold and each decorated with garlands and bunting, left Hanwell Depot and travelled along the new route through Ealing and Acton to Shepherds Bush Central London Railway station. 10 July was a brilliant day and contemporary reports speak of the exceptional weather. The cars reversed at Shepherds Bush and, accompanied by George White and Clifton Robinson, the company's guests for the day embarked for the inaugural journey to Southall. Some 450 guests had accepted the company's invitation to the ceremony and to the luncheon which followed. Among those boarding the cars were the Marquess of Lansdowne, Earl Grey, the Earl of Rosse, Lord Rothschild, the Rt. Hon, A.J. Balfour, MP, Sir John Kennaway, MP, Lord Hillingdon and Lord Herries. Charles Tyson Yerkes and J. Pierpont Morgan Jr., both of whom were later to play a prominent part in the affairs of the LUT were present, together with numerous members of the financial world and many distinguished members of the electrical industry, and the formalities were presided over by George White in his capacity as LUT Chairman.

At the start of the inaugural run, Lord Rothschild, in a short speech, declared the system and the new extension open, following which the procession set off to Southall, which was reached in forty-five minutes. The traction poles and other suitable fixtures along the whole route were decorated with flags and bunting, and in Ealing additional lavish floral and other decorations associated with the town's own celebrations added to the general festive atmosphere. At the Southall terminus the Town Hall with its decorations provided a backdrop for the many photographers who took advantage of the brief halt there for the reversal to record the scene for posterity. The reversal accomplished, the procession set off for Shepherds Bush which was reached in forty minutes, where once again the cars reversed and took the route along Goldhawk Road to the power station and depot at Chiswick, arriving there at 1.45 pm.

At Chiswick the party inspected the generating station and depot. The depot floor had been boarded over and carpeted with red baize and tables set out for an elaborate luncheon, details of which were described at length in the *Ealing Gazette*. Following this, George White, who presided, proposed the Loyal Toast and the Rt. Hon. Arthur Balfour proposed "Success to the London United Tramways", speaking in glowing terms of the company's achievements. He said nothing Parliament could do could match the benefits to the public of such enterprises as the LUT in improving the lot of people in crowded areas by providing cheap and speedy transport to the outskirts of London. He understood that the LUT, when completed, would carry 150,000,000 people per year; he gave the company the Toast, coupled with the name of George White. White responded saying that the day was the culmination of some six years of pioneering work and reviewed the progress the company had made since 1895. He referred to the Kew Observatory problem and opposition to the company's proposals by Middlesex County Council: the amicable settlement with the Treasury of the Kew problem, agreement with the MCC and support from many of the district councils were all gracefully acknowledged. Forty miles of route were now authorised and the LUT was looking ahead to a total of eighty miles and intended to press forward to get these new lines opened as soon as possible.

White went on to say that Kew Gardens was now within easy reach of the London working man, and Hanwell and Southall men working in London were able to reach their work rapidly and at a small outlay. White mentioned the decision of the directors to have no advertisements on the cars: this entailed foregoing £3,000 per annum which would ultimately rise to £10,000. White finally referred to the master-mind behind the company's achievements, "who did not have to be named". Dr. Silvanus P. Thompson, the eminent electrical engineer proposed a toast to James Clifton Robinson – "a jolly good fellow" – who contented himself with a brief and modest acknowledgement, remarking that too many words from him might prove the truth of an old "chestnut" – "why was George White?", "Because Robinson Crusoe".

During the Charter celebrations during the afternoon Lord Rothschild with Sir Montague Nelson, the Charter Mayor of Ealing, councillors and other distinguished personalities were joined by White and Robinson on a dais outside Ealing

Town Hall, where Sir Montague welcomed the LUT to Ealing, saying that times had changed and the tramways were now welcome in the town, he having earlier opposed their coming. He hoped that the tramways would bring increased population and prosperity to the town. Lord Rothschild responded, saying he had earlier that day had much pleasure in formally opening the London United Tramways electric system, which he felt would bring greatly improved facilities to the districts through which they passed. He had great pleasure in congratulating George White and his fellow directors of the company. Thus ended the inaugural ceremonies of the first electric street tramways, worked from a fixed source of power, in the London area. The day's arrangements had cost no less than £1,307.10s. 0d, a very large sum at that time.

The events of 10 July provided a brief interlude in the unremitting task of constructing the authorised lines and fighting the Parliamentary battles for new ones. The next thrust in the expansion scheme would be towards the Middlesex bank of the River Thames, for which powers had been obtained in the Act of 1900. With the Ealing gap now closed the company shelved the construction of the Brentford – Hanwell line through Boston Road to concentrate upon these new lines. Meanwhile, the daily service between Shepherds Bush and Southall opened to the public on Thursday 11 July, using the new white cars, considered at the time to be the ultimate in tramcar design. They were built by G.F. Milnes & Co. of Birkenhead to Clifton Robinson's own designs and their design and technical details are chronicled in Chapter 11.

Services commencing on 11 July were remarkably frequent. On weekdays the first car left Hanwell Depot for Shepherds Bush at 6.50am, arriving at Shepherds Bush at 7.27am. The first departure from Southall to Shepherds Bush was at 7.30am, arriving at 8.18am and the first car left Shepherds Bush at 7.30am reaching Southall at 8.20am. A three-minute service operated throughout the day until the 11.05pm departure from Hanwell to Shepherds Bush following which a six-minute service operated until 11.17pm. From Southall to Shepherds Bush the three-minute service operated until the 10.54pm departure following which a six-minute service operated until 11.06pm, and from Shepherds Bush to Southall the three-minute service was worked until 11.42pm with departures every six minutes thence until

Bound for Southall, No. 132 is seen passing No. 107 at 'The Bell' public house in Ealing. Side poles were used to suspend the overhead wires on this section.

(Courtesy: National Tramway Museum)

12.50am. On weekdays late departures left Southall at 11.17pm, then every six minutes until 12.07am, and from Shepherds Bush to Southall late cars left at 12.10am and every ten minutes until 1.00am. Sunday services commenced with the first car from Hanwell Depot at 8.3 am and every three minutes thereafter until 11.43pm, the first car leaving Southall at 9.15am and running every three minutes until 11.37pm, while from Shepherds Bush for Hanwell and Southall the first car left at 9.15am, running every three minutes until 12.30am.

Workmen's cars were timed to leave the Depot every 20 minutes from 4.20am until 6.40am and from Shepherds Bush terminus from 5.00am to 7.00am. Workmen's fares were 1d between Hanwell Depot and Shepherds Bush and the same from Shepherds Bush to Drayton Green Road, Ealing. Ordinary fares were 1d between Shepherds Bush and Birch Grove, Acton; Acton, Birch Grove and Eccleston Road, Ealing; Ealing Broadway Station Approach and Hanwell Broadway, and Hanwell Boundary (Eccleston Road) and South Road terminus, Southall. 2d ordinary fares were between Shepherds Bush terminus and Eccleston Road, Ealing and between Acton (Birch Grove) and South Road terminus, Southall, with 3d for the full journey between Shepherds Bush and Southall termini.

The frequencies at the commencement of these services soon gave rise to complaint from residents, almost all in Ealing with houses in Uxbridge Road. There was still a large body of anti-tram opinion in the town and this influential lobby started to make itself heard with petitions to the Borough Council demanding less use of the gong, the reduction of late night services and decreased frequency of services generally. The Council, despite having sanctioned the Company's 1900 Bill had nevertheless indicated that the company's operations would be subject to close scrutiny, and as a result of this the rapproachment between the company and the Council was short-lived. The Council enlisted the co-operation of the Acton, Chiswick and Southall councils in bringing pressure to bear upon the company and Clifton Robinson, having gained the goodwill of Ealing and the other councils at considerable cost, set about placating them, especially Ealing. The interlacing between Hanwell boundary and Eccleston Road was a source of complaint and once the road had been widened this was quickly replaced with double track. Robinson undertook to minimise the use of the gong, especially at night and to ensure that speed limits were strictly observed. On the question of speeds, he was able to point out that where some sections of the community called for speed reductions, others wanted speeds increased.

A dewirement in Acton on 7 February 1902 brought down a length of overhead wire which remained live, killing two horses. The Clerk of Acton Council wrote to the Board of Trade on 11 February asking for a speed restriction not to exceed 12 mile/h to be enforced, and said that a councillor had witnessed the accident and stated that the car involved had been travelling "at a great speed". Local users of the trams in the three districts distributed handbills in the cars and throughout the area protesting against the councils' proposals to reduce speeds and drew up a memorial to the Board of Trade requesting the Board to take no notice of such proposals. Those protesting said the omnibus proprietors were behind the councils' moves to limit the speeds of the electric trams to those of the recently-ousted horse trams. Clifton Robinson received a copy of Acton Council's letter to the Board of Trade and he acknowledged this on 15 February in a terse three-line letter devoid of comment. The residents' memorial to the Board of Trade was signed by 50,211 persons. Meanwhile, Heston & Isleworth Urban District Council, on the Hounslow route, was taking the opposite view to that of its Uxbridge Road neighbours and sent a memorial to the Board of Trade on 13 February asking for more cars to be run and for "the speed of travelling to be increased with due regard to safety".

Further along Uxbridge Road, Southall-Norwood UDC asked the Board of Trade to insist that the cars should be fitted with speed indicators to register maximum speeds, the indicators to be sealed and periodically inspected by officers of the Board. The UDC also asked that the indicators should be linked to a speed governor and that such governors should cut off power when a speed of 12 mile/h was reached and have a registering device to record each operation of the governor. Other requirements of this council were that the brakes should be capable of pulling up a car within two lengths and for wire guards to be fitted between the trucks; also for the ventilation of the cars "to be adequately secured by a simple method of communication between the passengers and the driver or conductor"; for spitting in the cars to be made an offence; for a distance of 100 yards to be maintained between cars on the same track, and for electric lamps to be fitted on the top decks of all cars (the first 100 cars did not have these, though later batches were so fitted), Southall-Norwood UDC rounded off its list of requirements with demands for shelters to be erected "at exchange points such as Hanwell Depot and Southall terminus" and for motormen to signal their intention to stop "by means of a flag or other signal which will be seen by persons in other vehicles following the cars".

A P. Trotter, the Board of Trade's electrical inspecting officer was a resident in Chiswick and his help was sought by the councils in respect of "unnecessary gonging". He told the councils that he would do what he could as a private resident, but felt that it would be undesirable that he should take such a course in his official capacity. Col. Yorke, however in an internal memorandum said that the gong nuisance was "an abuse by the company of the privileges accorded to them".

Col. Yorke commented internally to the Board of Trade officers that nearly all the requests by the councils were unnecessary; speed registering devices had been considered in other cases and decided against. He did not think upper deck lamps were desirable, noting that they had been fitted on later cars. He also said that a request for illuminated stop signs was unnecessary and did not accede to a request by Middlesex County Council to inspect the cars when they thought fit and to prohibit their use "if thought unfit". The Board of Trade officers discussed the conflicting demands of the councils and observations by Clifton Robinson and Col. Yorke's final word, on 14 February was "no further action required, I think".

These exchanges between the parties were all part of the process of agreeing the Board of Trade's Rules and Regulations for electric working of the LUT, delayed mainly by the difficulties with the Kew Geomagnetic Observatory. The Statutory Rules and Regulations were finally settled and confirmed by the Board of Trade under the seal of Sir Herbert Jekyll on 20 February 1902.

In September 1902 the track in Acton was the subject of complaints by Acton UDC; this track had been reconstructed as a single line with loops in 80lb/yd rails in 1895. It was relaid in 1900 making use mainly of the 1895 rails as double and interlacing track, there being no fewer than six interlacings in the High Street within five-eighths of a mile, for electric traction. These interlacings were beneath the North London Railway bridge; between Birkbeck Road and Grove Road; at the end of Winchester Street and outside the Public Library; between Oldham's Terrace and Church Road; between the George and Dragon and Mill Hill Grove and between the Fire Station and Steyne Road.

The track was not standing up to the heavy stresses imposed by the electric trams and moreover the six interlacings in such a short distance were a source of complaints by residents and others. The Board of Trade had been critical of this layout from the outset but had not pressed the company to make any alterations. The LUT and Acton UDC negotiated an agreement in September 1905 for reconstruction of the line in the town in 100lb/yd rails as double track except for the interlacing between the George and Dragon and Mill Hill Grove. The Council had opened proceedings in the High Court to force the company to begin the reconstruction but withdrew their action pending conclusion of the agreement. On 4 December the council refused to exchange agreements owing to difficulties which had arisen between the UDC and Middlesex County Council over widenings and footpaths in High Street, and the LUT directors resolved to take court action to compel the UDC to conclude the agreement.

By 20 March 1906 Acton UDC was willing to conclude the agreement provided that the LUT retained the interlacing line beneath the North London Railway bridge, where the carriageway was 26ft wide with correspondingly narrow footpaths, particularly on the north side of the road. Whilst double track could have been accommodated at this point there were objections to the reduction of the space between the outer rails and the kerb and the LUT directors agreed to retain the interlacing with a view to getting the work carried out without further delay. However, the parties were still unable to come to a final agreement on a number of minor points and on 15 April 1907 the directors of the LUT learned that the agreement was under consideration by the Attorney-General and it was hoped that his decision would be known shortly. By 4 June the Attorney-General had approved the terms of the agreement and Clifton Robinson told the directors that the work had commenced, retaining only the interlacings beneath the railway bridge and between the George and Dragon and Mill Hill Grove. At the same time as the directors learned this they were told that the Board of Trade had complained of the condition of the track between the railway bridge and the London county boundary at Askew Road and they approved Robinson's recommendation that this section should be reconstructed to the same standard as the rest of the section, i.e. between Mansell Road east of the bridge and Acton Depot.

Under the terms of the agreement between the company and Acton UDC the forecourt of Acton Library was set back at the company's expense to provide for doubling the interlacing at that point and handrails were fitted along the edge of the pavement below the North London railway bridge. Adjustments were made to the pavements in High Street and some frontages were set back. The work of reconstruction started on 27 May 1907 and was completed by 15 April 1908. The work was carried out in 100lb/yd rail with sole-plates and girder anchors to the same standards as those adopted for the lines in Kingston and Wimbledon. The paving throughout was in Jarrah hardwood blocks and the cost of the work amounted to £14,325 after credit for the sale of scrap rails amounting to £619.

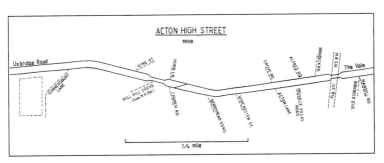

Plan of the track in High Street, Acton as relaid in 1907/8.

From the start of electric operation the LUT operated exceptionally intensive services, at intervals of three minutes and often less on the trunk routes radiating from Shepherds Bush and Hammersmith, and at a very early stage it became apparent that a form of track more capable of withstanding the strains imposed by the use of cars which, fully laden weighed some seventeen tons, was required. A result of this was that after a very short time the joints commenced to work loose and once this happened the rail ends became dished, creating a hammering effect on the ends which compounded the damage still further. In 1904, after the first electric lines had been in service for some three years an anonymous writer in the *Tramway and Railway World* foresaw the problems which this type of construction would bring and made suggestions which the LUT took up when the time came to build the Thames Valley lines in Surrey.

Meanwhile, the company's problems arising from this factor had attracted serious complaints from the Acton and Ealing councils. The councils had at first directed their complaints to Robinson but later went direct to the Board of Trade. That body, having passed the Uxbridge Road tramway as satisfactory so recently was at first loath to take definite action against the LUT, but following complaints by Acton UDC on 27 June 1904 and by Southall-Norwood UDC on 30 June followed by a further letter from Acton UDC on 5 August complaining that "old cars from the Kew Bridge line" had been put on the Uxbridge Road service, the Board drew Robinson's attention to the complaints and received a promise that they would be dealt with.

Ealing Borough Council, keeping up a running battle with the company and bombarding the Board of Trade with complaints, was strongly supported by influential residents and other interests. Robinson continued to fend off the councils, while the company's engineers considered how best to deal with the problem. Ealing lost patience and in October 1905 the Council passed a resolution which placed upon record that the Council did not consider Robinson's promises "sufficiently binding" and called upon the Board of Trade to "insist upon a compulsory arrangement being made". This arose from a letter dated 12 September from Robinson to the Council in which he said that the Ealing and Hanwell cars would be fitted with Brill trucks in replacement of the McGuire bogies then in use under Nos. 101-150. He said that he had recommended his directors to take this step and that the McGuire trucks under this batch of cars had been used because of difficulties in obtaining the preferred Brill or Peckham trucks.

Under pressure from Ealing Council the Board of Trade detailed Col. Yorke to carry out an inspection of the track and cars in the Borough of Ealing. Robinson had received notice of the inspection which was due to take place on 29 November 1905 and he instructed C.R. Holmes, resident engineer at Chiswick Works to "at once organise the closest inspection of all rolling stock on the Uxbridge Road, to press on with the rail grinding and have everything spick and span" in time for Col. Yorke's visit, which was due to take place at 11am at Acton Depot. Col. Yorke reported to the Board of Trade on 13 December: he found that most of the noise from the cars came from defects in the construction of their trucks. He had examined the 101-150 group of cars at Acton Depot, finding that the arrangement

From c1903 the Uxbridge Road service was augmented with cars Nos. 201-210, at first in white livery, but yellow from 1904. No. 210 is seen in High Street, Acton in 1907, on its way to Shepherds Bush.
(Courtesy: Ealing Libraries)

of the brake rigging on the trucks was unsatisfactory, working loose after a short period of use and causing severe rattling. The cars had been withdrawn from service pending correction of these faults and meanwhile car No. 117 had been fitted with Brill 22E maximum traction bogies and was running satisfactorily. Col. Yorke remarked that the track would very shortly have to be relaid in heavier rail and Robinson agreed with the Colonel that the track bed was insufficient for the work it had to do: no proper joints were fitted and there was no support at the rail ends. Corrugations were being dealt with by an electric track grinder which Robinson had designed, and he told Col. Yorke that he would experiment with the Thermit rail welding process to see if improvements could be made at the rail joints. Col. Yorke felt that the LUT was doing everything reasonable to meet the demands of the Council and told the Board of Trade that he did not think it necessary to make any recommendations at that time.

It appears that Ealing and the other councils accepted that, for the time being at least, they would receive little encouragement from the Board of Trade in pursuing what amounted to their vendetta against the LUT. However, Ealing Council were able to make capital in June 1906 when car 104 shed a motor gear case which caused alarming noises until the car was halted. The Council reported this to the Board of Trade, saying that the car had derailed and "several ladies on it had gone into hysterics". Ealing, once more with the bit between their teeth, called the safety of the system into question. They also (again) asked the Board of Trade to compel the company to reduce noise, saying that their committees were being forced to sit in rooms at the back of the Town Hall. Robinson told the Board that No. 104 did not derail; the gear case had fallen from the car because a bolt had sheared and the shearing of a bolt was a common minor mechanical mishap; there had never been any danger to any person on the car.

From this time Ealing kept up pressure upon the company as a matter of routine. Col. Yorke paid another visit to the town in August 1907, making an inspection of the track and cars. This time he found that Ealing had little cause for complaint and reported briefly on 30 August that he "was not wholly in sympathy with the Council's views'. On 18 October 1907 the Council told the Board of Trade that a conference of local authorities had taken place at the Town Hall on 26 July, the councils of Ealing, Hammersmith, Hampton Wick, Hanwell, Teddington and Twickenham being represented. It was resolved that the Board of Trade be asked to receive a deputation from the conference.

Hanwell UDC added their voice to those of Ealing and the other bodies on 5 December 1907 when they asked the Board of Trade to look into the condition of the track and the cars. This council also took its complaint to the Commissioner of Police for the Metropolis, who said that his jurisdiction over the LUT extended only to the cars and the track was the responsibility of the Board of Trade. Hanwell UDC found it advisable later in a letter to the Board of Trade of March 1908 to stress that their complaints were "not inspired by Ealing Borough Council". The records clearly show that Ealing Borough Council was actively promoting and co-ordinating complaints by local interests in the LUT area.

The LUT directors did not sanction the retrucking of the rest of Nos. 101-150. Instead modifications were made to the brake rigging which Robinson told the Board of Trade would eliminate rattling; No. 117 retained Brill 22E bogies for the remainder of its life. During 1907 some nearly new cars from Nos. 301-340 were transferred from the Kingston routes to Uxbridge Road and two of these, Nos. 323 and 333 are mentioned in a letter dated 7 January 1908 from Ealing Council to the Police Commissioner. These two cars and nine of the 101-150 group were described as being "noisy at 8 mile/h". The Commissioner was asked to make an inspection "without notice" and to withhold the issue of licenses. The Police inspected several cars later, on 30 July and found two only were noisy and blamed the track. Again, the majority of the complaints concerned cars in the 101-150 group, which were shortly afterwards removed from Uxbridge Road and placed in storage, seeing little use thereafter. The top-covered cars working the Kingston routes were transferred to Middlesex, ten of them to work the Hounslow route and the

No. 223, an early example of a blue car working on Uxbridge Road services, c1909 is seen crossing Brent Bridge, Hanwell on its way to Shepherds Bush. Side pole and bracket arm overhead wire suspension may just be seen in the background. It also looks as if the roadway is in need of considerable cleaning.

(Commercial view)

remainder to Uxbridge Road. Their places in Kingston were taken, in the Summer of 1908, by a number of Uxbridge Road cars, possibly Nos. 201-210. These, together with 101-150 had been repainted yellow in 1904 and a witness in Kingston records returning to the town from boarding school and seeing all the trams on the local routes painted in "glaring canary yellow". The transfer was short-lived, Nos. 101-150 and 201-210 were all repainted red by 1909 and 201-210 thereafter worked on various duties in Middlesex and Surrey.

The transfer of the 301-340 group of cars appears to have been completed by the late Summer of 1908 as Col. Yorke, once again summoned to Ealing, reported on 12 August that the line was "not in such a state as to be a source of danger". By this time cars of four batches were running on Uxbridge Road. On 14 August the *Daily Mail* reported Col. Yorke's visit to the town under the heading "Hustled Mayor – Disconcerting rapidity of Col. Yorke". Col. Yorke, in company with the Mayor, some councillors and the Borough Surveyor walked the route, and the *Daily Mail* said he had covered the two miles of line in 27 minutes. The Mayor protested and Yorke said he would if the Mayor wished cover the route again in a motor-car or a tram. Robinson was represented at this inspection by C. R. Holmes and G.E. Cummings. Col. Yorke lost patience with the Council and asked Charles Jones, the Surveyor to "show him something of which he complains". Col. Yorke said he had other business to attend to "and could not waste all the morning". Jones said "if you have not time to do your work properly you ought to leave". Col Yorke raised his hat, said "Good morning, Mr. Mayor, good morning, Mr. Surveyor", turned on his heel and walked away.

Col. Yorke made a further visit very soon after this and on 17 August 1908 he reported that "the joints are in good order and whatever noise is made on this line is due to maintenance of the cars. I noticed that some cars coloured yellow rattled a certain amount, others did not". He considered that the track was passable. A petition by Hanwell residents about noise resulted in Col. Yorke visiting the town in November 1908 and on 17 December he reported that the cars were the cause of much of the noise but the track was bad and complete reconstruction was necessary.

Throughout the period during which Ealing Council kept up its campaign of complaint the LUT had gangs continuously working on the track in the borough, probably at the expense of maintenance elsewhere on the system, where the councils were not so persistent with their demands. Nevertheless the basic problem of the track on the lines in Middlesex and in the County of London persisted throughout Robinson's reign and by February 1910 the mantle of Robinson had fallen upon Albert Stanley, managing director of the Underground Electric Railways group. One of Stanley's first tasks was to tell the Board of Trade that every car in the fleet was about to undergo a thorough overhaul. Rail joints were being cast-welded and the work would be pressed forward as fast as resources would allow. This work necessitated rearrangement of the works at Chiswick and it was not until 1913 that all the arrears of maintenance had been cleared. Even then much of the work was of a temporary nature, most of the track mileage still requiring complete reconstruction to modern standards.

The Hammersmith – Uxbridge Road Link

The 1898 powers for the link between Brentford and Hanwell via Boston Road ensured that LUT cars could reach points along Uxbridge Road west ot Ealing directly from Hammersmith, avoiding the barrier west of Acton set by Ealing Urban District Council's initial refusal to consent to the LUT line through the town. When Ealing finally consented to the 1900 LUT Bill, the importance of the Boston Road link diminished and the company closed the Ealing gap by completing the line then terminating at Acton Depot, through Ealing and Hanwell to Southall, together with the authorised extension from Kew Bridge through Brentford and Isleworth to The Bell at Hounslow.

There was still a need for a link between Hammersmith and the towns along Uxbridge Road east of Hanwell, and in November 1901 the LUT Bill for 1902 was deposited in Parliament. This included inter alia a scheme for the Hammersmith – Uxbridge Road link from Glenthorne Road via Dalling Road, Paddenswick Road and Askew Road to meet the Uxbridge Road line at the Askew Arms, a little over a mile east of the centre of Acton.

The 1902 Act, which received the Royal Assent on 8 August, gave the necessary powers for the line to be built, but only after agreeing with the London County Council that it would be included with those in Hammersmith which were to be available for compulsory purchase in 1909. Clifton Robinson had been able to secure extensions of tenure beyond the normal 21 years provided for in the 1870 Tramways Act by agreement with some of the local authorities, and had hoped to do the same with the LCC, but without success. As things turned out, all lines in Hammersmith remained in the hands of the company until May 1922, owing to protracted litigation followed by the onset of the Great War in 1914.

The 1902 powers authorised 1.09 miles of route commencing at the corner of Studland Street and Glenthorne Road, Hammersmith and along and into Dalling Road and Paddenswick Road to and along Goldhawk Road. After about 35 yards, the line was to turn into Askew Road, reaching Uxbridge Road at the Askew Arms, where it joined the line to Acton by a south-to-west double junction.

Construction of the line was carried out by the company's own workforce at the same time as the extension of the line was being built between Southall and Uxbridge. All was double except for a 78-yard single section in Askew Road between Hadyn Park Road and Askew Crescent, together with the south-to-west curve from Studland Street into Glenthorne Road and the east-to-north curve from King Street into Studland Street. This allowed cars from Uxbridge Road to proceed to the Broadway via Glenthorne Road and Beadon Road, and to return by way of King Street and Studland Street.

The work was completed late in May 1904 end Col. Yorke carried out the Board of Trade inspection on 31 May, immediately after his inspection of the Southall-Uxbridge extension. Being satisfied, he recommended the issue of the certificate to enable public service to begin, subject to a speed limit of 10 mile/h in Glenthorne, Dalling and Paddenswick Roads, and in Askew Road from Goldhawk

Ealing Common.

Upper: The view of No. 330 crossing Ealing Common, shown on this card, postmarked 15 Sept 1907, gives a good indication of when this type of car was put into service on the Uxbridge Road line.   (Commercial view, Courtesy: J.H. Price)
Lower: No. 327, bound for Uxbridge, is seen in High Street, Southall, c1909. The lack of general street traffic is noticeable.   (Commercial view, AES series)

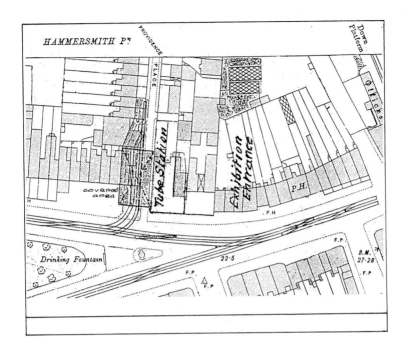

Diagram of proposed tram station.

Looking across to Providence Place and the site of the proposed tram station, next to the "Tuppenny Tube" station of the Central London railway. Had it been built, it would have meant the demolition of the premises of the antique dealer, the auctioneer and the "certified bailiff". (Commercial view)

Road to Uxbridge Road, except between Hadyn Park Road and Askew Crescent, where a 6 mile/h limit was imposed. At all facing points and on curves between King Street and Uxbridge Road, maximum speed was to be 4 mile/h. Compulsory stops were imposed in both directions at these points also, and in Askew Road between Askew Crescent and Becklow Road. The certificate was signed on 7 June 1904.

A brief opening ceremony took place immediately following the inspection, with the first car being driven by Clifton Robinson Jnr. Public service commenced on 1 June between Hammersmith, Acton, Southall and Uxbridge. The fare from Hammersmith Broadway to the Acton-Ealing boundary at Birch Grove, a distance of 2.90 miles, was 1d. The short single line section in Askew Road was doubled after the necessary land was acquired, but speed was always restricted at this point. Construction costs amounted to £24,045, of which £13,027 was for permanent way, £3,044 for cables and overhead equipment, with £7,027 being the cost of acquisition of land and road widenings.

Shepherds Bush Terminus

There were termini at Shepherds Bush for two main routes, in Uxbridge Road for cars to Acton and on to Uxbridge, and in Goldhawk Road for Kew Bridge, Hounslow and Hampton Court. The Central London Railway station was the busiest point and was situated immediately west of the Uxbridge Road – Goldhawk Road junction. This was the unloading point for the Uxbridge Road cars and, at first, cars also loaded there for westbound journeys. Goldhawk Road cars at first ran to the end of the track outside the Uxbridge Road station of the West London Railway. Both points saw much congestion at ordinary times, but at Bank Holidays and on summer weekends the traffic was extremely heavy, and later, to ease the difficulties thrown up by the Goldhawk Road cars crossing the Uxbridge Road traffic stream, these were cut back to a point at the eastern extremity of Shepherds Bush Green at the end of Goldhawk Road.

Traffic congestion continued to be a problem, however, and when the White City exhibition centre opened in 1908 heavy traffic developed to and from the Central London Railway station, which led Hammersmith Borough Council making representations to the LUT with a view to improving the situation.

Various proposals were put forward by the company and other parties, and on 15 January 1907, Robinson submitted a scheme to provide an off-street terminal and loading point for Uxbridge Road cars in Providence Place, immediately west of the Central London Railway station. This provided for a widening at the south end of Providence Place (now Shepherds Bush Place) to allow a 50-yard layby to be provided, of which 30 yards was double line with the rest as a single line reversing stub. The double track section was to be under cover. This would allow Uxbridge Road cars to stop alongside the station entrance, to unload and load and return to the Uxbridge direction. The scheme necessitated the demolition of two properties in Uxbridge Road and part of the frontages of two properties in Providence Place.

Hammersmith Council discussed the proposals at length and various amendments were suggested. The MBC in June 1908 called the existing terminus "a danger to life and limb", and other schemes were considered. On 16 December 1908, however, the Hammersmith Council Works Committee said that they were not prepared to recommend the Council to take any definite action, and the terminus remained virtually unaltered until the end of tramway operation.

CHAPTER SIX

HAMMERSMITH, CHISWICK AND HOUNSLOW.

Hammersmith is situated at the westerly extremity of the Central London area with Shepherds Bush, also in the Borough of Hammersmith a little to the north and at about the same distance of two and a half miles from the central West End area. Early in the 19th century it was still a comparatively quiet district on the Middlesex bank of the River Thames but development was rapid from that time and Hammersmith became heavily built up by the third quarter of the century and is now an important commercial and administrative centre, with major shopping centres and entertainment facilities. Hammersmith lies at the confluence of major roads out of London to the west and south-west and by 1874 was a terminus for the District Railway, was served by many omnibus services and from 16 December 1882 was served from Kew Bridge, Brentford and Chiswick by the West Metropolitan Tramways Company.

Up to 1889 Hammersmith was in the geographical county of Middlesex and local government for the area was through the Metropolitan Board of Works, the Fulham Local Board of Health and the Hammersmith Vestry. From 1889 the responsibilities of the Metropolitan Board of Works passed to the new London County Council, which absorbed parts of Middlesex including Hammersmith. In 1900 Hammersmith Vestry became one of the new Metropolitan Borough Councils which together covered the area of the administrative County of London and today Hammersmith has rejoined Fulham as the London Borough of Hammersmith and Fulham.

Hammersmith boasted a large number of important houses, and its riverside situation attracted many notable figures in the world of the arts, science and literature. The western extremity of Hammersmith, at Young's Corner, where Goldhawk Road, from the Shepherds Bush direction meets Hammersmith's main thoroughfare, King Street met Chiswick, formerly in the county of Middlesex at a distance of 0.875 miles from Hammersmith Broadway. Chiswick, with Brentford and Heston & Isleworth were, until the creation of the Greater London Council separate local authority areas but are now merged in the London Borough of Hounslow. Prior to this Hounslow had no status as a local authority in its own right.

Chiswick is a place of some antiquity, occupying a favoured situation on the north bank of the River Thames. Among the better-known edifices in Chiswick are the sixteenth-century Chiswick House and the house built for Hogarth, while numerous eighteenth-century houses of a grand type are situated along the river front. It is at Chiswick that the first of the western suburbs of London starts. Beyond Chiswick lies Brentford, an ancient township and a place of considerable industrial importance, with riverside enterprises in boatbuilding, marine engineering, warehousing and other industries having been established there for many centuries. The Victorian era saw the establishment of two landmarks in this area close to the Thames, the large gas-works and nearby the Metropolitan Water Board's pumping station close to Kew Bridge. Brentford was, and still is to a large extent, a town of very narrow streets and densely-packed dwellings, which still today carries much evidence of its ancient origins.

From Kew Bridge it is a journey of one and a half miles through Brentford until the important road junction at Busch Corner, Isleworth is reached. Busch Corner is named after an Austrian who built the large house, Busch House and named it Bush House. Years later it was renamed Busch House in his memory. From Busch Corner the road branches south towards Twickenham and Hampton

Upper: James Clifton Robinson with his son, Clifton, about to open the ground at Brentford on 20 March 1899, in preparation for laying the first electric line of the London United Tramways. (Photo: LUT)

Lower: Car No. 95, one of the first trams to arrive at Hounslow, 'The Bell', on 6 July 1901, apparently being welcomed by an appreciative audience. (Photo: LUT)

Court, the river having turned at Kew Bridge from a south-westerly to a southerly direction. The main road, however, continues south-west through Isleworth, a pleasantly-situated small town about five miles distant from Hammersmith Broadway. Isleworth is still largely a residential area, and that part of it which lies south of Busch Corner flanks the river, where the usual riverside activities predominate; to the west of Busch Corner the town lies either side of London Road and it is in London Road that the celebrated A.& F. Pears' soap factory was one of the first large industrial concerns to be built in the town. The founder, Alfred Pears, was a local benefactor in whose memory an impressive fountain was erected in the town. Alfred Pears was also a member of a group of businessmen which attempted to establish horse tramways in the district.

From Isleworth the London Road continues for 1½ miles until the town of Hounslow is reached. Hounslow, still a small place at the end of the nineteenth century fell in the administrative area of Heston & Isleworth and is a place of some antiquity which has developed extensively during the twentieth century and is now almost merged in the London Airport complex at Heathrow. Hounslow Heath, once the haunt of highwaymen and footpads, was to become a short-lived terminus of the London United Tramways and the Heath, still open land but greatly reduced in area, is bounded to the west by the heavily built-up area of Hounslow West and Whitton Park, while to the west of the Heath and bounded by the Great South West Road, Heathrow Airport has covered a huge tract of former farmland.

Transport services in the area beyond Hammersmith became progressively sparse as the road progressed south-westward. The District Railway reached Hounslow Town (now Hounslow Central) in 1883 and Hounslow Barracks (now Hounslow West) in 1884, but initial services were far from frequent and better road transport facilities were still needed.

The London United Tramways 1895 Provisional Order and subsequent Confirmation Act, empowered the company to electrify their existing tramways, to reconstruct as double lines the tramways in Hammersmith and Acton, and to construct a short extension in Acton to reach the new depot under construction there. As related in Chapter 3, the attitude of the London County Council in refusing sanction for electric traction, resulted in the company reconstructing the lines in Hammersmith and Acton for horse traction and this, together with the demands of the authorities responsible for the Kew Geomagnetic Observatory, resulted in the introduction of electric traction on the LUT system being delayed until April, 1901.

The company's second Act, that of 1898 which received the Royal Assent on 12 August sanctioned two tramways. One was a continuation of the existing line at Kew Bridge as a double track tramway 3.620 miles in length terminating at The Bell at the west end of High Street, Hounslow. The other line was a cross-country route linking Brentford with Hanwell by way of Boston Road and is described in Chapter 7. Other powers sought in this Bill extended from the new depot at Acton along Uxbridge Road to Hanwell but this route was lost owing to opposition by Ealing Urban District Council. The Act also empowered the company to erect generating stations at Chiswick Depot and the new depot at Acton. In the event only the Chiswick station was built and details of this will be found in Chapter 15. The Act also contained a clause for the protection of Kew Observatory which is detailed in Chapter 4.

The LUT powers in Hammersmith were derived from those of their predecessors, the Southall, Ealing & Shepherds Bush Tram Railway Company and the West Metropolitan Tramways. These powers had passed to the LUT on the company's acquisition of the WMT undertaking in 1894 and the same situation applied in the case of the lines in Acton and Chiswick. The WMT tramway between Young's Corner through Chiswick to Kew Bridge, originally a single line with passing loops, had been reconstructed in 1893 by the WMT as a double line as far as the Chiswick-Brentford boundary at Wellesley Road, a little over 200 yards east of Kew Bridge. The remaining 200 yards as far as Kew Bridge was not then rebuilt. It was at the Brentford boundary that the ground-breaking ceremony for the first electric street tramway in the London area was performed by Clifton Robinson on 20 March 1899. This new line was the extension of the existing line to The Bell, Hounslow. Robinson drove the first pick, accompanied by an assembly of local dignitaries, members of learned societies and others connected with the electrical engineering industry.

The new line was driven forward to The Bell at some speed and was laid in 92½lb/yd girder rail for electric traction on the overhead trolley system with side poles and spanwire suspension. The opening of the line was delayed by the protracted difficulties posed by objections by the Kew Observatory authorities. It had been expected that electric trams would commence working from Hammersmith and Shepherds Bush by the early Summer of 1900 but as related in Chapter 4 the requirements of Kew Observatory became a major obstacle to the inauguration of electric traction which was not removed until April 1901, when electric trams at last started to operate, but, at first, still only as far as Kew Bridge.

The westward advance of the LUT was not achieved without lengthy and expensive battles with local authorities and other interests who had demands to make. In the case of Chiswick Urban District Council a deposit against non-fulfilment of obligations under the WMT Act of 1882, amounting to £1,000 was still held by the UDC. This body also demanded an annual wayleave for the right to work through the district, which was fixed at £350 per annum for the first five years from 12 August 1898, increasing for the succeeding seven years to £500 per annum and thereafter £750 annually until 1919. The extension of the line at Kew Bridge through Brentford and Isleworth to Hounslow, and the new line through Boston Road from Brentford to Hanwell, were purchaseable by the respective authorities in 1919, and the wayleaves payable to Chiswick were in consideration of the Council's agreement to postpone its power to purchase until 1919 in conformity with the new lines empowered by the 1898 Act in the urban districts of Brentford and Heston & Isleworth. Under the terms of the WMT Acts the Chiswick lines had been purchaseable in 1903 and 1910.

An early view of Hammersmith Broadway, with the tram in King Street to the left and Beadon Road to the right. Of interest is the tricycle upon which the delivery lad carries his goods.
(Photo: LUT)

From Chiswick the line entered the urban district of Brentford at Wellesley Road, some 200 yards east of Kew Bridge, whence it continued past the bridge through High Street, Brentford for a distance of 1.320 miles to the boundary with the Heston & Isleworth urban district. High Street, Brentford has always been a busy thoroughfare and has today been extensively widened. When the line was constructed through the town in 1899 the road was exceptionally narrow. Nevertheless a double line was laid through the town, and to ease congestion caused by the numerous carts and vans stopping outside the many shops and other commercial premises along the road no fewer than twelve crossovers, of which five were facing and the remainder trailing were laid on the 1.10 miles of line between the Wagon and Horses public house and the Brent County Bridge immediately west of the Heston & Isleworth boundary. This arrangement allowed a tramcar obstructed by a standing vehicle to gain the opposite track to pass the obstruction and reach its correct side of the road after the obstruction had been passed, permitting a reasonably free flow of traffic, especially at busy times. Notwithstanding these measures, frequent stoppages resulted in long lines of trams moving slowly through the town as they moved over the crossovers from one side to the other.

Brentford UDC foresaw traffic difficulties in the High Street and had obtained a clause in the LUT 1898 Act obliging the LUT to pay one third of the costs of widening parts of the High Street up to a limit of £5,000 into a deposit account with the London & County Bank on the passing of the Act, and before construction commenced. Half Acre, leading from the High Street into Boston Road was to be widened by at least fifteen feet between High Street and The Butts. Again, on account of the difficult conditions in the High Street the Act provided that no cars should stop between a point west of Kew Bridge and No. 271, High Street "other than is required for the ordinary traffic of the tramways", and cars working to Brentford (only) could, if required reverse outside No. 271, High Street. The company spent £20,000 on widenings and other improvements in the High Street and in the course of time the Council made further demands for improvements; these problems contributed to the abandonment of later proposals for extensions.

The tramways in Brentford were initially purchaseable by the UDC on 12 August 1919. The company's 1899 Act provided for the UDC to pay half of the costs of widenings in Half Acre and Back Lane but the LUT released the Council from this obligation on the Council's agreement to extend the purchase date for all tramways in the district to 1 August 1928. The line in Chiswick was also purchaseable from 12 August 1919 and by agreement with the Council the earliest date of purchase was postponed until 12 August 1935 and this change was confirmed in the company's 1912 Act.

The line from Brentford entered the urban district of Heston & Isleworth at a point 100 yards east of Brentford Bridge which was a county bridge across the confluence of the River Brent and the Grand Junction Canal. Before constructing the tramway across the bridge, the company was obliged by the 1898 Act to widen the carriageway on the bridge by throwing the existing footpaths into the roadway and extending the bridge by making equivalent new footpaths. A time limit of six months was imposed for completion of this work which resulted in a handsome structure brought about at the sole expense of the London United Tramways.

The 1898 Act stipulated that the whole line through Isleworth and Hounslow should be double track and that construction of the line in Heston & Isleworth should not be started until the whole of the double line through Brentford from Kew Bridge was completed. The line from Brentford to Hounslow was, in fact the first new tramway route to be constructed by the LUT, and as in the case of all new tramway construction until 1905 all these works were carried out by the company using its own workforce.

A widening in High Street, Hounslow on the south side near Douglas Road was necessary to provide for double track at this point and the LUT was obliged under the terms of the 1898 Act to pay Heston & Isleworth UDC half the cost of

Upper: No. 86 at Hounslow Broadway c1910. The car was taken out of service shortly after the Great War and scrapped in 1923. (Commercial view. Courtesy: J.H. Price)

Lower: King Street, Hammersmith had an almost 'provincial' air about it when this photograph was taken of car No. 5 having just passed No. 107 near Rivercourt Methodist Church. (London Borough of Hammersmith & Fulham Libraries)

acquisition of the necessary lands, the widenings themselves and the council's Parliamentary powers in connection with the work.

The rails used were 92½lb/yd and paving was in Jarrah wood blocks throughout. The Council was empowered to request the company to erect "sufficient electric lamps of such a height, character and design as the Surveyor shall approve at the Brent County Bridge, at which point the tramways entered the district, at the terminus at The Bell public house in Hounslow and at eight other points along the route at the junctions of principal roads with the tramway route. These lamps were to be fed from the tramway overhead line and to be supplied with current and maintained by the company and always illuminated at the times when the council's own lighting was in operation.

In accordance with the terms of the Tramways Act 1870 and the Acts of the LUT the company deposited a bond in the sum of £1,000 as security for its carrying out obligations in connection with construction and subsequent maintenance of the tramways The company's agreement with Heston & Isleworth UDC of 23 February 1900 provided for the Council purchase powers to commence from 17 August 1926 and this was confirmed in the LUT Act of 1900.

The new line to Hounslow, The Bell was completed and ready for electric traction by Spring, 1900 except for connection of the feeders to the power station. The differences between the company and the Kew Observatory authorities dating from early 1898 remained unresolved, the discussions between the company, the Board of Trade and the Observatory authorities having started as early as February 1898. The matter remained deadlocked until the early Spring of 1901 when George White finally broke the impasse with his offer to the Treasury to contribute to the costs of removing the Observatory's instruments to another site.

Meanwhile the powers for the new electric line between Kew Bridge and Hounslow were due to expire on 12 August 1900 and, with the work completed several months earlier Robinson, to avoid the necessity to apply for an extension of time to complete the line (technically incomplete until inspected and certified by the Board of Trade) asked the Board on 4 August for an inspection, having advised them on 26 July that track construction was complete. Lt. Col. H.A.Yorke, RE inspected the section on 11 August, using a horse tram and finding the track and paving in excellent order. The line still awaited an inspection by the Board's electrical inspecting Officer, A.P. Trotter, so a certificate of fitness in respect of the track and paving was signed by F.J.S. Hopwood, a senior officer at the Board of Trade immediately following the inspection. The company was at liberty to work a service of horse trams on the new line, but Robinson told the Board the company would not do this.

As related in Chapter 4, negotiations between the parties concerned with Kew Observatory continued throughout this period during which time continued electrification of the old lines and construction of authorised new ones. Meanwhile, George White was becoming increasingly perturbed over the delays in getting the electrified lines into operation. Tests were being carried out on the electrical installation from the Autumn of 1900 and in early 1901 and White, mindful of the heavy losses to the shareholders arising from the delays made his personal approach to Sir Courtenay Boyle at the Board of Trade on 11 March 1901, with his offer to defray the costs of moving the Kew instruments. All the parties now realised that the matter could not be further delayed, as The Times had made it the subject of a leading article on 29 December 1900 and questions had been asked in Parliament.

A.P. Trotter inspected the electrical installation on the Hammersmith – Kew Bridge, Shepherds Bush – Young's Corner and Shepherds Bush – Acton routes on 15 March 1901; the new extension from Kew Bridge to Hounslow had to await an electrical inspection until 2 July owing to last-minute discussions between the company, the Board of Trade and the Observatory authorities over possible stray currents from this line, which was the closest to the Observatory of the company's lines so far built. Meanwhile, Col. Yorke inspected the electrified lines in Hammersmith including the loop line, the line in Goldhawk Road and that in

Chiswick as far as Kew Bridge together with the line from Shepherds Bush to Acton Depot, on Saturday, 30 March 1901, using a horse tram.

The refusal of the London County Council in 1895 to sanction electric traction in Hammersmith resulted in the company resolving to reconstruct the worn-out West Metropolitan tracks for horse tram operation, and as a consequence the track in Goldhawk Road between Shepherds Bush and Young's Corner was replaced with new rails of 80lb/yard girder pattern as a double line, in 1897. The same had applied to the Shepherds Bush – Acton line, reconstructed between Shepherds Bush and Mansell Road, Acton as double line in 1895. The line in King Street, Hammersmith between Young's Corner and the Broadway with the loop line via Studland Street, Glenthorne Road and Beadon Road, with the short relief line in The Grove between Beadon Road and King Street were reconstructed in 1900, using heavier rails of 92½lb/yd, the company having by this time overcome the opposition of the London County Council to electric traction in Hammersmith. The line in Chiswick between Young's Corner and the boundary with Brentford had been reconstructed by the West Metropolitan Tramways Company in 1893, as a double line with 80lb/yd rails, and these sections had been converted for electric traction by bonding the rails, making the necessary electrical connections and improving the rail joints. However, none of this reconstruction of the original horse tramways had sole plates or girder joints, the plain fished joint being thought at the time sufficient to cater for the heavier electric trams.

Col. Yorke found the track on all these sections satisfactory; he recommended speed limits of 10 mile/h along Goldhawk Road and High Road, Chiswick from Young's Corner to Kew Bridge; 8 mile/h in King Street, Hammersmith between Goldhawk Road (Young's Corner) and The Broadway and 6 mile/h in Studland Street, Glenthorne Road and Beadon Road. Col. Yorke did not consider that the Board of Trade would find it necessary to institute any compulsory stops as the company had indicated that it intended to adopt "all cars" stops at certain points on the route, which he regarded as sufficient for safety reasons but he asked for a 4 mile/h limit round all curves and through facing points.

A group of cars seen in High Road, Chiswick by Turnham Green Church, probably on a summer Sunday, Car No. 89 is bound for Shepherds Bush. (Photo: LUT)

Col. Yorke commented adversely upon the width of the cars, which were 7ft 3in at their widest point. This dimension contravened Clause 34 of the 1870 Tramways Act. Moreover this excess width left considerably less than the requisite fifteen inches clearance between passing cars. However, as the railings around the upper deck was unusually high, he did not suggest that authority to work the lines by electric power should be withheld on that account. He regarded the braking as adequate, with the handbrake for normal service stops and the rheostatic brake for use in emergencies. He was, however, critical of the lifeguards and the absence of a speed governor. The lifeguards fitted to the first electric cars were to a design by W. Wood, of Brecknell Munro & Rogers and after a short time in service, during which there had been a number of accidents, the Board of Trade indicated that they should be replaced. All subsequent cars up to 1905 were fitted with Wilson & Bennett guards actuated by pilot gates or if necessary by motormen.

On 23 March, a week before the inspection, George White again asked Sir Courtenay Boyle for an assurance that the lines could be opened for service in time for the Easter holiday traffic. The Treasury was still delaying final implementation of the agreement on the Kew instruments and White asked Boyle to use his good offices in expediting the matter. At last the Treasury moved and on 3 April White and Sir Francis Mowatt, Permanent Under-Secretary to the Treasury signed the agreement. Meanwhile, Col. Yorke had gone to Glasgow, with the certificate for the lines still not signed. The Board of Trade telegraphed him there on 2 April and he wired back saying that there was no objection to the lines being opened subject to the speed limits "and other points which will be specified in my report". The Board thereupon sanctioned the use of the lines and the certificate was signed on 3 April by Sir Thomas Blomefield. The certificate was conveyed by special messenger to Robinson who acknowledged its receipt in like manner immediately. In fact, Col. Yorke's report was not compiled until 17 April, following internal discussions between Col. Yorke and his colleagues at the Board of Trade.

As previously mentioned part of the line between Brentford and Hounslow was only a very short distance from Kew Observatory and the opening of this section was further delayed during final discussions between the parties. Meanwhile a speed limit of 6 mile/h was fixed through the bottleneck in High Street, Brentford from the Gas Works to Brentford Bridge. The limit between the bridge and a point 250 yards to the west was 8 mile/h, from the latter point to the

A busy scene at Kew Bridge terminal siding at the commencement of electric operation on 4 April 1901. (Photo: LUT)

99

junction of Hanworth Road, 10 mile/h and from Hanworth Road to Hounslow (The Bell) 8 mile/h.

With the final obstacle to electric working removed and with everything standing ready the horse trams made their final runs on the night of 3 April and on the following morning electric trams made their first journeys, with services from Hammersmith to Kew Bridge, Shepherds Bush to Kew Bridge via Goldhawk Road and from Shepherds Bush to Acton Depot. The maximum fare on the routes opened was 2d. These first services started at 7am on 4 April 1901 without ceremony; this was reserved for a later date. The Easter traffic upon which George White and Clifton Robinson had set such store came up to their expectations, some 385,000 passengers having been carried over the holiday period. Horse trams had been banished from the LUT lines in London and Middlesex but would continue for years to come in Surrey between the south side of Kew Bridge and Richmond, as a result of dogged opposition to the company's electrification proposals by the local authorities in Richmond.

The new electric tram services were provided by one hundred double-deck bogie cars (1-100) which had been supplied through the company's contractors, the British Thomson-Houston Co. Ltd by Hurst, Nelson & Co. Ltd. of Motherwell. They were of elegant design, seating 30 in the lower saloon and 39 on the upper deck. They were painted in a bold livery of Venetian red and white, with luxurious button-back seats upholstered in brown Utrecht velvet in the saloon, with curtains at the windows and three heavy coir floor mats, the centre one in each car lettered LUTL in elegant script. The monitor-type ceilings were finished in bird's eye maple veneer, with opening vents glazed with ruby glass etched with a formal design, and internal woodwork was finished in light oak. These were short-canopy cars with straight two-flight staircases with a landing between the flights, a feature designed by Clifton Robinson which would endure on all new double-deck cars on the system until 1931. The cars' electrical equipment consisted of BTH B18 controllers with eight power and seven brake notches and two BTH GE58 25 hp motors. The trucks were Peckham type 14D2 maximum traction swing-bolster bogies of 4ft 6in wheelbase. Full details and dimensions of these cars will be found in the rolling stock chapter.

With the first electric services in full swing and final details of the Kew agreement settled the Board of Trade and the company were engaged in the lengthy task of formulating electrical regulations for the company's operations. The extension from Kew Bridge to Hounslow was finally opened on 6 July 1901 with services to that point from the Shepherds Bush and Hammersmith termini. The fare for the full journey between Shepherds Bush or Hammersmith and Hounslow (The Bell) was 4d, with workmen's fares of 1d single or 2d return.

By the time the extension to Hounslow opened both Shepherds Bush and Hammersmith were scenes of bustling activity throughout the day up to the times the last trams ran into their depots. At Shepherds Bush and Hounslow automatic trolley reversers had been installed at Robinson's instance (these having earlier been introduced on the Bristol tramways under his management). The company wished to extend the line at Hounslow to Baber Bridge, the bridge carrying the road across the river Crane at the western boundary of the Heston & Isleworth urban district. They decided to use the provisions of the 1896 Light Railways Act to secure this and other objectives and in May 1899 an application for an Order was lodged with the Light Railway Commissioners covering the Baber Bridge extension and new lines from Isleworth through Twickenham, Hampton and Hampton Court and returning to Twickenham via Teddinton, thus forming a loop. A branch from Twickenham to the Middlesex side of Richmond Bridge was also sought. As described in Chapter 7 this method of obtaining powers had proved successful in the case of the extension from Hanwell to Uxbridge, but in this instance the application failed on account of opposition by the London and South Western Railway Company. The Light Railway Commissioners held an inquiry at Twickenham in June 1899 and found they had to take into account the LSWR objection on the grounds of competition and refuse the application. The

Chiswick High Road

2514 Photo Tourists Association. Turnham Green S.W.

Six cars can be seen in this 1903 view in Chiswick High Road, with No. 263 making for
Shepherds Bush and No. 35 working between Hammersmith and Kew Bridge.
(Commercial view: Tourist Association)

A rare view of a car in Glenthorne Road Hammersmith, No. 133 is seen c1909 on the single
track section heading for the Hammersmith terminus. The conductor is busy adjusting the
rear indicator blind ready for the journey to Kew Bridge. This group of cars seldom worked
further westwards than that.   (London Borough of Hammersmith & Fulham Libraries)

101

Commissioners advised the LUT to seek the powers they required in Parliament, as a result of which the company submitted a Bill in November 1899 for the 1900 Session.

The 1900 Bill was a comprehensive measure, which sought not only the Baber Bridge extension and the lines to Hampton Court and Richmond Bridge but also the Acton – Hanwell line. The Bill had a comparatively easy passage through Parliament and received the Royal Assent on 6 August 1900. It sanctioned the extension of the line at The Bell, Hounslow for a distance of 1.648 miles of double track to the point known today as North Feltham at the east side of Baber Bridge and wholly in the district of Heston & Isleworth. This line traversed Staines Road westward from The Bell, passing the open country at Hounslow Heath adjacent to Hounslow Barracks. Much of the Heath is still open land at the time of writing and Baber Bridge is within less than a mile from the perimeter of Heathrow Airport.

Similar terms to the 1898 Act applied to the extensions authorised in 1900. In the new Act Heston & Isleworth UDC gained twenty electric lamps to be placed on the Baber Bridge extension and the part of the Hampton Court route along Twickenham Road between Busch Corner, Isleworth and the Heston & Isleworth boundary. The council's power to purchase was to become effective on 6 August 1925 and this date would apply also to the line terminating at The Bell. The Council was also empowered to call upon the company to provide and maintain at its own expense a waiting room and public convenience at any point of the Council's choice along the routes in their district.

Middlesex County Council had objected to the use of the Light Railways Act by the LUT to gain their powers for the Hanwell – Uxbridge line. The success of the company in obtaining these powers in their 1898 Light Railways Order brought about a change in the approach of the MCC to the tramways and light railways question. The LUT had been able to obtain the Hanwell – Uxbridge powers because the Light Railways Act did not define, in precise terms, what constituted a light railway. The MCC saw that the situation could be turned to its advantage and on 23 February 1899 Middlesex resolved to use the Light Railways Act to promote its own scheme for the county and the County Surveyor, Henry Titus Wakelam, was instructed to draw it up.

The County Council had endeavoured to obtain the support of the district and other councils in its opposition to privately promoted schemes, and in the north and north-western parts of the county a number of schemes, which were not successful had been submitted from 1897.

With the LUT in possession of parts of west and south-west Middlesex it was already in a strong position to resist further incursions by the County Council in that part of the county. However, the MCC was, as has been seen, in a sufficiently strong position to obstruct the company's schemes and when the opportunity arose it did not hesitate to do so.

The LUT did not consider Baber Bridge as the limit of possible extensions in the south-westerly direction; in itself it was no useful traffic objective. The town of Staines, already well populated and growing fast, lay some 5.125 miles beyond the bridge and was a natural terminus for the group of LUT lines projected for south-west Middlesex. Beyond Baber Bridge the route lay within the areas of East Bedfont Parish Council, the Rural and Urban District Councils of Staines, with the MCC being the overall road authority.

The MCC, notwithstanding the strong position of the LUT in west and south-west Middlesex submitted an application in May 1901 to the Light Railway Commissioners for a group of lines in areas in which the LUT were also interested. These were Hounslow – Staines, Hounslow – Colnbrook, Hounslow – Southall and Twickenham – Sunbury. There was also a projected line from Acton across Uxbridge Road through Bedford Park and across High Road, Chiswick to the north bank of the Thames and return by a loop. The Light Railway Commissioners held an inquiry at Hounslow on 22 July 1901 at which the LUT opposed these

Car No. 141 seen outside Hammersmith GWR & Metropolitan Railway Station c1909 and, for this group of cars, on an unusual working to Hampton Court, Bracket-arm overhead wire suspension, seen in this view, was little used on the LUT. (Courtesy: A.D. Packer)

proposals. The majority of the local district councils favoured the LUT scheme for the Staines and Hounslow group of lines and the MCC application was rejected.

Later in 1901, on 28 November the Middlesex County Council came to an agreement with the LUT which defined the parties' spheres of influence in the county. This agreement divided Middlesex into north and south-west portions, along a line between a point south of Willesden Junction station in the east and Uxbridge in the west, north of which schemes would be promoted by the MCC and south of the line would be LUT territory. The County Council agreed to withdraw pending applications south of the line except that for the intended light railway from Willesden via Horn Lane to Acton. It was agreed that the LUT would not oppose the County Council's application for this line and the County Council would permit its lessees, the Metropolitan Tramways & Omnibus Co. Ltd. to arrange with the LUT which of the two companies would work the line when constructed. The agreement was to remain in force until 31 December 1919.

Because the MCC had attempted to obtain powers in the LUT area some delay occurred in starting construction of the line beyond The Bell at Hounslow to Baber Bridge, doubt having been cast upon the possibility of reaching Staines. Work finally commenced early in 1902 but the line was carried only as far as Barrack Road, Hounslow (The Hussar), a distance of about one mile. There was no traffic objective at Baber Bridge, the authorised terminus, and it had probably been decided that until the position in regard to the planned line to Staines was clearer the line would not be taken beyond The Hussar.

Work on this section was completed by June 1902 and consisted of 1.016 miles of double track. Col. Yorke carried out an inspection of the section on 20 June and found the construction in good order. The paving was in the almost universal Jarrah hardwood blocks throughout. A speed limit of 12 mile/h throughout was recommended with a compulsory stop at the junction of Bath Road and Staines Road (The Bell). Some delay ensued before the Board of Trade issued a certificate of fitness on 12 August and on the following day services commenced between the

103

new terminus and Shepherds Bush and Hammersmith. A depot had been constructed, with a sub-station on a site in London Road one mile east of The Bell. It was on the north side of the road, on a site of three quarters of an acre, known locally on that account as "Three Rood Piece".

The 4d fare between the London termini and The Bell was not increased when the line was extended to The Hussar, giving a mileage for the full journey of a little over 8.25 miles. Workmen's fares were 1d single and 2d return for the full journey.

By the Spring of 1903 the loop line through Hampton Court had been opened and the resources devoted to this major extension were available for completion of a number of authorised lines. On 18 July 1903 Robinson wrote to C. T. Yerkes, Chairman of the LUT and the UERL, on the urgency of completing some of these lines while the powers were still alive, and the desirability of seeking powers for extensions to those lines already authorised or built.

The authorised line to Baber Bridge still remained to be completed. The exact reasons for the line stopping short at Hounslow Heath have not been made clear, but demands by Middlesex County Council in respect of this section, together with the uncertainty of securing powers to reach the natural terminus, Staines, appear to have influenced the directors' decision to proceed no further. The MCC required widenings to fifty feet with made-up footpaths along what was at the time a rural highway, and indeed, on 11 April 1904 the County Council told the LUT that they wanted all the poles between Hounslow Heath and Baber Bridge to be lighted at the company's expense. Earlier, on 14 March 1903 Heston & Isleworth UDC had asked the LUT to complete the line to Baber Bridge and Robinson had replied saying that the matter was deferred "until extensions further in the direction of Staines had been decided upon". Both the MCC and the UDC had pressed the company a number of times to clarify their intentions, citing the necessity for improvements to the road.

Notwithstanding the problems posed by the MCC, the LUT still took the view that the Staines route was of considerable value and in his letter to Yerkes of 18 July 1903 Robinson urged upon him the desirability of seeking powers for a number of new routes, one of which was a continuation of the authorised line at Baber Bridge via Staines Road and London Road to Staines and on to Virginia Water to terminate at the Wheatsheaf Hotel, a total distance from Baber Bridge of 9.5 miles. Another proposal in Robinson's letter was revival of a 1902 proposal to extend the authorised line at Cranford to Windsor Road, Slough via Bath Road, Cranford, Sipson Green, Longford, a new road and bridge at Colnbrook GWR station to avoid the necessity for a level crossing and a new road south of Colnbrook avoiding the narrow High Street. From this point the proposed line continued along Bath Road, Langley Marsh and High Street, Slough and along Bath Road to Maidenhead, across the Thames at Maidenhead Bridge through Bridge Road, Bridge Street and High Street to a terminus at the Bear Hotel. Branches to Windsor and Datchet from Slough were not repeated in this scheme, which included a line connecting Ealing Broadway and High Street, Brentford and a short line connecting the Uxbridge Road line at Acton with the authorised MCC line in Horn Lane via Acton Market Place with running powers over the MCC line in Horn Lane to reach a proposed LUT line commencing at the junction of Horn Lane with Willesden Lane and reaching the Royal Agricultural Society's show grounds at Park Royal via Willesden Lane (now Park Royal Road). This last proposal did not proceed because the Royal Agricultural Society, which had earlier asked the MCC to provide services to the grounds, found the site unsuitable and it was sold to be developed as the Park Royal Industrial Estate.

Other unsupportable demands by the local authorities resulted in withdrawal of most of the rest of the scheme. Brentford UDC demanded a pedestrian subway under Kew Bridge Road and part of the High Street to be widened to 80ft at a cost of £500,000 against a cost of £250,000 to widen to 50ft. At another point in High Street between the east side of the waterworks and Ealing Road a widening to 80ft was demanded at a cost of £120,000 with the addition of an annual £1,000 wayleave.

Car No. 36 for Hammersmith and another for Shepherds Bush stand at Kew Bridge terminus mid-1903, No. 269, on the left, is bound for Hampton Court.
(Photo: LUT)

105

Ealing Borough Council asked for £7,000 of works in addition to the £13,536 the company had provided for widenings and other improvements, on less than a mile of line linking Ealing with Brentford. In Slough the company proposed widenings costing £32,000 to provide a 50ft roadway throughout. The Council demanded an 80ft roadway, wood-paved throughout from kerb to kerb at total costs of £97,000 and in addition, conduit traction through the town was demanded, which would have doubled construction costs as well as adding interruptions to the working of the tramway.

With all the tramway provisions in the 1904 Tramways Bill lost except the extension of the line at Baber Bridge as far only as Staines, some 5.25 miles of double track (the part beyond Staines through Egham to Virginia Water having been withdrawn on account of excessive demands by the local authorities in Surrey) the 1904 Bill received the Royal Assent on 15 August. Other provisions in the Bill covered powers to acquire lands for widenings on the Hampton Court lines and at various points on other routes. Extensions of time were granted to construct the Boston Road line, junctions between the Boston Road and Lower Boston Road lines with Uxbridge Road at Hanwell and lines in Kingston and Surbiton.

The line between the London county boundary at Young's Corner and the Chiswick – Brentford boundary at Wellesley Road, immediately east of Kew Bridge, had been relaid as double track by the West Metropolitan Tramways Company in 1893, using 80 lb/yd rails and adapted for electric traction in 1900 by the LUT. By 1904 the track was showing signs of serious deterioration and this stretch, 1.790 miles in length was reconstructed by the LUT during 1904, using new 92½lb/yd rails with soleplates beneath the joints, this being only the second LUT example of the use of sole plates, the first being the new line between The Bell, Hounslow and The Hussar at Hounslow Heath.

A triangular junction was laid at Busch Corner, Isleworth, allowing access from the Hounslow direction to the Hampton Court lines via Twickenham and Teddington, but no regular cars used the west to south curve. An experimental service from Hounslow to Hampton Court was operated on Sunday afternoon, 3 July 1904, and again on the following Sunday afternoon, 10 July. The service was withdrawn on Sunday, 17 July but was reinstated on Sunday afternoons from 24 July to 25 September after which it was withdrawn and as far as is known did not operate again.

When the Brentford – Hanwell via Boston Road line opened on 26 May 1906 a service from Hammersmith via Chiswick and Brentford, Boston Road, Lower Boston Road, Hanwell and Southall to Uxbridge was instituted; this was later cut back to Southall and by 1910 was withdrawn altogether, leaving the track in Lower Boston Road, Hanwell unused except for occasional special journeys and works car movements.

The older sections of track in Hammersmith, which dated from between 1896 and 1900 had begun to deteriorate. Hammersmith Metropolitan Borough Council made a number of complaints to the company from late 1907, to which Robinson responded by making repairs to some of the track joints and paving. Hammersmith MBC was not satisfied and following exchanges of correspondence during September 1908 the MBC applied for nine summonses against the company at West London Police Court for non- compliance with the terms of the Tramways Act respecting track and paving maintenance. The LUT responded by asking for arbitration but the MBC insisted upon the matter being dealt with summarily. Both parties were in touch with the Board of Trade and the summonses were withdrawn pending the possibility of a mutual settlement. By June 1909 the MBC had changed their mind and on 3 June asked the Board of Trade to appoint an arbitrator to settle the differences between the parties. The LUT withdrew their request for arbitration on 17 August and allowed Hammersmith to go to arbitration, meanwhile carrying out repairs on various sections of route. The Board of Trade appointed William Worby Beaumont as Arbitrator and his hearing was fixed to take place on 16 December. Meanwhile, at the outset C.R. Holmes, Resident

Engineer at LUT headquarters had on 24 September 1908 sent Robinson a detailed analysis of the state of the Hammersmith tracks, in which it was stated that the condition of the road outside the tramway was very poor, a point strongly emphasised by the LUT in their submission to the Board of Trade that the company's part of the paving was in generally better condition than the Council's portion.

The company had sought the views of W.B. Hopkins, MICE., MIEE and the Leeds Tramways Manager, J.B. Hamilton on the state of the Hammersmith track. Hopkins was the son of George Hopkins, Engineer to the North Metropolitan Tramways Company and the Calcutta Tramways Company, among others. Hopkins visited Hammersmith on 11 and 12 November 1909 accompanied by C.R. Holmes, and reported that he had found the wood paving in generally good condition, The track in Uxbridge Road half a mile from Shepherds Bush showed considerable wear with worn joints and rough paving. Several defects of which Hammersmith MBC had complained had been rectified. In Goldhawk Road the track was generally good, the paving having sunk in a few places. The rest of Uxbridge Road as far as Askew Road was in good condition, Askew Road in excellent condition and in King Street and the loop Hopkins found no fault. Hopkins commented that Hammersmith's complaint was "couched in nebulous terms" with nothing definite stated.

J.B. Hamilton wrote to Robinson on 20 November saying that he found the routes in very good condition and submitted his views in the case of arbitration. He had no hesitation in saying that the LUT had "absolutely fulfilled their obligations with regard to the rails and the paved surfaces in Hammersmith and the loop".

Meanwhile, the LUT had entered into negotiations with the London County Council on the latter's notice of intention to purchase the Hammersmith lines and on 9 December Hammersmith MBC withdrew their application for arbitration "as the LUT had carried out some repairs". The matter rested until 21 February 1911,

Numerous trailing and facing crossovers were provided in narrow High Street, Brentford to allow trams to pass the many carts which obstructed the tracks at times. Car 60 is about to regain the eastbound track. (Commercial view)

by which time Robinson had been replaced as Managing Director of the LUT by Albert Stanley and as Engineer by Zac Ellis Knapp. Stanley, accompanied by A.L.C. Fell, the LCC Tramways Manager met officers of the Board of Trade seeking a solution of the Hammersmith track problem, which had become embroiled in the negotiations between the same parties on the intended purchase of the lines by the LCC. Hammersmith MBC tried to get the LCC to reconstruct the track before they purchased it, but in a letter to the Board of Trade dated 24 March 1911 the LCC declined to take this course.

Following this, Hammersmith MBC again requested arbitration and on 6 November 1911 William Worby Beaumont was again nominated by the Board of Trade and appointed as arbitrator. Beaumont produced his award on 3 May 1912. He found that the MBC had frequently notified to the company of defects in the track at specified places and that these defects had always been rectified by the LUT in a proper manner and that repair work was done as and when required to the reasonable satisfaction of the Council, who had at no time deemed it necessary to make such repairs themselves. He found that the request by the MBC for reconstruction of the lines was not reasonable and that the work done by the LUT was such as ought reasonably to satisfy the MBC. He ruled that Hammersmith MBC should pay the costs of the arbitration and of his award.

Hammersmith was not satisfied, and on 25 June 1912 the Borough Surveyor's department inspected every piece of rail in the Borough and reported to the Board of Trade full details of wear and other claimed defects. Meanwhile, on 21 June the LUT had written to the Board of Trade saying that every car in their fleet had been inspected "and all were in good condition and perfectly safe". But by 7 June the Board of Trade had nevertheless reached the conclusion that complete reconstruction of the track was necessary and on 25 July an agreement was signed between the LCC and LUT for reconstruction of the track along Uxbridge Road between the Askew Arms and Shepherds Bush terminus. Costs of work in the Borough of Hammersmith to the end of 1912 amounted to £13,874 and the work in Uxbridge Road had been completed by the end of November. The Uxbridge Road track was the first to be reconstructed after the LUT had come into possession of the West Metropolitan Tramways undertaking.

A view of High Street, Hounslow, with car No. 50 standing almost outside the Town Hall.
(Commercial view)

On 1 February 1913 the LCC voted £16,100 to reconstruct parts of King Street and Goldhawk Road, the LUT to carry out the work under the terms of an agreement between the parties. This work was commenced on 21 May. On 22 July the LCC Highways Committee recommended that arrangements should be made with the LUT to reconstruct the track in King Street between Shaftesbury Road and the Broadway, in Goldhawk Road between Paddenswick Road and Young's Corner and the Hammersmith Loop through Studland Street, Glenthorne Road and Beadon Road. £19,700 was voted to carry out this work, and again an agreement was made with the LUT for the company to carry out the work. All these reconstructions were carried out in 100 lb/yd rails with anchor joints. With the completion of this work all the original track in Hammersmith had been reconstructed except that in Askew Road and Paddenswick Road, which had been laid in 1904 in 92½lb/yd rail and was reconstructed after the Great War of 1914 – 18.

Some reconstruction was found necessary before the war in the Heston & Isleworth district. Here the track between the boundary with Brentford at Brentford Bridge and The Bell at Hounslow had been the first new track to be laid specifically for electric traction, in 1899. It went into use for electric trams on 6 July 1901. This section had been laid with 92½lb/yd rails with plain fished joints, while the section from The Bell to Hounslow Heath, opened on 13 August 1902 had been laid with the same rails but with the addition of ⅜in thick sole plates beneath the joints. The section to The Bell had deteriorated by 1913 and in June Heston & Isleworth UDC asked the company to reconstruct it. Negotiations with the UDC were carried out on behalf of the company by James Devonshire, who had succeeded Albert Stanley as Managing Director on 18 December 1912. These negotiations resulted in an agreement for reconstruction of this section; in consideration of the Council postponing their power to purchase the tramways in their district until 31 December 1930 the company undertook to reconstruct the tramway between Brentford Bridge and Hounslow (The Bell), with new rails and paving. An agreement between the parties was sealed in July 1913 and this varied the terms of the original agreement which had obliged the company to maintain the paving for 2ft outside the outer rails; the more common 18in margin was substituted for this.

The 1 July 1913 agreement between the company and the UDC also covered some repair work on the track in Twickenham Road, Isleworth between Linkfield Road and the UDC boundary with Twickenham at Ivy Bridge. The reconstruction between Brentford Bridge and The Bell was carried out by Dick, Kerr & Co. Ltd. but was not completed until after the 1914 – 18 war had commenced.

The metal cap badge issued to traffic staff in the early years of LUT operation.

CHAPTER SEVEN

SOUTHALL TO UXBRIDGE AND THE BOSTON ROAD LINE

At the same time as the Southall Ealing and Shepherds Bush Tram Railway Company obtained their powers in 1873 for the line between Southall and Shepherds Bush, another company, the London and County Tramway Company Limited obtained a Provisional Order from the Board of Trade to continue the line westward from Southall for a little over six miles through Hayes and Hillingdon to Uxbridge. The powers were confirmed in the Metropolitan Tramways Confirmation (No. 2) Act which received the Royal Assent on 7 July 1873 and also confirmed the powers of the Southall company. The L&CTC was unable to attract sufficient capital to carry out its schemes; a number of its promoters were associated with the Southall company and the failure of this undertaking to complete its scheme ensured the demise of the London & County company, which was ultimately wound up.

No further powers were sought for the line between Southall and Uxbridge until 31 May 1898, when the London United Tramways applied to the Light Railway Commissioners for an Order under the Light Railways Act 1896 to empower them to construct a line from Hanwell along Uxbridge Road through Southall, Hayes and Hillingdon to Uxbridge, a distance of 7.25 miles.

Westward from Southall to Uxbridge the route was largely rural in character, with Uxbridge Road being little more than a winding country lane beyond Southall, at some points no more than 16ft wide. Clifton Robinson foresaw that the already built-up part of the Uxbridge Road in Ealing, and the growing settlements of Hanwell and Southall would develop rapidly and become densely populated once travelling facilities between these places and London were improved. Uxbridge, the westerly terminus of the proposed new line was already a prosperous small town with its own shopping and business centre and a number of smaller light industries serving the mainly agricultural population of the surrounding area. Uxbridge was the county town of Middlesex and close to the Buckinghamshire border. The link between the town and London was by way of a branch line of the Great Western Railway and services were sparse. The London United Tramways Act of 1898, which authorised the Boston Road line linking Uxbridge Road, Hanwell and High Street, Brentford ensured that the LUT could reach the westernmost parts of Uxbridge Road beyond Ealing despite Ealing Council's continued refusal to consent to the line through their town. The failure of the company's Ealing proposals in the 1898 Bill and a later application under the Light Railways Act were thus no longer a barrier to an unbroken link between the central termini at Shepherds Bush and Hammersmith and the towns west of Ealing.

The difficulties created by the councils in Ealing and other towns were not repeated by their counterparts in Hayes, Hillingdon and Uxbridge. As early as 11 February 1898 William Garner, Clerk of Uxbridge Urban District Council wrote to Clifton Robinson saying that they were in favour of a proposal by the LUT to extend the line beyond Ealing and Southall to Uxbridge. Robinson, replying the next day said that his directors would give the matter serious consideration.

Opinion in Uxbridge was firmly in favour of the proposal and was led by John King, proprietor of the *Uxbridge Gazette* and was a partner in the firm of King & Hutchings, which published the *Middlesex County Times, Acton Gazette* and *Ealing Gazette* and had championed the cause of the LUT tramway proposals. This firm also produced Robinson's propaganda broadsheets, the *Ealing Election News* and the *Chiswick Electric Tramways News.* King wrote to the Chairman of Uxbridge

UDC on 14 February 1898 telling him that some 90% of the population of Uxbridge and the surrounding districts had signed a petition asking for the promotion of a tramway connecting Uxbridge with London and suggesting that the Council should convene a public meeting to consider the matter. King felt strongly that every opportunity should be taken to promote the interests and prosperity of the town of Uxbridge: he pointed out that no local expenditure would be involved, and asked the Urban District Council to give the petition he had raised their favourable consideration. A bound volume containing the six thousand signatures to the petition was presented to the Council, to which the seal of the Council was affixed for presentation to the LUT directors at their meeting on 22 February 1898, the Council having agreed *nem.con.* to consent to the LUT's proposal.

On 25 February 1898 Uxbridge Rural District Council took a similar decision and on 10 March Clifton Robinson advised the councils that the company had started to survey the route two days previously and the directors hoped to advise them of their decision in a few weeks. Other councils affected by the scheme were Southall-Norwood UDC and the parish councils of Hillingdon East, Hillingdon West and Hayes, the latter three forming part of the Uxbridge Rural District. Southall-Norwood UDC met on 27 May, with George White and Clifton Robinson present; the council agreed to the proposal, subject to the company paving part of the roadway with wood blocks and to the company giving the council the right to use the traction poles for lighting and other purposes. Hillingdon East Parish Council, meeting on 2 June was a dissenting voice and resolved on the casting vote of the Chairman to oppose the application and to ask Middlesex County Council to co-operate by supporting their opposition. The Parish Council also resolved that a committee, consisting of Parish Councillors W.G. Allen, C.M. Harvey, C. Fane de Salis and the Rev. A. Mitchell be formed to consider which clauses in the application were objectionable. The Parish Council had been favourable at the outset but raised objections later to press their case for wood paving. Hayes Parish Council met on 3 June with Hugh Godfray, one of the LUT directors in attendance and a resolution in favour of the scheme was carried with two dissentients.

At a meeting of Uxbridge UDC on 7 June Clifton Robinson attended and the council approved the company's proposals *nem. con.* At this meeting it was stated that the consent of Ealing UDC had not been obtained for the line through that town, but the company would construct a line from Hanwell to Uxbridge irrespective of opposition by Ealing UDC, obtaining the through route to London by using the authorised line from Brentford via Boston Road and Lower Boston Road to Hanwell. Minor requirements of the UDC, such as for the council to have the right to use the traction poles for lighting and other purposes and for the poles to be of a design approved by the council were agreed, and the LUT undertook to commence construction as soon as the Order was confirmed by the Board of Trade and to provide, if required, a waiting room at Uxbridge terminus.

On Wednesday, 29 June 1898 the Light Railway Commissioners, the Earl of Jersey and Col. George Boughey, RE, CSI and their Secretary, H. Allan Steward held an inquiry into the application at St. John's Hall, Southall Green. Finding little objectionable in the application they decided to recommend an Order to the Board of Trade. The draft Order was approved by Uxbridge UDC on 30 August but Hillingdon East Parish Council, which had expressed reservations earlier, drew the attention of the Commissioners to Clifton Robinson's promise to pave the road through the parish with Jarrah wood blocks. On 28 October the draft Order was submitted to the Board of Trade for consideration of clauses and ultimate confirmation. The Commissioners said that the line would be taken to a point in Uxbridge a little short of Osborne & Stevens' timber yard, On 28 October the Commissioners wrote to Hillingdon East Parish Council advising them that a clause had been inserted in the Order under the terms of which the LUT would pave with Jarrah wood blocks the whole width of the road flanking Hillingdon Churchyard.

The opposition of Ealing UDC to the tramway proposals was at this time implacable and it would be another year before they moved from this position. At

The route to Uxbridge was through long stretches of open country. The section along Hillingdon Hill with its single track illustrates the rural nature of the line.

(Courtesy: J.H. Price)

a meeting of Uxbridge UDC on 28 November 1898 it was resolved that the council should send a deputation to Ealing UDC on 1 December to bring to their notice the importance of improved travelling facilities between the western suburbs and the Metropolis. Despite the deputation's best efforts Ealing UDC's sixteen members decided by a majority of one to continue to oppose tramways in the town.

The Board of Trade Committee sat again on 22 December and ruled that opposition to the scheme by the Great Western Railway on grounds of competition had failed, as had objections by some frontagers along the route. The Committee settled a number of other points, including requests for wood paving by Uxbridge Urban and Rural District Councils. The LUT proposed to use granite sett paving on most of the route, and the Committee upheld this but specified wood paving across the whole of the road flanking Hillingdon Churchyard and alongside churches. The Committee met again on 20 January 1899 to consider objections by some frontagers that the line was not a proper proposal for legislation under the Light Railways Act. The frontagers had also asked the Board of Trade to delete clauses relating to the carriage of goods from the Order. On this point the Board of Trade Committee agreed that power to make bye-laws should be given to Middlesex County Council rather than the local bodies, these bye-laws to include the conditions under which heavy goods might be carried.

On 26 May 1898 Middlesex County Council had resolved to oppose the application for the Order and maintained their opposition on a number of points. Among these was a submission that the roads in the county should not be allowed to fall into the hands of private companies. They also feared that county bridges and culverts might be damaged during construction work and the subsequent running of the trams. They objected to the use of the overhead trolley system, saying that this had not yet been proved satisfactory in practical use elsewhere. The County Council also said that there were no electric tramways or light railways in Middlesex and that they "objected to an experiment on such a scale being carried out in the county". Moreover, the county council held that the line "would not confer any advantage on agriculturists, the class whom the Light Railways Act was intended to benefit" and they also objected to "a profit-making monopoly taking over for a profit a main road which belongs to the inhabitants of the county at large".

The Board of Trade Committee disposed of most of the objections by Middlesex County Council, decided the preamble of the Order had been proved and sat again on 2 February 1899 to consider clauses. Some further minor objections were upheld and the Order amended to conform to these. The Board confirmed the Order on 9 May 1899 as the London United Tramways Limited (Light Railways Extensions) Order 1898.

The Order as amended allowed the company two years to construct the line, subject to any extension of time granted by the Board of Trade. If called upon to do so, the company was obliged to strengthen or reconstruct the bridge across the Grand Junction Canal at Southall, and at the insistence of the Kew Geomagnetic Observatory the whole of the return circuit along the line was to be insulated to the satisfaction of the Commissioners of Works and Public Buildings. Other provisions in the Order confirmed the proposed local fares as prescribed in the Shepherds Bush and Hammersmith Tramways Order 1881. Workmen's fares were fixed at half the ordinary fares and the company was obliged to run at least one workmen's car each way every morning and every evening except on Sundays, Good Friday and Christmas Day, not later than 7am or earlier than 5.30pm.

For much of the route beyond Southall there were sparsely populated stretches administered by the parish councils where street lighting was not provided and the Order called for the cars to carry a minimum of one light at the front and rear of each car, these lights to be of such colour and illuminating power as the local authority might prescribe. The Middlesex County Council was the road authority and consequently the county council was empowered to make bye-laws respecting such matters as speed limits, stopping places, overcrowding of the cars and similar matters.

The company applied in 1901 for an extension of time to complete the Uxbridge extension but on 28 May Middlesex County Council lodged an objection. The MCC pointed out that in February 1899 they had resolved to avail themselves of the provisions of the Light Railways Act with a view to becoming the tramway

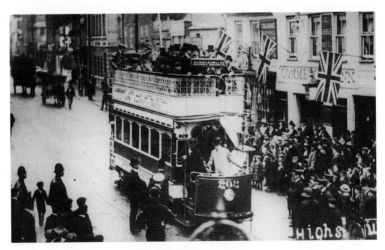

Car No. 202, in yellow livery, seen outside the 'Chequers Hotel', High Street, Uxbridge, on 31 May 1904, after the Board of Trade inspection by Lt. Col. Yorke of the extension from Southall, Clifton Robinson Jnr stands at the controls.

(Commercial view, Courtesy: London Borough of Hillingdon)

authority for the county. Their objective was "a uniform and comprehensive scheme which would be for the convenience of the public and the county generally". At this time the county council had gained approval from the Light Railway Commissioners for a group of lines in the north of the county and was seeking sanction for a further 73 miles of line covering nearly all the urban districts in the county. They were considering the question of acquiring the whole of the existing tramways in the county including the LUT system, compulsorily, to complete their objective of becoming the light railway and tramway authority for the whole of the county.

The company replied by pointing out that the county council had also resolved not to work any tramways or light railways they promoted, but to lease them to a company for operation. An agreement between the county council and the Metropolitan Tramways & Omnibus Company Ltd. for such leasing arrangements gave the first option to the MTOC. On 20 May 1899 this company, on learning of the county council's proposal to promote a further 73 miles of route, said that in their opinion the lines proposed would not be of any commercial value for some considerable time to come, and it was essential that the county council and their lessees should be careful not to embark upon any schemes of an unprofitable nature. The MTOC went on to say that they would not be prepared to take a lease of some half of the 73 miles of line in the county council's application.

It transpired that the MTOC's letter to the county council was never read to the meeting of the council on 23 May, the members of which were allowed to vote entirely in ignorance of such an important letter. The county council said the LUT had not used the powers of their 1898 Light Railway Order, and that they believed the company was asking for the extension of time to complete the lines merely in order to prevent the county council from applying for powers to construct lines over the route (Hanwell to Uxbridge) authorised by the Order. Further, the county council alleged that the company were endeavouring to obtain powers to construct several other lines which they had no intention of working, solely for the purpose of preventing the county council from constructing light railways in order that the LUT may have a monopoly of the most profitable portions of roads in the western part of the county.

The LUT referred to the delay caused by the Kew Observatory question, but with this close to resolution the directors had decided to press forward with the line west of Acton. The county council had blocked this move for several months. They had also delayed approval of the working plans for the portion of the 1898 Order in Hanwell and Southall during 1900 and the company had been compelled to threaten that they would proceed with construction of that section without the council's approval of the drawings. This was part of the line from Acton to Southall opened on 10 July 1901. The company reminded the Board of Trade of its record in the promotion and construction of the first electric lines in the London area, pointing out that nearly a million pounds had been spent on the new power station, several depots and sub-stations and 16 miles of route out of a total authorised of 30 miles, and that they intended to proceed with construction of the remaining authorised 22 miles forthwith. Samuel White, the LUT Secretary, in his submission to the Board of Trade dated 14 June 1901, suggested that with such a record the company was entitled to decide in what order their various works should proceed.

Samuel White roundly condemned the county council's attitude, especially the allegations about the company's intentions with respect to their powers, branding these allegations as "libellous". White said it was reasonable that the extension of time to complete the remaining portion of the Light Railway between Hanwell and Uxbridge should be granted, and expressed the hope that the Board of Trade would be pleased to grant a two years' extension of time. The Board of Trade was suitably impressed by the company's submission and after dealing with a few minor local objections an extension of time, for one year from 9 May 1901 was granted.

While the company had promised the local authorities to construct and commence operation of the line within the time prescribed in the Order, they had been unable to achieve this target. The Kew Observatory question was not finally resolved until 3 April 1901 and there had been uncertainty through much of 1900 as to whether or not the overhead trolley system could finally be adopted. The company had meanwhile suffered heavy loss of revenue owing to the delays in getting other lines into service, notably the potentially profitable extension from the Hounslow line through Twickenham to Hampton Court and return via Teddington, forming the Hampton Court Loop tramway, sanctioned in the 1900 Act. George White and Clifton Robinson recognised this line as one which would be highly profitable, with immense pleasure traffic potential to the popular riverside resorts, and with this in mind the company's efforts were diverted from earlier projects towards getting this route into operation, The Hampton Court Loop was opened in April 1903 and the company then again turned its attention in the direction of Uxbridge.

In the meantime the ownership of the company had passed from the White interests to the Underground Electric Railways Company of London, George White being replaced as Chairman on 19 March 1903 by Charles Tyson Yerkes, Chairman of the Underground company. Robinson now had to justify his actions to a new master and in a letter to Yerkes dated 18 July 1903 he stressed the importance of completing the company's authorised lines and pointed out that the preparatory work for the line from Hammersmith to Acton via Askew Road and for the line to Uxbridge was already in hand. He stressed the importance of commencing track laying on the Uxbridge section without delay as the light railway powers would expire on 9 September 1903. An extension of time had been obtained from the Board of Trade until 9 May 1903 with a further extension until 9 September 1903.

Robinson's letter to Yerkes gave a detailed account of work recently completed, in progress and awaiting commencement. He said that estimates had been prepared for construction of the 5.77 mile Southall - Uxbridge line early in July. The estimated cost of permanent way was £56,942; overhead £9,880; cables

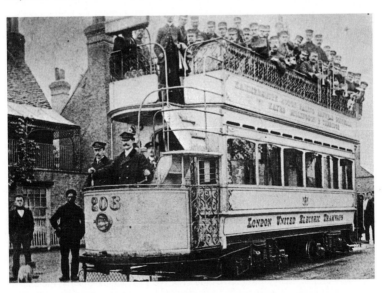

The official car was followed by No. 206 in white livery and carried the Hillingdon Prize Band on the open top deck. The "photo stop" is at Hayes, 'Adam & Eve' public house.
(Courtesy: London Borough of Hillingdon)

115

Car No. 149 passing through Uxbridge shortly after the extension was opened. The car is in the newly adopted yellow livery.   (Courtesy: J.H. Price)

and switch pillars, £6,596; car shed for 20 cars and offices at Hillingdon, £5,400; land for depot and car shed, £1,000; sub-station at depot, building, £2,500; plant at sub-station, £5,400; high-tension feeders from Hanwell sub-station, £4,398; widenings and works, £1,385 and twenty bogie cars at £873 each, £17,460. The total estimated cost was £110,961 to which was added engineering and contingencies of 15% £16,444.

Construction from Southall to Uxbridge commenced on 27 July 1903 and continued in tandem with the work on the Hammersmith – Acton link via Askew Road. When the Board of Trade granted the extension of time until 9 September 1903 they told the company that they would have considerable difficulty in allowing further extensions but the company having begun the work in July, the Board found itself able to grant an extension until 9 April 1904, by which time the company was confident that the work would be completed. However, an unexpected difficulty arose with the depot and sub-station site at Hillingdon, which was being obtained from Lord Hillingdon, who had extensive estates in the locality. The nature of this difficulty is not recorded, but Clifton Robinson was able to obtain another site about half a mile west of the original site for £728; this site was larger and less expensive than the earlier one. The delay resulted in the company finding it necessary to seek further extensions of time, which were granted, until May 1904 with a final one until 9 June.

On 15 July 1903 Uxbridge UDC approved the LUT working plans, subject to the LUT agreeing to pave the main road through the town with wood blocks, and to the company ensuring that when the line was laid, sufficient space was left on either side of the road for a cart or a van to stand. On 28 July the council resolved to oppose the company's current application for an extension of time, and urged Middlesex County Council to refuse any application for further extensions anywhere in the county of Middlesex until the company had completed the line in Uxbridge. However, the Board of Trade granted the requisite extension of time.

Hillingdon East Parish Council had formed a Tramways Committee at the time of the LUT application for the Light Railway Order. Their demands had been for wood paving in the parish and for conduit working – "poles and wires would be

116

objectionable" – but "if poles had to be used they should be ornamental and the Parish Council allowed their use for lighting purposes". There was to be "no ringing or other noises within 100 yards of a church during the hours of Divine Service on Sundays", and as the road through the village was only 21 ft wide, a single line was asked for between Harlington Road and Hillingdon Hill.

As with the construction of the earlier lines the whole of the work was carried out by the company's own staff. By February 1904 the work was well advanced and it was at this time that the depot site at Hillingdon unexpectedly became unavailable. Once the new site was found the work was pressed forward, and the costs of the depot and sub-station were lower than had been estimated, the land costing £728, buildings, £7,779 and £2,134 for machinery, a total of £10,641 against the estimated £14,300. The depot site was 120 yards west of the Hayes – Hillingdon boundary and half a mile west of the earlier site in Hayes Parish and on the north side of Uxbridge Road. Separate buildings were provided for the car shed, sub-station, offices and staff mess-room and the site allowed space for future extension.

Construction had reached Heath Road, Hillingdon by the end of 1903 and by late March 1904 the line had reached Uxbridge. Owing to the delay caused by the change of depot site, the line could not yet be fed by the Hillingdon sub-station and a connection was therefore made to Hanwell sub-station. A trial car was run to Uxbridge on the evening of Monday 28 March 1904.

The depot and sub-station had not been fully completed by late May but nevertheless Clifton Robinson requested a Board of Trade inspection of the line, which was carried out by Col. Yorke on 31 May. He duly reported that the line consisted of 5.77miles of route, of which 2.438 miles was double and 3.151 miles single track. By agreement the line had been curtailed slightly east of the authorised Uxbridge terminus near the Grand Junction Canal bridge. Through Uxbridge the line was double track for 0.725 miles as it was in Hillingdon village for 0.262 miles, The line was laid in 92½lb/yard rails with fished joints and the rail ends were supported on steel soleplates. Overhead construction was in side poles and span wires, Col. Yorke found the installation in good order and recommended

High Street, Uxbridge.

Another view of High Street, Uxbridge c1910/11, with car No. 117 seen heading for Hammersmith, experimentally fitted with Brill 22E trucks, No. 21, in the background, is approaching the terminus.   (Commercial view, Courtesy: J.H. Price)

117

the Board of Trade to certify the line fit for public service. He imposed a general speed limit of 12 mile/h, except 8 mile/h through Hillingdon from the bridge across the River Pinn to Park Terrace; opposite St. Andrew's Schools and through Uxbridge from the parish boundary to the terminus, with 4 mile/h at all facing points. He also required each car to carry oil lamps for use as head and tail lights in the case of power failure at night. Robinson accepted all the Colonel's requirements but objected in vain to the call for oil lamps. This recommendation had been made on account of the many unlit lengths of road on the rural sections of line. The Board of Trade duly issued their certificate on 7 June but Col. Yorke had meanwhile given verbal permission for public service to commence on 1 June.

Col. Yorke's visit to Uxbridge was something of a gala occasion. Immediately following the inspection a formal opening of the line took place, with Clifton Robinson Jr. driving the opening car, No. 202 which had also been used for the inspection. The car, in a new yellow and white livery which had just been adopted for the Uxbridge route was decorated for the occasion and the main street through Uxbridge was likewise beflagged and strung across with banners proclaiming "WELCOME TO THE TRAMS". The formal opening was followed by a grand luncheon at the Chequers Hotel, given by John King, proprietor of the *Uxbridge Gazette*. King had played a leading part in promoting the acceptance of the LUT proposals in Uxbridge and the townships along the route. At this function toasts were proposed and drunk to HM The King; the Board of Trade; the London United Tramways and the Town of Uxbridge. Throughout these proceedings the Uxbridge and Hillingdon Prize Band was in attendance, having passed along the route playing the whole way on white car No. 206. The Guest of Honour was Col. Yorke and among a large guest list were Sir Frederick Dixon Hartland, MP for Uxbridge; the chairmen of the councils along the route, local clergy, businessmen, members of Middlesex County Council and the County Surveyor, H.T. Wakelam

A view of High Street, Hanwell, with car No. 97 bound for Shepherds Bush.

(Commercial view)

118

and the directors and officials of the London United Tramways. After this function Col. Yorke and the LUT contingent left Uxbridge to carry out the inspection and formal opening during the afternoon of the other new line between Hammersmith and Uxbridge Road, Acton via Askew Road.

Public service commenced at 8am on Wednesday 1 June 1904 with cars operating from Shepherds Bush and Hammersmith to Uxbridge with intermediate services to Hanwell and Southall. For some unexplained reason the Shepherds Bush – Uxbridge service was suspended during the week ending 10 June but was

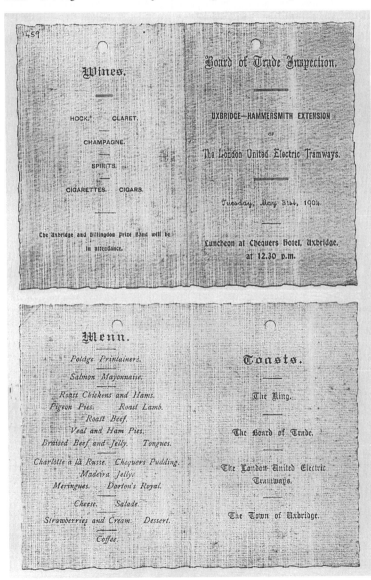

restored the following week. The cars initially used were those already operating to Southall, from the 101-150 series, augmented by ten Milnes-built cars from the 151-300 series, Nos. 201-210. The white cars Nos. 101-150 and Nos. 201-210 were at this time being repainted chrome yellow and white. Nos. 201-210 were originally blue, thus in a short space of time this group wore three different liveries. Later, as traffic increased, the Uxbridge service was augmented by some cars from the 1-100 batch, in red and white livery.

Fom an early date Ealing Borough Council had complained to the company and the Board of Trade about alleged noise from the cars and had actively enlisted the co-operation of neighbouring councils to exert pressure upon the LUT and the Board to obtain reductions of noise levels which Ealing considered objectionable. On 28 May 1907 Uxbridge UDC considered letters from Ealing and Chiswick councils seeking co-operation from Uxbridge UDC to put pressure upon the company on the noise question and, in the case of Chiswick UDC, their objection to the company's methods of snow clearance. Uxbridge UDC resolved to take no action.

On 25 August 1908 Uxbridge UDC was told that complaints had been made to the Commissioner of Police for the Metropolis about the state of the track in the Uxbridge district, and an inspection had been made on the Commissioner's behalf. The Commissioner's office had sent a detailed schedule of track defects to the council's Surveyor and had recommended that the Surveyor should call upon the company to rectify the faults listed in the schedule. On 29 December the council was told that Sir Clifton Robinson had arranged for the track through Uxbridge to be repaired. The nature of these repairs is not recorded, but evidently were of a reasonably substantial nature, as in the autumn of 1909 Robinson reported to the LUT directors that track reconstruction between Southall and Uxbridge would not be necessary until 1919 in the case of the single line sections and 1924 for the double track.

By the autumn of 1910 Wimbledon Borough Council had approached Uxbridge UDC asking the UDC to appoint a representative to attend a conference of local authorities on the noise question. The UDC appointed two councillors to attend on their behalf, and meanwhile the management of the LUT, following the resignation of Sir Clifton Robinson, came into the hands of Albert Stanley who had been appointed Managing Director on 2 March. In October 1910 Stanley wrote to the UDC and the Board of Trade saying that all of the company's cars were being put through the shops for complete overhaul, and improvements were being made to the track throughout the system.

The Boston Road Line

At the time the LUT were drafting their tramway extensions Boston Road, some two and a quarter miles in length, was a straggling thoroughfare with much open land on either side, linking High Street, Brentford via Half Acre and Boston Road with The Broadway, Uxbridge Road, Hanwell, following a roughly north-westerly route from Brentford. For much of its length it was an unmade road of no great width but at the time legislation was sought for the route it was of strategic importance to the LUT.

The LUT had a major objective to extend the Uxbridge Road line beyond its authorised terminus at Acton to Ealing, Southall and Uxbridge, and in 1898 was in the process of obtaining a Light Railway Order covering the part of the Uxbridge Road between Hanwell and Uxbridge. Ealing Urban District Council refused their consent to the LUT applications for tramway or light railway powers through the town and in November 1897 the LUT deposited plans for a number of lines, one of which was the Hanwell – Brentford tramway, to consist of 2.385 miles of route, all double track except for a 22 yard piece of single line. This line was authorised in the resulting Act, which received the Royal Assent on 12 August 1898. As matters stood, therefore, this authorised line provided the link between the inner London terminus at Hammersmith Broadway via Chiswick and Brentford with the soon to be authorised line from Hanwell to Uxbridge. The Act also authorised the continuation of the existing line at Kew Bridge through High Street, Brentford and London Road, Isleworth to The Bell, Hounslow.

These two sections set at naught the barrier to the westerly part of Uxbridge Road set by Ealing Urban District Council's refusal to consent to the LUT proposals for lines through the town. Clifton Robinson, however, did not relinquish his objective of gaining powers through Ealing, and later, in 1900, after much activity in Parliament and at local levels the Ealing powers were obtained. No time was lost in utilising these powers and a stated intention to quickly construct the line through Boston Road was shelved and the line from Acton to Ealing and Southall was pressed forward at all speed, to be opened on 10 July 1901.

The LUT now had the powers for the direct route to Uxbridge and the Boston Road line was no longer of vital importance, except that it did provide a through route from Hammersmith to points along Uxbridge Road west of Ealing, as well as from Shepherds Bush. At a later date the importance of the Boston Road route was reduced still further when the link between Hammersmith and the Uxbridge Road via Askew Road opened on 31 May 1904.

In the meantime the company had gained powers for the important Hampton Court and Surrey lines and a great effort was concentrated upon securing the opening of the Hampton Court line by Easter, 1903, followed by the Southall – Uxbridge section on 31 May 1904. There was now little likelihood of Parliament granting further extensions of time to complete the Boston Road line. Extensions had been granted in the 1900 Act, for two years to 12 August 1902, and in the 1901 Act an extension was sanctioned for two years from 12 August 1902 until 12 August 1904, the 1904 Act allowing a final extension to 12 August 1906.

During the late summer of 1904 the LUT directors gave consideration to completing construction of outstanding authorised mileage, this amounting to the lines in Kingston and Wimbledon to Tooting and the Boston Road line. Estimates were prepared for construction of the Boston Road tramway, which consisted of the double line from High Street, Brentford into Half Acre, through Boston Road and Lower Boston Road to meet the Uxbridge Road line in the Broadway, Hanwell approximately 70 yards east of the Hanwell – Southall boundary, the authorised length of this section being 2.397 miles, all of which was double track, and including a double west to north junction into Half Acre from High Street,

Car No. 117, in yellow livery, was one of three used on the Boston Road shuttle service when it opened on 26 May 1906. It is being reversed at Half Acre, Brentford for the return to Hanwell.
(Courtesy: National Tramway Museum)

121

Brentford and a double north to west junction from Lower Boston Road into the Broadway, Hanwell. The company evidently felt that there was a need for a south to east connection with Uxbridge Road and in the 1900 Act powers were gained for an 0.231 miles branch from Boston Road into Upper Boston Road with a double south to east junction with Uxbridge Road 100 yards west of Hanwell Depot. This branch contained two short single line sections separated by a 75 yard loop and allowed a more direct access to Hanwell Depot as well as providing a terminus at Uxbridge Road closer to the centre of Hanwell.

Two sets of estimates were prepared for construction and equipment of the line. The first dated July 1903, amounted to £69,432 and included £35,693 for permanent way, £4,662 for overhead on the span wire system, £1,889 10s 0d for low tension cabling, including switch pillars, £13,460 for widening and works, £5,000 to extend Hanwell Depot and ten bogie cars at £873 each, £8,730. An addition of £10,415 covering engineering and contingencies, at 15% brought the grand total up to £79,847.

Up to this time all construction work had been carried out by the company's own workforce and by 1904 the company's financial backers, Speyer Brothers and the Underground Electric Railways of London Ltd. were becoming concerned at the financial position of the LUT. It was felt that some economies could be made, and in September 1904, with the powers for the Boston Road and other lines running short, further estimates were prepared. These, dated 22 September provided for £34,337 for the permanent way, £4,662 for overhead, £1,852 for low-tension cables and switch pillars, £14,382 for widenings and works, an extension for Hanwell Depot at £5,000 and ten bogie cars at £700 each, £7,000, a total of £67,233 plus an addition of £6,723 for engineering and contingencies bringing the total to £73,956, a reduction of £5,891 on the earlier estimate.

Discussions between the LUT directors, Speyer Brothers and the UERL directors, centred upon the advisability of continuing to carry out construction as previously, or to place the work out to tender by outside contractors. The LUT directors met on 20 October 1904 and approved the estimates presented on 22 September, and on 4 November they resolved to construct the lines in Kingston and Wimbledon together with the Boston Road line, and a decision was taken to place the work with outside contractors. On 19 December Robinson reported on tenders received but no details were given at the time.

Car No. 117 again, at the Brentford end of Boston Road, bound for Hanwell. This part of the road had been widened before the tramway was completed, but further north several more years elapsed before work was completed.   (Courtesy: A.D. Packer)

The Boston Road contract, for permanent way and overhead was placed with J.G. White & Co. Ltd. of London and was part of the contract for constructing the lines in Kingston, Surbiton and Malden, the price for the whole being £170,777, including permanent way construction and overhead. On an average mileage basis this represents a cost of £31,570 for the track and overhead. The contract with J.G. White & Co. was signed on 1 March 1905 and a contract for low-tension cabling with four switch pillars was awarded on 8 March to W.T. Henley's Telegraph Works Co. Ltd., for £2,594. No additional cars were ordered for the Boston Road line, nor was any extension made to Hanwell Depot. Widenings and road improvements on this section amounted to £20,778, much of the route being narrow and the road of poor construction.

Work on the Boston Road tramway commenced on 5 June 1905, and took the greater part of a year. The company was under pressure from Kingston Corporation and the other councils on the Surrey lines to expedite work in their districts, and the Boston Road line, of secondary importance, suffered on account of the contractors' men being taken off the work to the Surrey lines. There were some complaints about this, but as the route was very sparsely populated at that time, the company was not subjected to any great volume of opprobrium.

Some bad winter weather also slowed work down, but by May 1906 all was ready for the Board of Trade inspection, which was carried out by Col. Yorke on 23 May 1906. His report, dated 24 May expressed satisfaction with the construction, which was in heavier rails than the earlier lines, 100 lb/yard on straight track and 106 lb/yard on curves. The rail joints were also an improvement on earlier practice, being of heavy girder construction set in concrete as described in Chapter 12. The overhead construction was in side poles and span-wires throughout, and paving was of Jarrah hardwood blocks throughout.

In addition to the 2.397 miles of double line between High Street, Brentford and the Broadway, Hanwell in Half Acre, Boston Road and Lower Boston Road and the short 0.213 miles of line from the junction of Boston Road and lower Boston Road through Upper Boston Road to the Broadway an additional south to east double junction had been laid at the Lower Boston Road – Broadway intersection. This had been laid without sanction but by agreement with Hanwell UDC, and Col. Yorke raised no objection to it, remarking that as it had been laid without Parliamentary sanction, the Board of Trade could not certify it, but use of it was not debarred. Col. Yorke recommended speed limits of 14 mile/h in Boston Road between Elthorne Park Road and the bridge over the London and South Western Railway at Brentford station and 8 mile/h in Upper Boston Road and Boston Road between Hanwell Broadway and Elthorne Park Road and in Boston Road and Half Acre between Brentford station and High Street, Brentford. A 4 mile/hour limit was imposed through all facing points and compulsory stops set at the junction between Upper and Lower Boston Roads, and before passing round the curves at the junctions between the Broadway and Lower Boston Road and between the Broadway and Upper Boston Road. The use of magnetic track brakes was required on the cars using the route. The Board of Trade certificate was issued on 26 May 1906.

Service commenced between Brentford and the Hanwell terminus at the end of Upper Boston Road on 26 May 1906, with a ten-minute service throughout the day commencing at 7am until 11pm, with workmen's cars from 5am and returning from 3pm, and from noon on Saturdays. A through service from Hammersmith to Uxbridge via Brentford and Lower Boston Road was also operated, details of which are sparse. This service was at an unknown date cut back to Southall and by 1910 had ceased to operate. On 16 April 1907 it was announced that the three-car ten-minute service between Hanwell and Brentford would become a fifteen-minute service, operated by two cars, and this pattern persisted throughout the period covered by this chapter. Other service reductions were announced at the same time and late night services curtailed. It may have been at this time that the through Hammersmith – Uxbridge service was cut back to Southall.

The Boston Road shuttle had, by its nature, an uneventful life. At an unrecorded date the cars working the service, initially No. 117 and another from the 101-150 group, and No. 212 were divested of their magnetic track brakes and this became the subject of correspondence between the company and the Board of Trade at a later date, details of which will be found in Volume 2.

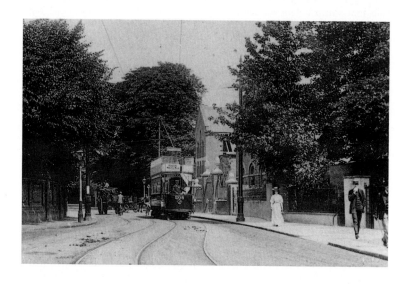

Upper: Another yellow car, No. 208, seen working on the Boston Road line near the junction of Boston Road with Half Acre, Brentford. (Commercial view)

Lower: A later view on a still-rural part of Boston Road, prior to the Great War. No. 37, fitted with a top cover in 1910-11, is seen on its way to Brentford.
(Commercial view: Courtesy: J.H. Price)

CHAPTER EIGHT

TWICKENHAM AND HAMPTON COURT

Busch Corner, Isleworth is situated some four miles west of Hammersmith at the intersection of London Road and the Twickenham Road. The latter diverges south through Isleworth and Twickenham to Hampton, where the Middlesex bank of the River Thames is reached at the intersection of Church Street, Thames Street and Hampton Court Road. From this point Hampton Court Road continues east along the Middlesex bank of the Thames for a little under one mile until Hampton Court Bridge is reached, at which point Hampton Court Road turns sharply north for about 250 yards before again turning east on a direct route to Kingston Bridge at Hampton Wick. Between Hampton Court and Kingston bridges the river diverges south from Hampton Court Road and in this large semi-circular area lies Hampton Court Park with Hampton Court Palace situated south of Hampton Court Road east of Hampton Court Bridge, while the north side of Hampton Court Road nearly as far as Kingston Bridge is flanked by Bushy Park. Hampton Court is one of the most southerly points in Middlesex and the county of Surrey is reached by the bridges across the Thames at Hampton Court, Richmond and Kingston.

This area of south and south-west Middlesex is rich in historical associations. Chief among these is Hampton Court Palace, built by Cardinal Thomas Wolsey in 1516 and later the residence of King Henry VIII followed by later kings and queens until the reign of King George III, during which time it was converted to "Grace and Favour" apartments for persons who had rendered service to the Crown or the State. Two years after Queen Victoria came to the throne the State apartments were opened to the public, and the Palace and its environs remain today one of the premier tourist attractions in the Greater London area.

Numerous historical personages have resided in the area covered by this chapter, apart from the Royal figures associated with Hampton Court Palace. Among them are Sir Francis Bacon, Horace Walpole, Alexander Pope, J.M.W. Turner, Alfred Lord Tennyson and Henry Fielding, all of whom had residences in and around Twickenham. Charles Dickens had a summer residence there in 1838 at which *Oliver Twist* is believed to have been written. These are but a few of the many important historical figures who in bygone years lived in and around the Twickenham and Hampton Court area.

In Isleworth and North Twickenham considerable housing development took place in the Victorian era and some industrial enterprises had been established. South of Busch Corner and Isleworth the shopping and business centre of Twickenham was centred upon the Twickenham station of the LSWR and further south lay the district known today as Fulwell, sparsely built up at the turn of the century. South from this point lay the urban district of Hampton, through which the main thoroughfares are Hampton Hill, High Street and Church Street before Hampton Court Road and the River Thames is reached. At the turn of the century these thoroughfares were mainly country lanes, flanked on either side by much open land with some large residences spaced widely apart on the west side, the east side forming the west boundary of Bushy Park. At the point where Church Street, Hampton reaches the river bank stands Garrick's Villa, one-time residence of the celebrated actor-manager, David Garrick, of which more will be found in another part of this book.

Several attempts had been made to obtain powers for tramways in this area. One company had obtained powers and had actually laid part of its authorised mileage in Brentford and Isleworth but lack of capital had prevented its completion. The line already laid was never used, ultimately taken up and the powers abandoned. The West Metropolitan Tramways Company had hoped to reach Hampton Court from Richmond but the necessary powers were not granted.

The riverside location of Hampton Court and the added attractions of the Thames pleasure boats and launches, with Kempton Park racecourse only a short distance across Hampton Court Bridge had, by the late Victorian era, made it a popular rendezvous for week-end and holiday traffic from Central London, but public transport in the locality was hampered by the narrow roads approaching the area. These roads were mostly poorly maintained and some local interests did not wish to see improvements which might bring increases in traffic to a district which consisted mainly of large residences in extensive grounds and would have a detrimental effect on local amenities.

Notwithstanding these difficulties much traffic did reach such a popular holiday venue, largely by means of horse-drawn omnibuses, while the LSWR station at Hampton Court provided a direct, if infrequent service from Waterloo. Bank Holidays and Summer Sundays brought large numbers of horse-drawn brakes with parties from Central London, and George White and Clifton Robinson had perceived at an early date the traffic potential of direct services to Hampton Court and beyond for fast high capacity electric tramcars from the Central London and District Railway termini at Shepherds Bush and Hammersmith respectively. There was also useful local traffic to be tapped in and around the built-up area of Twickenham, whilst south and west of Twickenham much of the area was ripe for residential development with the prospect of future tramway extensions. Later extensions were envisaged across the Hampton Court and Kingston bridges to reach the Moleseys, the Dittons, Kingston and Wimbledon, and it was anticipated that when the London County Council's electric tramways, then being planned, became a reality agreements would be made with that body for through services over their lines into Central London.

The LUT accordingly deposited a Bill in November 1899 for the 1900 Parliamentary Session, This Bill, which included the important Uxbridge Road line between Acton and Ealing, referred to elsewhere in this book, contained provisions for a line to commence by a double junction, at Busch Corner at the junction of London Road and Twickenham Road at Isleworth, and to follow Twickenham Road in the urban district of Heston & Isleworth, thence into the urban district of Twickenham through London Road, King Street, Heath Road, The Green and Hampton Road and continuing along Wellington Road in the urban District of Teddington and through the Hampton urban district via Hampton Hill, High Street, Church Street and Hampton Court Road, terminating at a double track stub immediately west of the Hampton – Hampton Wick boundary at Hampton Court. From this point another line was connected to the first by a double track junction curve but commencing at another double track stub at right angles to the first, some 300 yards west of the boundary. This line took a northerly and easterly path past The Green along Hampton Court Road through the urban district of Hampton Wick past Kingston Bridge, through High Street, Hampton Wick and Upper Teddington Road, re-entering the Teddington urban district via Kingston Road and continuing through Teddington along Ferry Road, High Street, Teddington, Bridge Parade, Broad Street and Stanley Road, where the urban district of Twickenham was again met, and the Hampton Court Loop formed by a junction with the line from Twickenham to Hampton Court via Hampton. The total length of this line from its commencement at Busch Corner was 10.882 miles of which 9.313 miles was authorised as double and 1.568 miles as single track.

In Twickenham a branch diverged from the line in King Street 23 yards north of the King's Head Hotel and traversed York Street, a newly-built thoroughfare, into Richmond Road, to terminate at a point 98 yards south-west from Willoughby Road at the south-west side of Richmond Bridge. This was the nearest point at which electric trams reached to the centre of Richmond, but was nearly a mile from

The scene at Ivy Bridge, Twickenham on 23 April 1902, as preparatory work is being undertaken prior to the beginning of track laying. As was usual in those days, a member of the local police force was on hand to ensure that order was maintained.

(Courtesy: Bristol Record Office)

the LUT's other terminus in Kew Road. This line was authorised as 0.89 miles of double and 0.214 miles of single track. The whole of this mileage (the loop and its branch) was situated in the county of Middlesex.

In November 1898 the company had applied for a Light Railway Order for a number of routes amounting to 16.75 miles, the costs of which were estimated at £199,045. These were Acton – Hanwell, Hounslow – Baber Bridge and the Hampton Court lines described above. The Acton – Hanwell section had been rejected by Parliament earlier in 1898 and was withdrawn from the application on this account. This line and the Hounslow – Baber Bridge extension were later sanctioned by Parliament as related elsewhere. The local authorities in the area covered by the Hampton Court scheme had been generally in favour of the proposal but the London and South Western Railway Company had opposed the application on the grounds of competition, and at the inquiry into the scheme at Twickenham on 12 May 1899 the Light Railway Commissioners had no choice but to uphold the railway company's objections. The LSWR had also stated that the scheme should have been submitted to Parliament and the Commissioners, the Earl of Jersey and Col. Geo. Boughey, having heard that the local authorities were in favour of the scheme, advised the company to submit their application to Parliament.

The support of the local councils, who had received promises of extensive road and other improvements in their districts, helped to ensure the success of the company's 1900 Bill, all the tramway provisions of which were sanctioned, with the Bill receiving the Royal Assent on 6 August 1900 as the London United Tramways Act 1900.

The easy passage of the 1900 Act had been facilitated largely by the company agreeing to extensive street widenings and other improvements, especially in Twickenham and Teddington. Heston & Isleworth UDC secured a clause in the Act which obliged the company to complete construction of and open the double line authorised in the 1898 Act from Kew Bridge to Brentford Bridge before commencing work on any of the lines authorised in the 1900 Act "so as to provide a continuous double line of tramways from Kew Bridge to the commencement of Tramway No. 6 authorised by the said (1898) Act", i.e. to Hounslow (The Bell). However the council's consent was required before the company should commence construction of any other tramway in the district until the line from Kew Bridge to Hounslow was opened with through cars from Hammersmith.

Widenings were required at four places in the urban district of Heston & Isleworth between Busch Corner and the boundary with Twickenham, a distance of 1.5 miles. The council undertook to bear half the costs of these widenings and an obligation was placed upon the company to erect at twenty places along this section electric lamps of a design to be approved by the Council and to be lit and maintained by the LUT. If required by the Council the Company was obliged to provide and maintain a waiting room at a place along the route selected by the council, together with a public convenience. This was duly placed at Busch Corner. The Council also gained the power to condemn any car or equipment on the section within their district which in their opinion might be unfit for public use, and, exceptionally, to require the company to pave and maintain the roadway for a space of at least 24in outside the two outer rails of the track with wood blocks. The 1870 Tramways Act requirement was for paving outside the outer rails was eighteen inches and there were very few exceptions to this.

Twickenham UDC laid the onus upon the company to bear the full costs of land acquisitions and widenings in their district and could require the LUT to lay double track throughout the whole of York Street and widen the carriageway there to 32ft and relay the footpaths. The council could also call upon the company to lay either double or interlacing track in London Road from Amyand Park Road to Holly Road. The company was required to erect lamp standards opposite the King's Head Hotel in King Street and at the junction of Hampton and Stanley Roads, and to supply current and maintain them at their own expense and, if required by the Council, to provide and maintain a waiting room at the junction of London Road and York Street. The demands of Twickenham UDC were considerably fewer than those of Heston & Isleworth UDC, whose requirements for numerous concessions covered some twelve pages in the printed Act.

Hampton UDC required the levels in High Street to be raised and the whole width of the road and footpaths to be reconstructed for 112 yards north of The Triangle. Another provision in the Act stipulated that the company should maintain the road on both sides of the track for six months after completion of the line in the Hampton district. The 1900 Act also obliged the company before commencing the line in Hampton Court Road to widen the road near the junction with Church Street and for some 250 yards to the east by purchasing a strip of land flanking a large house, Garrick's Villa, situated at the corner of Church Street and Hampton Court Road, adding the land purchased to the road and remaking the roadway, footpaths and kerbing to the Council's satisfaction. In addition to these requirements the LUT was to pay the Council £500 to cover the cost of constructing a footbridge beside Pantile Bridge in High Street, Hampton, a further £200 for widening the footpath in another part of the High Street and £300 to enable the Council to set back the bank on a portion of the north side of Hampton Court Road and to erect a retaining wall and iron railings flanking the adjacent footpath. The Council was also empowered to ask the company to provide and maintain a waiting room at a place to be chosen by the Council.

Hampton Wick UDC was granted a number of privileges in the Act. The Council was given the right to use the company's overhead poles for ventilating the drains along the route, for lighting purposes and for fixing street name tablets. Wood paving was called for throughout the line in the district except for 0.75 miles between the Dew Drop Inn and "Lynwood" in Hampton Court Road, where the Act allowed granite sett paving. This was the only stone sett paving authorised anywhere on the Hampton Court lines.

Upper: The track in Twickenham Road, Isleworth, immediately south of Busch Corner nears completion on 23 May 1902, with the laying of hardwood block paving
(Courtesy: Bristol Record Office)

Lower: At the opposite end of Twickenham Road, at Ivy Bridge, on the same day, work is about to start on stringing the overhead wires. Note the ornate scrollwork on the poles.
(Courtesy: Bristol record Office)

Teddington Urban District Council had asked for few concessions on the part of the LUT other than the standard requirements as to plans and constructional details but were empowered to call upon the company not to run fewer cars on race days at Kempton Park than on other days.

There were special provisions in the Act covering Royal property. Pantile Bridge in Hampton, across the River Longford, or The Queen's River was, like other Royal property, administered by the Office of Works. The widening of this bridge was to be carried out at the company's expense and to the satisfaction of the First Commissioner of the Office of Works on behalf of the Sovereign. The trees along Hampton Court Road and certain culverts, drains and gas mains were also Royal property and were not to be altered in any way without the permission of the First Commissioner. In the event, Pantile Bridge was widened and a separate footbridge thus became unnecessary.

Work on the new route commenced in March 1902. From the time of passing the Act prior to commencing construction the company had negotiated several further agreements with the councils along the route. The part of the line from Busch Corner, Isleworth to the Twickenham boundary was now authorised as a double line throughout, and of the remainder of the Hampton Court route much of which had been shown in the plans as single line was, by a number of agreements with the councils laid as double track. In 1903, 1904 and 1906 the company obtained powers to acquire lands for additional widening in Heston & Isleworth, Twickenham, Teddington and Hampton, some of which were not carried out for several years, although practically all the track on the Hampton Court routes had been doubled by 1909.

The Hampton Court lines were the largest single construction scheme of the LUT. Clifton Robinson and the LUT management embarked upon the task with customary vigour, the whole of the constructional work on the route being carried out by the company's own workforce except for some work on bridges. Only the structural steelwork for the new depot at Fulwell was supplied and erected by a contractor and the target date for opening the complete route was Easter 1903. At the same time as construction of the line commenced several large contracts were

No. 249, the first tram to reach Teddington, on the eastern side of the Hampton Court Loop, on 2 April 1903. The police, as usual, took a prominent part in the proceedings.
(Courtesy: National Tramway Museum)

Cars 159 and 223 pass in Heath Road, Twickenham in the early days of the Hampton Court
services.   (Commercial view)

placed for additional equipment at Chiswick power station, a new sub-station at the
depot, cars and equipment. These contracts covered the purchase of two new
boilers from Babcock & Wilcox Ltd., part of the necessary additional machinery at
the power station, one hundred and twenty-five new car bodies from Geo. F.
Milnes & Co. Ltd., twenty-five similar bodies from the British Electric Car Co. Ltd.,
150 pairs of Brill type 22E maximum traction bogies from the J.G. Brill Co. of
Philadelphia and one hundred and fifty sets of motors and controllers from the
British Westinghouse Electric & Manufacturing Co. Ltd. and 150 sets of lifeguards
from Gabriel & Co. Ltd. These contracts were sealed at a directors' meeting on 26
February 1902 but apart from the cost of the cars no other figures are recorded. The
cars are recorded as having cost £669 each including their equipment.

Traction poles for the new route were ordered from John Spencer & Co. Ltd.,
cabling from W.T. Henley's Telegraph Works Ltd., cast-iron pole bases, finials and
other pole fittings from James Allan Senior & Sons, span wires from Dixon Corbett
& Co. Ltd. and span wire and scroll brackets from Strachan & Henshaw Ltd.,
together with thirteen section and two feeder pillars from the Electric Transmission
Co. Ltd. A contract was also placed with Stephen Kavanagh & Co. Ltd. for the
reconstruction of Ivy Bridge, across the Duke of Northumberland's River at
Isleworth.

On 30 April 1902 the directors approved a contract with John Aird & Sons
Ltd. for the reconstruction of Cole's Bridge, an old brick structure across the River
Crane at North Twickenham for the sum of £4,450. At the same time the Secretary
reported that difficult negotiations with the Trustees of Sir Charles Freake had
been concluded for a 99 years building lease on a large piece of land with frontages
to Stanley Road and Wellington Road, Fulwell on which the depot and sub-station
serving the new lines was to be built. On 27 June 1902 further contracts were
approved, with John Aird & Sons Ltd. to widen the bridges across the LSWR at
Stanley Road and Broad Street, Teddington for the sum of £11,779 and with James
Crispin & Sons to install the central heating system at the new Fulwell Depot. A
tender by John Lysaght Ltd of Newport and Bristol was accepted to supply and
erect the steelwork for the new depot and sub-station. These buildings were
erected on what was at the time open country which rapidly became built up

following the opening of the new lines. On 27 June Clifton Robinson told the directors that additional generating plant was required at Chiswick power station, to serve the new lines and details of this will be found in Chapter 15.

Meanwhile construction of the new tramway from Busch Corner down to the north side of Cole's Bridge at North Twickenham had progressed and by late May 1902 Robinson had requested a Board of Trade inspection of the completed section, which took place on 20 June. This section consisted of 2.119 miles of double track and an interlacing section of eighty yards in Twickenham Road, Isleworth.

The inspection was carried out by Lt. Col. H.A.Yorke, RE and he found the construction in sound order, recommending a general speed limit of 10 mile/h except through the interlacing between Gumley House School and Worton Road, where 8 mile/h was recommended. Compulsory stops were imposed, on the inward journey (to London) at the Congregational Church at the corner of Worton Road and in both directions at the junction of Twickenham Road and St. John's Road. Although the inspection had been carried out on 20 June 1902 the certificate of fitness for traffic was not issued until 12 September. Meanwhile, on 13 August, a service commenced on this first section of the Thames Valley lines from the termini at Shepherds Bush and Hammersmith to the north side of Cole's Bridge, Twickenham. The fare from either London terminus to this point was 4d and the workmen's fare 1d. Pending completion of Fulwell Depot the depots at Chiswick and Hounslow worked these services.

When the Twickenham section opened the LUT issued a press release which stated that it was expected that the line to Hampton Court would be opened within two months "and frequent services of the LUT's "Palace" cars will open up all the beauties of Hampton Court and Richmond and all that is most interesting in this attractive part of the Thames Valley".

A further section of the line through Twickenham was completed by 12 September 1902. This extended from the north side of Cole's Bridge to Cross Deep, at the southern end of King Street in the centre of the town, together with the branch from the other end of King Street via York Street and Richmond Road to a point near Richmond Bridge. Extensive widenings had been carried out in London Road and King Street, while York Street was a new thoroughfare. At the same time as construction of the track was taking place many old buildings were demolished which, when the tramways were opened and the old buildings replaced resulted in the establishment of a fine shopping and business centre which attracted many large shops and other businesses to the town.

The reconstruction of Cole's Bridge had been delayed by the construction of a large new water main across the bridge. By 12 September 1902 all was ready for the inspection of the section to Cross Deep and the branch to Richmond Bridge, which was carried out by Lt. Col. P.G. Von Donop, RE. The section from north of Coles Bridge to Cross Deep consisted of 0.40 miles of double line and 100 yards of interlacing track, a total of 0.456 route miles, while the branch through York Street and Richmond Road to Richmond Road was 0.967 miles of double and 0.117 miles of single line, with a double junction at the intersection of London Road, York Street and King Street. At a number of places double track had replaced single lines shown on the plans by agreement with the local council and the Board of Trade. A double line had replaced single track over the railway bridge in London Road and Col. Von Donop expressed his view that this bridge should have been widened, He found the construction satisfactory and recommended the Board of Trade to impose speed limits of 8 mile/h in London Road except between Amyand Park Road and the brewery entrance north of the LSWR bridge where speed in the direction of Busch Corner was restricted to 4 mile/h. In York Street 10 mile/h was imposed and in Richmond Road between Beaufort Road and Montpelier Row and between Orleans Road and Sion Road, 12 mile/h, with 8 mile/h at all other places except round the curves in Richmond Road at Beaufort Road and Cambridge Park and round the junction curves at London Road, York Street and King Street where a limit of 4 mile/h was imposed. No limit had been fixed for the curves at the intersection of London Road and Twickenham Road at Busch Corner at the time of the inspection of the Busch Corner – Coles Bridge section on 20 June 1902 and this omission was rectified by the recommendation of a 4 mile/h limit round the curves. Compulsory stops were fixed in Richmond Road at Montpelier Row and Orleans Road and at the intersection of York Street and London Road in both directions in each case. The Board of Trade certificate for both sections was signed on 29 September 1902 but by agreement they opened for public service on Saturday 13 September, the Hammersmith and Shepherds Bush services being extended to a temporary terminus near the Post Office in King Street and a shuttle working between the same point and Richmond Bridge on the branch.

Construction of trackwork and buildings was, as customary carried out by the company's own workforce and this had outstripped the completion of the depot at Fulwell and its accompanying sub-station. This accommodation was now urgently needed if the target date for opening to Hampton Court by Easter was to be met, and despite Robinson's consistent pressure upon all concerned, some contractors were failing to meet delivery commitments. Robinson wrote some acrimonious letters to John Lysaght Ltd., contractors for the steelwork at the depot. This material had failed to arrive and was holding up bricklayers and other tradesmen, resulting in Robinson finding it necessary to ask Geo. F. Milnes & Co. to hold back delivery of fifteen cars ready for delivery in November. On 5 November 1902 he demanded of Lysaght's that they work night shifts to complete delivery of the material. Argument and counter-argument with Lysaght's claiming that the LUT had altered the drawings at a late stage continued until the matter was resolved on 8 December.

The delivery of cars from Milnes had been affected by delay in completing the depot, and Robinson found it necessary to write to them on 22 January 1903 saying that his programme was being delayed by late deliveries. Doubtless Robinson's request for deliveries to be held back in November had resulted in Milnes slowing down production, but in a letter dated 30 January 1903 G.F. Milnes told Robinson that all the cars ordered would be delivered by early March with most by the end of February. The twenty-five cars ordered from the British Electric Car Co. Ltd. appear to have been delivered in the late autumn of 1902.

Robinson was also experiencing difficulty in obtaining delivery of the 150 pairs of bogies ordered from the J.G. Brill Co. of Philadelphia. Sixty-five pairs were still outstanding at 27 November 1902 when Robinson wrote to the company asking for completion at an early date. There was an acrimonious correspondence between the parties between 22 October and 27 November, and in his final letter on 27 November Robinson protested against the treatment he had received from Brill and threatened the company with an action for damages. This evidently produced the desired result as there is no further entry in the relevant file. Meanwhile, Robinson had told his directors that he had placed orders with Brill and the McGuire Company because the preferred supplier, the Peckham Truck & Wheel Co. had full order books and was unable to deliver in the specified time. These delays meant that the LUT labour force had to be diverted from job to job when late deliveries of material and equipment held up work in progress.

By Autumn 1902 construction of the new lines had reached the boundary of the Twickenham and Teddington urban districts at a point immediately in line with the south side of South Road at Fulwell, immediately south of which lay the site of the new depot and sub-station. To the north of the boundary Stanley Road formed a junction with Hampton Road, the former taking the tramway through Stanley Road and Teddington and Hampton Wick to Hampton Court, returning via Hampton Hill to rejoin the route from Twickenham at Stanley Road Junction, forming the celebrated Hampton Court Loop. Completion of Fulwell depot was still outstanding at the time Stanley Road junction was reached from the Twickenham direction.

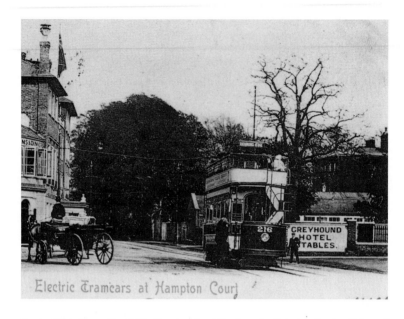

Electric Tramcars at Hampton Court

Upper: BEC-built car No. 216 in Hampton Court Road on the Hampton Court – Richmond Bridge working, outside the 'Greyhound Hotel' and opposite the Lion Gate entrance to Hampton Court Maze.   (Courtesy: J. Sheaf)

Lower: Car 168 loads up at Shepherds Bush on August Bank Holiday 1903. The board on the dashplate reads "CIRCULAR ROUTE, Teddington, Kingston Bridge, Hampton Court, Garrick's Villa, Hampton," the opposite way round to that shown on the legend on the upper deck side.
                                                          (Courtesy: London Transport Museum)

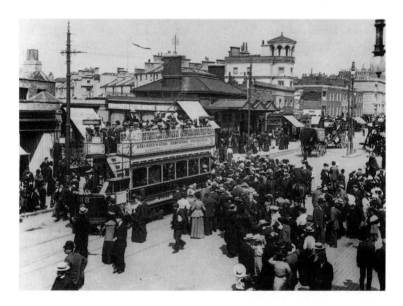

The Board of Trade inspection of the section between Cross Deep and South Road, Fulwell, taking in the two short sections along Stanley Road and Hampton Road to the depot was carried out by Col. Von Donop on 6 November 1902. The new section consisted of 1.445 miles of route of which 0.968 miles was double track, 0.156 miles single and 160 yards interlacing along King Street, Twickenham, Heath Road, The Green and Hampton Road to South Road and 0.23 miles from the junction of Hampton Road and Stanley Road along Stanley Road to the Twickenham – Teddington boundary at South Road. As in the case of the previous sections, widenings had been carried out at several points and double lines substituted for single and interlacing track on the deposited plans by agreement with Twickenham UDC and the Board of Trade. Additional widenings and doublings were to be undertaken when necessary legislation was secured.

Col. Von Donop found the new section in excellent order and advised the introduction of a general speed limit of 8 mile/h except in Hampton Road between South Road and Staines Road and along Heath Road between Lion Road and Cross Deep, where 10 mile/h was permitted. There was a 4 mile/h limit round the curve between Stanley Road and Hampton Road and compulsory stops were imposed in Hampton Road before entering Stanley Road, in Hampton Road at the junction with Staines Road and in Heath Road at Heath Gardens. The certificate of fitness for public service was issued on 22 November 1902 and the services of cars from Richmond Bridge and Shepherds Bush then terminating at Cross Deep were extended on Saturday 8 November to the Nelson public house at the Hampton Road – Stanley Road junction, while cars from Hammersmith continued to turn back at Cross Deep. The fare from Shepherds Bush to Stanley Road was fixed at 5d and from Richmond Bridge the 1d fare was extended to Stanley Road. Workmen's fares were 2d and 1d respectively. Construction of these new lines was in 92½lb/yard rails with fished joints and plain soleplates. Overhead construction was in side poles with span wires throughout.

While work continued at Fulwell depot and sub-station and on the Hampton Court Loop the company considered how best to handle the very heavy traffic anticipated at Hampton Court when the loop was opened. Robinson wrote to the Middlesex County Council in January 1903 asking for approval to construct a stub

Car No. 246 approaches Stanley Road Junction on its way to Shepherds Bush from Hampton Court. The line to Teddington diverges to the left. The "Kitsell" point switching indicator is just visible at the extreme left. (Courtesy: J.H. Price)

135

terminal in Vrow Walk, which lay along the south side of Hampton Court Road to the west of the south entrance to Bushy Park. He said this was required to facilitate the traffic flow at Summer holiday periods. The County Surveyor, H T.Wakelam advised the MCC Highways Committee that road traffic would be obstructed and as a result the County Council declined to agree to the proposal. In his report to the County Council Wakelam recommended that the LUT "should be told to obtain a piece of land off the highway to carry out their ideas". Robinson acknowledged the MCC's refusal on 2 March 1903, remarking that he regretted their decision.

During July 1902 Robinson had been negotiating with the First Commissioner of the Office of Works on a proposal to lay double track in Hampton Court Road where the 1900 Act authorised a single line, between Church Street, Hampton and The Green. The LUT wished to make double lines throughout the Hampton Court Loop in anticipation of heavy traffic once the whole route was completed. The negotiations with the First Commissioner, acting on behalf of the Crown, resulted in the LUT purchasing a strip of land in Bushy Park and Hampton Court Green to avoid difficult negotiations with several private owners of large properties on the side of the road flanking the river. The company had purchased Garrick's Villa in 1902 because it was found necessary to set back a high brick wall which screened the house and its grounds from Hampton Court Road, the result of this being that the LUT had to buy the whole property. The strip of land taken from Bushy Park was exchanged for a part of the grounds of the Villa and part of the frontage of the Villa was used in the widening scheme. The provision of new ornamental iron railings along the set back frontage of Bushy Park replacing a former wooden fence was done by the LUT at a cost in excess of £30,000.

Agreement had been reached with the First Commissioner of Works to widen Pantile Bridge across the Longford River at Hampton. The agreement provided for the LUT to pay £500 towards the cost of this work, which was carried out shortly after the line through Hampton opened, and the extensive widenings in High Street, Hampton and Hampton Hill were continuing up to the time the lines opened. Much work was done after the opening to Hampton Court, there having been differences of opinion between Hampton UDC and the company, the Council being dissatisfied with the progress of the work. There had been agreements for the LUT to widen these thoroughfares to 45ft and some of the work was to be carried out after legislation was obtained in 1903 and 1904.

As the route from Stanley Road junction was taken through Hampton, Hampton Court, Hampton Wick and Teddington the roads followed became progressively more rural in character as the banks of the River Thames were approached. These roads were little more than country lanes, especially those in Hampton and Hampton Court Road. In bad winter weather some of these roads became passable to traffic only with some difficulty. Many of the roads were on poor, sometimes non-existent foundations and before the track could be laid such roads had to be made up to the standards more in keeping with those in more densely populated areas. All this additional work, most of it carried out in the winter months, stretched the company's material and financial resources to the limit, and Robinson strained every nerve to secure his objective of the all-important opening of the whole loop by the Easter holiday. This meant that work on the depot and sub-station, already delayed, in its turn held up the erection of the cars and installation of the equipment in the sub-station. Bad weather early in 1903 had played its part in retarding progress but work went on apace until 22 March 1903 when a test run was made over the new route, starting from Fulwell Depot, which was now complete except for some minor details. The test car was driven by Clifton Robinson Jr., and was from one of the two batches ordered for the new group of lines. The trial was successful and the car attracted much attention in the districts through which it passed.

All was now ready for the Board of Trade inspection, which was carried out by Col. Yorke on 28 March 1903. No faults were found in the construction, which was once more pronounced to be to the highest standards. The inspection plan showed that the loop consisted of 6.93 miles of route, of which 5.530 miles was double line, 0.922 miles single and 0.365 interlacing track. Col. Yorke recommended speed limits of 12 mile/h in Hampton Court Road between the approaches to Kingston Bridge and the entrance to Bushy Park near the Greyhound Hotel, 10 mile/h along Hampton Court Road between the approach to Hampton Court Bridge and St. Alban's Bank, 8 mile/h along Stanley Road, Teddington between the Teddington boundary and the corner of Queen's Road and 6 mile/h along Kingston Road, Teddington between St. Alban's Road and Seymour Road and at all other places except for 4 mile/h on the curves at St. Alban's Church, Hampton Green and Hampton Court Bridge approach and through facing points. Compulsory stops were required at the top of the bridge across the LSWR at the east end of Broad Street, Teddington, the corner of High Street, Hampton Wick and Kingston Bridge Approach, before passing round Hampton Green curve and before passing in front of the Hampton Elementary Schools. These stops were required in both directions.

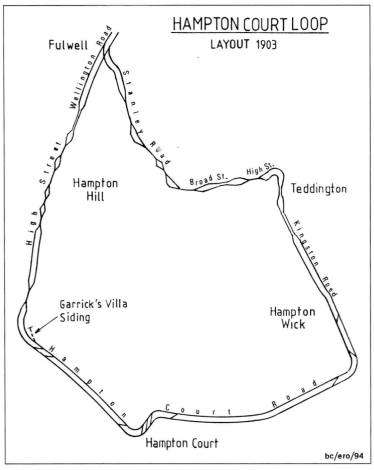

A diagram of the Hampton Court Loop as at the opening in 1903. It shows the position of the Garrick's Villa siding, which had been removed by 1911.

Although not shown on the inspection plan, two double track stubs with crossovers were laid at the right angle bend close to Hampton Court Bridge approach. These were laid in anticipation of taking the authorised line across Hampton Court Bridge. In the event this was not done but the stubs remained for many years as useful reversal points for cars reaching Hampton Court from opposite directions. Within a quarter of a mile of this point there were no fewer than five crossovers, with a further three within 200 yards near the approach to Kingston Bridge, one of these facing. The provision of these facilities was to stand the LUT in good stead from the day the lines opened, but modifications were made later in the light of experience.

Two Board of Trade certificates of fitness for the completed loop were issued. The first covered the section from the Nelson public house at Stanley Road Junction to the LSWR bridge at Fulwell and was signed on 22 November 1902. The second, signed on 30 April 1903, covered the remainder of the loop from Fulwell back to Stanley Road Junction. No reason is given for the delay in issuing the certificate for the second portion of the loop but the LUT received sanction to open the whole loop by Thursday, 2 April when the Thames Valley lines were formally opened.

The LUT had once again taken the opportunity to stage a grand occasion and this took place in a huge marquee which had been erected in the grounds of Garrick's Villa. The Company had made the house available to Robinson as his private residence, and although it had not been shown on the inspection plan a single line siding had been laid from Hampton Court Road into the grounds of the house. At some 120ft in length off the road it could accommodate three, possibly four tramcars and went into use for the first time on the occasion of the opening of the new lines.

Four new royal blue trams, built by the British Electric Car Company Ltd., arrived at Garrick's Villa on the morning of 2 April. They had conveyed some two hundred guests of the LUT from Fulwell Depot, where earlier they, the guests, had viewed the new depot and sub-station, having previously inspected the power station at Chiswick and the additions to the generating plant there. After leaving Chiswick the convoy proceeded through Brentford, Isleworth and Twickenham to Stanley Road Junction, where the Hampton Road was taken as far as Fulwell Depot. The cars passed through the depot, which allowed access from either end, into Stanley Road and continued through Teddington to Hampton Wick, traversing Hampton Court Road to arrive at Garrick's Villa, where the party disembarked and were welcomed by the recently elected Chairman of the LUT, Charles Tyson Yerkes, James Clifton Robinson, Engineer and Managing Director and Samuel White, a director and Secretary of the LUT.

The guests included Sir Charles Dalrymple, MP., Maj. L.H. Isaacs and Ernest Law, directors of the District Railway Company, Edgar Speyer and W.H. Brown of Speyer Brothers, the merchant bankers to the Underground Electric Railways Company of London Ltd. and numerous others including Members of Parliament, prominent electrical engineers and local dignitaries. After luncheon was served in the marquee in the Villa grounds Yerkes formally declared the new lines open for traffic. Yerkes was an American who had been involved in tramway and railway promotions in the USA for forty years and he told the LUT men and their guests that the LUT system was the best he had seen during that time. He thought it was too good, not necessarily for the riders, but from a commercial point of view. He expressed his view that London was backward in transport development and said that the UERL hoped to help in solving transport problems in London. The LUT was a valuable adjunct to this and he expected housing development to follow the Tube railways and the tramways to the suburbs to ease congestion in Central London. He emphasised that fares were low, and said that in his experience the flat fare system was by far the best and he hoped to do away with mileage fares on the associated UERL companies' systems.

Car No. 309 passes through High Street, Hampton Wick on its way from Hampton Court to Richmond Bridge, during the short time that cars of this type worked on the route.

(Commercial view)

Edgar Speyer replied and proposed the health of the Chairman and Clifton Robinson. Speyer was critical of British investors, who, he said were reluctant to support schemes like the underground railways, which had been largely financed by American capital. He anticipated that the UERL companies would soon require more capital and English investors would again have the opportunity to subscribe "but if the richest city in the world still could not find the money to settle its own transport problems, they would have to get it from abroad". Clifton Robinson responded by congratulating Yerkes on his first public appearance as Chairman of the LUT. He hoped the impression Yerkes had received would soon be strengthened and was convinced that the LUT had a future full of promise. He mentioned the work of George White, who had made the great effort to overcome the obstacles to electrification raised by the Kew Observatory authorities. The Company had paid out £240,000 in wages in two years and in that period some 2,300 men had been employed in the establishment and operation of the tramways. Following the conclusion of the speeches, the guests rejoined the trams and travelled over the Hampton side of the loop back to Fulwell and on to Shepherds Bush and Hammersmith, while during the afternoon public service commenced, with cars running from Shepherds Bush and Hammersmith to Hampton Court alternately every five minutes, the fare for the whole journey from either terminus being 6d, the workmen's fare 3d and the journey time 64 minutes from Hammersmith and 70 minutes from Shepherds Bush.

Some £200,000 had been spent on road and other improvements on the new route and the Tramway & Railway World commented that it was astonishing that the LUT had felt able to make such concessions to the local authorities, and that it appeared that some of these improvements were not essential to the operations of the tramways, and the responsibilities for these should have been shared by these bodies. The establishment of Twickenham as a well-planned town and the development of the road system on the Hampton Court route, especially in the Hampton district, where the roads had been the poorest in the county of Middlesex was a direct result of the coming of the tramways, while in Hampton Wick the necessary widenings had resulted in the elimination and replacement of a large amount of dilapidated property.

The day following the opening of the new route was Good Friday and once again Clifton Robinson's objective of opening a new route (with attendant Press publicity) had been achieved. In addition to the 6d ordinary fare between the London termini and Hampton Court circular tours were operated from Hammersmith and Shepherds Bush to Hampton Court and return, without change of car, at a fare of one shilling at Summer week-ends and Bank Holidays. At these times special cars for private picnic parties were operated in conjunction with the Immisch Electric Launch Company with river trips commencing from a landing stage near Garrick's Villa and the siding at the Villa accommodated the waiting trams, which were made available to passengers as "impromptu luncheon rooms". It is not known how long these special tours continued to operate after Easter 1903 but a traffic notice dated 1906 indicates that they were still operating at that time.

All these facilities proved immensely popular, and the traffic on Good Friday, 3 April 1903 over the LUT system amounted to nearly a quarter of a million passengers, the total of passengers carried over the Easter holiday period as a whole amounting to 646,000. There were now 300 cars in stock and at these holiday times cars were frequently on the road for more than eighteen hours per day. The maintenance facilities at Chiswick Depot and Works were now supplemented by additional accommodation at Fulwell Depot, which was the largest on the system and built to accommodate 189 cars.

The siding at Garrick's Villa became the subject of a dispute between the LUT and Middlesex County Council during 1903. The Council complained that the siding had been laid without authority and moreover was a danger to road traffic. Robinson wrote to the Council on 4 April 1903 in forthright terms, saying that he thought the LUT and MCC had common objectives and regretted "the captious criticisms of the County Council", and that he thought it was in the interests of both parties "that strife should cease". He went on to point out that the siding was for depot purposes and was on the company's own land and that it was "not necessary to show any such adjunct to the system on the plans". On 13 May Sir Richard Nicholson, Clerk of the MCC wrote to Robinson, again pointing out that the siding was a danger to road traffic, and Robinson replied saying that the LUT had

Crossing the widened Pantile Bridge over the Queen's River, Hampton Hill, No. 185 is seen on its way to Shepherds Bush c1904. An air of tranquility still seems to dominate the scene.
(Courtesy: National Tramway Museum)

A view showing the double track stub and crossover in line with Hampton Court Bridge c1901, BEC car No. 230 stands ready to depart for Richmond Bridge via Hampton Wick, while the Milnes car on the stub at the end of the line from Hampton awaits return to Hammersmith.
(Commercial view)

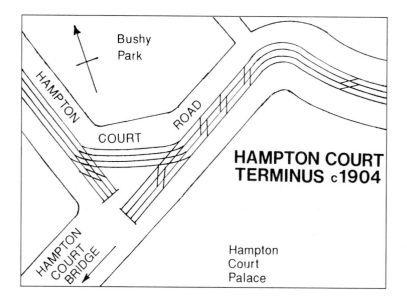

The Hampton Court terminus layout as seen c1904. The ambition to extend the tracks over the bridge was never fulfilled.

widened the road at Garrick's Villa for the purposes of the siding, which had been laid "to run in an occasional car which might be used privately on special occasions".

The MCC Highways Committee resolved on 6 June 1903 to tell the LUT that they were still of the opinion that plans should have been submitted for that part of the siding which was on the road not on LUT property. Robinson pointed out that Col. Yorke had inspected the line on 28 March and the Board of Trade had raised no objection. The matter was raised in the County Council again on 2 December by Cty. Cllr. De Wette. On this date the Highways Committee advised the County Council that the matter should be left as it stood, and the Committee "could not give any reasons". Evidently the MCC's objection to the siding was discussed at the Board of Trade and may have been the reason for the certificate for the route between Fulwell station and Stanley Road Junction via Hampton Court being delayed until 30 April 1903.

Shortly after the Hampton Court services commenced Hampton Wick UDC complained about fares. At the Council's meeting on 27 April it was reported that on Sundays and Bank Holidays the Richmond Bridge trams were running only one way round the loop. The Council complained that this resulted in a higher fare being charged between Richmond and Kingston bridges, and it appears from this that the cars from Richmond Bridge were all running to Hampton Court by way of Hampton and Hampton Hill at these times. The LUT stated that cars ran in one direction only round the loop at these times until further widenings could be carried out and more single and interlacing sections could be doubled. There appears to have been no alteration to fare scales.

While much of the single track on the Thames Valley lines authorised in the 1900 Act had been laid as double by agreement with the Board of Trade and the local authorities, a considerable amount of widenings and doubling still remained to be carried out, and for this further legislation was required. The company's Act of 11 August 1903 authorised the purchase of lands in Twickenham, Teddington and Hampton, which in many cases amounted to no more than a narrow strip along a frontage at various points along the route. The Act also empowered the purchase

Car No. 292 coming from Richmond Bridge and No. 303 from New Malden meet at the junction on the west side of Kingston Bridge. Both are bound for Hampton Court.

(Courtesy: A.D. Packer)

Standing outside the 'White Hart Hotel', Hampton Wick to pick up passengers is No. 212, one of twenty-five cars built by the British Electric Car Co. It is on the Richmond Bridge – Hampton Court via Teddington service. (Commercial view)

of land and buildings on the north side of High Street, Teddington and the east side of High Street, Hampton Hill and the powers for compulsory purchase of these lands were valid for three years from 11 August 1903. Further powers were granted in the Act of 15 August 1904 to acquire strips of land in Twickenham, Teddington and Hampton, to be exercised within three years of passing the Act . The widening and doublings were carried out over a number of years until 4 November 1909 when only 130 yards of single line remained in Richmond Road, Twickenham, 129 yards of single line in The Green and 85 yards in Heath Road. The single line in Richmond Road remained to the end of tramway operation as did that in The Green, while the interlacing track in Heath Road was doubled in May 1931. At the time the doublings were being carried out up to 1909 the line across Pantile Bridge over the Longford (or Queen's) River in High Street, Hampton was doubled, the LUT contributed £500 towards the cost of the work.

Hampton UDC had opposed the 1904 LUT Bill, which contained proposals for additional lines in Middlesex with the clauses covering land acquisitions, but withdrew their opposition upon the LUT agreeing to widen High Street, Hampton Hill to 45ft for a distance of 30 yards between the Brewery Tap public house and the Coffee Tavern. The company also undertook to pay forty guineas to the Council, this being the costs of the Council's opposition to the Bill. At the same time the company undertook to carry out a further widening in the High Street, between Pantile Bridge and Devonshire Villa, again to 45ft, the first of these widenings to be carried out within 18 months after the passing of the Act and the second twelve months following acquisition of the land by the company. Costs of the acquisitions and works covered in the 1903 and 1904 Acts amounted to £122,700.

At a meeting of the LUT directors on 19 March 1905 it was stated that Twickenham UDC was pressing the company to erect a shelter and waiting room at the London Road – York Street junction. The Council was making extensive improvements at the junction and Robinson had arranged with the Council to alter the track and curves to accord with the street improvements. Discussions between Robinson and the Council resulted in the Council agreeing to waive their request for the shelter if the company would make a lump sum payment of £250. Following some discussion the directors agreed.

The heavy traffic on the Hampton Court lines soon made itself felt on the track, and following early initiatives on the part of Ealing Borough Council, Twickenham UDC raised the question of noise and track maintenance with the Board of Trade during 1905. Extra maintenance gangs were deployed on the lines concerned but Twickenham UDC made a further complaint in June 1909, followed on 14 July when Hampton Wick and Teddington UDCs joined forces with complaints about the track, Hampton Wick also complaining about the condition of the cars. By February 1910 Albert Stanley had assumed the mantle of Clifton Robinson and Stanley wrote to the Board of Trade on 13 August saying that all cars were going through the shops for systematic overhaul and the track was being improved. Teddington UDC asked the Board of Trade to inspect the track in their district and Col. Yorke visited the town on 26 July, finding the track worn, the rails badly corrugated and paving in poor condition, but conditions were "not dangerous".

A widening had been outstanding for several years in Teddington, although all track had been doubled earlier. The directors completed the purchase of the St. Albans Club premises to facilitate this on 26 July 1911 and agreed to hand the strip of land to the Council for them to carry out the work. No record of the costs involved has been seen. Under an agreement of 20 April 1900 the company and Twickenham UDC had agreed that as part of the road widening scheme in Heath Road the Council would acquire the necessary land and the company would pay half the cost of the widening. The LUT's share of this amounted to £2,000 and on 12 February 1913 the directors agreed to proceed accordingly.

Clifton Robinson had left Garrick's Villa by May 1910 and the property was later sold. At a date prior to 1912 the turnout into the grounds was removed and some alterations to the track layout on the Hampton Court Loop were made by about 1914, notably the removal of three of the five crossovers originally situated close to the approach to Hampton Court Bridge.

This view, probably taken c1911 in High Street, Hampton Wick, near the 'Swan Hotel', shows car 189 in a simplified livery, bound for Richmond Bridge.   (Commercial view)

CHAPTER NINE

KINGSTON AND WIMBLEDON

The ancient town of Kingston lies on the Surrey side of the River Thames and faces the town of Hampton Wick on the north side; adjacent to the latter are Bushy Park and also Hampton Court Park, while at about a mile to the west Hampton Court Palace lies close to the north bank of the river near Hampton Court Bridge, on the opposite side of which the Moleseys and Dittons are among the most northerly of the pleasant Surrey suburbs. Kingston is approached from the Middlesex side of the Thames by way of Kingston Bridge, a handsome structure which leads directly into the town by way of Clarence Street, which is almost at the centre of the shopping and administrative district. To the south the town is bounded by Surbiton, a small residential town in the early years of the twentieth century, with Tolworth to the south-east, while to the north of Kingston are Ham Common, Petersham and Richmond. East of the town the erstwhile urban district of The Maldens & Coombe commences 1¼ miles east of Kingston Bridge, and the road from the centre of Kingston passes via Kingston Road, Burlington Road, West Barnes Lane and Coombe Lane to Raynes Park, where the boundary with the old borough of Wimbledon is reached near Raynes Park London & South Western Railway station. The centre of Kingston is situated at a distance of twelve miles to the west of London Bridge.

Kingston received its first charter as a market town from King John in the year 1200 and seven Saxon kings were crowned on the Coronation Stone next to the Guild Hall. In 1481 King Edward IV granted the town a charter of incorporation as a borough and in 1927 the status of a Royal Borough was conferred upon the town by King George V. Kingston is one of only four Royal Boroughs in England and Wales. Later, in 1965, as a result of the London Government Act of 1963 the new Royal Borough of Kingston-upon-Thames was created which was enlarged by taking in the existing boroughs of Surbiton and Malden. Kingston was, up to 1965, the county town of Surrey, but became a part of the new Greater London Council area in that year. Some parts of the administration of the county of Surrey remain in the town to the present day.

Between Kingston and Wimbledon the road passes through what are now thickly populated suburbs, but which in the mid-nineteenth century were small settlements where market gardens and other semi-rural activities predominated. Housing development was slow until the later years of the century. The town of Wimbledon is bordered by Merton to the south, Malden to the west, Putney and Wandsworth to the north and Mitcham to the east. The extensive open spaces of Wimbledon Common lie to the north and the famous landmark of Caesar's Camp was built on the Common between the years 750 and 250 BC. Wimbledon started to build up from 1860 and some industrial development took place in South Wimbledon and Merton around the turn of the century. Wimbledon is probably best known as the headquarters of the All-England Lawn Tennis Championships, which were first held in 1870, under the aegis of the All-England Croquet and Lawn Tennis Club, formed in 1868. The Club's first headquarters were established in Worple Road in 1869 and now occupy an extensive site in Church Road.

From about 1865 horse 'bus services developed in the built-up areas around Kingston and Wimbledon, and while Kingston proper was not reached by the London & South Western Railway until 1863, the line from Waterloo had reached Woking on 21 May 1838, the station at the then-small settlement of Surbiton opening on the same day, together with those at Wimbledon and New Malden. The station at Surbiton was at first called "Kingston on Railway" but in 1840 it was re-named as Surbiton. From the time horse 'buses started to operate in the Kingston and Wimbledon areas competition between them and the LSWR was intense. Fares on the LSWR were high, one example being 9d from Kingston to Richmond, the omnibus proprietors charging 6d for this journey. Despite the competition services provided by both forms of transport were slow and infrequent.

Kingston Corporation had determined that it should be the tramway authority for the town and submitted a Bill for lines in the town on 20 November 1899 for the 1900 Parliamentary Session. Following a brief consideration of the proposals the Bill was thrown out in March 1900 on the grounds that it was insufficiently comprehensive. The Corporation still insisted that it should be the tramway authority for the Borough and should have the necessary powers to exercise that authority. Wimbledon Urban District Council considered promoting tramways in the town and surrounding areas in 1900, and in 1901 drew up a scheme covering a group of lines, one of which was planned to meet the future London County Council electric tramway at Tooting.

As related in an earlier chapter, the London United Tramways, having obtained powers in 1900 for the Hampton Court Loop group of lines, was now poised to take the leap across the Thames into Surrey with the ultimate objective of entering London from the south. The company's Bill for the 1901 Session was placed before Parliament in November 1900. This was a comprehensive measure for lines into and within the County of London. In the County of Surrey the Bill contained proposals to construct a line from Hampton Court across Hampton Court Bridge and through Bridge Road, East Molesey, Esher Road, Embercourt Road, Station Road and across High Street, Thames Ditton and along a new street to be constructed between High Street and Portsmouth Avenue, Portsmouth Road, Brighton Road, Surbiton, Claremont Road and Surbiton Road, reaching Kingston at Penrhyn Road and passing through St. James's Road, Eden Street and Clarence Street and across Kingston Bridge to rejoin the authorised line at Hampton Wick, thus forming a loop making two crossings of the Thames. These sections of line passed through the urban districts of East & West Molesey, Esher & The Dittons, Surbiton and the Borough of Kingston respectively for a distance of 5.112 miles, of which 4.829 miles was double line and 0.284 miles single track.

From the centre of Kingston, commencing by a junction with the above line in Eden Street the Bill provided for a line along London Road and Kingston Hill to terminate at the boundary with the urban district of The Maldens & Coombe to the south of George Road, a distance of 0.819 miles, of which all was to be double line except a 22-yard single line terminal stub. From The Maldens & Coombe boundary in Norbiton at the junction of Kingston Road and Malden Road (now Coombe Road) a line was projected through Kingston Road, Cambridge Road, London Road and Richmond Road to the northern boundary of Kingston with Richmond at Ham, consisting of 3.072 miles of route of which three miles was double line and 125 yards single, and a branch left Richmond Road via King's Road to terminate at the Kingston Gate of Richmond Park, for a distance of 0.702 miles, all double line except for the terminal stub.

In Surbiton, from the Kingston-Surbiton boundary in Claremont Road a line branched by way of Claremont Road, Victoria Road, St. Mark's Hill and Ewell Road as far as the Red Lion Hotel in Ewell Road immediately south-east of Red Lion Lane (now Red Lion Road), Tolworth. This was projected as 3.031 route miles, all double line except the 22-yard single line stub at Tolworth terminus. From the Tolworth branch the line branched again at the junction of Beaconsfield Road with Ewell Road into Ditton Road and Hook Road (then known as Brighton Road) to terminate in Hook Village, 1.380 miles from the junction of Ewell and Beaconsfield Roads, double line except for a 22-yard terminal stub in Hook Village.

The Act authorising this complex of lines received the Royal Assent on 17 August 1901. However, before this milestone was reached many hurdles had to be surmounted. Kingston Corporation, despite the rejection of its own Bill in March 1900 still harboured ambitions to control tramway operation in the town and had succeeded in gaining considerable local support for this view. The Corporation had considered making a further attempt to obtain powers to construct and own tramways and, if not able to secure powers to work them, to construct and own them and lease them to a company for operation. The LUT Act covered the same ground as the Corporation's 1900 Bill with minor differences and included some lines and extensions additional to the Corporation's measure.

The hardest battle was in Kingston itself; some of the other districts did not raise serious opposition. The Surbiton Commissioners (later Urban District Council) expressed criticisms on matters of detail but did not seriously oppose, while The Maldens & Coombe UDC followed the more usual local authority line by opposing the proposals as a matter of principle and demanding expensive street widenings and other improvements as the price for their consent to the Bill, as did the two urban districts of East & West Molesey and Esher & The Dittons. These last two bodies, whose roads at that time were mostly ill-kept and unlit country lanes, demanded extensive widenings, provision of footpaths at points where none had previously existed, kerbing, channelling and wood paving. As in the case of the earlier LUT schemes, such demands were acceded to and given the force of law in the Act. Exceptionally heavy expenditure was called for in Kingston where numerous shops, houses, forecourts and other properties had to be acquired, frequently at inflated prices, wholly or in part for these purposes.

Kingston Corporation was empowered to require the company to work a service of cars at not less than ten-minute intervals on the lines in the town between the hours of 8am and 10pm at fares not exceeding one penny on the routes between Surbiton station and Ham Boundary, Surbiton station and Kingston Hill and the

An early view of Kingston Bridge from the riverside, before the tramway was extended over it.   (Courtesy: Kingston Museum & Heritage Service)

whole of the line from the Middlesex side of Kingston Bridge at Hampton Wick as far as the boundary with The Maldens & Coombe at Surbiton, a distance of 1.350 miles. In addition the company was obliged to charge not more than one penny between any two points in the borough or between Surbiton station and Hampton Wick, or between any point in the borough and Surbiton station or Hampton Wick if a through service existed between these points. The usual half fares for workmen at one halfpenny per mile were delineated in the Act but Esher & The Dittons UDC obtained a clause allowing workmen's fares in their district at a farthing (¼d) per mile with a minimum of one penny and a return fare of 1d for a distance of under two miles.

Further provisions for the lines in Kingston insisted that all trams used in the town should be "of the best modern type" and to the Corporation's approval and that the street widenings and improvements in the Act should be completed and construction of all the authorised lines in Kingston completed and opened at the same time. Wood paving was called for throughout, and where the tramways passed in front of schools, churches, chapels and other public buildings the LUT was obliged to pave at its own expense the whole width of the carriageway in wood blocks.

The provision for compulsory purchase by the Corporation under section 43 of the Tramways Act was varied to the extent that the Corporation could first exercise its power to purchase the lines in the borough from six months after the expiry of twenty-five years after the passing of the Act, i.e., 17 February 1927 or six months after the expiry of each subsequent period of seven years. The same terms applied to the lines in the urban districts of Surbiton, The Maldens & Coombe, Esher & The Dittons and East & West Molesey. The purchase terms were later modified by agreement in the case of some of the authorities. An agreement giving effect to the arrangements in respect of the Kingston lines was signed by the LUT and the Corporation on 18 April 1901.

In common with the Middlesex authorities the Surrey councils demanded payments in the form of wayleaves. Kingston Corporation enforced payments on a rising scale at annual rates of £225 for the first five years, £450 for the next ten years and £700 for ten years thereafter. The Maldens & Coombe UDC demanded an annual payment of £1,500 and part of this was to defray the cost of a local improvement anywhere in the district, whether or not on a tram route. Esher & Dittons UDC asked for an annual sum of £150 in respect of the mileage in their district and the East & West Molesey demand was £100 per annum. Surbiton UDC asked for an annual payment of £100 and Surrey County Council, over some of whose main roads the LUT was authorised to work, made an annual charge of £100 per mile in respect of the 4.87 miles concerned. Some of the wayleave charges became payable following the passing of the Bill, others from the times the lines were constructed.

As was the case with the earlier routes the various authorities in Surrey had other demands to make of the LUT. One common requirement was for street lighting to be provided and maintained at the company's expense where none had previously existed. The Maldens & Coombe UDC asked for an electric lamp to be placed upon the drinking fountain column or a standard opposite the Norbiton Park Hotel at New Malden. The company was obliged to supply current for this lamp, free of charge, when the trams were running during the hours of darkness. Other improvements obtained by this body were the filling in and piping of the ditch on the south side of Kingston Road, New Malden, between the LSWR bridge and the Kingston boundary, and the forming of a footpath and kerbing on this section, and when the road below the bridge was lowered the company was obliged to construct a twelve-inch clean water drain to debouch into the Hogg's Mill River.

Esher & Dittons UDC made several expensive demands; they required the parts of Ember Lane, Embercourt Road and Station Road, Thames Ditton which lay in their district and would be traversed by the tramways, together with the new road to be built between High Street, Thames Ditton and Portsmouth Avenue to be made up to a width of forty-five feet. Curves at right-angled turnings of the line were to be eased to provide a radius and footpath of not less than twenty feet; an elevated path in Station Road to be lowered to match the levels of the rest of the path in that road. At the cross-roads at Thames Ditton LSWR station the gradients below the railway arches were to be modified to the satisfaction of the UDC surveyor and water mains at these points were required to be "efficiently protected from damage due to the passage over such roads by the steam rollers of the council". The Council also called upon the company to construct the new road between High Street, Thames Ditton and Portsmouth Avenue to the standards laid down in the Private Streets Act of 1892 and to maintain it for twelve months from the date on which it opened to public traffic.

Surbiton UDC made few demands against the company other than the near-universal one for wood paving, some widenings and improvements to kerbing and footpaths, but Surrey County Council, as the authority for main roads in the district required extensive widenings in Claremont Road, Brighton Road and Hook Road, where, in the last case the carriageway was to be widened to 24ft., these works to be executed by the LUT before lines opened to public traffic.

The urban district of East and West Molesey was, at the turn of the century, rural and sparsely populated at the Surrey side of Hampton Court Bridge, and the roads there were mostly country lanes suitable to carry only light traffic. Here, extensive widenings were demanded in Bridge Road, at the Hampton Court Bridge approach. The LUT route in the UDC's area was less than half a mile in extent and the UDC insisted that these narrow and ill-made streets be widened to provide a minimum 9ft 6in between the outer rails and the kerbs. Moreover the bridges across the Ember and Mole rivers in Esher and Bridge Roads respectively were required to be widened at estimated costs of £4,000.

At the turn of the century Hampton Court Bridge had become the responsibility of the Middlesex and Surrey County Councils. This old bridge was in a very poor condition and it was estimated that expenditure of some £30,000 was required to put it into a serviceable condition. A similar amount was required to widen Kingston Bridge for a double track tramway, and another bridge on these routes, Windows (or Winters) Bridge across the Rythe, a small stream feeding into the Thames at Thames Ditton required widening at a cost of £2,500.

The old bridge over the Thames at Hampton Court was unsuitable for tram tracks, and proved to be the barrier to tramway extension into Surrey from the Hampton Court terminus.
(Commercial view)

149

The company's hard-fought battle with Kingston Corporation had started in 1900, despite Parliament's rejection of the Corporation's Bill. As early as March 1899 the LUT suggested that they might take a lease of the lines if the Corporation gained their powers, and the Corporation's Tramways Committee continued to stress the importance of the municipality being the owners of any tramways in the town. The Corporation wanted a tramway system in the town, but a resolution was adopted to oppose the LUT Bill. The Corporation envisaged the possibility of a second attempt to obtain powers and a powerful campaign was mounted against the LUT proposals. Numerous public meetings were held, at some of which passions ran high as the twin factions pressed their respective arguments.

The LUT mounted an impressive campaign. Clifton Robinson had mastered the arts of publicity and persuasion during his battles with the Middlesex and London authorities. At a ratepayers' meeting called to discuss the Corporation's proposal to make a fresh application for powers and to oppose the LUT Bill there were rowdy scenes as opposing factions howled down their opponents. It transpired at this meeting that a telegram had been received by a respected figure in the town, Dr. E.W. Finny, assuring him of 500 LUT debentures if he refrained from supporting a motion to oppose the LUT Bill. This was unsigned and found to be a forgery. Dr. Finny had the distinction of being seven times Mayor of Kingston. A resolution to authorise the Corporation to re-apply for tramway powers was lost but another to oppose the LUT Bill was carried.

The battle for Kingston was nearly won. Early in 1901 a ratepayers' poll was heavily in favour of the LUT scheme and opposition in the neighbouring districts tailed off. The Bill passed through its remaining stages and received the Royal Assent on 17 August 1901.

There followed a period during which construction of the Twickenham and Hampton Court lines commenced. The LUT directors were meanwhile considering extensions to the Surrey lines in the direction of Wimbledon, Epsom, Sutton, Mitcham, Croydon, Esher, Petersham and Richmond, with extensions in the County of London from Shepherds Bush to Marble Arch and from Hammersmith Broadway across Hammersmith Bridge to Barnes and Richmond. Other promoters were interested in these areas at this time and details of their proposed schemes will be found in another chapter. After consideration of prospective traffic development many of the proposed extensions and new lines were dropped as it was thought that they were of a semi-rural character and likely to remain unprofitable for the foreseeable future. Accordingly the scope of the 1902 Bill was scaled down and placed before Parliament in November 1901. This chapter is concerned with the lines in the Kingston and Wimbledon areas and lines in the Bill outside these areas are described in Chapter 10.

The 1902 Bill sought powers to extend the line authorised in the 1901 Act from the Kingston-Maldens & Coombe boundary at Norbiton along Kingston Road, New Malden, Burlington Road, West Barnes Lane and Coombe Lane, Raynes Park, entering Wimbledon via Pepys Road and continuing into Worple Road for most of its length as far as Raymond Road. This section passed through the urban districts of Maldens & Coombe, Merton and Wimbledon, consisting of 2.833 miles of route of which 2.395 miles was double and 0.437 miles single track.

The main route through Wimbledon and Merton commenced in Wimbledon Hill Road opposite Mansel Road and followed Wimbledon Hill Road, The Broadway, Merton Road, High Street, Merton and High Street, Colliers Wood as far as Longley Road. This route passed through the urban district of Wimbledon and the rural district of Croydon, and consisted of 2.168 miles of track of which 1.731 miles was double and 0.378 miles single line. At the time this legislation was enacted the whole of this mileage was in the county of Surrey but a later revision of boundaries resulted in the first eighty-two yards of track at Longley Road terminus being transferred to the county of London and the Metropolitan Borough of Wandsworth. Other alterations to the municipal borders resulted in the parishes of Merton and Mitcham and Colliers Wood being absorbed in a new urban district of Merton & Morden and the whole of the area, except the small piece at Longley Road is now absorbed in the present-day London Borough of Merton.

Worple Road was connected to Wimbledon Hill Road by a single line loop leaving Worple Road at Raymond Road and turning into Francis Grove and St. George's Road and these single line connections totalled 0.189 miles A branch left High Street, Merton at Haydon's Road, passing along that road and Plough Lane as far as the London county boundary near the Plough public house at Summerstown and close to a future LCC electric tramway in Garratt Lane, Wandsworth. The whole of this route was double track and totalled 1.247 miles.

The 1902 Bill was opposed in Parliament by the London & South Western Railway Company on the grounds of competition. Their Counsel said competition from trams was costing them £10,000 annually and cited examples of heavy expenditure by the company on improvements to their services. There was little other opposition to the Bill and it finally received the Royal Assent on 8 August 1902. With these powers secured a period of intense activity ensued, with the object of completing the Hampton Court lines in time for the Easter 1903 Bank Holiday. Robinson and the LUT directors reviewed the costs involved in completing mileage for which the powers were running out and following an appraisal of the costs of constructing the first sections of the Surrey lines, Robinson wrote to the LUT Chairman, Charles Tyson Yerkes, on 18 July 1902. Yerkes was also Chairman of the Underground Electric Railways of London Ltd., the parent company of the LUT. In his letter, Robinson referred to the recent opening of the Hampton Court lines "which had absorbed all our energies for a considerable time", and said that the extension from Southall to Uxbridge and the new line linking Hammersmith to Uxbridge Road were under construction and being pressed forward with all speed.

In his letter Robinson stressed the importance to the LUT of the Surrey lines, which would meet the newly-electrified lines of the London County Council at Tooting and a future LCC electric line at Summerstown, pointing out that the only outlet in Surrey and the Thames Valley for the millions of passengers to be carried over the LCC electric lines would be over the LUT lines from the London-Surrey boundary at Wimbledon. He also stressed the fact that the Surrey lines would give the LUT a great advantage over the LCC when that body's power to purchase the LUT lines in Hammersmith arose in 1909. He mentioned the heavy and increasing summer traffic on the new Hampton Court lines which would see little traffic in the winter months if left as they stood. Connected across the river with large and growing districts, a valuable local and cross-river traffic would develop and go far to counterbalance the loss of summer traffic. He said the lines along the new routes

The windmill on Wimbledon Common as seen from Windmill Road. The site of the N.R.A. shooting butts was nearby. (Courtesy: Merton Library Service)

were all of a high-class residential nature and he looked for a very large and increasing traffic from them which would more than justify the capital expenditure involved. He also said that a large amount of money was still being spent on the Hampton Court Loop street widenings and improvements, with the object of doubling the tracks over the whole route.

Robinson reminded Yerkes that annual payments to the local authorities became payable at varying times, some from the opening of the lines and others began from the passing of the respective Acts. The date for completion of the Kingston group of lines was 17 February 1905, those in Surbiton, the Moleseys, the Maldens, Esher & The Dittons 17 August 1905 and the lines in Wimbledon and Merton authorised by the 1902 Act, 8 August 1906. Robinson concluded by saying that he thought Yerkes would be convinced that early construction of these and other lines described elsewhere in this book was of utmost importance to the company and that immediate steps should be taken to enable him to go forward with the necessary work. Much preliminary work needed to be done before track laying could commence, and he hoped Yerkes would find the time to give the matter his earnest consideration with a view to the preparation of a comprehensive plan for early construction of the authorised lines, "and, concurrently with the practical work, the provision of the capital entailed".

Robinson convinced Yerkes and, through him, the LUT and UERL directors together with the companies' financiers, Speyer Brothers, of the importance of completing the lines and after estimates had been prepared and considered the LUT directors resolved on 17 March 1904 to increase the company's capital to £2,500,000 by an issue of 50,000 £10 shares, half of which were Ordinary and half preference. The LUT shares were still a good market, the new issue was quickly subscribed and capital for the new works secured. Meanwhile, a small committee consisting of Robinson and Walter Abbott was formed, to which George White was co-opted in an advisory capacity. The function of this committee was to oversee the construction of the lines. Abbott was a director of both the LUT and the UERL.

A preliminary estimate dated July 1903 covered construction of the Kingston routes authorised in 1901 and the continuation of the line from New Malden on to Raynes Park and Wimbledon to Tooting and Summerstown authorised in the 1902 Act. This first estimate provided for road works, permanent way and overhead construction, provision of additional sub-stations and the necessary electrical equipment, a depot in Wimbledon, acquisition of lands and the provision of one hundred new cars of the same type as those bought for the Hampton Court route. £30,000 was estimated to widen Kingston Bridge, £10,000 to strengthen Hampton Court Bridge and £6,500 to widen the bridges across the Rythe at Thames Ditton and across the Mole and Ember rivers at East Molesey. The intention at this time was to construct the whole of the lines authorised in 1901 and 1902 together with the connecting line between Brentford and Hanwell authorised in 1898, and the grand total of this work was £813,704. By mid-1904 the estimates had been revised and the figures for the Brentford-Hanwell line removed from the total and for a proposed 100 new cars revised, reducing the total estimate from £813,704 to £789,288, The estimates were subjected to detail modification from time to time and it is evident that the LUT directors and, perhaps, the company's financiers were pressing Robinson to make reductions wherever possible in the projected expenditure.

The company was discussing with the authorities responsible for the Thames bridges the conditions under which the tramways would be constructed on the bridges at Kingston and Hampton Court. Kingston Bridge at that time was owned by the Kingston Municipal Charities and Hampton Court Bridge jointly by the Middlesex and Surrey county councils. The LUT and the Joint Middlesex-Surrey County Councils Committee responsible for the latter bridge had come to an agreement whereby the LUT would strengthen the bridge to carry the tramway and was liable to contribute £10,000 towards the work on the bridge before the Committee was liable for any expense. However, a meeting of Middlesex County

Council on 16 March 1904 heard that the LUT had written to the county council saying that they were about to construct the tramways across the two bridges, and that the county councils were about to confer on the matter. On the same day, H.T. Wakelam, the Middlesex county surveyor, reported to the MCC, saying that the bridge at Hampton Court would have to be both strengthened and widened before trams could run across it. He recommended that it was possible to satisfactorily strengthen and widen the bridge but the best course would be to completely rebuild it to a width of fifty feet. The MCC accordingly resolved that consent to construct tramways across both Hampton Court and Kingston bridges be withheld until they had been rebuilt and widened to the satisfaction of both county councils.

This effectively ruled out immediate construction of the lines across Hampton Court Bridge but in the case of Kingston Bridge the county councils were not the owners and had little, if any, power to give or withhold consent to the LUT proposals. On 26 July 1904 Robinson met the Joint MCC/SCC Bridges Committee. He pointed out that the tramways across Hampton Court Bridge were due to be completed by 17 August 1904 and an extension of time to complete the work was being considered. He asked for the question of the line across Hampton Court Bridge to be held over until after the Long Vacation, i.e., until October.

Robinson submitted a scheme for widening Kingston Bridge which involved leaving the main structure intact and constructing footpaths on cantilevers on each side of the bridge, each 7ft wide to give a carriageway of 27ft wide and a total width of 41ft. The Committee decided that this scheme was "not to be entertained" but the final decision lay with the Trustees of the Kingston Municipal Charities. That Hampton Court Bridge would have to be reconstructed is evidenced by the fact that the old structure had deteriorated and was already becoming unfit for heavy traffic at the time the LUT gained their 1901 Act. The decking consisted of oak planking covered with asphalt, which was in poor condition and a heavy barge had come adrift earlier and damaged one of the dolphins. The Joint Bridges Committee was anxious to obtain control of Kingston Bridge but the Bridge Trustees had not come to agreement for the transfer of the bridge to the county councils and the Committee resolved to recommend the two councils to take steps to obtain ownership of the bridge.

Robinson appears to have been in error in saying that the powers for certain lines in the 1901 Act were due to expire on 17 August 1904 as the Act states that these powers were due to expire three and a half years after passing the Act in the case of the Kingston lines and four years in the case of the rest of the lines in the Act. An Act of 15 August 1904 extended the time by two years in each case, to 17 February and 17 August 1907 respectively.

The LUT directors met on 20 October 1904 and approved estimates, plans and schedules for construction of the Kingston and Wimbledon extensions. On 4 November they resolved to proceed with construction of the Kingston and Wimbledon extensions authorised in the 1901 and 1902 Acts, with the exception of the section between the east side of Windows Bridge at Thames Ditton to the Moleseys and across Hampton Court Bridge to the line in Hampton on the Middlesex side of the Thames. On the advice of the committee appointed to oversee construction of these lines tenders for the work by outside contractors had been obtained and on 19 December Robinson reported on these to the directors. Meanwhile, at the same time Kingston Corporation pressed their demand for superior cars to be used on the lines in the borough, while The Maldens & Coombe UDC asked for additional widenings in Kingston Road, New Malden and for double track to be laid below the LSWR bridge in that road. This council complained to the Board of Trade that the LUT had sent out notices of intention to start construction too close to the Christmas holiday in order to minimise the time available in which to lodge objections.

The Trustees of the Kingston Municipal Charities declined to agree to proposals by the MCC and SCC to purchase Kingston Bridge and the charities' estates and funds and went against the wishes of the councils by coming to an agreement with the LUT allowing construction of a double track tramway across the bridge without any widening or alteration of the bridge structure. A survey of Hampton Court Bridge confirmed the precarious condition of this bridge and this effectively blocked completion of the connection across the Thames to the lines at Hampton Court, and since Windows Bridge, across the Rythe at Thames Ditton also required widening for trams, together with the two bridges across the Mole and the Ember at East Molesey the company decided to construct the line only as far as the east side of Windows Bridge.

The decision taken on 4 November 1904 to construct the lines in the 1901 and 1902 Acts did not remain unchanged. As well as the section west of Windows Bridge another short section was removed from the construction programme, this being between the Kingston-Richmond boundary at Ham in Richmond Road and King's Road from which point a short branch led to Richmond Park Gates at the end of King's Road. The directors had concluded that the authorised section beyond King's Road was of little value as it stood, while reasonable holiday traffic was expected to develop on the Richmond Park Gates branch. At the same time discussions were proceeding with Wimbledon UDC on the council's requirements for construction of the lines in their district. One of the council's demands was the construction of a new sewerage system in the streets through which the tramways were to be laid. Pending settlement of this the LUT directors postponed arrangements in hand for the lines in the 1902 Act and pressed forward work on the Kingston group of lines.

Up to the construction of the Southall-Uxbridge line and the line connecting Hammersmith with Uxbridge Road in 1904, all the LUT electric lines had been built by the company's own workforce under the direct supervision of Robinson, large numbers of men being engaged as and when required to carry out the work, The committee appointed to oversee construction of the Surrey lines had advised the directors to obtain tenders from contractors to construct the lines in Kingston

The Mayor of Kingston-upon-Thames, Ald. H.C. Minnitt, drives the first pick in Kingston Road at the Kingston – Malden boundary on 3 April 1905. Also present were the Chairman of Maldens & Coombe UDC and James Clifton Robinson.   (Photo: LUT)

154

and through the Maldens to Raynes Park, together with the line linking Brentford and Hanwell via Boston Road.

After consideration of a number of tenders contracts were awarded for the construction and equipment of the line from Hampton Wick across Kingston Bridge through Kingston and Malden to Raynes Park LSWR station together with the branches to Windows Bridge, Thames Ditton, Tolworth and Kingston Hill. This contract covered the Richmond Road line only as far as King's Road and the short branch along King's Road to Richmond Park Gates and did not include the 0.375 miles to the authorised terminus at Ham Boundary. The contract was awarded to J.G.White & Co, Ltd., on 1 March 1905 in the sum of £170,777, which figure included the Boston Road line, which had been estimated at £38,999. The work consisted of track and overhead construction, and after failure of some of the earlier track construction to stand up to the wear imposed by heavy bogie cars and frequent services, the specification included the use of 100 and 106lb/yard rails to an improved metallurgical standard, stronger track bed and heavy girder rail joints. The contract was later amended to cover an additional £28,862 to cover extra work involved in altering the positions of some gas and water mains.

Contracts for cabling along the new routes were awarded to W.T. Henley's Telegraph Works Co. Ltd., on 8 March 1905, covering the supply and installation of high and low tension and telephone cables from the Middlesex side of Kingston Bridge across the bridge, through Kingston and the Maldens to Raynes Park together with the branches to Kingston Hill, Thames Ditton, Tolworth and Ham Boundary. The total value of these contracts was £41,444. Work on these new lines commenced at the Kingston-Maldens boundary by J.G. White & Co. Ltd., on 3 April 1905 when, following speeches by Clifton Robinson, the Mayor of Kingston, Alderman H.C. Minnitt and the Chairman of The Maldens & Coombe UDC, Councillor A. Streeter, Ald. Minnitt drove the first pick, saying "with this pick we bury the hatchet", and after some short speeches some four hundred members of of J.G. White & Co's workforce commenced work. Earlier, on 27 March, Henley's had started the work of cable laying.

Shortly after the main construction contracts were placed tenders for the supply of cars, equipment for sub-stations and other works were considered. When the first estimates for the Surrey lines were produced the addition of a hundred new trams was contemplated, which was later reduced to eighty. Both Kingston and Wimbledon councils had insisted upon the use of the latest pattern of trams in their districts but the specifications attached to the early estimates provided for vehicles to the exact designs and dimensions of the 150 cars purchased in 1902 for the Hampton Court routes. The insistence of the Surrey councils on later designs resulted in Clifton Robinson relaxing his rigid adherence to open-top vehicles, and quotations were sought from a number of car builders, including the Electric Railway & Tramway Carriage Works Ltd., of Preston. The last estimate for 80 cars was meanwhile reduced to cover forty, to a superior specification, with open-balcony top-covers and plain arch ceilings in the lower saloons. At the time these estimates were under consideration the Electric Railway & Tramway Carriage Works Ltd., was engaged in negotiations to take over Geo. F. Milnes & Co., and the contract for the forty new cars was awarded on 27 July 1905 to the newly incorporated United Electric Car Company Ltd. The order for forty bodies, at the price of £413 each was to be fulfilled by delivering ten bodies by 10 October 1905, ten by 25 October, ten by 10 November and the remainder by 25 November.

The contract for the cars' electrical equipment was awarded to the British Westinghouse Electric & Manufacturing Co. Ltd., on 15 September 1905, for controllers, motors, trolley equipment and switches, for the sum of £8,545 and at the same time an order was placed with the Bergische Stahl-Industrie of Remscheid, Germany, for 80 pairs each of driving and pony wheels and axles for £1,084. Further orders were placed with the J.G. Brill Company for 40 pairs of Type 22E maximum traction trucks for £2,720 and with Gabriel & Co., for forty sets of lifeguards to an improved design by Hudson & Bowring for £284.

The section in Burlington Road, New Malden and West Barnes Lane consisted of narrow lanes which were quite unmade, without lighting or surface drainage, especially in the case of West Barnes Lane, which was formerly a private lane leading to a farm. The LSWR main line crossed the lane by means of a cattle arch which was reconstructed for the LUT by John Aird & Sons, the contract price of this work being £7,250. Part of the J.G. White contract covered the rebuilding of an old, narrow bridge across the Beverley Brook in Burlington Road, which was replaced with a steel-decked brick structure. Other expenditure on these lines was £46,981 for acquisitions of land and extensive widenings between Kingston and Raynes Park, a payment of £3,386 to Surbiton UDC for a widening in Ewell Road and an addition to J.G. White & Co.'s contract was made to cover re-routing gas and water mains for £28,862.

The LUT found a site for a sub-station to serve the Kingston group of lines in Surbiton, but negotiations for this failed and another site was found in Clarence Street, Kingston. Kingston Corporation objected to the use of this site and after some delay a suitable site was found at London Road, Kingston, which was bought for £750 and a contract awarded to Courtney & Fairbairn to construct the building for £1,669. A £4,395 contract was awarded to the British Westinghouse Electric & Manufacturing Co. Ltd., on 3 August 1905 to supply and erect the equipment in the sub-station and details of this will be found in Chapter 15.

The contract for construction of the lines excluded the 0.375 miles in Richmond Road between King's Road and Ham Boundary and the LUT had notified Kingston Corporation that this section would not be constructed for the time being. The Corporation insisted that the whole of the authorised lines in the town and to Surbiton be completed and opened at the same time, and at a directors' meeting on 2 August 1905 Robinson was authorised to arrange with J.G. White & Co., to complete the disputed section at the schedule prices of their existing contract.

Meanwhile, work was proceeding in the Kingston area and the directors turned their attention to the lines in the Wimbledon area authorised in the Act of 1902. This subject had been discussed in the Summer of 1905 and there had been misgivings over the financial position, the money markets at the time being unfavourable for financing large-scale projects, and on 30 October 1905 the directors resolved to defer proceeding with the work There were other consider-ations, chief among these being a demand by the recently-incorporated Wimbledon Borough Council that the LUT should build a new sewerage system in the streets through which the tramways would operate. Robinson was authorised to continue negotiations with the council on the latter's demand that the LUT should contribute to the cost of this work.

The question of Kingston Bridge was the subject of correspondence between the LUT and the Board of Trade in late 1904 and early 1905 and on 4 February 1905 the Chief Inspecting Officer of the Board advised the latter that there was no objection to the LUT taking a double line across the bridge. There was much adverse comment in the town on this point, and the joint MCC/SCC Bridges Committee endeavoured to persuade the owners of the bridge, the Kingston Municipal Charities Trustees, to sell it to the county councils, or alternatively to withhold consent for the double line across the bridge. Despite the Board of Trade's approval of the LUT plans for the bridge, the Kingston Chamber of Trade and other local interests persisted in calling for the bridge to be rebuilt or widened and on 5 October 1905 the Chamber resolved to send a deputation to the President of the Board of Trade to ask him to bar trams from crossing the bridge until it was widened. The President, Lord Salisbury, declined to receive such a deputation, saying Parliament had authorised the lines and the question of widening the bridge rested with the Kingston Municipal Charities Trustees.

Work on constructing the lines in the Kingston area was delayed by several factors. The contractors were held up by alterations required to a gas main in Surbiton, and the UDC had complained to the Board of Trade and the LUT about the work in Portsmouth Road and levels in Victoria and Claremont Roads. The

The Board of Trade Inspection of the Kingston routes took place on 21 February 1906, using new top-covered car, No. 321, seen at Claremont Road, Surbiton. The recently knighted Sir Clifton Robinson is seated on the open balcony of the car. (Courtesy: Bryan Woodriff)

UDC resolved to take action against the LUT under the terms of the 1870 Tramways Act "to ensure that the works are promptly and satisfactorily completed". The contractors were held to be at fault and following strong representations by Robinson to J.G. White & Co., the lines outward from Kingston to Surbiton, Thames Ditton and Tolworth were completed. However, some work remained to be completed in Kingston, and the company's agreement with Kingston Corporation precluded the opening of any section in the town until all the authorised mileage in the town and into Surbiton was complete and ready for opening.

The LUT contract with J.G. White & Co., stipulated that all work in Kingston, Surbiton and Maldens & Coombe should be completed by 1 November 1905. Robinson wrote to Whites on 11 November pointing out that the work was falling behind schedule and threatened them with a claim for penalties. The LUT was receiving a stream of complaints from the councils, frontagers and other interests about delays in finishing the work, which were causing difficulties for traffic and obstructing footpaths. The Board of Trade were also receiving complaints at regular intervals from the councils, especially Kingston Corporation, who pointed out that the most important streets in the town had been obstructed for several months. The Corporation wanted the Board of Trade to take action to compel the LUT to complete all work without further delay. These complaints were reinforced by innumerable objections by the councils about matters of detail such as the position of poles, minute deviations from the plans, paving and other matters. An immense file accumulated at the Board of Trade on all this and the Board was drawn into acting as a mediator in resolving differences between the LUT, the councils, chambers of trade, frontagers and other interests.

Some of the delays had arisen from the fact that extra work was found necessary on mains and sewers and J.G. White had been asked to do this as an addition to their contract. Robinson wrote to Kingston Corporation on 11

November 1905 saying that he would make every endeavour to complete the lines "and to have them in operation not later than New Year's Day". Later, on 7 December, Maldens & Coombe UDC wrote to the Board of Trade saying that the LUT had planted two anchor poles in their district during September without consulting the council or their surveyor. The UDC insisted on the poles' removal and stood firm on this point for a considerable time. At the same time the UDC complained about works in Burlington Road, and after lengthy argument the parties resolved their differences. The poles in question had been erected at the Kingston Hill terminus, where the track ended right on the Kingston-Maldens boundary and consequently the anchor poles were perforce over the border and in the UDC's district.

Notwithstanding the agreement with Kingston Corporation stipulating that all lines in the borough were to be completed and opened at once, Robinson asked for the Corporation's consent to open the sections so far completed, consisting of the lines from Hampton Wick into central Kingston, the branch to Kingston Hill and the line in Surbiton to Thames Ditton and the branch to Tolworth. Surbiton UDC had asked Robinson when the lines in their district would be opened and he had suggested that they might ask Kingston Corporation to approve opening the line from Kingston through Surbiton, but the UDC felt that they could not take this course, and matters were left as they stood until 11 February 1906 when a trial run over the lines already completed was undertaken.

The trial run was carried out using two of the new top-covered cars specially ordered for the Surrey lines. One of these, No. 309, carried Robinson and senior members of the LUT staff, the second a number of staff of other grades. Robinson drove No. 309 across Kingston Bridge from Hampton Wick, thereby becoming the first man to drive an electric tram over a Thames bridge. The cars reached the bridge at midnight and despite the lateness of the hour some 500 people had assembled at the bridge to see the car across into the town. There were scenes of enthusiasm among the crowd and a number of people managed to climb aboard No. 309 as it negotiated the town centre junctions on the return journey across the bridge to Fulwell Depot.

The councils maintained their positions on opening the routes but Robinson was finally able to persuade Kingston Corporation to sanction opening the sections from Kingston through to Thames Ditton, Tolworth and Kingston Hill. An inspection took place on 21 February 1906 by Col. Yorke, who reported to the Board of Trade on 27 February, having found the construction satisfactory, and recommended the Board of Trade to issue the certificate of fitness for public service, which was done on 1 March. The lines inspected consisted of the track from Hampton Wick across Kingston Bridge through Clarence Street, Eden Street, St, James's Road and Penrhyn Road in Kingston, and into Surbiton through Surbiton Road, Surbiton Crescent, Claremont Road, Victoria Road and Portsmouth Road to the terminus at Windows Bridge, Thames Ditton, the total length of this stretch being 2.618 miles. Of which 2.503 miles was double, 0.347 miles single and 31 yards interlaced track. The section continuing from Clarence Street in the centre of Kingston along London Road comprised 0.363 miles of route of which 0.159 was double and 0.214 miles single line, and at the London Road-Cambridge Road junction 0.819 miles of route, consisting of 0.382 miles of double and 0.437 miles of single track, diverged to Kingston Hill where it terminated at the borough boundary near George Road. The line at Hampton Wick was connected to that across Kingston Bridge by a double north to east curve, and a south to east double curve 41 yards in length completed the triangular junction in front of the bridge.

Col. Yorke made a number of comments, remarking that some 42 yards of authorised double line in Eden Street had been laid as interlaced track while 88 yards in Clarence Street, shown as single on the plans, had been laid as double line. These changes had been made by agreement between the LUT and the Corporation. Some other sections in London Road and Kingston Hill shown as double line had been laid as single, and a number of curves were of less than 50ft radius, some being no more than 35ft. The track was well laid, and the new top-covered car used for the inspection was No. 321. Col. Yorke pointed out that the car did not have folding platform steps and said he wished to have the company's attention drawn to this important matter.

As there were a number of sharp junction curves and some gradients on the sections inspected Col. Yorke recommended speed limits and compulsory stops at a number of places. A 14 mile/h limit was allowed in Claremont Road, Surbiton, in Portsmouth Road between Windows Bridge and the junction with Brighton Road, Surbiton and in Ewell Road, Surbiton between Victoria Road and the terminus at Tolworth. 12 mile/h was prescribed on the approach to Kingston Bridge at Hampton Wick, in Kingston Hill and London Road between the terminus at Kingston Hill and Alexandra Terrace, in Penrhyn Road and Surbiton Crescent, in Brighton Road, Surbiton between Victoria Road and Claremont Road and in Cambridge Road and Kingston Road, Richmond Road and King's Road, Kingston. An eight mile/h limit was imposed in Clarence Street and London Road between the east side of Kingston Bridge and Alexandra Terrace, in Eden Street between Clarence Street and St. James's Road, in Victoria Road, Surbiton between Brighton Road and Claremont Road. The limit on Kingston Bridge was 6 mile/h and on the curve between London Road and Richmond Road and all other curves of 66ft radius or less and through all facing points 4 mile/h was imposed, with ten mile/h at all other places.

Numerous compulsory stops were called for. These were at the junction of Clarence Street and Thames Street; London Road and Eden Street; Eden Street and St. James's Road; Surbiton Road and Surbiton Crescent; Surbiton Crescent and Claremont Road; Claremont Road and Victoria Road; Victoria Road and Ewell Road; Brighton Road and Portsmouth Road and the junction curves at Richmond Road and King's Road.

Heavier rails were used on the Surrey lines than on the earlier routes. Stronger foundations and specially reinforced girder joints were used after trials on the earlier routes, where the track had failed to withstand intensive services with heavy

The line-up of cars used for the formal opening of the Kingston routes on 1 March 1906, No. 320 was driven by Ald. H.C. Minnitt under the guidance of senior LUT motorman Lewis Bruce, Sir Clifton stands on the step. (Courtesy: Bryan Woodriff)

No. 320 about to be driven over Kingston Bridge by Ald. Minnitt, Sir Clifton is in front of the car on the right, with Clifton Robinson Jnr on the left with one foot on the step.

(Courtesy: Bryan Woodriff)

bogie trams. Details of track and overhead construction will be found in Chapter 14. The construction work in Kingston had been the subject of much controversy in the town while the main streets were obstructed for several months during widenings and alterations to mains. In Kingston, Clarence Street was widened at heavy expense and in the process became a fine shopping and business thoroughfare. Other streets in the town suffered similar inconvenience to a greater or lesser degree but the final result was always a great advantage to the town. Kingston Chamber of Trade relaxed their opposition to the tramways across Kingston Bridge after assurances that the bridge would be widened following the Middlesex and Surrey county councils' declaration of their intention to acquire the bridge from its owners and ultimately carry out the work.

The sections inspected and approved, across Kingston Bridge to Surbiton and Thames Ditton and the branches to Kingston Hill and Tolworth were formally opened on Friday, 1 March 1906. The weather was indifferent but Kingston was now in festive mood and the LUT had lavishly decorated Kingston Bridge, while many of the town's shops and businesses had similarly decorated their premises. The opening procession of trams consisted of three of the new top-covered cars headed by No. 320 which, under the supervision of Robinson was driven by the Mayor of Kingston, Ald. H.C. Minnitt, and led the way from Hampton Wick across the bridge through Clarence Street and London Road and up Kingston Hill to the terminus, where a brief halt was made. For the return journey Ald. Minnitt relinquished the controller to one of the senior motormen of the LUT, Lewis Bruce, who piloted the car for the rest of the tour. On the return journey down the hill the car encountered two brewer's drays, the second of which collided with the front of the leading tram when one of the horses shied. Robinson, standing on the platform was caught between the tram and the dray, falling from the car onto the road and suffering severe bruising and a sprained ankle. He made light of the incident and declined aid and, in some pain continued with the tour. The tram was damaged, a window being smashed and some of the bodywork suffered. At the end

160

of the tour, the party, numbering some two hundred, adjourned to Nuthall's Restaurant in Kingston, where, as on previous similar occasions an elaborate luncheon was served, the dining hall being elaborately decorated on tramway themes.

Following the luncheon, Ald. Minnitt made a gracious speech in which he complimented the LUT on its perseverance in attaining its objects. He expressed the hope that the LUT would prosper and expand; he also hoped that the LUT would be able to maintain low fares and excellent services. Charles James Cater Scott, who had earlier succeeded Charles Tyson Yerkes as LUT Chairman expressed the hope that the inconvenience suffered by the town during construction of the lines would soon be forgotten and one of the guests, Sir James Szlumper, the Mayor of Richmond, said he regretted his town's attitude to the LUT and thought that the trams would bring excellent business to Kingston. Robinson responded, making the point that the LUT had, since electrification, carried 201,720,930 passengers and £1,200,479 of revenue had been derived from an average fare of less than 1½d.

Completion of the remaining lines in Kingston and the Maldens followed hard on the heels of those radiating from the centre of Kingston, and on Monday, 14 May 1906 a trial run was made over the line as far as Raynes Park LSWR station. A water car led the way, spraying the track, and was followed by Clifton Robinson in a motor-car and lastly, one of the new trams. The trial run was successful and an inspection took place on Wednesday, 23 May and as customary was carried out by Col. Yorke, using car No. 320. The sections inspected consisted of the line from the centre of Kingston along Richmond Road to the Kingston-Richmond boundary near Ham Common comprising 0.874 miles of route, of which 0.384 miles was double and 0.490 single track with three passing loops. From the line in Richmond Road a branch along King's Road, consisting of 0.690 miles of route, of which 0.671 miles was double track with a 33-yard single line terminal stub ran as far as the Kingston Gate of Richmond Park. From London Road a line diverged through Cambridge Road to terminate in Kingston Road at the junction with Malden Road near the Norbiton Park Hotel (since re-named The Fountain). This section consisted of 1.770 miles of route of which 1.697 miles was double and 0.063 miles single track. The single track consisted of two short sections, one in Cambridge Road and the other in Kingston Road below the narrow skew arch bridge carrying

No. 320 leads the inaugural procession across the decorated Kingston Bridge from Hampton Wick, Ald. Minnitt remains at the controls. (Courtesy: Bryan Woodriff)

the LSWR main line across Kingston Road. From the Norbiton Park Hotel the line continued into Burlington Road, New Malden and along West Barnes Lane and Coombe Lane for 1.75 miles, all double track to a point close to Raynes Park LSWR station at the boundary with the Croydon Rural District and the Borough of Wimbledon,

Col. Yorke found the construction in good order but was exceptionally critical of the single line beneath the LSWR bridge in Kingston Road. He noted that gradients on either side descended towards the bridge and he condemned the arrangement as objectionable and a possible danger to both tramway and general traffic. He expressed his firm view that the bridge should be widened and the track below doubled. He found no other fault with the layout or its construction and was able to recommend the Board of Trade to certify the line fit for public traffic subject to various speed limits and compulsory stops. A limit of 14 mile/h was imposed on the section between Raynes Park station and the Norbiton Park Hotel. This section traversed Coombe Lane, West Barnes Lane and Burlington Road. The limit between London Road, Kingston and Kingston Road, New Malden and on the lines in Richmond Road, Kingston and the branch in King's Road was 12 mile/h and a limit of 4 mile/h was imposed on the curves between London Road and Richmond Road and all curves of less than 66ft radius. At all other places the limit was 10 mile/h. Compulsory stops were fixed at the junction of Richmond Road and King's Road and before passing beneath the LSWR bridge in Kingston Road. The certificate of fitness for public service was signed at the Board of Trade on 26 May and on the same day traffic commenced on all the lines passed except the section between the Norbiton Park Hotel and Raynes Park station.

No reason was given at the time these sections opened for the failure to open the 1.75 miles between the Norbiton Park Hotel and Raynes Park station but a study of local records indicates that the Maldens & Coombe UDC were still concerned about the narrow single line section under the LSWR bridge in Kingston Road, Norbiton. On 1 May 1906 Robinson told the LUT directors of differences with the UDC over constructional details, especially the track under the bridge and the lack of a footpath on one side of the road there. A major improvement scheme involving the demolition of a large house, Derby Lodge, and alterations at the Malden Road-Kingston Road junction was the subject of a clause in the LUT 1902 Act, which precluded the company from opening the line in the Maldens district until these works had been carried out to the council's satisfaction, but did not debar the company from constructing the tramway in the interim. The council feared there would be danger to pedestrians using the narrow footpath under the railway bridge, and weight was added to these concerns when a schoolchild was killed at this spot on 1 May 1906.

On 9 June 1906 a special meeting of the Maldens & Coombe UDC discussed the footpath and the road beneath the bridge. They wanted the road under the bridge widened, the adjacent track doubled and footpaths provided on both sides of the road below the bridge. They also wanted additional widenings in Kingston Road.

Following Col. Yorke's report on the new line and his criticisms of the line under the bridge the LSWR was induced by the council to agree to widen the bridge at the cost of £6,000, subject to the LUT bearing one third of this cost, the LSWR and the UDC financing the remainder. At their meeting on 31 July the LUT directors declined to enter into this arrangement and nothing further was done until 1932 by which time the trams had been replaced by trolleybuses. Meanwhile, the LUT and the UDC were at loggerheads over several related matters, including the acquisition of land in Kingston Road required for widenings. Work at the Malden Road-Kingston Road junction was slow, as there were several mains which had to be re-routed at the new crossroads The UDC had agreed that the line could be opened as far as the Norbiton Park Hotel, but the section on to Raynes Park station did not open until 27 April 1907.

In the summer of 1905 the LUT directors considered the construction of the

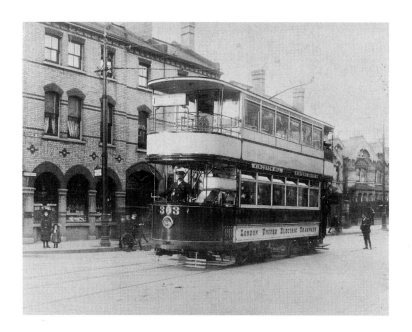

Upper: Almost brand new, No. 303 is seen on the Winters Bridge – Kingston Hill service soon after operations began. As yet, there were no advertisements placed upon the panels of the car. (Courtesy: Bryan Woodriff)

Lower: No. 330 in London Road, Kingston, on its way to Kingston Hill. The first advertisements have now made their appearance on the cars. The old buildings in this view have given way to large stores. (Commercial view)

This view of central Kingston shows car No. 277 on its way between Kingston Hill and Surbiton. By this time all Surrey routes were worked by cars of the 151-300 batch, with only rare workings with cars from other groups. A mechanical points switch had also been added at the Kingston Hill junction. (Courtesy: A.D. Packer)

The Board of Trade Inspection of the line between Norbiton Church and Raynes Park Station took place on 23 May 1906. Car 321, carrying the inspector, Lt. Col. Yorke, together with Sir Clifton Robinson and others, is seen at Malden. (Courtesy: A.D. Packer)

lines in the 1902 Act, from Raynes Park to Wimbledon, Tooting and Summerstown. Discussions had taken place between the LUT and UERL directors and the companies' financiers, Speyer Brothers when it was agreed to defer commencing work on these lines until the Kingston lines were completed. During these discussions it was agreed that, notwithstanding the clause in the company's agreement with Wimbledon council which provided for all the authorised lines in the town to be completed and opened at once, the lines would be constructed in two stages. On 30 October 1905 the directors deferred a decision on the lines pending a close examination of estimates and in February 1906 tenders were sought for construction of the lines in the 1902 Act. Meanhile the LUT had obtained an extension of time to complete the lines, the powers for which were due to expire on 8 August 1906 and were extended for two years from that date in the Company's 1905 Act, This same Act extended the time to complete the lines in the Maldens & Coombe for two years from 17 August 1905.

One of the reasons for deferring construction of the Wimbledon lines was the demand by Wimbledon Borough Council that the LUT should construct a new sewerage system in the streets through which the tramways would be constructed. Robinson had been negotiating with the Borough Council and its predecessor, the Urban District Council and the Borough Council had suggested that the LUT should contribute a part of the cost of this work. On 5 March 1906 the LUT directors agreed to leave the matter with Robinson to continue negotiations and to obtain the best possible compromise, with any outlay by the company not to exceed £5,000. Robinson was able to arrive at a satisfactory arrangement with the Borough Council and on 23 March the directors resolved to construct the section between Raynes Park station and Wimbledon Hill Road via Worple Road immediately, leaving Robinson to arrange the necessary contracts.

The first of these contracts covered the continuation of the line from Raynes Park station into Coombe Lane, Pepys Road and along Worple Road as far as Wimbledon Hill Road for a distance of 1.362 miles, which included a single line loop from the end of Worple Road into Wimbledon Hill Road, St. George's Road and Francis Grove to rejoin Worple Road. The contract was awarded to J.G. White & Co. Ltd., on 12 May 1906 for £17,812, of which £15,655 covered the cost of track and foundations and £2,257 the erection of the overhead wiring. Another contract went to W.T. Henley's Telegraph Works Co. Ltd., for cabling on 13 June 1906 and on 12 July the British Westinghouse Electric & Manufacturing Co. Ltd., was awarded a contract for additional equipment at Kingston sub-station and the machinery for Wimbledon sub-station, for £6,998 to which was later added provision for additional equipment at £1,611. The LUT purchased three large houses on the south side of Worple Road for widenings. They were Nos. 60, 62 and 64, and No. 60, on the west corner of Salisbury Road had a large garden in which the sub-station was built. Details of track and overhead construction and power supply will be found in Chapters 14 and 15 respectively.

J.G. White & Co., had commenced work on the Raynes Park-Wimbledon Hill section by 7 June 1906 and part of the cableways through this route were laid at the same time as the Kingston lines were constructed. On 3 July 1906 an agreement was concluded with Wimbledon Borough Council and a cheque in the sum of £5,000 sent to the council as the LUT's contribution to the cost of alterations to the sewer system in the town. Extensive widenings were carried out in Worple Road, and at a number of places shown on the plans as single lines, double track was laid by agreement with the Borough Council. By July 1906 construction as far as Wimbledon Hill Road had been completed and on 31 July a trial run was made over the new section using one of the top-covered cars, led by Robinson in one of his motor-cars. Unlike earlier trial runs this one was attended by some difficulties. The tram derailed at the junction curve at Worple and Wimbledon Hill Roads and again at the St. George's Road-Francis Grove junction. There were difficulties at other curves and after this trial the rails were taken up on the St. George's Road-Francis Grove junction and relaid with rails of a different section. A second trial

Services between New Malden and Hampton Court started on 26 May 1906, using the new cars. This early view of No. 320, together with an interested group of young bystanders, was taken at the New Malden terminus. (Courtesy: National Tramway Museum)

took place on 3 August and all went well. The car used on these trials carried boards reading "Haydon's Road and Colliers Wood" but much work remained to be done before those destinations were reached.

Notwithstanding Wimbledon Borough Council's insistence that all authorised lines in the town should be completed and opened at the same time, Robinson took steps with a view to opening the new section, despite the fact that contracts for the remaining sections had not then been placed. An inspection of the Worple Road line took place on 9 August 1906 and was carried out by Col. Yorke. The section inspected consisted of the line from Raynes Park station into Pepys Road and along Worple Road as far as Francis Grove for 1.097 miles, of which 0.700 was single track, accounted for by three short and a longer single track section of 0.133 miles in length from a point between Arterberry and Crescent Roads and Albert Road. The single line loop in Worple Road, Wimbledon Hill Road, St. George's Road and Francis Grove back to Worple Road amounted to 0.302 miles as inspected. The line in Wimbledon Hill Road was under construction at the time of the inspection and not all the junctions had been connected. In addition, by arrangement with Wimbledon Borough Council the LUT had agreed that a short length of single line in Wimbledon Hill Road between Worple Road and St. George's Road would be doubled and a widening there carried out.

Col. Yorke approved the construction, noting there were no severe gradients and recommended speed limits of 14 mile/h throughout Worple Road except opposite the intersection with The Downs where 8 mile/h was imposed owing to the single track there. In Francis Grove and St. George's Road the limit was 8 mile/h with 4 mile/h round curves of less than 22 yards radius and through facing points. Col. Yorke recommended the issue of the certificate of fitness for public use which was signed at the Board of Trade on 13 August. On 15 August the Board of Trade approved the road widening in Wimbledon Hill Road, then under construction. Meanwhile, the LUT was unable to work the new line, which was effectively isolated from Fulwell Depot and the rest of the system while improvements in the Maldens remained uncompleted, and in any case, Wimbledon were to insist, at first, that all the authorised lines in their district should be completed and opened at the same time, which did not occur until 2 May 1907.

While tenders had been invited for construction of all the Wimbledon mileage with a view to undertaking all the work at once, the LUT directors had taken a cautious view of the financial position and deferred placing contracts for the lines in Wimbledon Hill Road, The Broadway, Merton Road and the branches to Summerstown and Tooting pending discussions with the UERL directors and Speyer Brothers. Meanwhile, Wimbledon Borough Council had become suspicious that the LUT intended to postpone indefinitely construction of the lines from Worple Road to the south. Work on the improvements in Malden had progressed to the point at which it would soon be possible to open the section from the Norbiton Park Hotel to Raynes Park station and Robinson asked Wimbledon Borough Council to approve opening the Raynes Park-Wimbledon Hill Road section to provide a continuous service between Wimbledon and Kingston. The council and residents were divided on the issue and a large number had petitioned the Borough Council to withhold sanction to open the Worple Road line until work in Wimbledon Hlll Road had been completed.

The company's request for permission to open the Worple Road section was the subject of a meeting of Wimbledon councillors and residents on 11 August 1906, Robinson was present and made a forceful speech, alleging that the meeting had been "packed" by opponents of the LUT with people from outside the town. The opposition, in turn, made a similar accusation against the LUT. Robinson was furious at the suggestion that he had "packed" the meeting, while Ald. Porter denounced the man sitting next to him as a non-resident. The meeting centred on the delay in starting work on the remainder of the lines in the town, and Cllr. R.D Pond asked Robinson for a definite date for this. Pond said he would give his vote to allow Worple Road to open if Robinson gave the assurance he asked for. Pond said he wanted the trams in all parts of the borough; as it stood the line in the north of the town had been built where it was not wanted, and there was no line in the south, where it was needed.

At a later meeting on 5 September it emerged that delays in completing the lines lay in the lack of money. Robinson, accompanied by the LUT Chairman, Charles James Cater Scott had met the councillors and told them it had been

Coombe Lane, Raynes Park c1908, with car 287 on its way to Wimbledon, about to pass the corner of Durham Road. This area still retained its unspoilt character for several more years to come.   (Commercial view)

167

difficult to raise money and the market was worsening. Robinson told the Mayor that the company did not expect to raise finance for further work for four to five months and said that it was desired to open the Worple Road line to recoup some of the money already spent. The councillors feared that the line to Tooting might be shelved indefinitely and a suggestion was put forward for an agreement by which Worple Road could be opened if outstanding widenings were dealt with forthwith, and if not the council would be at liberty to give the LUT seven days' notice to cease running the trams and to be liable for £20,000 damages. This did not proceed and the councillors voted unanimously to refuse consent to open the section.

It is possible that uncertainty over negotiations which had been started with the LCC on through running at Tooting was behind the LUT wish to delay completing the lines in Wimbledon, Following the decisive rejection of Robinson's request to open Worple Road the LUT and UERL directors had hurried discussions with the result that tenders for constructing the rest of the lines already in hand were accepted and contracts drawn up. The contract to carry out widenings where necessary and construct the track and overhead connecting the Worple Road line with Wimbledon Hill Road, The Broadway and through Merton and Colliers Wood to the London county boundary at Longley Road, Tooting, together with the branch from High Street, Merton through Haydon's Road and Plough Lane to the London county boundary at Summerstown was placed with John Mowlem & Co. Ltd., for the sum of £48,960. This covered necessary street widenings, track foundations and rails, accounting for £44,006 and overhead construction for the balance of £4,954. The contract for cabling and telephone lines was placed with W.T. Henley's Telegraph Works Co. Ltd., for £6,227 and these contracts were sealed on 29 September 1906. Work commenced without delay and meanwhile the directors allowed the question of opening the line between New Malden and Raynes Park station to remain in abeyance while the Maldens & Coombe UDC continued to raise difficulties over the LSWR bridge across in Kingston Road and road improvements elsewhere along the route. Until this section opened no through service could be opened betweeen Kingston and Wimbledon and the Worple Road section, even if sanctioned, would be of little value to the LUT.

During this period Kingston Corporation raised objections to a reduction in the service frequency on the short section in Richmond Road between King's Road and Ham Boundary. The ten-minute service on this section had been reduced to a fifteen-minute frequency and the Corporation demanded the reinstatement of the ten-minute service. The LUT told the Corporation that all other routes in the town had a ten-minute service interval or better and that demand on the section was slight, especially in the winter months. The Corporation insisted that the ten-minute service should be reinstated and Robinson ignored their demands. The Corporation then gave notice that failing reinstatement of the ten-minute service they would apply to the Board of Trade for enforcement of the terms of the agreement between the LUT and the Corporation which laid down a ten-minute frequency throughout the borough between 8am and 8pm. Robinson wrote to the Town Clerk on 5 December 1906 saying that the Corporation had not shown that the public were inconvenienced by the service alteration.

The Corporation themselves were divided on the issue, some members taking the view that the new service frequency was adequate. After lengthy discussions the Corporation took the matter to the Board of Trade who, by 19 March 1907 had asked the Corporation if they would submit their case to arbitration. They agreed to this, subject to their rights under the LUT 1901 Act. At a later date service alterations resulted in the section being covered by a single car shuttle between Ham Boundary and King's Road, with a journey time of 3 minutes and a ten-minute frequency. This service remained unchanged until it was withdrawn in 1920.

A large number of widenings and other improvements were carried out throughout the South Wimbledon lines. Some 3.80 miles of road were widened from 40ft to 50ft and part of Merton Road to 57ft. In Plough Lane much of the road was widened from 30ft to 50ft and the bridge carrying Plough Lane across the River Wandle was increased from 30 to 50ft wide, while the bridge carrying High Street, Merton across the Wandle was widened from 37ft to 48ft. The bridge over the railway in Haydon's Road was not widened but was structurally altered and its approaches widened to allow a future widening from 26ft to 50ft.

By February 1907 construction of the lines in Wimbledon, Merton and Colliers Wood had reached the stage where Robinson felt that he could make a further attempt to obtain the Borough Council's consent to open the Worple Road line. He wrote to the Town Clerk on 18 February asking for this consent. The Tramways Sub-Committee met Robinson on 23 February and he outlined the progress the company was making on the new lines. The Sub-Committee saw no reason why consent should not be given for the Worple Road section subject to the council's right to withhold consent to open any other tramway in the town. A further letter from Robinson to the council of 25 February said that the line to The Grove Hotel

(at the Wimbledon-Merton boundary in High Sreet, Merton) would be inspected by 31 March and he would be able to open that section and the one beyond, to Tooting, on Easter Monday.

The Town Clerk met officers of the Board of Trade on 25 February and discussed the forthcoming inspection. The Chairman of the Tramways Sub-Committee reported all this to a meeting of the General Purposes Committee on 27 February. At this meeting a petition was read, signed by sixty-six tradesmen and residents in High Street, Merton and Haydon's Road, asking the council not to allow any tramway in Wimbledon to be opened until all widenings and improvements the LUT was bound to make in the town had been completed. The Committee,"with regret", resolved that having considered the Tramway Sub-Committee's report and the petition they were unable to assent to the tramway in Worple Road being opened.

Progress was delayed as a result of these conditions and the proposed inspection was deferred. At the General Purposes Committee's meeting on 24 April a letter from Robinson, dated 12 April was read, in which he said that all the works as far as The Grove Hotel were complete and strenuous efforts were being made to complete the remaining sections to Summerstown and Tooting ready for the Whitsun traffic. He made a further appeal for consent to open the line from North Wimbledon to The Grove Hotel, which was considered by the Tramways Sub-Committee on 18 April, who recommended that the line between Raynes Park and The Grove Hotel be allowed to open for service on and after 2 May 1907. The General Purposes Committee accepted this recommendation and resolved accordingly, subject to inspection by the Board of Trade and a number of outstanding works being completed by 2 May. Another condition was for all outstanding work to be completed as soon as possible and the acceptance of a clause in the Board of Trade regulations stipulating that no more than one car should stand in Wimbledon Hill Road near Mansel Road and, until the line in High Street, Merton was opened for traffic cars should not run in Merton Road south of its junction with Balfour Road.

Prior to this, on 27 April 1907, the section between the Norbiton Park Hotel and Raynes Park station had at last opened, with an interim service of cars between Raynes Park station and Hampton Court and following Wimbledon Borough Council's meeting on 2 May the service of cars from Hampton Court to Raynes Park was extended along Worple Road to the terminus at the junction of Worple Road and Wimbledon Hill Road.

Wimbledon Borough Council's amended resolution of 1 May meant that the rest of the lines in the town had to be completed in every detail and all widenings and street improvements carried out to the Borough Surveyor's satisfaction before an opening to traffic could be contemplated. These requirements perforce included the sections of track in the Croydon Rural District and the 82 yards of line in the Metropolitan Borough of Wandsworth at the Tooting terminus. This was a further setback to the plans of the LUT and efforts were made to ensure that the Borough Council could not further delay the opening on the grounds of uncompleted work.

By mid-June 1907 work was very nearly finished and on 24 June a trial car was run over the new sections. Col. Yorke arrived in Wimbledon on 25 June to carry out the last inspection of authorised new tramways on the LUT system. The sections inspected were the line from Wimbledon Hill terminus down through Wimbledon Hill Road, The Broadway, Merton Road, High Street, Merton and High Street, Colliers Wood and High Street, Tooting as far as Longley Road, Tooting to within a few yards of the London County Council tramway terminus. In addition the branch to Summerstown from High Street, Merton through Haydon's Road and Plough Lane to the LCC boundary near the Plough public house, and the remainder of the junction lines at the Worple Road Wimbledon Hill Road-St. George's Road-Francis Grove loop were viewed. Col. Yorke was accompanied by Robinson and representatives of the various local authorities.

The line from Wimbledon Hill terminus to Tooting consisted of 2.069 miles of

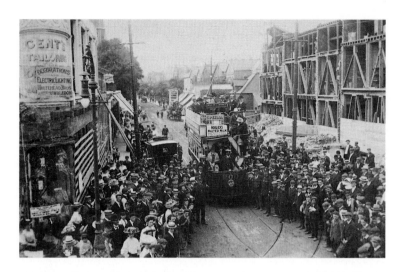

Services on the extension between Raynes Park and Wimbledon Hill Road were initiated on 2 May 1907, using car No. 200. An appreciative audience of local people was at Wimbledon to greet it. As was usual on such occasions, several police officers were in attendance.
(Courtesy: J.H. Price)

route, of which 1.923 miles was double line and 0.146 miles single track, this last being two short sections in Merton Road. The branch to Summerstown was double track throughout and was 1.247 miles in length. The connections between the line in Worple Road and Wimbledon Hill Road consisted of a double west to north junction, a single line west to south junction, a single line continuation in Worple Road from the junction into Francis Grove and St. George's Road to meet the line in Wimbledon Hill Road by a south junction, and a single line north to west junction from Wimbledon Hill Road into St. George's Road. The north junction from Worple Road into Wimbledon Hill Road was authorised as a single line but by agreement with Wimbledon Borough Council this and the section in Wimbledon Hill Road between Worple Road and George's Road authorised as single track were laid as double and the road in the section was widened. The connections totalled 0.313 miles of which 0.177 miles was single line and the remainder double.

Col. Yorke's report on the new lines was favourable. He noted that rails of 100lb/yard and 106lb/yard had been used on all the Surrey lines and in addition heavy girder joints had replaced the earlier plain joints, and construction generally strengthened. A difficulty arose over a short section in Haydon's Road where a resident, Henry Paxton complained that there was insufficient space for a tram to pass when his carriage stood outside his house. Col. Yorke arranged for Paxton's carriage to be placed by the kerb and a tram passed "with ample clearance". There was, however, a "narrow place" at this point where the space between the outer rail and the kerb was only 6ft 6in, and an error in measurements when the plans were produced caused the narrow place to be overlooked. The error was not noticed by the Board of Trade and could have resulted in the LUT scheme being thrown out of Parliament under Standing Orders because the narrow place was not noted on the plans. Paxton was the only complainant, but the matter caused a stir at the Board of Trade, where senior officers arranged to make careful checks of future tramway Bills and to refer the plans to an inspecting officer in every case for examination. The Board said that the matter would be allowed to stand over in this instance, but notes of the case would be retained for future reference.

Apart from this difficulty, Col. Yorke was able to pass the new lines as

171

satisfactory for public service subject to a special speed restriction at the narrow place in Haydon's Road. In Plough Lane the limit was 16 mile/h and 14 mile/h in Haydon's Road between High Street, Merton and Plough Lane except at the narrow place south of Hubert Road where 12 mile/h was imposed, as in High Street, Merton and High Street, Colliers Wood between Merton Road and Blackshaw Road. 12 mile/h was also imposed in Wimbledon Hill Road between Mansel Road and the main entrance to Wimbledon station and in Merton Road between Latimer Road and Kingston Road, with 8 mile/h over the LSWR bridge between the main entrance to Wimbledon station and Hartfield Road, and 6 mile/h under all low bridges. A four mile/h limit was instituted on the curves between Wimbledon Hill Road and Worple Road, Wimbledon Hill Road and St. George's Road, in Merton Road opposite Latimer Road, between Merton Road and High Street, Merton and between High Street, Merton and Haydon's Road. Compulsory stops were prescribed at the junction of Wimbledon Hill Road and Worple Road, the junction of Wimbledon Hill Road and St. George's Road, the curve in Merton Road opposite Latimer Road, the junction of Merton Road and High Street, Merton, the junction of Merton Road and Trinity Road on eastbound journeys, on the south side of Wimbledon station at the footbridge exit on journeys in the Tooting direction and opposite the main entrance on journeys towards Wimbledon Hill. Following discussion of a few minor points between Robinson and the Board of Trade the certificate of fitness for public use was signed at the Board of Trade on 29 June 1907. Meanwhile, with the verbal permission of Col. Yorke cars started running between Hampton Court and Tooting and on the branch to Summerstown on Thursday 27 June.

A traffic notice published at the time the extensions went into use stated that services would operate in close conjunction with the London County Council electric trams at Tooting, allowing speedy access to Westminster, Blackfriars, south London and the beauty spots of Surrey and West Middlesex. The Hampton Court-Raynes Park-Wimbledon Hill Road service was extended to Longley Road, Tooting and the loop from the end of Worple Road into Wimbledon Hill Road, St. George's Road and Francis Grove back to Worple Road went into use for

No. 287, seen c1907, departs from Wimbledon Hill terminus for Summerstown via Merton and Haydons Road. Almost alongside it is a sign of things to come – one of the early motor cars.
(Courtesy: J.H. Price)

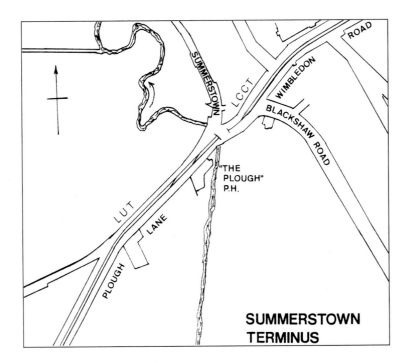

SUMMERSTOWN TERMINUS

reversing Wimbledon-only cars. At first various services were tried out, details of which will be found in Volume 2.

The line in Haydon's Road was built to meet a London County Council line authorised in 1903, projected from the conduit line in Garratt Lane, Wandsworth as a double line 0.225 miles in length, leaving Garratt Lane by a double junction and proceeding via Wimbledon Road to meet the LUT line (which was constructed two yards short of the LCC boundary at Summerstown). Clifton Robinson and the LCC Tramways Manager, Alfred Baker, had discussed closing the gap between Summerstown and Garratt Lane in 1902, when it was proposed that the LCC should construct the connection on the overhead system to allow LUT cars to run to Garratt Lane to make the interchange with LCC conduit cars. The LCC included the connection in their 1903 Bill.

Aubrey Llewellyn Coventry Fell, who succeeded Baker in July 1903, held different views on the subject of joint operations, and while the Wimbledon Road line was authorised in the 1903 LCC Act, the LUT made numerous requests to the LCC to make the connection. Baker, in evidence to Parliament on the LCC 1903 Bill had said "I think Tramway No.6 (the Wimbledon Road connection) will be a useful physical connection between the London United Tramways and the Council's projected tramways in Garratt Lane and with a view to mutual exchange of running powers, I think it is very desirable". The suggestion had received the support of John Williams Benn, at that time the Chairman of the LCC Highways Committee. Despite numerous attempts by the LUT to get the LCC to make the connection, one suggestion being for the LCC to lay the track on the overhead system to allow LUT cars to interchange with the LCC cars in Garratt Lane, it was many years before it was made, in 1931 on the conduit system, which will be chronicled in Volume 2. A similar fate befell various attempts by the LUT to obtain the connection at Longley Road, Tooting, which was realised early in 1922.

The extension of the LUT lines to the Tooting and Summerstown termini placed them at a distance of nearly twelve miles from Fulwell Depot and it was realised that depot accommodation closer to these termini was desirable to eliminate the large amount of dead mileage this entailed. Negotiations during 1905 to buy a plot of land in Haydon's Road adjacent to the Recreation Ground at the south end of the road did not materialise and another site came under consideration, in High Street, Colliers Wood, on the east side between Cavendish Road and Christchurch Road. This large site of nearly eight acres was nearly rectangular in form and was approached from High Street by a narrow entry into the north-western corner of the site, and the LUT was empowered in their 1906 Act to purchase as much of this site as was not occupied by the Mitcham Public Elementary Schools. On a plan of the entire LUT system attached to the 1906 Bill this site has been marked, in Indian ink, as "Tooting Depot". The LUT did not purchase the land, for unexplained reasons, but the site is clearly that which earlier researchers have understood to be that of a depot in the Tooting area. Other sites were considered for an additional depot but none were bought and Fulwell Depot accommodated cars for the Surrey lines throughout the life of the system. Details of depots and proposed sites will be found in Volume 2.

Elsewhere on the Surrey lines, difficulties in the Maldens & Coombe district continued in 1907. Work at the re-aligned road junction at Kingston Road and Burlington Road was not completed entirely to the council's satisfaction by May, and despite extensive improvements at this spot the council erected "DANGER CROSSROADS-DRIVE SLOWLY" there. The UDC continued to complain about work in Kingston Road and at the crossroads throughout 1906 and early 1907, all of which resulted in the late opening of the line to Raynes Park, and difficulties with Wimbledon Corporation added to these delays. At the crossroads a triangular island was made and the UDC asked the LUT to place a cluster lamp on this island in lieu of one at the fountain near the Norbiton Park Hotel as called for in the Act.

The company's Bill for the 1907 Session was deposited in Parliament in November 1906 and contained provisions for mutual through running over the LUT and LCC lines. Robinson had been involved in discussions with the LCC

Turning from Merton Road, South Wimbledon into High Street, Merton, No. 260 is seen travelling between Wimbledon Hill and Summerstown via Haydons Road c1908.

(Courtesy: J.H. Price)

officers on this subject from as early as 1902 but the LCC still refused to come to an agreement and the provisions were withdrawn from the Bill. Extensions of time to complete the line across Windows Bridge at The Dittons and across the Thames by way of Hampton Court Bridge to join the line in Hampton Court Road and that continuing southward from the Red Lion Hotel at Tolworth to Hook Village were granted until 17 August 1909, while powers to acquire land for widenings in the Moleseys UDC were extended until 8 August 1909. The 1907 Act received the Royal Assent on 26 July.

Whilst the 1907 Bill was proceeding through Parliament, Robinson was pressing Sir Edgar Speyer and the UERL directors to facilitate completion of the remaining authorised LUT lines. In January Speyer had asked Robinson for a resumé of the purchase dates of the tramways and light railways and the general financial position of the company. Robinson supplied the information asked for in the form of a detailed table detailing the authorised lines yet to be built, and this was accompanied by a letter dated 9 February 1907 giving an outline of the financial position to date. At this time the LUT was being pressed by Surrey County Council and the Esher & Dittons UDC about the approach to Windows Bridge, where the tram terminus had made a widening necessary. The UDC pressed the SCC on the matter on 15 February 1907 saying that the bridge approach was a danger to traffic with the tram terminus hard by the end of the bridge and a widening was a matter of urgency.

Earlier, Robinson had agreed to refund the cost of widening Windows Bridge if the SCC were to carry out the work and the trams were subsequently taken across. The UDC asked the county council to widen the bridge and its approaches and to negotiate with the LUT on the subject. If the company did not agree to carry out the work the UDC asked the SCC to oppose the 1907 Blll. At a meeting of the Highways and Bridges Committee on 14 May with Robinson present the SCC made it plain that the presence of the tram terminus near Windows Bridge necessitated a widening there.

The meeting of the SCC Highways and Bridges Committee on 10 July heard

No. 172 stands at the Longley Road, Tooting terminus of the LUT ready for departure to Hampton Court, while London County Council class E car No. 485 waits on the other side of the gap between the two systems to return to Blackfriars.   (Courtesy: A.D. Packer)

details of the offer by the LUT to pay for part of the cost of widening the bridge approach on the east side and the bridge itself if at a later date the LUT took the trams across. This was accepted and the councils withdrew their opposition to the Bill. Meanwhile the question of Hampton Court Bridge remained unresolved and later, at a meeting of the SCC/MCC Joint Bridges Committee on 28 July 1908 it emerged that the bridge required complete reconstruction, was in a dangerous state and it was remarked that "it is probable that several years will elapse before arrangements can be made and the money found for rebuilding the bridge". The bridge was not in fact rebuilt until 1933, and then on a different alignment to the old one. This effectively meant that the line across Windows Bridge to Hampton Court would not be built and the powers were ultimately abandoned.

Meanwhile, services on the Surrey lines continued through 1907 and 1908 with few changes, these being detailed in Volume 2. The year 1908 saw the introduction in November of a Bill for the 1909 Session of Parliament. Attempts by the LUT to secure agreement with the London County Council for mutual through running over the LCC lines via Wimbledon had been consistently repulsed by the LCC and the company again sought the help of Parliament to attain its objects. The 1909 Bill contained proposals for the postponement until 1919 and 1924 of the LCC's power to purchase the lines in Hammersmith, which became purchaseable in July 1909. The LUT Surrey lines were affected by proposals to obtain powers granting the LUT the right to run over the LCC lines south of the Thames to the extent of 17 miles and to give the LCC similar rights for a distance of 10½ miles. The proposed reciprocal powers were for the LCC to work over the LUT tramways in Plough Lane, Summerstown and through Colliers Wood, Merton and Wimbledon to Hampton Court. The proposed LUT powers over the LCC were to run over the authorised link from the LCC boundary at Plough Lane along Wimbledon Road to connect with the LCC line in Garratt Lane to reach Victoria via Wandsworth Road and Vauxhall Bridge and to join the LCC line at the LCC boundary at Longley Road, Merton reaching the inner London terminus at Victoria Embankment .

The 1909 Bill also sought renewal of the powers to construct the authorised extension of the line at Tolworth to Hook Village, and across Windows Bridge at The Dittons to Hampton Court, and the transfer to the LUT of the powers granted in 1903 to the LCC to construct the short piece of tramway in Wimbledon Road between the LCC line in Garratt Lane and the LCC boundary at the Plough Inn in Plough Lane if that line was not built by the LCC within 6 months of passing the Bill. There was fierce opposition to the Bill by the LCC, and other major objections were by Wimbledon Borough Council and the Maldens & Coombe UDC. Wimbledon Borough Council's terms for their consent to the Bill were for the LUT to contribute £6,000 towards widening Worple Road for a distance of 100 yards between Worple Mews and Raymond Road to fifty-five feet and in return the LUT would be permitted to double the single line at that point, which lay immediately opposite Francis Grove, a little short of Wimbledon Hill Road. The Borough Council also insisted that the annual wayleave paid by the LUT should be increased from £100 to £200 per mile and that the LUT should not supply current to the LCC for any purpose except for running their cars through Wimbledon and beyond. In addition all LCC cars working through Wimbledon were required to be of the best modern type, trailer cars debarred and workmen's fares to be available on LCC cars as defined in the LUT 1902 Act.

The Maldens & Coombe UDC also opposed the Bill. In evidence before the Select Committee of the House of Lords the UDC alleged that the object of the Bill was to increase the value of the LUT undertaking as a going concern, the LCC having also made this allegation. The UDC said that as a result of Col. Yorke's comments on the bridge in Kingston Road, New Malden the LSWR was induced by the UDC to agree to widen the bridge at the cost of £6,000, the LSWR, LUT and the UDC each to pay one third of this, but the LUT refused to enter into the arrangement. The UDC said in evidence that the tramways in Kingston Road, New Malden were a danger to the public and "injuriously affected property owners along the route, and the UDC was alarmed that another body (the LCC) would get

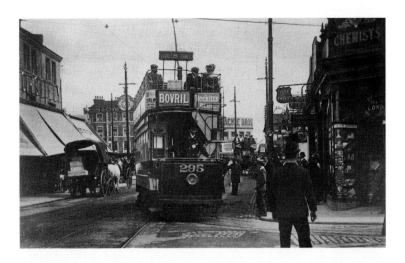

No. 295, in the busy Wimbledon Hill Road, is seen being slowly driven round the curve into St. George's Road on its journey from Tooting to Kingston and Hampton Court. The indicator lamp of the point-switching mechanism can just be seen in front of the traction pole on the right of the picture. (Courtesy: National Tramway Museum)

powers to run over the route". The extra traffic would be to the detriment of the district and its inhabitants, and the UDC would consent to the introduction of the Bill only if the LSWR bridge was widened and provisions relating to the powers of the UDC to purchase the lines in the district in the 1902 Act were repealed and the purchase powers made subject to the 1870 Tramways Act. The LUT 1902 Act provided for purchase of the lines in the district to commence in 1932 on the basis of a fair market price as a going concern. The 1870 Tramways Act provided for purchase at the construction cost less depreciation, contingent upon the condition of the undertaking at the time of purchase.

The Board of Trade had been approached by Robinson, seeking their support against the LCC's proposals for the purchase of the LUT Hammersmith lines. Robinson and his directors had been convinced that their case was unanswerable but the Board of Trade stood aside. The result was that, mainly on the case submitted by the LCC the Bill failed, which meant that the powers to extend the time to construct the line to Hook and the line across Windows Bridge to Hampton Court were not secured and no further application for them was made.

One result of the failure of the 1909 Bill was a request by the LUT to Surrey County Council for wayleave payments of £112 per annum in respect of the Hook extension to be waived. These payments had commenced on 17 February 1903 at the rate of £100 per annum per mile of main road traversed by the tramways and on 9 November 1909 Surrey County Council agreed to release the LUT from the obligation, the powers having lapsed. At this meeting councillors were told that the powers for the line over Windows Bridge to Hampton Court had expired on 8 August. The line would not now be built and the county council voted to take no further action in the matter. Earlier, plans for reconstruction of the bridge had been sent to the LUT, whereupon Robinson had advised the council that the powers had lapsed and no further application would be made to revive the powers. The LUT received repayment of moneys overpaid for the wayleave in October 1910.

During 1909 W.G. Verdon Smith, the LUT Secretary, presented to the directors a statement of the costs of the construction and equipment of the Surrey lines at 4 February. This amounted to £763,596, of which £53,782 was accounted for by the provision of 75 cars, and an additional estimated sum of £30,000 was included in the statement covering the proposed depot for the Wimbledon routes. It was estimated that the average number of cars required to work the Surrey lines was 62 per day with a maximum of 96 for holidays and a maximum of 200 per day for the system as a whole and 309 per day for holidays.

Services continued in Wimbledon and Kingston with little alteration through

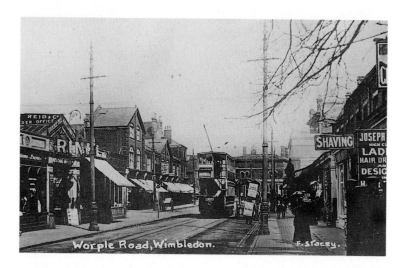

Upper: A number of cars from the 151-300 group received top covers in 1910-11, No. 285 passes through Worple Road, Wimbledon on its way to Tooting, shortly after this modification was carried out. (Courtesy: G.E. Baddeley)

Lower: Car No. 186 on its way to Tooting and another bound for Hampton Court are seen at Raynes Park (L&SWR) station bridge c1910. Of interest is the railway signal gantry, which dominates the skyline. (Courtesy: National Tramway Museum)

1909 until 1912, with a revision of fares in 1910, detailed in Volume 2. The original rolling stock bought for the Surrey lines in 1905 had a short life there, and by the time the Wimbledon lines opened in 1907 most of the new open-balcony top-covered cars had been transferred to the Middlesex lines and replaced by cars from the 1902 and 1903 batches, this notwithstanding clauses in agreements with both Kingston and Wimbledon Corporations which required the company to operate cars to the latest and best patterns in their districts.

Wimbledon Borough Council also had a clause in their agreement which forbade the display of "trade advertisements" on the cars running in the town. This point was raised in the council chamber at various times, and the Town Clerk was asked to write to the LUT pointing out that the display of advertisements was a breach of the agreement with the council and that the council reserved to themselves the right at any time to object to advertising. Evidently the councillors had come to accept the position as advertisements continued to adorn the exteriors of the cars throughout the life of the trams in the town.

The question of Kingston Bridge came closer to a settlement in May 1909 when the Middlesex and Surrey County Councils Joint Bridges Committee reported to Surrey County Council that the Trustees of the Kingston Municipal Charities were willing to support a Bill to be promoted by Surrey County Council for powers to transfer the bridge, the funds and estates of the Charities to the County Councils. Discussions between the parties continued up to November 1910 when a Bill was deposited in Parliament to facilitate the transfer of ownership, which received the Royal Assent as the Kingston-upon-Thames Bridge Act on 18 August 1911. The bridge, however, was not rebuilt until 1914 and its subsequent history will appear in Volume 2 of this work.

Surbiton, Victoria Road.

Entering a single track section in Victoria Road, Surbiton, No. 252 is on a journey between Winters Bridge, Thames Ditton and Richmond Bridge c1907.
(Commercial view: Courtesy: A.D. Packer)

179

CHAPTER TEN

UNREALISED LUT PROPOSALS

If all the schemes envisaged by the LUT had come to fruition, the resulting system would have extended from Reading, some forty miles distant from the centre of London, through rural areas in Berkshire, Buckinghamshire and Middlesex, and also from rural Surrey through the south-west suburbs to inner London termini at Marble Arch at the heart of the West End, to the north bank of the Thames at Westminster, Vauxhall and Blackfriars bridges, and to the inner London suburbs north of the Thames at Regents Park and Camden Town. Almost all proposed extensions in the County of London failed in the face of resolute opposition by the London County Council which had adopted a policy of owning all tramways within the County.

However, the LUT was exceptional in that it did own lines in London, these being the erstwhile West Metropolitan tracks in Hammersmith which were authorised and opened before the creation of the County of London in 1889, together with a line connecting the tramway in Hammersmith with that in Uxbridge Road which was authorised in 1902. There was also a short piece of track just 82 yards in length in the Metropolitan Borough of Wandsworth, also sanctioned in 1902, which when built, lay in the County of Surrey, meeting the LCC boundary immediately north of Longley Road Tooting. A boundary revision in April 1904 transferred this piece of tramway into London, but it remained the property of the LUT throughout the company's existence.

The 1898 LUT Bill

The company's first powers were obtained in the Provisional Order of 1895, and all were confirmed in the subsequent Confirmation Act of that year. This was followed by a Bill submitted for consideration in the 1898 Session of Parliament, seeking powers to construct new tramways in Hammersmith, Acton, Hanwell, Brentford and Hounslow. It also sought to link the termini at Shepherds Bush and Hammersmith by way of Richmond Road, Netherwood Road and Shepherds Bush Road. A short link with this extension was planned to leave the Uxbridge Road line at the west end of Shepherds Bush Green and pass along Shepherds Bush Road to connect at Netherwood Road. Lastly, it was proposed to reconstruct and extend the isolated line on the Surrey side of Kew Bridge, details of which are given in a later section of this chapter. These schemes involved approximately 14 miles of route.

The Bill also sought powers to build generating stations at Acton, Chiswick, Shepherds Bush and Richmond depots, and to make arrangements with the Central London Railway Company for mutual power supplies. It was expected that these schemes would cost £165,357. The lines in Shepherds Bush and Hammersmith were opposed by the LCC, while the Acton-Hanwell line was blocked by Ealing UDC. This only left the Kew Bridge-Hounslow extension and the Brentford-Hanwell tramway to receive sanction in the 1898 Act, which obtained the Royal Assent on 12 August. Both of these are described in other chapters. With regard to the power stations, only those at Chiswick and Acton were authorised, while Chiswick was the only one to be eventually built.

The 1898 Light Railway Application

The failure of the 1898 proposal for the Acton-Hanwell line resulted in Robinson and LUT directors seeking to obtain an Order for the route under the

Light Railways Act of 1896. Although the Act as written was intended to allow for the construction of mainly rural lines, it had been used as a way of obtaining authority to build what were, to all intents and purposes, electric tramways. Robinson, however, had seen that the lack of definition of a light railway in the preamble to the Act offered an opportunity to make use of its provisions as a cheaper and quicker way of gaining authority to build lines, rather than to go through the Parliamentary process, with all that it entailed.

On 21 April 1898 an application was lodged for an Order covering a line between Hanwell and Uxbridge, which was granted, and for a greatly extended line from the south side of Kew Bridge, through Sandycombe Road to Richmond, then via Petersham Road, Ham Common, Richmond Road, Clarence Street, Kingston, Kingston Bridge and on to Hampton Court, which was to be a mixture of double and single line. This was opposed by residents of Richmond and other parties, and there was also objection to the use of the Light Railways Act, resulting in the application for this section being withdrawn.

The Second 1898 Light Railway Application

This was submitted in November 1898 and made another attempt to secure powers for the Uxbridge Road line between Acton and Hanwell. It also sought to gain authority to build an extension from Hounslow (The Bell), along Staines Road to the east side of Baber Bridge at North Feltham, together with a branch from the authorised tramway in London Road, Isleworth at Busch Corner, through Twickenham and Hampton, to reach the River Thames at the foot of Church Street, and then to pass along the Middlesex side of the river, past Hampton Court Palace as far as Kingston Bridge, there to pass through Hampton Wick and Teddington, and at Stanley Road to rejoin Hampton Road, thus forming the "Hampton Court Loop". A further branch line was envisaged to pass through York Street to the Middlesex side of Richmond Bridge.

Apart from the Acton-Hanwell proposal, which was withdrawn prior to the Light Railway Commissioner's Inquiry, it appeared that the local authorities, with the exception of Ealing, were generally in favour of the remainder of the scheme, but the LSWR opposed on the grounds of competition with their services. At the inquiry at Twickenham on 12 June 1899 the Commissioners, the Earl of Jersey and Col. T. Boughey, declined to grant the Order, saying that the proposals should go before Parliament.

The 1900 Act

This sanctioned all mileage rejected by the Light Railway Commissioners in June 1899. However, in the Bill was a request for powers to construct lines from the authorised tramway at Acton, through Gunnersbury Lane, Bollo Lane, Bollo Bridge Road, Acton Lane, South Parade, Turnham Green Terrace and, after crossing High Road Chiswick, to continue along Annandale and Devonshire Roads and into Mawson Lane, to reach the north bank of the Thames near Chiswick Mall. Following local objections, this section was withdrawn, as was a variation at Devonshire Road, where it was suggested that the line went over open land.

The 1901 Light Railway Applications

The first of these was placed before the Light Railway Commissioners in May. It was an extensive scheme, the proposals covering about 22 miles of route in the outer west Middlesex area, and a revised north to south route to that shown in the 1900 Bill, from Willesden via Acton to the north bank of the Thames at Chiswick. Also included was an extension from The Bell at Hounslow, along High Street and Bath Road to Cranford, another from Church Street Hampton, along Thames Street, Kempton Park Road and Staines Road to Hanworth and back to The Green Twickenham. From the Brown Bear Hotel in Hanworth, a 3 mile line was projected northward to reach the tramway in High Street, Hounslow, with another between Hanworth and Southall via Lampton Road, Heston Road and Norwood Green Road.

The second part of this scheme centred upon the existing main routes through Acton and Chiswick, and asked for lines from Willesden Lane, along Horn Lane, Churchfield Road, Grove Road and then into Acton Lane as far as Bollo Bridge Road; from Horn Lane into King Street, Mill Hill Grove and Road, and along Gunnersbury Lane to Bollo Bridge Road. From here a similar route to that withdrawn from the 1900 Bill was proposed to Mawson Lane near Chiswick Mall, and then to return via Burlington Lane and Sutton Court Road to High Road and Beaconsfield Road. It was intended that junctions would be made with the lines in High Street, Acton and High Road, Chiswick.

At an inquiry held by the Light Railway Commissioners at Middlesex Guildhall on 23 July 1901, the application was opposed by Southall-Norwood UDC and the Metropolitan District Railway Company. Resulting from this, and from the fact that no notices had been served on frontagers for acquisition of land for widening purposes, all mileage was rejected with the exception of the sections between Cranford and Hounslow, Hounslow and Hanworth and Hanworth and Twickenham.

A further application was made to the Commissioners in November 1901 which again sought powers for the Southall-Hounslow route, and for lines from Hampton through Sunbury to Hanworth, and also for the Willesden-Acton route. At the inquiry held at Hounslow Town Hall on 19 March 1902, it was stated that the local authorities involved had raised many objections and had demanded extensive road widenings, most to 50ft.

The Willesden-Acton route was again included in this application, but this time to start from the Uxbridge Road tramway at the Askew Arms and pass into Old Oak Road, East Acton Lane, Friars Place Lane, Horn Lane, Edward Road and Victoria Road North Acton, Old Oak Lane and Station Road Harlesden, to meet intended MET lines from Cricklewood and Paddington. A triangular junction in Horn Lane and Friars Place Lane took the line south to the centre of Acton to meet the tramway in High Street. It all amounted to a length of four miles.

It was originally intended that the Acton-Willesden line should branch from Horn Lane into Willesden Lane (now Park Royal Road) to serve the showgrounds of the Royal Horticultural Society, and continuing into a proposed new road to Twyford Abbey and Hanger Lane to join the Uxbridge Road tramway at Ealing Common. It was hoped by Robinson that this branch would be useful in conveying passengers to and from the showground at Park Royal, and much traffic would develop.

Following an agreement between the LUT and MCC to which the Metropolitan Tramways & Omnibus Co. Ltd. was also a party, whereby they defined their spheres of influence in the area, the Horn Lane proposal was withdrawn. Henceforth, the LUT were to restrict their activities to a line south of, but including Uxbridge Road.

The 1901 Bill

As well as proposals for tramways in Kingston, Richmond, Barnes, the Maldens, Surbiton, Esher, Tolworth and the Moleseys in Surrey, this Bill contained provisions for lines in Acton, Ealing, Heston & Isleworth, Brentford, Teddington, Twickenham, Hampton and Hampton Wick in Middlesex, and in Fulham, Hammersmith, Kensington, Marylebone, Paddington, and St. Pancras in London. Those in Kingston, Surbiton, the Maldens, Esher & The Dittons and the Moleseys were authorised in the resulting Act and are described elsewhere. However, of the lines in Surrey, two sections were not built; firstly, the 1.5 miles between Hampton Court and Thames Ditton (Winters Bridge) via Hampton Court Bridge; secondly the proposed continuation from Tolworth to Hook Village, a distance of 1.13 miles. The whole of the proposals written into the Bill covered about 63 route miles, while costs were estimated to be some £655,943 if all were constructed.

Powers were also sought for extensions within the County of London; from Hammersmith to Harrow Road; Harlesden via Shepherds Bush Road and Scrubs

Lane; Shepherds Bush to Harrow Road via Latimer, Lancaster, Westbourne Park and Porchester Roads, then along Harrow Road and Edgware Road to Marble Arch; northwards along Edgware Road to St. Johns Wood, then through Prince Albert Road to a point about a quarter of a mile short of Camden Town.

Also proposed were lines between Hammersmith and Hyde Park Corner via Knightsbridge; Shepherds Bush and Kensington via Holland Road; Hammersmith and Uxbridge Road via Askew Road; Hammersmith and Richmond via Putney, Roehampton and Mortlake. Due to objections made by the LCC and others, all were struck out. However, had the lines been built, connection would have been made with the Harrow Road & Paddington Tramway at Scrubs Lane and Porchester Road.

In Middlesex, there were proposals for tramways between North Ealing and Brentford via Castlebar Road, High Street and South Ealing Road; Teddington and Hampton Hill via Hampton Road; Twickenham Road and Richmond Road via St. Margarets. These also were struck out by the House of Lords Select Committee following local opposition. All that survived were the group of lines in and around Kingston.

The 1902 Bill

Arising from the Bill of 1902, an Act was obtained on 8 August which empowered the company to construct lines from New Malden to Raynes Park, Wimbledon and Merton (Tooting), with a branch line along Haydons Road to Summerstown. It also gave the company the right to construct the link between King Street, Hammersmith and Uxbridge Road via Askew Road, and to build a line from the south side of Hammersmith Bridge, through Barnes to Richmond, both of which had been previously been struck from the 1901 Bill. The Askew Road line was built; the other was not.

As originally drafted, the Bill sought to cover some 40 route miles of lines in Mitcham, Morden, Croydon, Epsom, Ewell and Esher. It was proposed that the authorised line at Kingston Hill be extended to Kingston Vale; that lines be constructed from Ham to Petersham; Thames Ditton to Broom Hill via Portsmouth Road; Ember Court, Molesey to Esher via Sandown Park; and Tolworth to Croydon via Cheam and Sutton.

In the Wimbledon and Merton areas, proposals were made for a line from Merton via Morden Road and Stonecot Hill to Ewell and Epsom; others from Stonecot Hill via Sutton Common to Sutton Station (LB & SCR); from Colliers Wood through Mitcham and Carshalton Road to Wallington Corner, where the proposed line from Tolworth would be met; and from Worple Road, Wimbledon, up Wimbledon Hill and along Wimbledon Common to the London boundary at Parkside. All were subsequently withdrawn, except for the Kingston Hill-Vale and Wimbledon Common proposals, which in turn were deleted by a House of Commons Committee on 29 May 1902 because of objections made by frontagers on the proposed lines of route.

By this time, the British Electric Traction Co., through their subsidiary undertaking, the South Metropolitan Electric Tramways & Lighting Co. had made an agreement with the LUT in which the areas to the south of a line drawn between Wimbledon, Sutton and Leatherhead be considered as the preserve of the SMET Co.

The Bill also contained a proposal making another attempt by the company to reach central London, this time from the existing line at Shepherds Bush, through Holland Park Avenue, Notting Hill Gate and Bayswater Road to Marble Arch. It also sought, once again, to gain powers to cross Hammersmith Bridge, and then to build the line to Barnes and Richmond. Due, however, to continued objection from the LCC, the Marble Arch line was withdrawn, as was the Hammersmith Bridge crossing, leaving only the lines on the south side of the river as candidates for construction.

The LUT, as part of its bargaining, had agreed to make a 60ft wide roadway along the riverside at The Terrace and Lonsdale Road, Barnes, and to construct a retaining wall on the river side of the road to prevent flooding on spring tides. This was expected to cost the company an estimated £198,750, but in the event, was never carried out.

The 1902 Light Railway Application

In this, the LUT applied to the Commissioners for authority to build a line to start from the authorised terminus at Cranford in Middlesex and to enter Buckinghamshire at Colnbrook, reaching Maidenhead via Slough and Taplow. Short branch lines, north from Slough to Langley and south to Datchet were also called for, in all amounting to 17.25 miles of route. Plans were also drawn to allow a bypass road to be built at Colnbrook. Except for Slough, most of this mileage was through rural areas.

The Commissioners held an inquiry at Slough on 22 October 1902 and, after hearing objections from the GWR, who stated that the proposed lines would run almost parallel to the railway and compete with it, and also from many frontagers, the Commissioners rejected the application, advising the company to submit the scheme to Parliament.

The 1904 Tramways Bill

The rejection of the 1902 Application did not deter Robinson's enthusiasm to extend the system westward. In writing to the LUT Chairman, C.T. Yerkes on 18 July 1903, in which he reported progress on current works, he commented on the importance of making the crossing of Kew Bridge to link up lines on either side of it. He also submitted several schemes for the 1904 Session. There was a variation of the 1901 attempt to reach the Royal Agricultural Society showgrounds at Park Royal, by linking the LUT line in Acton with the MCC terminus in Horn Lane by a junction line in Market Place about 142 yards in length. He also suggested building a branch line about 1,200 yards long, to the showground from Horn Lane. The MCC declined to allow this, and the proposal was not included. It transpired later that the showground was not a success, and the site was sold.

Another suggestion made by Robinson was that a short line in Gunnersbury Lane, Acton from the High Street to the MDR Mill Hill Park (now Acton Town) station, just under one half mile in length be built. An additional link was also proposed between Ealing and Brentford via Ealing Road, a distance of about 2.9 miles. There was also a proposal that the as yet unbuilt line to Baber Bridge be extended to Staines and Virginia Water via Egham, a distance of 9.5 miles. Lastly, there was a review of the proposed line to Cranford, Colnbrook and Maidenhead, which had been the subject of the 1902 Light Railway Application.

As had happened before, much of the planned mileage was withdrawn from the Bill at an early stage, owing to excessive demands by various local authorities. It had been estimated that £530,000 would be sufficient to undertake all work, but Brentford UDC alone demanded £556,659 to pay for the complete widening of the High Street, together with other improvements. Slough UDC, Buckinghamshire County Council and Ealing Borough Council all demanded extensive additional works, which would have cost considerable sums. The proposed Kew Bridge link was again struck out, leaving only the extension from Baber Bridge to Staines, for which Royal Assent was given on 15 August 1904. Even this, however, was never built, due to the failure of a future Bill in 1909, in which an extension of the time allowed in which to undertake the construction was applied for.

The London United Tramways (Railways) Bill 1904

The LUT terminus at Hammersmith was close to the MDR station, and a scheme was devised to allow a direct interchange to be made by tram and railway passengers, and at the same time to connect the authorised tramway in Lonsdale

Road, Barnes with the Hammersmith terminus. Plans were deposited in November 1903.

The LCC had vetoed LUT attempts to cross Hammersmith Bridge, and the company decided to ask Parliament to allow the construction of twin tunnels beneath the Thames at a point a little to the east of the bridge. The tracks in the 1,143-yard long tunnels would be connected with lines laid from the station at platform level where reversing facilities would be provided, then across Queen Street into Bridge Road where they would diverge to the east, and so enter 1 in 10 ramps leading to the tunnels. At the other end, 1 in 30 ramps would carry the tracks to Lonsdale Road. The tunnels, to be bored using the Greathead Shield system, were planned to be of sufficient height to allow for the passage of double deck tramcars working on the overhead wire system.

For trams reaching Hammersmith from Acton or Chiswick, a junction with the existing single line in The Grove was planned to diverge east, across the Broadway to meet the line in the station. On the return journey, these cars were to return to The Grove, there to go, via an east-to-south junction on to the one-way system in King Street. It was expected that the whole 1.28 mile scheme would cost approximately £732,000, while of this £213,263 would be required for purchase of lands and property, including the King Street-Grove-Beadon Road site, and £367,500 for the tunnels, etc.

The Bill was opposed by the LCC, who informed Parliament that they were authorised to construct tramways in the streets in the area, including part of Bridge Road, and also that construction of these by the company would tend to impair the foundations for their own authorised tramways. There were many other objections made on traffic, safety and legal grounds.

When the Bill came before the House of Commons Select Committee on Standing Orders, the Examiner reported that Standing Orders had not been complied with. The lines were described as railways, but were not railways as defined, as they were intended to be in part constructed on the surface of a road or street. Also, part of the line in Lonsdale Road was intended to be laid at a less distance than 9ft 6in from the kerbline. Moreover, the gauge of the lines had not been specified; a 6in to one mile Ordnance Survey map had not been deposited with the Board of Trade; and the LCC had stated that the proposal was for a tramway, not a railway. The Bill was thrown out.

The 1905 Light Railways Scheme

Preliminary estimates were submitted to the directors of the LUT by Robinson on 19 December 1904 for a system of light railways striking westward from the authorised terminus at Cranford to Reading, and another from the terminus at Uxbridge to High Wycombe. Slough was, once again, an important focal point, as a branch line was to diverge southward to Datchet and Windsor, while northward from Slough a line through Burnham Beeches was projected to join the Uxbridge-High Wycombe line at Beaconsfield. Most of the 50.92 miles of route lay in Buckinghamshire over country roads through sparsely populated areas.

Details of the scheme were that the 13.6 miles between Uxbridge and High Wycombe were to be single line with loops at an estimated £112,229 for permanent way, widenings at £20,250 civil engineering works and land acquisitions to be £7,500. For the 25.7 miles between Cranford and Reading, it was expected that costs for the double line would be £340,930 for permanent way, £20,250 for widenings, £78,367 for civil engineering works and land. The 6.4-mile link between Reading and High Wycombe would cost £53,787, plus £12,800 for works and land. The branches to Datchet and Beaconsfield were expected to add another £50,000 to costs. To all this must be added another £132,500 for power cables, £255,000 for rolling stock, plus £5,000 for Parliamentary expenses. It was expected that the whole scheme would amount to about £1,109,952. No figures were given for extension to the power station, or for sub-stations or depots.

At the meeting of the directors, it was decided to defer consideration of the scheme. Subsequent minutes of company meetings are silent on the subject; there is no further record of the proposals, and no application was submitted to the Light Railway Commission.

The 1907 Bill

One result of the LUT coming under the control of the UERL was an early assessment of the advantages of through bookings being arranged with the MDR and the tube railways. As a result of this, a series of these was introduced on 15 December 1906, which may have come earlier if the 1904 scheme had succeeded.

However, the failure of the 1904 Railways Bill did not deter the LUT from making another attempt to improve interchange facilities between the trams and railways at Hammersmith. Plans for the 1907 Bill, deposited in November 1906 gave details of a scheme to provide a pedestrian subway beneath the Broadway from the approach to the Hammersmith & City Metropolitan Railway station in Beadon Road to the north end of the eastbound platform of the MDR station.

This scheme fared no better than its predecessor. The LCC objected that the subway would seriously affect the foundations of their authorised tramway across Hammersmith Broadway, but equally, the Metropolitan Railway Company and Hammersmith Borough Council also opposed the plan. It was withdrawn. The Bill had also contained proposals for mutual through running arrangements to be made between the LUT and LCC, but these did not come about at this time. This aspect of operations was also included in the unsuccessful LUT Bill for 1909. Further details of this and subsequent proposals, Bills and Acts, together with their outcome will be discussed in Volume Two of this work.

The Richmond Proposals

The LUT made several attempts to reconstruct, extend and electrify the 1883 Kew Bridge-Richmond horse tramway, none of which came to fruition. The first powers sought in Richmond were for a light railway, 4.87 miles in extent, from the north side of Kew Bridge, through Sandycombe Road, Kew Road and Manor Road to Queen's Road Richmond, and on to Star & Garter Hill and Ham to Kingston. This was an alternative route from Kew to the centre of Richmond, avoiding Kew Road, but the application failed in the face of objections from local residents.

The eighteenth-century Kew Bridge across the Thames was unsuitable even for horse trams, and was a barrier to the direct link between the LUT lines on either side of it. The Middlesex and Surrey County Councils obtained powers in 1898 to reconstruct it, and while the MCC opposed the construction of a tramway across the bridge, Surrey did not stand in the way of the company. The Corporation of Richmond, a Royal Borough, did not favour further company-owned tramways in the town, and were considering a scheme of their own.

In November 1900 the LUT deposited plans for lines which included an extension of the Kew Road tramway from Richmond, through East Sheen and Barnes Common to Putney, and also to continue the Hammersmith line across Hammersmith Bridge, to join the proposed line at Barnes Common. The LCC and local interests in Richmond opposed the scheme, while the Putney proposal failed, which in turn caused the Corporation to withdraw their implied support for electrification of the Key Road line.

The company made another attempt in the 1902 Session of Parliament; this Bill proposed the reconstruction of the Kew Road line as a mainly double track electric tramway as far as the centre of Richmond, and then its continuation through Lower Mortlake Road, Lower Richmond Road, High Street Mortlake, The Terrace, Barnes, Lonsdale Road, and back across Hammersmith Bridge to meet the line in Hammersmith Broadway. With a total length of 5.40 miles, only 165 yards was to be single track, and 44 yards of this was at the northern end of Kew Road. The LCC again refused to consent to the Hammersmith Bridge crossing, while Richmond also opposed the Bill, and objected to the proposed terminus of the line.

On 21 February 1902, Robinson, in an attempt to mollify Richmond Corporation, offered £20,000 towards the cost of obtaining a right of way to a point near the Talbot Hotel, by making a new street via The Quadrant, Eton Street, Paradise Road and Ormond Road, or via the new Red Lion Street, to a terminus near the Town Hall. Richmond, however, would not give a decision on this. Meanwhile their Tramways Committee were busy in another direction by recommending that overhead wires should not be used on the Kew Road electrification, neither should any of the proposed lines be built until all street widenings had been carried out.

The LUT solicitor, H.G. Doggett and Clifton Robinson met the Tramways Committee and agreed to accept numerous conditions to gain the consent of the Corporation. Among these were the veto on the use of overhead wires along Kew Road, a scale of fares to be set by the Committee, and the use of small cars on the Kew Road line similar to those used at Bristol. Frequency of service along Kew Road was also to be restricted to not more than one car every three minutes, while car gongs were to be of an approved pattern, and their use to be subject to Corporation regulations. The company also undertook not to build a generating station, or to supply electric current within the borough except for their own tramway purposes, nor to promote an extension of the Middlesex lines across Kew Bridge, except at the request of the Tramways Committee.

The right to purchase the tramways after a certain period was also the subject of much discussion. The company asked for a 42-year term, the Corporation insisting on 30 years. At a later meeting between the Tramways Committee, Doggett, Robinson and LUT director Samuel White, a 30-year term and an annual wayleave of £1,250 were agreed. Fares were to be at the rate of $\frac{1}{2}$d a mile, with a minimum of 1d, together with a 2d fare between Richmond and Hammersmith, while workmen were to be able to travel this distance for 1d, or between the Gas Works and Richmond terminus for 1d return. On 11 March 1902, the two parties signed an agreement to this effect, and the LUT Act for 1902 received Royal Assent on 8 August.

Meanwhile, Middlesex and Surrey County Councils were jointly dealing with the reconstruction of Kew Bridge, and by early 1903 the work was almost complete. On 25 February, Robinson asked Richmond Tramways Committee to request the LUT to promote a connecting tramway across the bridge. He also pointed out the advantages to be obtained by the citizens of Richmond to such a connection, and the desirability of laying the tracks over the bridge before the final carriageway surfacing was carried out. However, on 10 March, the Corporation, without discussion, resolved to withhold consent to the company's application.

On 18 July 1903, Robinson, together with the LUT chairman, C.T. Yerkes, tried again, this time with a scheme to reconstruct the Kew Road line as a one-way northbound track, and to lay a southbound line to run close to and parallel with Kew Road via Sandycombe Road and Lower Mortlake Road, and to rejoin Kew Road in the centre of Richmond, but still using overhead wires to provide power to the cars. It was expected that this would cost an estimated £63,480 and, after approval by Yerkes, a Bill was prepared for the Parliamentary Session of 1904. This was submitted to Richmond Corporation on 12 October, but their Tramways Committee recommended that it should not be approved. Instead it was resolved that the Corporation would not assent to any alteration to the March 1902 agreement, as suggested by Robinson.

However, the Committee's refusal was opposed by many local bodies, and at a Town Meeting which had been held on 29 October, it had already been agreed that the cheap fares offered be accepted, and that the Corporation should ask the LUT to promote the Kew Bridge Bill. Despite this, the Tramways Committee still declined to recommend to the Corporation that it should make the request.

In the meantime, in anticipation of the inclusion of the Richmond and Barnes lines in a future construction programme, the company prepared estimates in July

1903 for doing this work, and also, again, for the conversion of the Kew Road line. Costs were expected to be £44,542 for Kew Road, £61,112 for Richmond and Barnes, £5,687 for cables etc., £8,700 for car shed and offices, £2,500 for a sub-station, and £1,000 for land. High tension feeders from Lots Road power station via the Metropolitan District Railway would cost £10,920, 35 double-deck bogie tramcars would account for £30,555, while land acquisitions for widenings, etc. would cost £218,315 and, together with an allowance of 15% for contingencies, would make a grand total of £449,927.

Robinson again wrote to Richmond Corporation on 1 December, stating that in the event of favourable consideration, the company would be prepared to defer construction of the bridge tramway until reconstruction of the Kew Road line was completed. He also said that the company was prepared to stand by the 1902 agreement in any way that the Tramways Committee though necessary. This brought the response from Richmond on 3 December that the Committee had finally recommended to the Corporation that the request be made subject to approval by Middlesex and Surrey County Councils; that no overhead wires were used on the bridge; that the Kew Road line be ready and opened for traffic by 1 January 1905 and that the conduit system be used; and the Kew Bridge line, if authorised, be opened on the same date.

Other conditions imposed were the introduction of the fare scale as originally proposed by the company, and the completion of the Richmond-Barnes line by 1 January 1905. The Corporation would also require two bonds from the company, each of £10,000, as security for the fulfilment of the agreed conditions, to be delivered before the request was made. The proposal to build the Kew Bridge crossing was then included in the 1904 Bill, but was again withdrawn in February 1904 due to demands made by Brentford UDC, which the company found to be unacceptable.

Discussions dragged on through 1905 and 1906, but the only thing to be gained was an extension of the time allowed by the Acts obtained in which to undertake the work. But during all this time, Robinson had still not given up. Early in 1906 he had attempted to placate Richmond Corporation and the residents of Kew Road by obtaining a quotation from G.F. Miles & Co. for six single-deck combination cars, each fitted with maximum traction bogies, at an estimated cost of £320 each, but nothing more came of this.

The company tried again early in 1907. This time the Richmond Tramways Committee were in favour of the LUT proposals, but the Kew Road frontagers were not. They insisted that no overhead wires should be strung along the road. This was to cause more delay, and nothing was achieved in that year.

It was at this point that the British Electric Traction Company entered upon the field with a proposal to construct lines over almost all the mileage that the LUT had been trying to achieve. Their Parliamentary Bill for 1908 sought to carry out construction in Richmond and its environs, including the Kew Road and Kew Bridge lines, together with a line to and across Hammersmith Bridge. The BET scheme, however, was soon withdrawn, due to the opposition of the LCC for the parts of the proposed lines in London.

At the same time, the LUT were again negotiating with Richmond Corporation with regard to the Kew Bridge crossing, but at the same time were trying to obtain a reduction on the annual sum to be paid to Richmond as wayleave for the continued use of the Kew Road line and for the right to cross Kew Bridge, which at £2,250 they thought excessive. Tied up with this, Robinson tried, once again, to gain approval for the use of overhead wires along Kew Road, on the understanding that, if that failed, the Kew Bridge clause would be removed from the Bill for 1908, which was then in course of being written.

It did fail, but Sir George White and the Imperial Tramways Company, both of whom had holdings of LUT preference shares, became concerned at this prospect, and offered to provide sufficient capital to reconstruct the Kew Road line and also to build the bridge crossing. The clause was retained, the Bill presented and the 1908 Act received the Royal Assent on 1 August. In it, a further extension of time until 8 August 1910 was granted in which to carry out the work.

But still Richmond Corporation would not agree to the use of overhead wires along Kew Road, resulting in the LUT deciding to ask Parliament to remove the embargo. A clause was inserted into the LUT Bill for 1909 to this effect, but opposition by Richmond ensured the loss of the clause, and the whole Bill was thrown out by the House of Commons Select Committee on 14 May 1909. The loan of £15,000 suggested by ITC did not materialise, and the financial position of the LUT, which had been deteriorating for some time, became critical. As a result, Robinson relinquished the post of Managing Director of the company on 4 February 1910.

Acts of Parliament were obtained in 1910 and 1911 to extend further the time allowed in which to complete all outstanding work, the later one extending the limit to 1 August 1912, but still nothing was achieved. The Kew Road electrification was still the main stumbling block to the scheme; the frontagers, would not have overhead wires, and some suggested that perhaps the surface contact method would be acceptable. Albert Stanley, by then Managing Director in place of Robinson, sought to explain the advantages and disadvantages of the various options open to the company, stating that the overhead trolley wire system was the only reliable method as well as being the cheapest to construct and maintain.

Differences of opinion still were to be seen, resulting in more delay. Eventually, the company decided, in discussions with Richmond Corporation, that the Kew Road tramway should be abandoned together with the proposal for the Kew Bridge connecting line, this to be done in anticipation of the passing of an authorising Act later in 1912. The last horse car, No. 22 ran into the depot at 11.20 p.m. on 20 April 1912, the trams being replaced the next day by an extension of the "General" omnibus service then terminating at Richmond. Formal abandonment of the line took place on 31 May 1912. An Act of Parliament, subsequently obtained on 7 August, gave the necessary authority for the action already taken by the company.

Farewell to the last of the horse cars operated by the London United Tramways.
(Courtesy: London Transport Museum U7863)

CHAPTER ELEVEN

THE LONDON UNITED ELECTRIC RAILWAYS SCHEME

The LUT made several abortive attempts to continue their tramways eastward beyond Hammersmith and Shepherds Bush into Central London, all of which failed in the face of unbending opposition by the London County Council. In 1901 the Central London Tube Railway, operating between the Bank and Shepherds Bush, was devising a scheme to continue its line at Shepherds Bush south to Hammersmith and then east through Kensington and the Strand back to their City terminus at the Bank, thus creating a circular, or more accurately, an elliptical route.

The LUT saw this as a threat to their interests, and George White and Clifton Robinson took the bold step of entering the fight for underground electric railway powers which, in 1901 and 1902, was at its height, with several competing promoters in the field. Consequently, on 18 November 1901 the LUT directors deposited a Bill which sought, *inter alia,* to incorporate the London United Electric Railways Company as a statutory undertaking with powers to construct and work underground "tube" railways and to build generating, stations, depots and workshops. There were two main contenders for underground electric railway powers at this time, both Americans. These were Charles Tyson Yerkes, who had visited London in 1896 with the object of assessing the scope for such schemes, and John Pierpont Morgan Jnr., of the huge American finance and industrial undertaking of J.S.Morgan & Company. Yerkes had already established a foothold in London, having bought the powers of the Charing Cross Euston & Hampstead "tube" undertaking, which was authorised in 1893 but had failed to gain financial backers. Yerkes gained control of the District Railway in the spring of 1901 and later formed the Metropolitan District Electric Traction Company Ltd., to electrify the District Line and to build a huge generating station at Lots Road, Chelsea. The MDET was reconstructed on 9 April 1902 as the Underground Electric Railways Company of London Ltd., with capital of £5,000,000, almost all of which was subscribed by American interests such as J.G.White & Co., who had a large stake in railway and tramway construction, as well as shipping and other interests, but were not connected with the White family of Bristol.

The LUER scheme was originally planned to run from Hammersmith to Charing Cross via Kensington, Hyde Park Corner and Piccadilly Circus. At the Hammersmith end a double line line loop was planned, from Addison Road to Shepherds Bush and Hammersmith with alternate trains leaving for the City from Shepherds Bush and Hammersmith. From Hammersmith a cross-river line was planned to reach Barnes, where the soon to be authorised LUT tramways were to be met, and another line was proposed from Clapham Junction to Marble Arch via Lavender Hill, Queen's (now Queenstown) Road, Battersea Park, Sloane Square and Sloane Street with an interchange with the line to the City at Sloane Street. The site chosen for a main generating station was on the Hammersmith side of the river Thames between Chancellor's Road and Crabtree Lane, a short distance downstream from Hammersmith Bridge and just within the Metropolitan Borough of Fulham. This site was also intended as a main depot and repair shops, and a smaller generating station was planned for a site on the north bank of the river immediately west of Chelsea Bridge.

The promoters of the LUER scheme were George and Samuel White, Edward Everard and James Clifton Robinson and Robinson was the Engineer. The earliest estimate of costs for the scheme amounted to £4,413,047 and a later, more detailed estimate dated 9 February 1902 totalled £5,413,250, covering construction costs of £3,510,000, with generation equipment at £300,000 and four sub-stations at £30,000 each and high and low tension cabling at £100,000. Fifty trains were included in the figures, with a total of 350 coaches, motor cars at £1,000 each and trailer cars at £500 per car. Engineering, Parliamentary and legal costs were estimated at £464,250 and interest on capital outlay during construction at £306,500.

A Joint Parliamentary Committee sat from 2 May to 26 July 1901 to examine the many underground railway proposals then before Parliament with a view to securing the best schemes for the London travelling public and ensuring that the promoters of such schemes were capable of carrying them out and working them on sound principles. This committee had to choose between a number of promoters who were competing for the same routes to the City, and one such route was the Charing Cross, Hammersmith & District Railway, promoted initially by the London & Provincial Electric Construction Co. Ltd., and backed later by two major engineering companies, Willans & Robinson Ltd., and Armstrong Whitworth & Co. Ltd. This scheme included a crossing of the Thames to Barnes from Hammersmith with a power station on the riverside at Barnes, and an end-on junction with a proposed Piccadilly – City line at Charing Cross was proposed. Both this and the Central London Railway circular scheme were rejected, and the committee insisted that the whole route, from Hammersmith through Piccadilly to the City and on to Southgate had to be built. The section north of Palmers Green to Southgate was later withdrawn by its promoters on account of objections from local landowners.

Another scheme before Parliament was the City and North East Suburban Railway, which consisted of 14 miles of route from Cannon Street through Victoria Park and Walthamstow to Waltham Abbey, and which J.S.Morgan & Co., were promoting with other parties. Early in the spring of 1902 George White was approached by Clinton Edward Dawkins, a former civil servant who was a director of the Electric Traction Construction and Equipment Co. Ltd., and the senior partner in the London offices of J.S.Morgan & Co. On Morgans' behalf Dawkins offered to join forces with the LUT directors with a view to the two undertakings constructing the through Hammersmith – Piccadilly – City – North East London line (the LUER and PCNEL schemes), as recommended by the Joint Parliamentary Committee. In essence this proposal involved the LUT side relinquishing their proposed section between Hyde Park Corner and Charing Cross and constructing as far as Hyde Park Corner, while the merged Piccadilly – City and North East London undertakings (Morgans) would carry the line through to the City from Hyde Park Corner and the proposed outer terminus at Southgate.

White and his associates agreed to the Morgan proposals and on 29 May 1902 the parties came to an agreement providing for through traffic facilities with through bookings and fares on the combined tube system, and another agreement signed on the same day, to which the London United Tramways was also a party, provided for through bookings and fares between any station on the combined undertaking and any fare stage on the London United Tramways. Examples of such fares, shown on a map of the proposed joint undertaking in June 1902 were Ealing – City (10 miles), 4d; Hounslow – City (14 miles), 6d and workmen's fares were the single fare for the return journey.

The promoters of the PCNEL scheme were John Pierpont Morgan Jnr., Clinton Edward Dawkins, Alexander Siemens, the Hon. Egremont John Mills and George von Chauvin. The proposed capital of the combined LUER and PCNEL undertaking was £11,380,000 of which the LUER was to be responsible for £4,500,000 and the PCNEL for £6,880,000. The 29 May 1902 agreement provided for both parties to share equally in the management of the joint undertaking. The construction and operation of the Clapham Junction – Marble Arch line was to be the sole responsibility of the LUER and there would be an interchange with the Hammersmith – City line at Sloane Street.

An estimate was prepared by C. Jenkins of Siemens Brothers & Co. Ltd., for the provision of the electrical equipment for the joint scheme. This company was associated with the PCNEL scheme. This estimate included the City and North-East Suburban scheme, from Cannon Street to Waltham Abbey, and covered 38 miles of route, 22½ miles of which was in tunnel. The two power stations, to generate up to 36,000 Kw were estimated at £920,000 including land and buildings at £200,000. Line equipment for 38 miles of double track accounted for £152,000 and high tension cabling, £80,000. Twenty-seven sub-stations were envisaged, each containing four rotary converters and one spare up to 300 Kw each set, and were costed at £135,000. Static transformers, batteries and switches were estimated at £205,000. Rolling stock for the LUER and PCNEL sections were estimated as 66 trains and for the CNES branch 44 trains, a total of 110 trains made up from 440 motor cars at a cost of £858,000 and 440 trailer cars at £349,800, the total cost amounting to £1,207,800. The grand total for electrical equipment amounted to £2,700,000. No additional details of estimated construction costs have come to light, and alterations to the estimates were made at various stages in the Parliamentary process.

Differences arose between the Morgan and the LUER sides by the summer of 1902. Morgans objected to the LUER having equal powers on the management committee of the joint undertaking, and the LUT directors countered this by pointing out that the huge volume of traffic to be brought to the Tube by the LUT trams entitled them to equal powers. Shortly after the parties had come to their agreement to join forces the Morgans had brought the CNES City – Waltham Abbey scheme into the partnership with no prior discussion with the LUER promoters. George White objected to this, saying that it had endangered the passage of the combined LUER – PCNEL Bill, as was evident by the fact that the House of Lords Select Committee had eliminated that part of the scheme. Later, Morgans' Parliamentary agent circulated a statement in the House of Commons Lobby which stated, *inter alia,* that "the promoters of the PCNEL Bill have nothing to do with the London United Tramways Company".

Notwithstanding these difficulties, the LUER side persevered in an attempt to secure an understanding with Morgans, and on 28 July 1902 George White submitted a proposed new agreement for the management of the joint undertaking. This still insisted upon equal voting rights for each party on a management committee of six, each company to nominate three and both companies to nominate a standing arbitrator to adjudicate on disputes in the committee. The financial clause in the agreement provided for the LUER to supply the whole of the capital for construction of the Clapham Junction – Marble Arch line, the PCNEL company (Morgans) that for the line between Palmers Green and Charing Cross and that for the construction of the line from the generating station at Hammersmith and on to Hammersmith station to Charing Cross (the "joint line") to be supplied by the parties in equal proportions. Electrical equipment at the power station at Hammersmith, rolling stock and electrical equipment of the combined undertaking was proposed to be provided by the two companies in proportion to their respective requirements from time to time. The new agreement also varied the liability of the LUER for construction costs of the Hammersmith eastward section, originally £1,555,744 to construct as far as Hyde Park Corner but reduced to £1,303,838, half the cost of construction of the joint line as far as Charing Cross.

Meanwhile, the House of Commons Committee had thrown out the LUER Addison Road – Shepherds Bush – Hammersmith loop. The preamble of the Clapham Junction – Marble Arch line was proved on 26 May 1902 and on that day the CNES withdrew their City – Walthamstow line (it had been withdrawn from Walthamstow northwards). On 8 July 1902 the House of Commons Standing Orders Committee approved the new combined Bills which received a Second Reading in the House of Commons on 16 July.

The Morgan group flatly refused to consider the terms of the proposed new agreement and denied that there had ever been any earlier agreement. On 2

August 1902 their solicitor told Hugh C. Godfray, the LUER solicitor, that Clinton Dawkins (who had since been knighted) and his associates "absolutely declined to discuss proposals on such a basis". From this moment George White resolved to wash his hands of the whole scheme. He was furious and roundly condemned the tactics of the Morgan group. Matters rested thus until 30 July when the House of Commons heard an application by Counsel for the LUER to postpone further consideration of the Bills until the Autumn Session, which was duly granted.

Chief among the other promoters seeking powers for tubes in London was the American financier and railway entrepreneur, Charles Tyson Yerkes (b. 1837), who had already come into possession of the Metropolitan District Railway Company and was preparing to extend underground electric railways throughout the Metropolis. Yerkes' company, the Underground Electric Railways Company of London Ltd., mentioned in an earlier paragraph, was largely financed by Speyer Brothers, the London branch of the Frankfurt finance house of Speyer Lazard Ellissen, which also had a branch in New York. From this date Speyer Brothers became the dominant partner in Yerkes' companies. The first directors of the UERL, appointed on 9 April 1902, were Yerkes, Walter Abbott, Frank Dawes, the Rt. Hon. Lord Farrer, Major Ernest St. Clair Pemberton, Charles James Cater Scott and C.A. Spofford, who was a director of Speyer & Company of New York. Walter Abbott was a director of the Metropolitan District Electric Traction Co. Ltd. Edgar Speyer loaned Yerkes £100,000 in March 1902 to form the UERL and on 5 April 1902 an agreement was signed between Yerkes, Speyer Brothers, Speyer & Co (New York) and the Old Colony Trust of Boston to form a syndicate to deal in UERL shares. This was effectively the beginnings of the "Combine" which dominated passenger transport in London for the next 31 years, and some of whose members remained in key positions for many years after the formation of the London Passenger Transport Board on 1 July 1933.

Following the rejection of George White's proposed agreement of 28 July 1902 by the Morgan interests events moved rapidly. A little later in August Edgar Speyer asked J.R. Chapman, the General Manager and Engineer of the UERL, for a report on the undertaking of the London United Tramways (this may have taken place even earlier, at a date prior to the proposed 28 July 1902 agreement, Chapman produced his report on 8 September, fully detailed as to finance, powers, equipment and future prospects. It was generally favourable, and said that "the general standards of polish and cleanliness are, if anything, too high for penny passengers". He made comparisons with tramway undertakings in New York and Boston which operated at a higher rate per car mile than the LUT, but foresaw improved profits as the authorised mileage was completed. He was critical of the location of Chiswick power station, where he noted that coal had to be carted and water bought from the public supply, although some artesian wells had been sunk. He concluded by saying that the LUT had to be regarded as a suburban line but had great value as a feeder to the underground lines.

The date of the next move in this story is not known precisely, but in September 1902 George White and the Imperial Tramways Company sold their majority holdings in the Ordinary shares of the LUT to Speyer Brothers. George White, in a letter dated 19 September from the Hotel Victoria, Newquay, made clear his contempt for the Morgans' tactics and that from 2 August he and Robinson had determined that they would have nothing further to do with the Morgan scheme. Morgans, in return, accused the LUT directors of making a secret deal with Speyer Brothers to allow Yerkes a free hand in developing the Great Northern and Piccadilly & Brompton schemes, whose powers Yerkes had acquired earlier. George White ignored an approach by Sir Clinton Dawkins' solicitor on 13 October 1902 to discuss the matter and on 21 October the LUT directors formally withdrew the LUER Bill.

On 29 October T.G.Ashton, MP., gave notice of a motion to re-commit the LUER Bill in the names of the Morgan syndicate, a move which was opposed by the LUT directors, who maintained that this attempt to take over and resuscitate

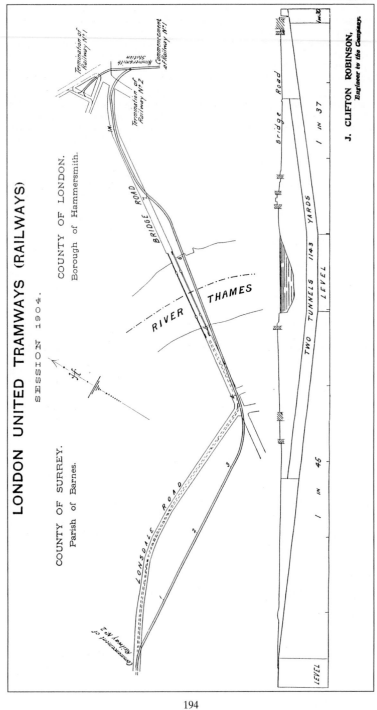

LONDON UNITED TRAMWAYS (RAILWAYS)

SESSION 1904.

COUNTY OF LONDON.
Borough of Hammersmith.

COUNTY OF SURREY.
Parish of Barnes.

RIVER THAMES

BRIDGE ROAD

LONSDALE ROAD

Commencement of Railway N°2

Termination of Railway N°2

Termination of Railway N°1

Hammersmith Station

Commencement of Railway N°1

LEVEL   1 IN 45   TWO TUNNELS 1143 YARDS   LEVEL   1 IN 37   Bridge Road

J. CLIFTON ROBINSON,
Engineer to the Company.

194

their Bill was wholly unwarranted, and that new arrangements (with Yerkes) had enabled the LUT directors to obtain a scheme of greater merit, allowing a more comprehensive integration of tramway and railway facilities. The new scheme entailed linking the LUT tramways with the District Railway and the authorised Piccadilly & Brompton tube and allowed, when the scheme was authorised completed, through fares and bookings between stages on the LUT tramways via Hammersmith District and Great Northern & Piccadilly & Brompton tube stations as far distant as Whitechapel and Finsbury Park. The first of these bookings commenced on 15 December 1906.

Ashton's motion for the re-committal of the LUER Bill was rejected by the Speaker of the House of Commons and following these events the Morgan syndicate made no further attempts to gain powers for underground railways in London. Yerkes went on to build up the London underground system, and in the meantime was appointed Chairman of the LUT in succession to George White on 19 March 1903. Later, in 1904, Edgar Speyer told the Royal Commission on London Traffic that the LUT shares had been initially offered to another party and no transaction had taken place, and when they were offered to his firm they were accepted "because the LUT undertaking made a useful alliance with the schemes of the UERL". It is possible that White had foreseen difficulties with the Morgans earlier than 2 August 1902 and had made tentative moves to withdraw from the London transport scene in anticipation of future difficulties.

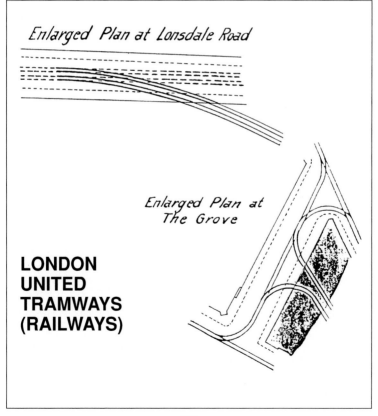

Enlarged Plan at Lonsdale Road

Enlarged Plan at The Grove

**LONDON
UNITED
TRAMWAYS
(RAILWAYS)**

CHAPTER TWELVE

LUT ELECTRIC ROLLING STOCK 1900-1912

When the newly-formed London United Tramways purchased the assets of the erstwhile West Metropolitan Tramways Company in 1894, the aims of George White and Clifton Robinson were twofold; first, to restore services which had ceased on 6 August by carrying out essential repairs to the track. especially in Acton and by placing in service new cars ordered in 1893 by the WMT and, as an interim measure, bringing up to serviceable condition the best of the cars taken over from that company. The Provisional Order and Confirmation Act of 1895 provided for an extension of the Acton line and for electrification of the system as described in Chapter 3, and it was intended that the electrification programme should start without delay. The 1895 legislation was followed by further Acts in 1898 and 1899, both of which had a close bearing upon the electrification programme, and followed a period of prolonged objections by and negotiations with the London County Council and the authorities responsible for the Geomagnetic Observatory at Kew,

The aim of early electrification was thwarted, initially, by the refusal of the London County Council to sanction the overhead trolley system in Hammersmith and by the Kew Observatory authorities, whose objections and the subsequent settlement are described in Chapter 4. Hammersmith Vestry had consented to the use of overhead electric traction at an early date and wished to have electric trams in their district, but following the LCC veto on the overhead system the Vestry resolved to approve the reconstruction of the old tramways in their district for horse traction. This resulted in the lines in Uxbridge and Goldhawk Roads, Shepherds Bush and Uxbridge Road in Acton and an extension in Acton being reconstructed in medium-weight rails of 80lb/yard. The section in High Road, Chiswick, between Young's Corner and Kew Bridge had been reconstructed as a double line with new 80lb/yard rail by the West Metropolitan Tramways Company in 1893.

The London County Council relaxed their insistence upon the use of conduit electric traction, first in Uxbridge Road. later in Goldhawk Road and finally, in late 1899, in King Street, Hammersmith and the Hammersmith Loop through Studland Street, Glenthorne Road and Beadon Road. Meanwhile, work had commenced early in March 1899 on construction of the generating station at Chiswick and the new electric lines authorised in the company's 1898 Act, as related in Chapter 3. At this time the difficulties between the LUT and Kew Observatory were partially resolved, but at a later stage further objections were raised, which delayed completion of the electrification scheme by several months pending final settlement of technical and financial questions.

Early electric trams were of the four-wheel three or four window bodied type, those of the Bristol system being typical of the period. The large double-deck bogie electric tram was, up to about 1896-7, comparatively rare, but by 1898 had found favour with a number of systems. one of these being that at Middlesbrough, which was a member of the Imperial Tramways Company group, to which the Bristol and London United companies were allied. Fifty cars of this type were supplied to the Middlesbrough system in 1898 by Geo. F. Milnes & Co. of Birkenhead, and this was the design, with detail modifications, adopted by the London United Tramways directors for their electric lines. Clifton Robinson drew up the basic design for the LUT electric tram fleet, as he had earlier for a number of horse trams built as an interim measure to reinstate services on the former West Metropolitan lines. The main feature of the Robinson design for electric cars was the "broken" staircase, consisting of two short straight flights of steps with an intermediate landing. This feature was retained for every batch of LUT cars up to and including forty top-covered trams built for extensions in Surrey, and Robinson said he was pleased to see his designs adopted by other operators, although a search of patent specifications has not revealed a registration of the design. Other features common to the first three hundred cars were the six-window body with Tudor arch windows and clerestory ceilings with ventilating lights of clear coloured glass with patterns peculiar to each batch. All had full-length platforms with double sliding doors into the saloons and short canopies.

While the first three batches of cars had minor detail differences in the overall design, Robinson had ensured that all main dimensions were identical, and this was largely continued with the forty top-covered cars ordered in 1905. The initial batch of one hundred vehicles had been built with a maximum overall width of 7ft 3in but this dimension was reduced in future batches at the instance of the Board of Trade, while certain internal measurements were standardised to conform with the requirements of the licensing authority which, in London, was the Metropolitan Police. The monitor roof design favoured by most early car builders and operators was giving way to the flat or plain arch ceiling by the early years of the twentieth century but was retained in all LUT cars built up to 1903. Robinson was a firm believer in the virtues of the open-top tramcar: on 31 March 1903 G.C. Milnes, Voss & Co., of Birkenhead wrote to him suggesting that he fit top covers to the LUT fleet, and Robinson, replying on 4 April said, "the matter has been before me in various ways for the past 30 years and I am not satisfied that any good results can accrue from their adoption". A brochure was enclosed with the Birkenhead firm's letter, showing something not unlike the top-covers fitted to some LUT cars in 1910-11, after Robinson had relinquished the management of the system.

Nos. 1-100

The first batch of one hundred cars formed part of a contract awarded to the British Thomson-Houston Co. Ltd., early in 1899. The contract included the supply and erection of the plant at Chiswick power station, details of which will be found

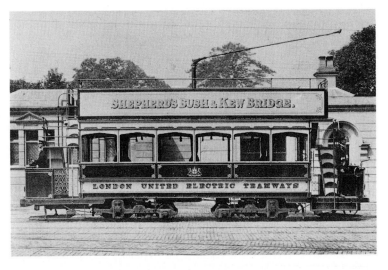

One of the first batch of one hundred cars seen at Chiswick depot just prior to the opening of services in 1901. The trucks are of the Peckham maximum traction type.

(LUT official brochure)

197

Car No. 1 was exhibited at the 1900 Tramways and Light Railways Exhibition at the Agricultural Hall, London. This view of the interior of the saloon shows the high standard of decoration achieved. (LUT official brochure)

in Chapter 15. The motors, controllers and other electrical equipment were supplied by British Thomson-Houston and manufactured by the General Electric Company of Schenectady, USA, before BTH began manufacture in Great Britain. The bodies of the cars were sub-contracted to Hurst, Nelson & Co. Ltd., of Motherwell, Lanarkshire, being the first major tramcar order carried out by this firm, who were primarily railway carriage and wagon builders, while the trucks were supplied by the Peckham Motor Truck & Wheel Company, of New York.

Each car seated 69 passengers, thirty in the saloon and 39 on the upper deck, there being one single seat on one side at the centre of the upper deck allowing the trolley mast to be set to one side to avoid blocking the gangway. The electrical equipment consisted of two BTH GE 58 six-turn 25 hp motors, and BTH B 18 controllers. Trolley masts of the "Dublin" pattern by R.W. Blackwell & Co. Ltd., with inside springs carried poles with swivel heads, and BTH resistances, cut-out switches and lightning arresters completed these cars' electrical equipment. Lifeguards were fitted, to a design by William Wood, a director of Brecknell, Munro & Rogers, who manufactured them. This design consisted of an elongated and slightly tapered tray formed from steel mesh on a rigid steel frame, suspended close to the road and provided with two small wheels which, in the event of the car pitching or rolling came into contact with the rails and prevented the tray from dragging along the track. The tray was not of the drop pattern and there was therefore no pilot gate, the leading edge of the tray being fixed at a distance of three inches from the road surface. Following a number of accidents and the introduction of the Wilson & Bennett guard with pilot gate and automatic drop tray, the Board of Trade recommended the replacement of the Wood guards with the new type and this had been done by 1904.

The first drawings of LUT cars show Brill type 22E bogies, but Nos. 1-100 were fitted with maximum traction trucks to the 14D2 design of the Peckham Motor Truck & Wheel Co. These bogies were of the swing bolster type of 4ft 6in wheelbase and the wheelsets, at first with chilled iron driving and pony wheels were supplied by the Bergische Stahl-Industrie of Remscheid, Germany. The bogies each carried one motor and the handbrake worked on all the wheels. The 1901 LUT rule book states that motormen should use the electric brake for service stops and the handbrake "for emergencies and for holding at a stop". This instruction was revised at an early date and the electric brake was reserved for emergencies, and the handbrake used for service stops.

The bodies of the cars were of a handsome appearance which was somewhat spoiled by the short canopies which moreover offered no protection against the weather for the platform staff, especially the motormen. Interior appointments were especially luxurious, the saloon longitudinal seats being upholstered in the button-back Victorian style in red patterned Utrecht velvet. The underside of these cushions was covered with imitation Morocco leather; when the cars were engaged on workmen's journeys and during bad weather the cushions were turned over with the leather side uppermost. The floors were covered with three heavy coconut fibre mats, the centre one being lettered "LUTL" in large, flowing script. Cut-glass pineapple globes protected three electric lamps along the ceilings on either side and the ceilings were finished with polished bird's eye maple veneer, the quarter-lights on each side of the clerestories being glazed with clear glass with a formal pattern in red. Six tasselled and braided handgrabs were spaced along either side of the clerestory above the seats and electric bells were fitted, with bell pushes spaced at intervals above the seats. These bells communicated with the conductor who in turn communicated with the motorman via a bell-push on the rear lantern panel, the motorman being likewise enabled to communicate with the conductor. There was also a bell-push at each end of the upper deck and these bells were worked from three Leclanché cells. Curtains in a patterned material were hung at the saloon windows and the clerestory ceilings were embellished with moulded walnut strips in natural finish picked out in gold and arranged in diamond patterns, in the centre of each was a diamond-shaped plaque of the same wood and finish. The ceiling lamps were mounted on walnut plaques of similar material and finish and the double doors in the bulkheads were surmounted by ornamental carved lintels. Interior panelling was in natural timbers of contrasting colours.

Externally the cars were finished in Venetian red and white, details of which are given in Chapter 13. Wooden decency boards, rather higher than those on most double-deck trams were placed along the upper deck sides and at the ends, and were surmounted by shallow wrought-iron grilles of a decorative pattern, Similar grilles were placed between the offside ends of the dashes and corner pillars. The upper-deck end panels and grilles differed in some cars. About half of the cars, mostly in the lower numbers up to No. 40 had a wider panel above the short canopy which was taken round to the adjacent side panel. This end panel had a quarter-round segment cut away at the bottom right-hand corner, while a narrow panel at the top of the stairs to the right was brought to the same height as this panel, both being surmounted by the grille-work. On the remainder of the batch the left-hand end panel was not brought round to the side panel, leaving a gap at the corner which presented a slightly unfinished appearance. This panel was about a foot less in width than that on the other cars and did not have the quarter-round cut-out at the bottom, while the smaller right-hand panel was shorter and the grille-work correspondingly deeper. There is no apparent reason for these differences, as views of the cars being erected at Chiswick Works show both varieties being worked on at once. Those cars with the narrow panels had as a consequence a gap about 12in wide immediately above the platform which could have allowed a small child to fall through. The panels were exchanged for wider ones after a time, but on this batch of cars minor differences in the top-deck ends persisted throughout their lives in the case of those which never received top-covers.

The upper-deck seats were of the reversible garden-seat type, made from wood finished in natural grain, and were of the "Brawn" dry-seat patent. The seat backs were of two patterns, some cars having a single rail of wood with the remainder of the back below this being filled with a panel of steel-wire mesh, others having a back consisting of four equally spaced wooden rails about 3in wide. The use of the mesh was to deter pickpockets, widespread at the turn of the century. It was found that in time the mesh deteriorated and it was replaced with closely-spaced wooden rails.

At the commencement of services destinations were indicated by the use of paper stickers on the upper-deck side and end panels, e.g., SHEPHERDS BUSH AND ACTON; sometimes the fare was shown. Later, as the network of routes expanded single-line roller-blind indicators were placed at the upper deck ends and destinations with intermediate points displayed on the upper-deck decency boards by means of transfer lettering. During the hours of darkness a cluster-light in the bulkhead lantern panel indicated terminal points by means of movable illuminated colour lenses. Details of destination indication equipment will be given in Volume 2.

The cost of these cars was £750 each, made up as £368 10s 0d for the body; £271 10s 0d per set for motors, controllers, resistances and trolley equipment, and £110 per pair for the trucks, including wheelsets. At an unknown date between 1902 and 1918 all the first 300 cars in the LUT fleet underwent a modification to the electrical equipment, probably the controllers, at the cost of £15 per car. The Nos. 1-100 batch worked the first LUT electric services, from 4 April 1901, initially between Shepherds Bush and Acton, Shepherds Bush and Kew Bridge and Hammersmith and Kew Bridge. During their first years in service they kept mainly to the Kew Bridge and Hounslow route from Shepherds Bush and Hammersmith, but later saw service over most of the system as the lines were extended and new routes opened.

A number of accidents occurred in the first few years' operation of these cars resulting in the fitting of the improved pattern of lifeguards; trials were undertaken with metal shields closely surrounding the leading ends of the driving wheels. The first three hundred LUT cars were not fitted with dog-gates as built and at least one serious accident resulted from this omission. Car No. 41 and another from a later batch were fitted with the metal shields and dog-gates fitting closely round the pony wheels. No. 41 was also fitted with Westinghouse magnetic track brakes, together with No. 87, during 1904.

The LUT was not given to experimenting with equipment, but trials were undertaken during 1909 and 1910 with a six-wheel radial truck designed by Thomas Walter Barber, using car No. 52. No record has been seen of the result of these trials, but two other systems, the Metropolitan Electric Tramways of London and

The 'Barber' six-wheeled radial truck fitted beneath car No. 52 in 1909. The centre pair of wheels guided the driving wheel sets through connecting links. (Tramway & Railway World)

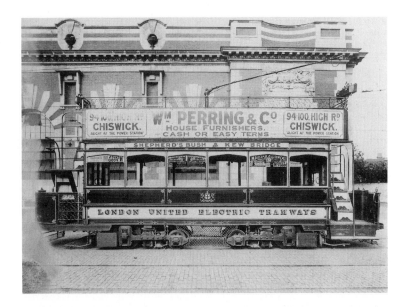

Car No. 41 in Chiswick yard. In 1905, this and several others were fitted with magnetic track brakes and metal guards in front of the driving wheels, but these were removed after a trial period. Note the destination indicators set at different levels.
(Photo: S.J. Muir, Courtesy: London Transport Museum)

Southampton Corporation also tried Barber's truck up to about 1911, and both reported on it in favourable terms but did not place production orders. No. 52 ran with the truck on the Uxbridge Road route and after trials ceased was re-fitted with Peckham bogies.

By 1909 most of the LUT car fleet required major overhauls, and with the replacement in 1910 of Sir Clifton Robinson by Albert Stanley steps were taken to rehabilitate the fleet at the same time as a major programme of track overhaul, improvements to Chiswick power station and re-organisation of the repair shops. This affected Nos. 1-100 to the extent that in addition to the outstanding mechanical and electrical refurbishment, sixty-six of them, Nos. 1, 2, 4, 7, 9, 10, 12-15, 17-19, 22, 24-25, 27-32, 35-39, 41, 43, 47-51, 56, 59, 61, 62, 64-72, 78,79, 82, 84-88, 91-95 and 98-100 were fitted with top-covers at the cost of £7,865. These covers were of light-weight construction, the financial position of the company at this time precluding all but necessary expenditure.

The covers consisted of light-timber framing with equally light T-section steel roof supports and ribs with 3in tongued and grooved boards, canvassed over. The original decency boards and metal grilles were retained but the grilles were removed from the ends and replaced with wooden panels. The ends were glazed and the six side bays were at first fitted with canvas spring roller-blinds which could be lowered in bad weather. Later, four of the six openings on each side were glazed, leaving the two centre ones still open, which remained thus for many years. One car, No. 30, had all the windows glazed at this time. The top-covering programme was carried out as cheaply as possible to the extent that the original trolley masts were retained and increased in height by the insertion of a longer piece of steel tube allowing the top of the mast to protrude through a hole in the roof. To prevent rainwater from entering the upper-deck through this hole a shallow metal tray resembling an up-turned dustbin lid was fixed inside the roof around the top of the mast to catch the water, from which a small-bore tube was led down the mast to drain from the side of the car. The doors at the top of the stairs were set at an angle, leaving a triangular gap in the floor allowing a strong draught to run alone the floor when the car was in motion. The seating layout and capacity of the top deck remained unaltered, at 39.

Of the cars which received these top-covers, one, No.27, differed from the rest in having a cover of slightly different construction. The roof framing was of wood and there were other detail differences. The most noticeable feature was the tops of the side windows, which were flat instead of arched as with the rest of the batch. The programme, commenced in 1910 was completed in 1911 and the annual directors' report for that year stated that one hundred cars had been dealt with, but in fact, 101 are recorded (including thirty-five from a later batch).

One of these cars, No. 1, was displayed in original open-top form on the stand of Hurst, Nelson & Co. Ltd. at the June, 1900 Tramways and Light Railways Exhibition at the Agricultural Hall in London. Dimensions and other details of the group will be found in the detailed rolling stock schedule.

Nos. 101-150

It is evident that Nos. 1-100 had met the expectations of Robinson and his directors, and a contract was placed in 1900 with another builder, this time Geo. F. Milnes & Co. for the supply of a second batch of fifty similar cars. These closely followed the design and dimensions of Nos. 1-100 but had different electrical equipment and trucks. The bodies were not quite identical to the first batch externally, the main differences being in the configuration of the tops of the Tudor arch windows, which were less steeply angled than the previous batch. Whereas the top-deck decency boards and grilles surmounting them were of unequal depth in Nos. 1-100 both were of equal depth on the new cars. The grille-work was also of a more ornate pattern, but the most noticeable variation was in the shape of the dash-plates, In the first cars the more common semi-circular pattern dashes were fitted, but Nos. 101-150 had dashes of a compound formation, best described as a central convex portion which was developed to a pronounced concave shape equally on either side. The tops of the dashes were also slightly higher than in the preceding batch, being level with the tops of the waist panels rather than a little below. Additionally, unlike the normal semi-circular dash usually brought round from the rear off-side along the platform to meet the bulkhead or a point close to it, these dashes were symmetrical and the additional space on the offside of the platform was taken up with an extended grille to meet the bulkhead corner pillar. These dashes, being of a flatter form than the half-round type, slightly overhung the platforms at the extreme ends, so increasing the overhang on curves. The dashes were also slightly higher than those on the first cars, and the other noticeable feature differing from Nos. 1-100 was the rear nearside top-deck ends which were markedly more rounded.

The seating capacity of Nos. 101-150 remained at 69, 30 inside and 39 out, and with the exception of the overall width of the top-deck, which in Nos. 1-100 at 7ft 3in had exceeded the maximum requirements of the Board of Trade and the Metropolitan Police, all dimensions conformed to those of the first batch.

Nos. 1-100 had been fitted out to very high standards, but these new cars were taken to an even greater degree of interior decoration and finish. The livery was overall white, with lining and corner ornaments in blue and gold. Polished brass commode handles and grab-poles, grille-work finished in silver with names of destinations and intermediate points in transferred lettering on the top-deck side panels. The upper-deck seats were again of the "Brawn" dry-seat type, the backs made from steel-wire mesh on a wooden frame.

The saloon seating was of the same material as in the previous batch, but of a golden hue with a flowered pattern, matched by the valanced and tasselled curtains at the windows. The saloon lighting was the same as the first cars, as were the electric bells, worked by Leclanché cells, passengers signalling to the conductor and he in turn signalling the motorman from his platform. The same braided and tasselled handgrabs were hung from rails above the saloon seats and the saloon floors were covered with three coconut fibre mats, again lettered "LUTL". Interior woodwork was in natural grained finish in light and dark timbers and the clerestory ceilings consisted of three-ply bird's eye maple veneer, with once more the walnut strips in diamond pattern and matching plaques relieving the otherwise plain expanse of the ceiling. The ventilation panels in each side of the clerestory were each glazed in clear and red glass with a formal pattern. Destination equipment was at first revolving blocks set in a frame above the canopy, each of the four faces showing a single line display, and transferred lettering on the upper-deck decency boards. The revolving blocks were very short-lived and were replaced by roller-blind indicators in the same position, and after a time these were raised to a higher position above the top-deck guard rails.

The "Wood" pattern lifeguard had proved unsatisfactory in the short space of time it was in use on Nos. 1-100 and on the new cars an improved pattern was fitted, the Wilson & Bennett design, marketed by Gabriel & Co. This pattern and later improved versions almost universally adopted consisted of a pilot gate which, on meeting an obstruction on the track allowed a drop-tray to fall and pick up anyone unfortunate enough to fall in front of the car. The automatic guard could also be operated by the motorman and re-set by him should it fall accidentally.

While Nos. 1-100 had been ordered by the British Thomson-Houston Company as part of the contract which established the electric tramways, this second batch of cars was ordered directly by the LUT. Because the minute books of the company prior to late 1901 have not survived, the dates of the contracts with suppliers are not known, but it is evident that the bodies and equipments had been ordered by late 1900 or early 1901. The McGuire trucks are recorded in the trade journals as on order by February 1901. The contract for the bodies was placed with Geo. F. Milnes & Co. Ltd., who had by this time become established at their new factory at Hadley, Shropshire. The price of each body was £350, and the electrical equipment, consisting of two Westinghouse type 49B 25hp motors, Westinghouse type 90M controllers, resistances and trolley gear was placed with the British Westinghouse Electric & Manufacturing Co. Ltd., of Trafford Park, Manchester, at

A busy scene at Shepherds Bush c1904 with No. 133 being made ready for the journey to Hanwell, while No. 81 stands while its passengers dismount.   (Commercial view)

the price of £268 per car set. Delivery of tramcar trucks at this time was slow, and the LUT had wished to place the repeat order with the Peckham Motor Truck & Wheel Company. This company could not meet the required delivery date and the order was placed with the McGuire Manufacturing Company for 50 sets of maximum traction bogies for £99 10s 0d per pair, the complete car costing £717 10s 0d.

The cars were specifically ordered for the Uxbridge Road services, and doubtless their superior specification owed much to the LUT management's wish to make a favourable impression upon the Ealing local authorities, whose consent to the company's proposals had been obtained at such great pains. Whilst the initial scheme was to allocate cars of a specific colour group to individual routes, the LUT also, in the case of this batch, often referred to them in correspondence as "the Ealing cars". They were first used for the ceremonial inauguration of the electric system on 10 July 1901 as described in Chapter 5 and thereafter went into service between Shepherds Bush and Southall, this route being extended to Uxbridge in 1904.

The extension from Southall to Uxbridge and the opening of the link between Hammersmith and Uxbridge Road on 31 May 1904 saw an early change of livery, when Nos. 101-150 started to appear in a combination of yellow and white. By this time the company was experiencing difficulties with the McGuire trucks fitted to these cars, and Ealing Borough Council was keeping up a running battle with the LUT over noise, about which they had complained from the commencement of services. These complaints culminated in an inspection of the cars and of the track in Uxbridge Road, Ealing, which took place on 29 November 1905 and was carried out by Col. Yorke on behalf of the Board of Trade. At the same time Robinson had identified the source of the noise as the brake rigging on the McGuire trucks, which was of a design which worked loose quickly under service conditions, producing excessive rattling, brake chatter and other sounds. In an effort to obviate, this one car, No. 117 was experimentally fitted with Brill type 22E bogies, such bogies having been fitted to a new batch of cars delivered in 1902-3. Robinson told Ealing that he had recommended his directors to have the whole fifty cars retrucked with the Brill bogies, but evidently the Board did not feel able to sanction the expenditure and later Robinson told the Board of Trade and Ealing that it had been found that alterations could be made to the brake rigging which would obviate the causes for complaint. No. 117, however, retained the Brill bogies throughout the rest of its existence.

Nos. 101-150 continued to work the Uxbridge Road services from both Shepherds Bush and Hammersmith, but noise problems persisted. Ealing Borough Council resumed their complaints and were successful in mobilising the support of most of the other councils in whose areas the cars ran, notably Acton UDC. On 1 March 1906 the link between Brentford and Hanwell via Boston Road opened, and No. 117 and another, believed to be 138 worked the shuttle service on this route, with a third from a later batch, No. 212, all three being fitted with magnetic track brakes to comply with the Board of Trade's requirements for this route. After a short time the service frequency on the route was reduced and the number of cars reduced to two.

In 1908 the company was preparing to face the demands of the London County Council, whose powers to purchase the LUT lines in Hammersmith were due to arise in 1909. It was at this time that a further stage in the history of Nos. 101-150 was reached. The company had completed its construction programme by June 1907 and had more cars than were required for current services and a decision was taken to ensure that Nos. 101-150 should form part of the assets which the LCC would be required to buy when that body purchased the Hammersmith lines. Robinson had told the directors that forty-five cars were in use to serve the Hammersmith tramways at any one time. At a date commencing in late 1908 or early 1909 work commenced on replacing the curious "concave-convex-concave" dashes of some of the cars with the common half-round type, and at the same time

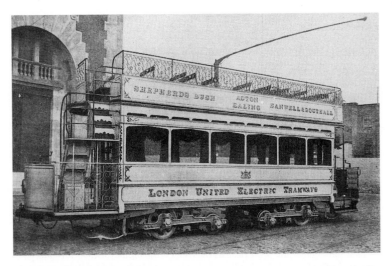

A newly delivered car of the 101-150 series standing in Chiswick depot yard. The all-white livery gave way to yellow and white in 1904, while the unusually shaped dash plates were eventually replaced with traditional ones. (The Engineer: Courtesy: J.H. Price)

the cars were repainted in the same red livery as Nos. 1-100 and the later open-balcony cars, 301-340. The cars had been repainted by the autumn of 1909, and some of them retained the original dashes until they were scrapped in 1924.

A fleet list attached to a report on the state of the system to the LUT Chairman, Charles James Cater Scott dated 11 October 1909, states that the cars were in a red livery and that two, which were not identified, were fitted with magnetic track brakes. The LUT had purchased forty-eight pairs of Westinghouse magnetic track brakes for use with McGuire trucks in 1904 and one set for the Brill type 22E trucks. There is no record of any other cars of this group having magnetic track brakes than the two mentioned in an earlier paragraph and these two cars are mentioned in the 1909 report.

Nos. 101-150 were removed from the Uxbridge Road services commencing in 1908 and most placed in store. For a short time, in 1908, when the cars in use on the Kingston routes were transferred to Middlesex, a number of cars in the yellow livery appeared on Kingston local routes, two of which were Nos. 107 and 123. A number of photographs taken in the summer of 1909 show cars from the 101-150 group in the red livery working the Kew Bridge services from Hammersmith and Shepherds Bush, and these cars have been fitted with the new dashes. Nos. 101-150 were rarely seen in use from this time and then only as breakdown cars or staff cars. From early 1910 most of them were stored at Fulwell and Hillingdon depots in anticipation of their becoming part of the settlement of the purchase of the Hammersmith lines by the London County Council. The place of Nos. 101-150 on the Uxbridge Road routes was taken by cars from other batches, chiefly the open-balcony cars originally ordered for the Surrey lines.

Nos. 151-300.

The extension of the LUT line from Busch Corner, Isleworth through Twickenham and Hampton to Hampton Court and return via Hampton Wick and Teddington to Stanley Road Junction and the secondary loop over Hampton Court Bridge through the Dittons and Surbiton and back via Kingston Bridge were expected to create exceptionally heavy holiday traffic to and from the riverside resorts centred on Hampton Court Palace, and to cope with this the LUT directors resolved to make large additions to the car fleet and the generating capacity at Chiswick power station. On 26 February 1902 they authorised the sealing of contracts for this work, those for rolling stock covering the purchase of 150 cars and their additional equipment. At this date it was intended that the whole of the Hampton Court lines including the line across Hampton Court Bridge through the Dittons to Kingston should be built at once, but these sections were removed from the construction programme when it was established that Hampton Court Bridge could not be used for tramway traffic without complete reconstruction.

The body design of Nos. 101-150 was retained for the new cars, and the electrical equipment was repeated except in the case of the controllers, which although of Westinghouse manufacture were to a slightly different pattern which did not provide for the operation of magnetic track braking.

The McGuire bogies of Nos. 101-150, having given trouble from the start, were not considered for this new batch and the new cars were fitted with maximum traction bogies of the type 22E pattern built by the J.G. Brill Company of Philadelphia, USA. The bodies scarcely differed from their predecessors, the main difference being the reversion from the oddly-shaped dashes on Nos. 101-150 to the more common halfround variety used on Nos. 1-100. The wrought-iron grille-work was slightly less ornate than on the earlier cars and the livery less flamboyant, being in royal blue and white with the customary gold lining and formal red and gold designs on the corner pillars. The bodies were supplied by two different manufacturers, and as a consequence there were two slightly varying patterns of grille-work on a class of otherwise identical vehicles.

The saloon interiors varied little from the first 150 cars, the interior panelling being, as previously, in natural timbers of contrasting colours and the clerestory ceilings of bird's eye maple with the same decorative diamond-shaped walnut strips and plaques on which were mounted the lamp fittings and bell-pushes. The seating was again in button-back Utrecht velvet, in blue with a flowered pattern and matching curtains were placed at the windows, all corresponding to the mainly

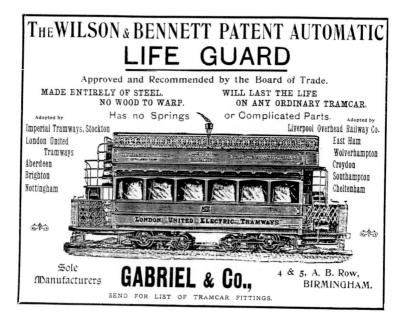

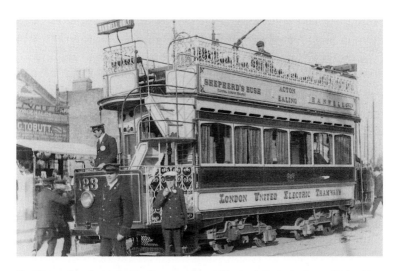

No. 123, now in yellow and white livery, standing at Shepherds Bush terminus, with the driver awaiting the signal to begin the journey to Hanwell.   (Courtesy: D.W.K. Jones)

royal blue exterior livery. The custom of elaborate decoration was continued in the ventilating lights in each side of the clerestories, which in these cars carried an exceptionally intricate design, in blue, of two dragons with tails intertwined, flanked by classical flower patterns, possibly derived from Chinese mythology.

The upper deck seating and its layout remained as in the earlier cars except that the wire-mesh seat-backs in some of 1-100 and in 101-150 had given way to an improved pattern, with "Brawn" dry seats and the backs made up of five lengths of natural grained timber spaced closely together to deter pickpockets. The seating layout remained as previously, at 30 inside and 39 on the upper deck, Roller blind destination indicators had become standard for the fleet, additional to the transferred lettering on the upper-deck side panels indicating terminal and intermediate points of fixed routes. The roller-blind indicators at each end now had bulls-eye lenses in the backs to illuminate the upper deck. The Wilson & Bennett lifeguards were repeated on these cars and an improved pattern of trolley-mast, the B/1 type made by Brecknell Munro & Rogers was used, replacing the Blackwell "Dublin" type used on the first 150 cars. As before, electric bell-pushes were arranged in the saloon, with one at the top of the staircases on the upper deck. These bells were again arranged to communicate with the conductor, who passed signals to the motorman through a mechanical bell worked by push-rods concealed in the brass curtain rails, these bells allowing communication between conductor and motorman

Contracts for the car bodies were placed with two different builders, 125 with Geo. F. Milnes & Co. Ltd., and the remaining twenty-five (Nos. 212-236) with the British Electric Car Company Ltd., of Trafford Park, Manchester, the contract price for each body in both cases being £324. The electrical equipment contract for all 150 cars was placed with the British Westinghouse Electric & Manufacturing Co. Ltd., also of Trafford Park, in the sum of £250 per car set, each set comprising two Westinghouse type 49B 25hp motors, two Westinghouse type 90 controllers, resistances, trolley equipment, cut-out switches and lightning arresters. The contract for the trucks was awarded to the J.G. Brill Company, who supplied 150 pairs of type 22E maximum traction bogies of 4ft wheelbase at £95 per pair including the wheelsets. The complete car cost £669.

Nos. 151-300 were the last open-top cars to be purchased by the LUT and the last to incorporate extravagant details of decoration and finish, which were being foregone by builders and operators by this time. In a letter to Robinson dated 7 April 1903 A.K.Baylor, Chairman of the British Electric Car Co., recommended the fitting of rattan or wooden seating in new cars, saying that most buyers were now specifying such seating, in the form of lath or plain veneer, and doing away with curtains and floor mats, all of which were difficult to keep clean. There is no trace of a reply by Robinson to this letter, but as will be seen later, the suggestion was taken up.

Meanwhile, the new "Royal Blue" cars (which were referred to in contemporary LUT press notices publicising the opening of the Hampton Court routes as "the new 'Palace' cars") were placed in service on each section of the new routes as they opened. The completion of the order created a surplus of cars for ordinary traffic pending extensions in other directions, and as traffic had developed rapidly on the Uxbridge Road route ten of the cars, Nos. 201-210 were transferred to the Shepherds Bush-Southall service. They were fitted with Westinghouse type 90M controllers for magnetic track braking, and while it is possible that the ten cars were delivered in the white livery common to 101-150 it is equally possible that they were repainted from the blue scheme after delivery. They were lettered for the Shepherds Bush-Southall service (and from 31 May 1904 for the Uxbridge services from Shepherds Bush and Hammersmith). Four of the BEC cars were used on the occasion of the formal opening of the Hampton Court routes on 2 April 1903, and another of these, No. 212, in blue livery was fitted with Westinghouse 90M controllers and magnetic track brakes for service on the Brentford-Hanwell line. where it joined No. 117 and another of the 101-150 group in 1906.

No. 275, a blue car, was fitted with a pair of maximum traction bogies supplied by Geo. F. Milnes & Co., at an unknown date, and is known to have worked on the Shepherds Bush-Hampton Court route by 1905, at which time it was known to the staff as "the Shepherds Bush rocker". Exactly what these bogies were is not recorded. As far as is known, only eight pairs of motored bogies were built by Milnes, in 1903, for Lowestoft and Gateshead. Robinson had experienced difficulty at an early date in obtaining deliveries of trucks, and it is possible that he had a

By now in red and white livery, No. 143 is seen in Goldhawk Road during the summer of 1909, bound for Shepherds Bush, with the 'Queen of England' public house in the background.
(Hammersmith & Fulham Archives)

sample pair made up by Milnes at the time Nos. 151-300 were on order, for trial purposes. No. 275 appears in a report on the system by J.G. White & Co., dated 11 October 1909 to the LUT Chairman, where it is described as a blue double-deck car with Milnes maximum traction bogies. A later schedule, of 1918 mentions No. 275 and describes it as the "pay car", single-decked and with the same bogies. During the early 1920s No. 275 was regularly seen in Chiswick taking wages boxes to the depots and transferring heavy wooden boxes of copper from the depots to the bank. The car was also noted on a track maintenance duty at the Dittons terminus at about the same time.

The cars which had been painted white for the Uxbridge Road services, Nos. 201-210, were repainted again in 1904, at the time the extension to Uxbridge and the link between Hammersmith and Acton were opened. In company with Nos. 101-150 they became yellow and white, and in this livery No. 202 was the Board of Trade inspection and ceremonial opening car when the extension from Southall to Uxbridge was opened on 31 May 1904.

By October 1909 twenty-five cars, Nos. 176-200 had exchanged the blue livery for red and thereafter there was a gradual change to red which was largely completed by 1914. Although primarily intended for the Hampton Court routes and the authorised sections which were not constructed, with the passage of time Nos. 151-300 found their way all over the system. By the time the Wimbledon and Tooting route was opened fully on 27 June 1907 they had largely replaced the later top-covered cars originally bought for the Surrey lines when the latter, after a comparatively short time in Surrey, were transferred to the Uxbridge and Hounslow routes.

In common with the rest of the fleet, by 1910 Nos. 151-300 had suffered heavily from lack of maintenance. The company's deteriorating financial position and consequent lack of attention to the track had accelerated the deterioration of the riding qualities of the cars. Following the appointment of Albert Stanley as Managing Director early in 1910, Zac Ellis Knapp, a colleague of his in the Underground Railways group was appointed as LUT General Manager and Engineer. It was found that every car in the fleet required a major overhaul and this work excluding Nos. 101-150, was put in hand without delay, the Chiswick workshops being re-organised to cope with it. Additional facilities were installed at

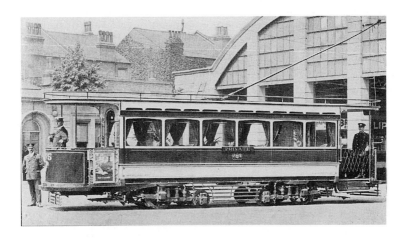

No. 175, altered for use as a saloon for private hire.   (Photo: LUT)

Fulwell Depot and the Chiswick paintshop was transferred there. At the same time top-covers, to the design as those fitted to Nos. 1-100 were fitted to Nos. 265-274 and 276-300. No. 275 was not included in this scheme, later appearing as a single-deck car for departmental use.

No. 175 was a double-deck blue car and photographs of it exist in that state from 1907, after the Wimbledon routes had opened. It has long been believed that this car was built as a single-deck private saloon for Robinson's use. Reports have now been found which establish that it was converted from a double-deck car in 1911. Both the *Tramway & Railway World* and the *Light Railway & Tramway Journal* carried descriptions of the car in their September 1911 issues, the reports indicating that the car was a new venture and suggesting that there was a potential source of income for tramway operators offering such cars for the use of private parties attending theatres or other entertainments. *The Tramway & Railway World* report described the car in some detail, stating that it had been converted "from an old double-deck car" and had been fitted out in the style of Pullman tramcars in America, with provision for a buffet at one end when required. Tables and wicker armchairs were provided, velvet curtains hung at the windows and a pile carpet covered the floor. Interior finish was in white enamel, and ornate light fittings were spaced along the ceiling. The car could accommodate twenty passengers or sixteen if a buffet was installed.

The car was used for the first time on the occasion of a wedding between members of two well-known Kingston families, which was reported at length in the *Surrey Comet* of 27 September 1911. This stated that the wedding took place on 23 September, and also described the car in detail. The motorman and conductor wore white shoes and gloves, with white caps and specially cut uniforms, and white buttonholes. The car attracted much attention in Kingston and the *Surrey Comet* reported that large numbers of people gathered in the streets, a crowd collected and the Police had to make way for the wedding guests. *The Tramway & Railway World* said that the car was available for hire to parties at a charge of 7/6d return for each distance covered by a one penny fare. It was advertised in the LUT route guides and timetables up to 1916 and thereafter private cars were advertised but the saloon was not mentioned.

It appears that the inspiration for No. 175 may have been the experience of both Stanley and Knapp in managing tramways in America, where private saloon cars were common. There is no evidence that Robinson was in any way associated with the introduction of the car or its existence before 1911. Robinson, in fact, was an enthusiastic motorist and had several motor-cars, which he used for business and private purposes. No. 175 carried no advertisements, except for an LUT poster for Kew Gardens which was displayed on the dash panels and was produced in 1910. Up to about 1913 the 151-300 group underwent few changes, continuing to work over the whole system. As a result of an accident on another system all open-top cars in service were fitted with guard rails round the top decks increasing in height from the centre to the ends to protect upper-deck passengers from injury in the case of a broken spring allowing a trolleypole to fall. This work had been carried out by the end of 1911.

From a comparatively early date, commencing from about 1903 most tramway operators were finding that upholstered velvet seating, floor mats, curtains and other luxury appointments, including cut-glass lampshades, were becoming a liability owing to the heavy expense of keeping them clean and the cost of replacements. The LUT was no exception to this experience, and from about 1906, following trials with vacuum cleaning equipment which had not proved successful, floor mats were dispensed with and seat cushions were being replaced with more durable materials. In the case of Nos. 151-300 rattan seats and backs replaced the velvet cushions as they became unusable, but curtains lasted rather longer, surviving throughout the Great War, when they gained a new lease of life owing to lighting restrictions. Other economies were the replacement of woven handgrabs with leather straps and the elimination of glass lampshades. The original electric

A maker's photograph of one of the forty open balcony cars built by the United Electric Car Co. in 1905/6, and numbered between 301 and 340 and considered to be a great improvement on the older cars. (UEC Co.: C.S. Smeeton collection)

bell signals were another casualty of the need for economies. The dual system of communication from passenger to conductor and on to the motorman fell into disuse as the equipment became due for replacement and gave way to the plain bell-rope along the ceiling. Some of the mechanical bells between conductor and motorman survived until about 1919 but the costs of maintaining the Leclanché cells working the electric bells ensured their demise at a comparatively early date.

Nos. 301-340

Clifton Robinson had been unshakeable in his faith in the virtues of the open-top tramcar. In fact, the double-deck tram in any form was disliked by him, and he only accepted it on account of the restrictions imposed upon trailer or multiple-unit operation in the British Isles. Early estimates for rolling stock for the LUT Surrey lines had provided for a further batch of open-top double-deck cars, and specifications indicating that they would be identical in almost every respect to the earlier trams were drawn up. However, Kingston Corporation insisted that the terms of their agreement with the LUT, which provided *inter alia* for the use of cars to the latest and best pattern within the borough, should be adhered to to the letter. As a result of this, tenders were sought for cars to meet these requirements, originally for a greater number of vehicles than were finally ordered. After tenders had been studied contracts for the supply of bodies and equipment for forty cars were awarded to the United Electric Car Co. Ltd., of Preston, Lancashire, the British Westinghouse Electric and Manufacturing Co. Ltd., the J.G. Brill Company, the Bergische Stahl-Industrie and Gabriel & Co. Details of these contracts will be found in Chapter 9.

Despite the earlier decision to reduce the opulent furnishings and finish which were the hallmark of the earlier cars the new vehicles were still built to a high standard, and at the time they were considered to be the best offered on the British market, and among other operators, Johannesburg took up the pattern and over a

211

period ordered a large number of them. Nos. 301-340 were double-deck bogie cars and a radical departure from the body design of Nos. 1-300. The familiar open-top short canopy body gave way to a fully canopied six-window body carrying an open-balcony top-cover of superior construction and pleasing outline. The only feature remaining from the earlier designs was the "Robinson" two-flight staircase, which was repeated unchanged but was rather less noticeable on account of its being partially surrounded by the upper-deck canopies and extended end panels. The monitor roof design had fallen out of favour with many systems from the earlier years of the century and given way to plain flat ceilings. Entry to the lower saloon was by double sliding doors.

The loss of the monitor ceilings meant that the twelve ventilating lights with their elaborate coloured glass decorations had been dispensed with and the six flat-top windows each side of the lower saloon were surmounted by shallow plain glass quarter-lights, hinged inward from the bottom. The ceiling was still of bird's eye maple veneer, however, and there were four external ventilators each side above the quarter-lights. Collapsible gates guarded the platforms and the only decorative grille-work to be seen was the customary section between the offside dash ends and the corner pillars. The upper saloon, constructed from stout timbers strengthened with steel sections was built with six windows a side which were arranged to be raised and lowered in groups of three through gearing operated by the conductor. Seating in the upper saloon consisted of reversible wooden seats, made up from single planks for seat and back from natural grain timber on iron frames, and accommodated 36 passengers in eighteen double seats. On each balcony four passengers were accommodated, on a fixed seat for three and a fixed single seat. With thirty seats in the lower saloon the total seating capacity of these cars was 74. The upper-deck sides were extended round the balconies with sheet metal screens surmounted by plain steel mesh strengthened by tubular steel stanchions, and above these were roller-blind destination indicators of the latest pattern in wooden boxes. Electric bells worked from Leclanché cells provided communication between passengers and car crews as in all the earlier cars. The full button-back upholstered velvet seat cushions were absent from the lower saloons of these cars and the almost universal longitudinal bench pattern seating consisted of wooden frames in which rested sprung cushions and seatbacks covered in durable woven rattan fibre.

The cars' electrical equipment consisted of two distinct batches of motors, supplied by British Westinghouse. Ten cars, Nos. 301-309 and 311 were fitted with Westinghouse No. 200 30hp motors and Nos. 310 and 312-340 received Westinghouse No. 80 40hp machines, The motors were mounted in Brill type 22E maximum traction bogies of 4ft wheelbase and the controllers were Westinghouse type 90M suitable for magnetic track brake operation, although the cars were not fitted with these brakes until much later in their lives. The electrical equipment was completed by trolleypoles and bases, lightning arresters and cut-out switches. Lifeguards were to an improved pattern by Hudson & Bowring and supplied by Gabriel & Co. The hand brakes on these cars were at first worked by a 16in diameter brass handwheel but these were replaced after a short time with the more common goose-neck handles.

The price for each car complete with equipment was £732 for those with the No. 80 motors and for those with the No. 200 motors it was £710. It will be seen that the costs of these cars, with the addition of top-covers differed little from those of the earlier open-top cars, this resulting from increased competition among carbuilders. The cars received the same red and white livery as Nos. 1-100, details of which will be found in Chapter 13, and this remained largely unchanged until a general simplification of exterior finishes commenced from early in 1914.

The two groups of cars had a distinct difference in their tractive effort, and this explains why, when the cars were moved from Surrey to Middlesex Nos. 301-309 and 311 went to the Hounslow routes and the remainder, with 40hp motors, went to the Uxbridge Road route with its steeper gradients. One car, No. 309, had the distinction of being the first electric tram to cross a Thames bridge on the night of 11 February 1906. The cars opened the services in Kingston on 1 March 1906.

The transfer of the 301-340 batch to Middlesex took place from the spring of 1907, shortly before the opening of the lines in Wimbledon. In 1908 a resident in Kingston, returning from a preparatory school prior to joining a public school, saw with surprise that all the trams in Kingston were yellow. Evidently some of the 101-150 group, or, possibly, Nos. 201-210 were transferred to the Kingston routes for a short period pending a more general redistribution of rolling stock arising from the problems with Nos. 101-150 on the Uxbridge Road route. The company's removal of the new cars from Surrey must have caused some hard feelings in Kingston and the other Surrey towns, and it is possible that the LUT was able to convince the councils that the heavier current consumption of their larger motors rendered their operation uneconomic, especially in view of the large amount of dead mileage involved in operating from the quite distant Fulwell Depot.

With the cars' transfer to Middlesex little of note affected them as they continued to provide the mainstay for services to Uxbridge and Hounslow. Few alterations were made to them in the first ten years of their life, the most noticeable being the removal of the destination indicators from their position above the balcony front rails to the inside of the balconies, where they were suspended from the roof immediately above the top of the stairs. This change took place in 1914 and coincided with the introduction of service numbers on the LUT system.

After the formation of the London & Suburban Traction Company in 1912, type letter system already in use on the MET was extended to the LUT and SMET, the LUT cars being allocated the letters between Z and T and, later S, but omitting V. No more passenger cars were added to the LUT fleet during the period up to 1913, but there were a few stores and service vehicles. Details of these and the acquisition of new cars in later years will appear in Volume 2.

LUT Car Dimensions

The main dimensions of all cars from 1 to 340 identical except where noted.

Length over collision fenders.............................	34ft	7^1/$_2$in
Length over platforms....................................	33	5^1/$_2$
Length over corner pillars	21	11^1/$_2$
Length over inside of saloon	21	4
Length of platforms.....................................	5	9
Width over pillars	6	7
Width over cantrails*	7	0
Height inside lower saloon deck (at centre)	6	9
Height to upper deck guard rails	13	1^3/$_4$

*This dimension applies only to open-top cars 101-300.
  (Nos. 1-100 were 7ft 3in – an infringement of B of T rules, but allowed.)

Type T cars varied as follows:

Height inside upper saloon...............................	6ft	0^1/$_2$in
Width over cantrails	7	2
Height: Rail to trolley plank	15	9^3/$_4$

Top-covered Type W and Z cars overall widths of upper deck as shown above. Height inside not shown in any record, but minimum of 6ft 0in was called for. Height from rail to top of trolley standard given as 16ft 2in.
(on these cars, trolley masts lengthened and protruded through hole in roof.)

Truck wheelbases: Nos. 1-100	4ft	6in
101-150	4	0
151-340	4	0
Total wheelbase of all cars:	14	7

CHAPTER THIRTEEN

LIVERIES, 1900 – 1912

An outstanding feature of the LUT electric trams was their exceptionally decorative liveries; unusually for electric trams, but common with horse trams, the cars operating the main routes were originally painted in distinctive colours. The other major system in the British Isles which adopted a similar scheme was that at Glasgow, which had a predominant colour scheme of bright orange, but distinguished routes by painting the upper-deck sides in distinctive colours. At the commencement of the twentieth century there was still a certain amount of illiteracy among the general public, and the different colours enabled everyone to identify the destination of a car with little or no difficulty.

The LUT system varied from the Glasgow scheme to the extent that the route colour, in the first years of the system, was the dominant feature of the livery, and thus the three main routes (north of the Thames) received deliveries of cars as they were opened, of three colours as described below. The general outline of the scheme was that red cars worked routes between the inner London termini at Shepherds Bush and Hammersmith out, at first to Kew Bridge and later to Hounslow. White cars worked from Shepherds Bush, at first to Southall and later, from both Shepherds Bush and Hammersmith to Uxbridge. Blue cars worked from Shepherds Bush and Hammersmith through Chiswick and Brentford to Twickenham and Hampton Court. Red was repeated later, in 1906, when the lines in Surrey opened with a fleet of new top-covered trams whose life in Surrey was short, being exchanged from c. 1907 for mainly blue and some red open-top cars.

Cars Nos. 1 – 100

The predominant shade for these cars was Venetian Red on the waist panels, dash plates and the upper portion of exterior bulkhead panels. Rocker panels, stair stringers, upper-deck sides and end panels, the lower portions of exterior bulkhead panels, lantern panels, the insides of stair stringers and risers, together with the backs of the stairs, were all white, while the insides of the dashes were grey. The collision fenders were black, as were controllers, stair stanchions, kick-plates and sole-bars. Upper-deck handrails, staircase handrails and commode handles were in polished brass, and all wrought-iron grille work was painted silver, together with the steel-mesh lifeguards. Trucks were finished in red oxide, and at first the trucks and collision fenders were lined out simply in white. On the upper-deck, trolley-masts and destination indicators were plain black and these latter were at first surmounted by a piece of decorative iron grille-work which was, like the rest of this work, finished in silver. These embellishments had a fairly short life and after the first few years were gradually removed as weather and general wear and tear took their toll.

Lining out of all panels was elaborate. The waist panels were lined in ⅝in wide gold strip, in three equal length sections, each having corner ornaments in gold strip to the Greek Triple Key pattern. This lining and decoration was extended to the dashes, which had the key pattern ornaments at all four corners. The rocker panels were relieved with a thin red line, the corners having the key pattern ornaments. All this lining-out and corner embellishments were extended to the exterior bulkhead panels. Blue and gold formal pattern ornaments were applied to the corner pillars and plain thin gold lining was applied to the outer stair stringers, cantrails and along the ventilation panels above the saloon windows and above each window, while a black line was applied from top to bottom of each window pillar.

The upper-deck side and end panels, white edged red, were in the initial days of electric traction plain and when electric services commenced on 4 April 1901 these panels carried paper stickers giving route terminals and fares. During this brief period the cars had not yet been fitted with destination indicators, but once these were installed the upper-deck side panels were lined out in gold with elaborate corner ornaments, and the terminal points of routes, e.g., SHEPHERDS BUSH AND KEW BRIDGE, were applied in large, gold-shaded red upper-case characters. The two larger end panels were similarly decorated, the ornaments and lettering being proportionate in size to that on the side panels.

The fleet numerals, large and of ornate design were in gold shaded blue, as was the legend on the rocker panels, LONDON UNITED ELECTRIC TRAMWAYS, in large upper-case characters. The centre of the waist panels carried a device which was based upon the arms of the City of London Corporation, from which the dagger and the motto had been omitted, the latter replaced by the legend LONDON UNITED TRAMWAYS LIMITED. Needless to say, this device had not received the approval of the College of Heralds.

These elaborate schemes persisted for the first four years of operation, but minor modifications were made fairly quickly; details such as lining out on fenders and trucks were the first to disappear, and following a contract for advertising on the cars taking effect from 1 January 1905 the upper-deck decency boards and end panels started to carry advertisements. It was, however, some time before every car lost these decorative features. All these ornate corner decorations, lines, letters and numerals were applied by transfers supplied by the London Transfer Depot, and such items as fleet numerals and ornaments varied slightly in design for each group of cars. Apart from the variations mentioned, the scheme for the red cars continued unchanged until major changes in the Company's administrative structure took place prior to the Great War of 1914-18.

Cars Nos. 101 – 150

Nos. 101 – 150 went into service when the Uxbridge Road route was extended from Acton Depot to Southall on 10 July 1901. There was a departure from the two-colour scheme of Nos. 1 – 100 and later batches in that the bodies were all over white, just possibly broken white. An old member of the Company staff referred to them in a letter to the author as "the Uxbridge Road Creams". Photographs of the

Seen at Shepherds Bush early in 1905, No. 87 is in its prominent livery of Venetian red and white, fully lined out, but now carrying advertising. This car was one of a small number to be fitted for a short period with Westinghouse magnetic track brakes.

(Commercial view: Courtesy: A.D. Packer)

cars when new show that if there was a little cream in the colour it was only very slight, probably due to the final coat of varnish. The white was applied to stair stringers, risers and inside the staircases.

There was some simplification in presentation in that fenders and trucks were not lined out, and the dashes were decorated with a plain blue line and a thinner gold line inside. There were no corner decorations on the dashes, but the scheme as a whole was equally decorative as that on Nos. 1 – 100. Lining, in blue and gold, was carried along the upper-deck side panels and on the end panels, the corners of the side panels having a floral decoration. On the waist panels the blue and gold lining was complemented by the same floral corner decorations as the upper-deck side panels, again in blue and gold. The corner pillars bore elaborate trails, in green, of ivy foliage. Rocker panels were lined in blue and gold and bore the fleet name, LONDON UNITED ELECTRIC TRAMWAYS in blue upper-case characters, the effect being slightly more ornate than the lettering on Nos. 1 – 100.

The upper-deck end panels were lined in blue and gold but without the corner decorations, and the side panels were at first lettered SHEPHERDS BUSH (Central London Railway) ACTON EALING HANWELL & SOUTHALL in gold, shaded blue. Later, in 1904 when services from Hammersmith to Uxbridge commenced, some cars were lettered HAMMERSMITH (District Railway) ACTON EALING HANWELL SOUTHALL HAYES HILLINGDON & UXBRIDGE. As in the previous batch this scheme was replaced by advertisements from the commencement of 1905 and destination boards were placed above the saloon ventilators.

Trucks were red oxide, solebars and fenders black and grille-work, handrails and lifeguards were all as in Nos. 1 – 100. The staircases, all white except for the black kick-plates and tread-plates were lined in blue and gold, including the backs of the step risers, and all other details were generally the same as the earlier cars. These cars did not retain the all-over white livery for long; from about the time of the opening of the extension from Southall to Uxbridge and the Hammersmith – Acton link on 31 May 1904 the waist panels, dashes and the space immediately above the side windows were repainted in mid-chrome yellow, the corner ornaments and other decorations were simplified, and the trails of ivy foliage on the corner pillars were replaced by dark blue and gold formal patterns. Lettering and lining remained unchanged but the fleet numerals, which were originally blue and gold shaded sans-serif figures were very short-lived and were replaced by ornate seriffed numbers, again in blue and gold and these numerals were carried over to the yellow livery. All other details remained unchanged.

The yellow livery was also short-lived. From an unrecorded date, but starting from late 1908 or early 1909, Nos. 101 – 150 underwent a second change. This time the change was to the same colours as Nos. 1 – 100, except that at about this time the company had started to buy in vermilion paint in place of the former Venetian Red. All livery details then became the same as Nos. 1 – 100 and the cars are listed as in red livery in a report on the system produced by management consultants in October 1909. The cars remained in this state until the end of their lives in service and their period in storage from late 1909-1910. This change foreshadowed a gradual change to red, which was carried out over a lengthy period, at the end of which red had become the standard colour for the LUT fleet.

Nos. 151 - 300

This batch of cars went into use on the Thames Valley routes from 1902, the first section opening on 13 September. Continuing the scheme of a distinctive dominant colour scheme for each main route this group, ordered for the Hampton Court services, had as its main colour ultramarine (described in a report on the Hampton Court opening as "Royal Blue"). This quite dark blue was applied to the waist panels and continued around the corresponding portions of the bulkheads and on the dashes, the strip above the saloon windows and the cantrails. As before the rocker panels were white, featuring also on the stair stringers and backs of the staircases, the upper deck side and end panels.

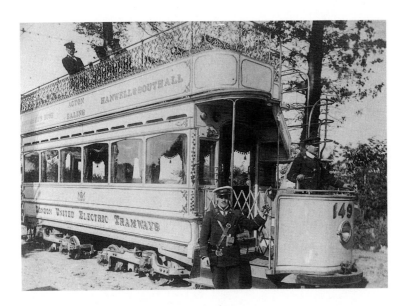

White car No. 149, fully lined out and decorated, and complete with lattice-work gates, photographed at a quiet spot on the extension to Southall. The picture may have been taken during a staff training duty prior to the opening of the extension.
(Courtesy: London Borough of Ealing Libraries)

Each group of cars had distinctive sets of ornaments, such as panel corners, corner pillar embellishments in gold and colours to contrast with the panel colours, all of which were applied by transfers, and Nos. 151 – 300 followed this pattern. The formal leaf pattern applied to the waist panel corners and abstract patterns applied to the upper deck side and end panels of the blue cars were peculiar to these cars and each is described in a surviving guard book listing contracts for supplies to the stores department, such as, e.g., "panel ornaments for red cars, H and H1". The corner pillar ornaments for the blue cars were plain gold on white, edged with red, from the top of the saloon window down to the top of the waist panel, where the pattern varied and became gold edged with red down to the top of the rocker panel. There were no dash corner ornaments, a plain double gold line being applied round the top, bottom and sides of each dash with a double gold line around the waist panels, which had formal leaf patterns in the corners. The white rocker panels were surrounded by a plain double gold line and the lettering, LONDON UNITED ELECTRIC TRAMWAYS was applied to the rocker panels, in gold shaded red. The upper deck side panels, white edged with a blue line carried destination lettering in gold shaded red, surrounded by a red line and a thin gold line, with corner ornaments peculiar to this batch, the end panels on the upper deck being similarly treated, but with no lettering.

In most other respects lining was similar to that on other batches, while black had become the standard finish for trolley masts, kick plates, fenders, controllers and sole bars. Trucks were again finished in red oxide, grillework, hand rails and stanchions followed the scheme set on the earlier cars while platforms, stairtreads and the insides of dashes were grey. Ten of these cars, Nos. 201 – 210 were allocated to the Uxbridge Road route when traffic built up after the extension through Ealing to Southall opened in July 1901. It is not known precisely when this took place, or if the ten cars were delivered in the blue livery and subsequently repainted white, but these ten cars did wear the white livery of the 101 – 150 group and the

Upper: Car No. 209 in yellow livery, seen in Paddenswick Road, Hammersmith on a journey to Uxbridge, early in 1905.
(Commercial card, C. Martin. Courtesy: Hammersmith & Fulham Archives)

Lower: Almost brand new and resplendent in its bright red and white livery, No. 327 seen at Tolworth, is being prepared for its return journey to Hampton Court.
(Courtesy: Bryan Woodriff)

October 1909 report mentioned earlier indicates that they entered service in 1903. The white livery was short-lived on 201 – 210, becoming yellow in 1904 in company with Nos. 101 – 150, when the Southall line was extended to Uxbridge.

At a later date, and prior to October 1909 Nos. 201 – 210 were repainted in the red livery described earlier in detail, together with Nos. 176 – 200. The remainder of this group were gradually repainted red from 1910 following the change of management earlier in that year, but this change was not finally completed until after the end of the Great War in 1918.

Nos. 301 – 340

These were the first top-covered cars to be acquired by the LUT, in 1905/6, and were as related elsewhere, bought specifically for the Surrey lines. All the previous batches had been delivered in distinctive colours, but these, probably because they were intended to work exclusively on the Surrey lines (but did not, in fact remain on those routes for very long) were delivered in the same colours as Nos. 1 – 100. There were minor differences and some simplification, but distinctive features such as the Greek triple key pattern ornaments on the dash corners and side panels were retained as was the ornate lettering on the rocker panels. Corner pillars were again embellished with formal blue and gold patterns and there were still formal patterns in blue and gold along the shallow panel above the lower saloon windows. The upper deck panels were white with plain red edging, these panels being continued round the balconies, with a vertical red line marking the ends of the upper-deck saloons, The ornate grille-work on the previous cars was not repeated on the upper decks of these cars, plain steel mesh taking its place finished in metallic silver paint, but the plain grilles at the dash sides were black in company with the fenders, stair kick plates and stair stanchions. There was no visible solebar, the rocker panels being brought down to conceal these. The fleet name was, as previously, in gold letters shaded blue, the fleet numerals to the same pattern as the first red cars.

This group did not undergo any livery changes until just prior to the Great War, when a much plainer style was beginning to be adopted. A maker's photograph of one shows the trucks in red oxide and lined out in some detail, but early photographs of the cars on Board of Trade inspection journeys indicate that this feature was not carried through the main batch. Contrary to some early suggestions, Nos. 301 – 340 carried the red livery from the outset, the evidence for this being the prominent Greek triple key pattern ornaments, stated in the company's records as peculiar to red cars only.

General

The change to the standard red and white livery of the Underground group of companies had started by 1905, but at 1909-10, when cars of the 151 – 300 were being fitted with top covers, the blue-livery was retained for those so fitted and the change to red commenced after 1918. Other than the changes described above liveries remained essentially unchanged until a comprehensive overhaul programme commenced in the 1920s.

Three water cars were delivered between 1901 and 1903; these were, at first, in blue, were brown by October 1909, but the ticket van delivered in 1903 still bore its original blue livery at that date, The brown/yellow horse cars retained after 4 April 1901 to work the isolated Kew Road line had become blue by October 1909.

219

CHAPTER FOURTEEN

TRACK AND OVERHEAD

The track used on horse tramways was at the outset made from steel with low carbon content often on poor foundations, and the first lines in the London area, those of George Francis Train's 1861 lines, used the notorious "step-rail" which did so much to delay the development of tramways in the capital. The introduction of the grooved rail removed much of the antagonism displayed towards tramways, but development of sound construction principles was slow and many early installations failed to stand up to the strains imposed upon them, necessitating expensive reconstruction after a comparatively short period of service.

The predecessors of the London United Tramways were no exception to such failures, The Southall, Ealing & Shepherds Bush Tram Railway Company's Shepherds Bush-Askew Crescent line of 1874 had been laid with light-weight rails of flat section on a flimsy track-bed. The Board of Trade had at first refused to pass the line for service until rectification of many faults in the construction had been carried out. Even then, it was of poor construction, and the company's successors, the West Metropolitan Tramways Company, found the line a continual drain on resources throughout their existence, The West Metropolitan company's own lines, built from 1882, were of a slightly more robust nature, but the rails themselves and their fixings, and the track-bed were still not sufficiently strong to carry continuous tram and heavy road traffic without frequent repair and maintenance work, which often went by default, The WMT tried out numerous different rail sections and fastenings in attempts to find the optimum profile and weight but without success. Pointwork was one of the weakest parts of much track construction, often being made up from the ordinary rail sections from steel of low carbon content, and without moveable blades, leading to excessive wear and frequent derailments.

The London United Tramways inherited a completely run-down system, except for the line between Young's Corner and Kew Bridge, which had been rebuilt as a double line with new rails, in 1893, as described in Chapter 2. The first task of the LUT was to make repairs to the existing tracks in Hammersmith, Shepherds Bush and Acton in order to resume services. The Kew Bridge-Richmond line, laid partly in 45lb/yard and partly in 50lb/yard rail in 1883 was never reconstructed but was refurbished and maintained in reasonable order until the line was abandoned in 1912.

Pending complete reconstruction of the lines in Hammersmith and Acton they were taken in hand with stop-gap repairs, and this was done as related elsewhere in this volume. Owing to delays in securing consent to use electric traction it was decided to reconstruct the lines in Hammersmith and Acton to horse tramway standards, albeit of a better quality than the original work, and in 1895 the line from Shepherds Bush to Acton was rebuilt as a double line as far as the North London Railway bridge in Acton Vale and extended from the west side of the bridge to the new depot as a single line with loops. In 1898 the line from Shepherds Bush along Goldhawk Road to Young's Corner was reconstructed as a double line, all these sections in 80lb/yard rails, and in 1899 the line in King Street, Hammersmith and the loop line via Studland Street, Glenthorne Road and Beadon Road to the Broadway back to King Street were relaid with 92½lb/yard rail, and a short line from Beadon Road through The Grove to King Street was added as a relief line to turn cars a little short of Hammersmith Broadway.

At its greatest extent the London United Tramways electric system consisted of 55.24 miles of route, of which all was double track except for 7.30 miles of single and 0.125 miles of interlaced line. All of this mileage was along the carriageway of streets and roads, most of which had been extensively widened and improved at the company's expense. An example of the high costs of these works was that of constructing the Surrey lines, the total costs of which, including Parliamentary expenses, construction of track and overhead, power supply equipment and rolling stock was reported to the LUT directors on 4 February 1909. This totalled £398,049, while the costs of acquiring property for widenings, paving and reconstruction of bridges amounted to no less than £365,547. These figures were not constant, and there were wide variations between the various routes, dependent upon local conditions. For many years after the first electric lines were opened in April 1901 the proportions of double, single and interlacing track changed as more track was doubled, this process continuing until as late as 1931, although the greater part of these works were completed by 1909.

Construction of the first new LUT electric lines commenced on 20 March 1899, extending the existing line at Kew Bridge to Hounslow (The Bell). This line and all subsequent mileage built up to 1904 was in 92½lb/yard rails supplied by Bolckow, Vaughan & Co. Ltd., of Middlesbrough. This rail was 6in deep and 7in wide at the base, the groove being ⅞in deep and 1in wide. The rails were supplied in 36ft lengths and were joined by fishplates weighing 56lb per pair. The rails were held to gauge by tie-bars measuring 2in by 3in at 6ft intervals and secured by nuts. Points and crossings were supplied by Askham Brothers & Wilson of Middlesbrough and were made from plain cast steel. The rails were double-bonded throughout; at each rail joint there were two copper bonds of B & S 0000 gauge with cross bonds every forty yards. The bed for the track was excavated to a depth of 12in and a concrete bed consisting of seven parts of Thames ballast to one part of Portland cement was laid in the trench. Overlying this was a floating of cement and sand and on this the paving rested.

On almost all the routes the paving consisted of blocks of Australian Jarrah hardwood measuring 3in by 9in by 4½in deep. On a few routes, notably in Hampton Wick and Uxbridge the LUT was able to obtain the consent of the local authorities to pave in hard-wearing granite setts 4in by 5in, both types of paving being grouted in with tar. The LUT was responsible for the paving between the rails and for 18in on either side of the outer rails, but in one instance the local council, that of the Heston & Isleworth urban district demanded a 24in paved margin outside the outer rails. In other cases, especially where the outer rail was closer to the kerb than 9ft 6in the LUT was obliged to pave the whole width of the carriageway in wood blocks to gain the necessary consent to deposit their Parliamentary Bill. Where the tramway area was paved in wood blocks there was usually a line of good quality granite setts laid either side of the tracks marking the division between the council's and the tramway paving.

Much of the LUT track was authorised as single line with passing loops or interlacings. By agreement with the respective councils some of this was laid as double line. Some, notably on the Hampton Court Loop, authorised as a mixture of double, single and interlaced lines, was initially laid as such and by arrangement with the councils was later doubled, in some cases further legislation being obtained to acquire the necessary lands for the street widenings. In these cases the transition to double track was carried out over several years. In High Street, Brentford special arrangements were made on account of the exceptionally narrow roadway. On this short stretch twelve strategically placed facing and trailing crossovers were laid in to enable the trams to pass the many carts and other wagons unloading and loading at the numerous commercial premises along the street. Details of these special instances are given in the respective route chapters. Points and crossings and other special work, at first in plain cast steel, was obtained from Askham Brothers & Wilson for all the lines constructed up to 1904 and for the lines constructed from 1905 to 1907 special work in manganese steel was obtained from

The track laying gang at work on the junction layout at Busch Corner, Isleworth in June 1899 on what appears to have been uncultivated land at that time.

(Courtesy: Bristol Record Office)

Edgar Allen & Co. Ltd., of Sheffield, who had taken over Askham Brothers & Wilson in 1904.

Except for the reconstruction of the old West Metropolitan Tramways Company's lines in Uxbridge Road, King Street, Hammersmith and the Hammersmith loop line in Studland Street, Glenthorne Road and Beadon Road, all LUT track construction up to 1904 was carried out by the company's own workforce under the supervision of Robinson's engineering staff. The extension from Southall to Uxbridge and the connecting line between Hammersmith and Acton via Askew Road were the last to be so built, and the 1905-7 Surrey lines and the Boston Road tramway were built by contractors.

Track construction costs naturally varied from job to job. An example of costs per mile is the 1.062 miles Hammersmith-Askew Arms section, which cost £13.974 for permanent way, equivalent to £13,157 per route mile or £6,578 per single track mile. The average cost of the Surrey lines, built by contractors was £9,970 per route mile or £5,077 per single track mile. Comparison of construction costs had to take into account differences between the earlier construction and that undertaken from 1905. For the Surrey lines and the Hanwell-Brentford link heavier rails of a higher specification were used, the 92½lb/yard rails with low carbon content giving way to 100lb/yard BS No 3 section on straight track with BS No 3C weighing 106lb/yard on curves. In addition the joints which had proved to be the weakness of earlier construction had been the subject of research by Robinson and his engineers and they had evolved a much stronger joint. replacing the plain fished joints at first used.

A major disadvantage of being one of the earliest operators of heavy bogie trams on street track lay in the fact that several engineering principles relating to such track were not fully understood at the outset. The first LUT lines laid specifically for electric traction, as described above and of low carbon content, were laid on a 6in concrete track-bed over which a floating of cement and sand was laid. The rails were joined by fishplates and in the case of the lines laid up to 1901 no soleplates were used. The first lines to be laid with plain soleplates were those between Hounslow (The Bell) and Hounslow Heath (The Hussar) and between Busch Corner, Isleworth and York Street, Twickenham, opened in 1902. The lines in Hammersmith reconstructed in 1896 and 1898, the 1895 reconstruction and extension in Acton carried out by the contractor for the LUT, and the section between Young's Corner and Kew Bridge reconstructed by contractors for the West Metropolitan Tramways Company in 1893 were all laid in light-weight rail, the last section being rebuilt with 92½lb yard rails with soleplates as early as 1904.

The new rail joint, described by Robinson as the "girder" joint consisted of the usual six-hole fishplates, in addition to which a half-inch soleplate measuring 2ft 6in by 12in was bolted to the underside of the rail, and below this a 2ft 6in length of heavy H-section steel girder, 5in wide by 8in deep was bolted through the soleplate by twelve heavy hook bolts. The concrete foundation was increased in depth by 1½in and at the joints the concrete base was increased in depth by a further 6in, ensuring that the whole joint assembly was embedded in a solid block of concrete which, in turn was mixed to s stronger specification. This was not the only improvement. At intervals of between 6 and 9ft a transverse sleeper consisting of a 6ft length of old rail was bolted, flange uppermost to the underside of the track rails and embedded in the concrete foundation.

There was a general requirement by the Board of Trade for track spacing to allow 15in clearance between passing trams. To achieve this the LUT tracks were

Newly laid rails in Richmond Road, Twickenham being levelled and packed in March 1902, on what was referred to as "Section 1" of the extension.   (Courtesy: Bristol Record Office)

spaced at 8ft centres, but at a number of places, especially at curves where tracks had been spaced to allow the barest minimum of 15in clearance notices were displayed on traction poles reading "Electric Cars Must Not Pass on This Curve". The most complicated trackwork on the LUT system was in Kingston, on the Surrey side of Kingston Bridge where the line from Hampton Wick entered Clarence Street. Within a few yards at the Clarence Street-Eden Street junction the line to Surbiton and The Dittons diverged at a triangular junction and, forty yards further a sharp turn in the opposite direction took the line into Richmond Road to reach Ham Boundary and Richmond Park Gates. About a quarter of a mile onward the main line diverged at the London Road junction to the Kingston Hill line, the other line continuing in the Maldens and Wimbledon direction. All this was complicated by the fact that there was a concentration of single line and loops in this area with an interlacing where Eden Street turned into St. James' Road.

An early track reconstruction took place in 1904 when the 1.790 miles section between Young's Corner, Chiswick and Wellesley Road, near Kew Bridge was found to be unfit for further use. This was the section reconstructed by the West Metropolitan Tramways Company in 1893, using 80lb/yard rails. The 1904 work was carried out in 92½lb/yard rails by the LUT, using fished joints with plain soleplates and no anchors. By 1909 this section had deteriorated to such an extent that its immediate reconstruction was recommended. It must be said that the section between Young's Corner and Kew Bridge saw some of the heaviest traffic on the LUT system. The recommendation for reconstruction was contained in a report called for early in 1909 by the LUT Chairman, Charles James Cater Scott after the UERL directors and Speyer Brothers had expressed concern about the general state of the company and its assets.

The report, by J. G. White & Co. Ltd. recommended that some of the sections originally constructed or reconstructed for electric traction in 1895-1900 should be renewed commencing from 1910, and all except the Surrey lines and the Brentford-Hanwell link and the track in Uxbridge should be rebuilt between 1911 and 1918. The line in Acton, already rebuilt in 1907-8 with heavier rails and girder joints was recommended for reconstruction in 1922-3, and the Surrey lines and the Brentford-Hanwell link at varying dates between 1916 and 1926. On routes with mixed single and double track the double line sections were given a life span of between four and six years more than single track. Whites' report was fully detailed. Every section had been examined closely, details of types of joints catalogued and the recommendations made.

The first indication that difficulties might arise with the track came with complaints from Ealing Borough Council about noise, immediately after services opened in July 1901. Ealing Borough was a vociferous critic and after a year or two other councils followed Ealing's lead, with Ealing actively canvassing support from the other authorities on the LUT system. Robinson started trials with different types of track joint from about 1904 and the first track to be laid with plain flat soleplates was the extension from Hounslow (The Bell) to The Hussar at Hounslow Heath, all construction prior to this having plain fished joints. From this time he developed the "girder" joint described in an earlier paragraph, which was decried in Whites' report. Whites advised the use of the "continuous" joint which, in simple terms consisted of a forged fishplate which was formed to clamp the rails together not only laterally, but around the base flange as well as the web, the object of this being to prevent vertical movement of the rail ends. Robinson did not accept this as a solution but he undertook trials with it. He also tried welded joints, which had been introduced to this country by the Tudor Accumulator Company of America, whose system had been successfully used in Berlin and Hamburg. Robinson thought this was a satisfactory system for existing track. The two rails were welded together at the joint and the fishplates were welded to the rails at six places. The cost of this system was estimated at £2 per joint including reinstatement of the paving. Other welding processes were tried, including the "Thermit" process, which was taken into general use.

Upper: The centre pole seen at Kasner's Corner, Uxbridge Road, Ealing also carried a 'stop if required' sign applicable to cars travelling in either direction. No. 148 is just about to move off.   (Courtesy: Middlesex County Times)

Lower: Youngs Corner, Chiswick, showing the side pole and span wire suspension, together with guard wires. The 'Kitsell' point and frog switching equipment is seen, sited on the pavement. Its indicator lamp showed a green light for cars turning left and white for car proceeding straight on.   (Courtesy: J.H. Price)

Robinson commented extensively on Whites' report to Cater Scott on 4 November 1909. He outlined early practice with rails and joints, remarking that early forms of construction, sufficient for horse tramways, had proved inadequate for electric traction. These methods had been applied to the first electric lines of the LUT but with slightly heavier rails. The heavier electric trams and intensive services, with higher speeds were found to cause movement at plain fished joints, and the joint, once loosened, progressively deteriorated until the rail ends were hammered to such an extent that they had to be cut short and lengths of new rail let in. The Ealing track had been fitted with girder joints after the borough council's complaints to the Board of Trade, corrugations ground out and the council now regarded the track as satisfactory. White had recommended the renewal of the concrete foundations, and proposed that this and other work should be done at expenditure of £420,000. Robinson insisted that renewal of the concrete was unnecessary. Whites' proposal covered all the LUT lines except the track in Acton, the Hanwell-Brentford link, the local routes in Kingston and the section between Haydon's Road Junction and Summerstown terminus.

Whites recommended that their renewal scheme should commence as early as 1910, Robinson proposing dates generally between three and six years later. His estimated renewal costs were £287,498. to which he added £4,397 to cover the costs of new points and crossings on sections proposed for reconstruction within three years. The Hammersmith lines were not included in these figures because by this time the London County Council had given notice of their intention to exercise their power to purchase them. White recommended that ten sections of line totalling 19.81 miles of single track be rebuilt over three years from 1910 at costs of £122,450, which Robinson categorised as excessive. At the time Robinson produced his report to Cater Scott he was about to be replaced as Managing Director and Engineer and from the start of 1910 the new regime was in place.

Albert Stanley and Zac Ellis Knapp, now respectively Managing Director and General Manager and Engineer had been brought in from the UERL and immediately set in train changes in management procedures and working methods. Full-scale reconstruction of the track was out of the question, and instead a programme of general refurbishment of the system as a whole, at the least possible expenditure, was embarked upon. Robinson's girder joints had one weakness in that it was necessary to cut away the foundation at the rail ends to make space for the 8in deep girder section to be put in place, and the concrete reinstated at a greater depth surrounding the joint than before. Welded joints had by this time been developed as a satisfactory alternative to mechanical joints and Knapp commenced a wholesale replacement of track joints by welding. At the 1911 shareholders' meeting, it was stated that 7,500 cast-welded joints had been made during the year and 3,750 in the previous year using, the "Thermit" system.

By late 1907 the track in Hammersmith became the subject of complaints by Hammersmith Metropolitan Borough Council, and on 5 October 1908 the council took out several summonses against the company at West London Police Court, on the grounds of non-compliance with the terms of the 1870 Tramways Act respecting track and paving repairs. The summonses were adjourned to allow the LUT to seek the opinion of the High Court, the MBC retracted and on 3 June 1909 asked the Board of Trade to appoint an arbitrator. The Board duly appointed W. Worby Beaumont on 8 October and Beaumont's hearing was arranged for 16 December. By this time negotiations between the LUT and the LCC on the latter's intended purchase of the Hammersmith lines had reached a critical stage, the LUT had carried out some repair work and the MBC withdrew their application for arbitration on 9 December.

The repairs were evidently minimal and further differences between the parties resulted in the re-appointment of Beaumont as arbitrator. Meanwhile, the discussions between the LUT, LCC and the Board of Trade on the purchase of the Hammersmith lines continued, and Hammersmith MBC attempted to get the LCC to reconstruct the lines, a suggestion declined by the LCC in a letter dated 24

A double track junction layout under construction at Wimbledon Hill Road in 1906. The curved section was to lead into Worple Road. Part of this layout was later removed.

(Courtesy: London Borough of Merton)

March 1911. Beaumont's award was given on 3 May 1912. He found that the LUT "had always rectified track defects when asked and Hammersmith MBC had not found it necessary to repair the track paving themselves from 9 December 1909". The request to reconstruct the track was unreasonable and the MBC was ordered to pay the costs of the arbitration and the award. However, by 7 June 1912 the Board of Trade was convinced that reconstruction was necessary, they having received numerous complaints about both track and cars. On 25 June the MBC inspected every piece of track in the borough and reported fully on its condition.

The financial position of the LUT was critical and the situation was worsening. The LCC took the matter in hand and an agreement between the LCC and LUT was sealed on 31 May 1912 for the reconstruction of the Uxbridge Road line between Shepherds Bush terminus and the Askew Arms, in heavy girder rails, and this work was completed at the end of November 1912. The LCC advanced the money for the work to the LUT with the LUT paying interest on the capital.

In January 1913 the LCC again agreed to advance funds to the LUT and on 12 March an agreement was sealed for reconstruction of the Goldhawk Road, King Street and the loop lines. On 17 July 1913 the LCC Highways Committee voted to arrange with the LUT to reconstruct the King Street track between Shaftesbury Road (now Dalling Road) and the Broadway, the loop line and Goldhawk Road between Young's Corner and Paddenswick Road. £19,700 was voted for this work, to be done in heavy rails with anchor joints.

The track between Brentford Bridge and Hounslow (The Bell) was laid in 1899 with 92½lb/yard rail, plain fished joints and without soleplates. It had become irreparable by 1912 and Heston & Isleworth UDC asked for it to be renewed. On 9 July 1913 the UDC Works Committee reported that agreement had been reached with the LUT for renewal of the rails and paving and that it had been agreed that the LUT should be responsible to maintain the margins for 18in outside the outer rails instead of the 24in stipulated in the original agreement. The UDC also granted

Upper: Rails being laid and track levelling in progress at Hampton Road, Twickenham in April 1902. Soleplates and rail anchors, together with tie-bars are to be seen, as is also a track gauge in the foreground.

Lower: Laying wood block paving on a previously completed section of track at Hampton Road, Twickenham in March 1902. After laying, molten tar was run in between the blocks to lock them in place. (Courtesy: Bristol Record Office) the company an extension of its tenure until 31 December 1930. The reconstruction was carried out by Dick, Kerr & Co. Ltd., but the cost of the work is not recorded in the company's minute books. Dick, Kerr & Co., had agreed to give the LUT an option to cover the cost of the work either by cash or on six months bills carrying interest at 6% per annum. The outcome of this is not recorded.

On 4 August 1914 the Great War started, and notwithstanding wartime conditions the councils of Ealing, Hanwell and Southall pressed for reconstruction of the track in their districts. On 9 December 1914 the LUT directors authorised £9,000 to reconstruct the half-mile of line in Uxbridge Road, Hanwell and entered into negotiations on the Ealing and Southall lines. On 13 January 1915 the directors were told that the position in Southall had become critical and James Devonshire, who had succeeded Albert Stanley as Managing Director, undertook to report on the costs involved. On 14 April £32,000 expenditure was approved to reconstruct the 1.543 miles of double line in Southall, but the company's financial position had worsened and the Hanwell reconstruction was postponed indefinitely.

On 27 July 1915 the proposed reconstruction of the Ealing track was postponed, but the question remained, and on 8 December the directors discussed an estimate from Dick, Kerr & Co. Ltd., to carry out the work for £40,000. The question of the Ealing track had been bedevilled since 1908 by the centre poles in the town, which the council had insisted upon in the first place but now wanted them removed, at the company's expense. By 2 February 1916 rails were unobtainable and all reconstruction was deferred indefinitely. Additionally, by this time the company had fallen into the hands of a Receiver and only expenditure of the utmost importance could he sanctioned.

On 6 March 1917 the Receiver's approval was obtained to carry out extremely urgent repair work in Ealing and Hanwell. To obtain additional life from some sections on the Hampton Court Loop the rail grooves were deepened; on 14 August a special directors' meeting sanctioned £1,000 for milling the grooves on a section of track at Hampton Wick. This work was carried out by the Woods-Gilbert Rail Planing Co. Ltd., it proved satisfactory and on 16 October the directors agreed to the treatment of a further ten miles of line. On 13 November it was learned that Woods-Gilbert were willing to treat the ten miles of line; an additional machine would have to be obtained and the work could commence in 4 to 6 weeks from the date of sealing the contract. Woods-Gilbert were also willing to extend the contract if the LUT exercised an option to do so three months before the completion of the first ten miles. War-time conditions delayed progress, and it was not until 25 June 1918 that the contract was finalised. Maximum expenditure was limited to £10,000 and the worst sections on the Hampton Court Loop were dealt with.

Meanwhile, the company had submitted a Bill for the 1918 Session which contained some important provisions. The future of the LUT was in grave doubt; the Bill sought powers for a financial restructuring of the company and for desperately needed increases in the fares fixed at the start of the company's operations. Parliament asked for a report on the company's position and this was provided by Alfred Baker, then General Manager of Birmingham Corporation Tramways. Baker's report, dated 24 May 1918 dealt with the physical condition of the system. In the case of the track the Young's Corner-Brentford Bridge section and Uxbridge Road from Acton Depot through Ealing, Hanwell and Southall as far as Hillingdon were all "absolutely worn out". On the Chiswick section, from Young's Corner to Kew Bridge the wheels were bottoming in the grooves, lengths of check were missing and there were signs of many derailments. Beyond Hillingdon the track required repairs but still had 7 to 9 years of life left in it. The concrete foundations were in generally good condition.

From Busch Corner, Isleworth to the Heston & Isleworth boundary at Ivy Bridge, Twickenham the track was worn out. The Hampton Court Loop was in slightly better condition but would require reconstruction later. The Brentford Bridge-Hounslow (The Bell) section, reconstructed in 1914 was satisfactory but beyond The Bell to The Hussar at Hounslow Heath the track was worn out. In

A section of interlaced track at Twickenham Green nearing completion and ready to have the wood blocks laid upon it. These can be seen stacked up on the pavement ready for use.
(Courtesy: Bristol Record Office)

Acton the 1907-8 reconstruction was good for another seven to eight years, and the Brentford-Hanwell link was in good condition as it had seen only infrequent services. This applied also to the Surrey lines in general except that the Kingston local routes had a little less life left in them than the 1907 Wimbledon sections. There was still some eight years' life left in the Surrey lines as a whole.

Baker's conclusion was that 29 miles of route required immediate reconstruction, 17.5 miles in eight years and 2.5 miles in fifteen years. Baker did not expect that materials would be available in quantity until two years after the end of the war (still six months in the future), and the company would meanwhile have great difficulty in operating its services safely. Baker recommended that heavier rails (BS No. 4 105lb/yard) should be used on straight track and BS No. 40 (111lb/yard) on curves. He estimated reconstruction costs at £406,000; essential repairs to existing track, £45,000 and £90,000 for renovation and re-equipment of rolling stock. He said that the company should have accumulated £500,000 as a reserve fund in the past fifteen years but had not done so, and recommended that £31,750 should be set aside annually in a fund to meet renewal costs at the next reconstruction period.

Parliament accepted Baker's figures and the 1918 Act, which received the Royal Assent on 21 November contained a clause whereby the company established a special reserve fund from 1 January 1919 to amount to £400,000 by 31 December 1927 and to set aside thereafter £30,000 annually for the same purpose. The company was placed under an obligation to commence the work of reconstruction as soon as practicable, and until the necessary works were carried out or the £400,000 had been placed aside no dividends were to be paid on the companys Preference and Ordinary shares. In addition, £235,000 payable by the

London County Council for the Hammersmith lines was to be placed towards the £400,000. Not less than £16,000 of the fund was to be spent on the Surrey lines and moneys forming the fund were to come from the revenue of the undertaking. The LUT was, in fact, able to meet the terms of the Act as by 31 December 1925 £400,811 had been laid aside and spent on reconstruction from the beginning of 1919. Meanwhile, in July 1919 the Woods-Gilbert company had come under the control of the Ministry of Munitions, work on the LUT contract could not start until 21 September and the LUT directors agreed to a postponement until 15 November 1918.

The Acton track reconstructed in 1907-8 had by this time deteriorated rapidly to the extent that immediate repairs were necessary and on 25 April 1919 the directors approved £2,704 expenditure to weld the track joints between the Askew Arms and Acton Depot. The first major post-war reconstruction was that of the long-delayed Acton Depot-Ealing-Hanwell section. This involved the removal of the centre poles in Ealing. The LUT came to an agreement with Ealing Borough Council on the poles as related in the second section of this chapter, and on 20 June 1919 the directors approved a contract with J.G.White & Co. Ltd., for reconstruction of the 2.696 miles of double line for £52,193, excluding rails and other ferrous materials, which would be supplied by the LUT. One director, W.C. Burton, a director of J.G.White & Co. did not vote. The contract covered the cost of replacing the Ealing centre poles with side poles and span wires, re-spacing the tracks and renewing the wood-block paving. The LUT had come to an agreement with the Borough Council whereby the company was responsible only for the paving 18in either side of the new track alignment.

Also on 20 June 1919 the directors were told that Maj. G.L. Hall, RE of the Board of Trade had inspected the track in Brentford three days earlier and reported that most of it required immediate reconstruction. Upon hearing this, the board resolved to carry out the work using the company's own resources. This was a reversion to the earlier LUT policy of carrying out its own engineering work. Expenditure of £90,000 was authorised and work commenced on 28 July 1919. Progress was delayed by the difficulty of obtaining the large amount of special work required in High Street, Brentford, where eleven crossovers were renewed. During this reconstruction the double north to east turnout from Half Acre into High Street was reduced to a single line curve. Brentford UDC asked for additional lighting at this point and the company agreed to provide the lamps and supply the current for them.

Shortages of materials caused long delays and it was not until 15 December 1920 that work on the south side of the High Street was completed, and the single line curve at Half Acre was finally laid in by 2 February 1921. Hardwood blocks were unobtainable and this resulted in the temporary use of granite setts. Here again, there were lengthy delays in replacing the setts with wood, and there was much acrimonious correspondence between the LUT and Brentford UDC. At 20 January 1925 some setts had still not been replaced and on 17 February the UDC demanded that the work be carried out without further delay and completed "without intermission". This work was financed by a loan from the London & Suburban Traction Co. Ltd. Shortly after the work had commenced the financial position caused the company to curtail expenditure pending settlement of outstanding, difficulties, which slowed the work. The 1.233 miles Brentford reconstruction was the most expensive undertaken by the company. The rails were imported from America.

Meanwhile, a decision was taken on 18 July 1919 to carry out extensive remedial work between Hayes Canal Bridge and Uxbridge terminus at estimated costs of £30,000. This section was in a better condition than the more easterly part of the Uxbridge Road route, and the work was to consist of the renewal of the many points and crossings at the loops, relaying paving and packing the rails. There were originally 24 loops between Southall and Uxbridge and it appears that one of these was taken out when this work was done. The work had been progressing for nearly six months when, on 5 December, work was curtailed. This lengthy section consisted of 5.851 route miles, of which 2.612 miles was double and 3.239 miles single track. Later, on 23 April the directors acceded to a request by J.G.White & Co. Ltd., to assign their Ealing contract to the Consolidated Construction Co. Ltd., which had been formed by a merger between J.G.White & Co. Ltd., and the contracting activities of the Dick, Kerr group. On 25 June an extension of the Woods-Gilbert contract was approved for further rail milling on the Hampton Court Loop, for £5,000. This firm had by this time been reconstructed as the Woods-Gilbert Rail Re-modelling Co. Ltd.

Work continued on the Ealing and other sections through this period and by 29 October the Manager, C.J. Spencer who had succeeded A.H. Pott on 1 November 1918 was able to report to the directors on the merits of track renewal by direct labour. His report (details of which were not given) was approved and the directors agreed to continue with the programme. At this time, the sister company, the Metropolitan Electric Tramways Ltd., had embarked upon a major track renewal scheme and Spencer, also Manager of that company had, with other senior officers of the Underground group of companies visited the USA, where Spencer inspected several large tramway systems where much of the construction and maintenance work had largely been mechanised.

On Spencer's return he devised equipment, based on machines he had seen working in America, designed to eliminate the use of horses for haulage, reduce manual labour and at the same time produce work of a higher standard at lower costs and in less time. This equipment was made available to the other two tramways in the "Combine" group, the LUT and the South Metropolitan Electric Tramways & Lighting Co. Ltd. A track-breaking car, based on the pile-driving hammer principle and built on the strengthened underframe of a redundant LUT car was prominent among these items, and machines such as stone crushers, conveyors and special purpose concrete mixers, handling large quantities of material at once were perfected and placed in commission from the early 1920's. Horses were replaced with American petrol driven end and side tipping trucks, and after some especially urgent reconstruction had been carried out on the MET system some of this equipment was loaned to the LUT, where the work of reconstruction was greatly reduced in both time and cost.

The directors considered the section between Boston Road, Hanwell and the Southall boundary at Hayes Canal Bridge on 22 April 1921 and Spencer was authorised to carry out reconstruction to a limit of £50,000 and asked to provide estimates. At this time the local authorities were suggesting the abandonment of the outer end of the Uxbridge Road route between Hanwell and Uxbridge. The LUT had included this proposal in the 1918 Bill but the clause was withdrawn and the company now opposed the proposal. On 28 August £1,300 was approved for the reconstruction of the terminus at Richmond Bridge, Twickenham but this was not implemented when it was found that the whole of the Richmond Bridge branch required reconstruction and it was abandoned as uneconomic. In Twickenham reconstruction of the 0.700 miles of line in London Road was authorised at the cost of £5,000 together with 1.543 miles in Uxbridge Road between Hanwell and Hayes Canal Bridge at the Southall-Hayes boundary at the cost of £36,000.

The LUT Hammersmith lines were still in the hands of the company at this time, and on 27 July 1920 the LCC Highways Committee had voted for reconstruction of the lines in Askew and Paddenswick Roads, the LUT to carry out the work with the LCC advancing the money, on which the LUT was to pay the LCC interest on the capital sum involved of £50,000. An agreement was sealed on 31 December 1920. The work was not all done at once but was completed by mid-1924, after the lines had passed into the ownership of the LCC. Reinforced concrete foundations with a steel mesh were used.

1922 commenced with the reconstruction programme well under way, and on 24 February the purchase of a petrol-driven "Tructractor" was authorised at a cost of £500. On 10 May the authorisation for reconstruction in Southall was revised;

£19,400 was voted for the section between Southall and Hayes Canal Bridge and £27,000 for the section eastward from the Town Hall to Hanwell. It was stated that this section would be rebuilt partly as standard and partly as open roadside construction sleeper track. At this time Middlesex County Council was considering improvement schemes on the main roads radiating outward from the inner suburbs and contemplated legislation which would have an effect on the LUT. Other work authorised at the 24 February meeting consisted of welding the rail joints between Kingston and Merton at a cost of £15,000 and reconstruction of the 2.221 miles of double line between Busch Corner, Isleworth and Twickenham junction at York Street for £70,700. On 26 May a continuation of this section, from York Street to Stanley Road Junction at Fulwell was authorised for renewal at costs of £32,700 for the 1.38 miles of route. At the same time £3,320 was sanctioned for the purchase of a "Jeffery" digger and loader, a Blake-Marsden stone crusher and conveyor and four "B" type bus chassis for conversion to lorries. On 30 June £82,451 was voted towards reconstruction costs and the directors asked Spencer to prepare a reconstruction programme for 1923 with expenditure up to £400,000. Some of this money was spent on rolling stock.

By mid-1922 negotiations had started with Middlesex County Council on the proposed reconstruction of the Brent Bridge, Hanwell to Green Drive, Southall section as a central reservation sleeper track. On 27 October the purchase of a generator and grinding machine for track welding was approved, for £650.

During 1922 and early 1923 Heston & Isleworth UDC were pressing the LUT to reconstruct the track and renew the paving in Twickenham Road between Busch Corner and the district boundary at Ivy Bridge, a distance of 1.540 miles of double line. The work started in 1923 and was being done in two stages, from Ivy Bridge to St. John's Road, which was to be followed later by the remainder from St. John's Road northwards to Busch Corner. In April 1923 the company told the UDC that

The rails in the approach road to Fulwell depot and the tracks inside were being laid at the same time as the outside walls of the building were being erected. Work had reached this stage by 10 July 1902. (Courtesy: Bristol Record Office)

work on the latter section had been postponed. and on 9 April the UDC resolved to press the LUT to reconstruct the whole of Twickenham Road in 1923-4 and to seek the aid of the Middlesex County Council in pressing their case. The LUT had told the UDC that the St. John's Road-Busch Corner section was in fair condition and its reconstruction should be deferred "until the rails were worn out". The UDC was insistent that the work be done in 1923-4 but a postponement was finally agreed and the work was completed in 1926, at which time the west to south junction at Busch Corner was removed.

With several reconstructions being carried out simultaneously there was inevitably some switching of gangs and equipment from one part of the system to another, and this was a source of irritation to the councils. More than one scheme was rescinded and reinstated but details of all such instances are not recorded. With the transfer of the Hammersmith lines to the LCC in May 1922 LCC trams from the Hop Exchange to Hammersmith were extended to Kew Bridge. The existing lay-by on Kew Bridge approach was extended and a new scissors crossover laid in at the cost of £2,100. The track and curves at the entrance to Chiswick Depot (now the property of the LCC) were reconstructed at the cost of £1,600, this expenditure being authorised on 1 June 1923. At the same time a further "B" type chassis and body were obtained for the use of the permanent way department for £300. Additional equipment for the department consisted of a pair of compressor sets and drills for which £720 was sanctioned.

On 29 June 1923 £2,100 was voted to reconstruct the two single line sections in Merton Road, Wimbledon, together with £910 to replace setts temporarily used when High Street, Brentford was finally re-paved with wood blocks. Twickenham UDC told the LUT that they were renewing the wood paving in York Street between Twickenham Junction and Richmond Bridge, and asked the company to renew the track at the same time. Spencer suggested that as the line was unremunerative it should be abandoned and a Railless (trolleybus) service instituted. The directors approved this proposal and resolved to promote a Bill for the 1924 Session to give effect to it.

In July 1923 the directors voted to reconstruct the two interlaced sections in High Street, Acton at the cost of £2,100. The 1924 Railless Bill failed on account of objections by Twickenham UDC to a proposed turning circle, and on 6 June 1924 Spencer told the directors that he had reached agreement with Middlesex County Council to abandon the Richmond Bridge branch and that the trams would be replaced by omnibuses of the London General Omnibus Company. The LUT undertook to pay the MCC £3,000 towards reinstatement of the roadway, the tram service ceased on 1 October 1924 and the track was lifted forthwith.

On 4 November the company was advised that the MCC were seeking powers in their 1925 Bill to provide that if any roads were widened to not less than 100ft the tracks on them may be reconstructed as a sleeper track not more than 35ft wide and separate from the carriageway. Spencer was asked to consult the company's solicitor on the position of the LUT and the question of protecting the company from any obligations arising from these powers.

Track reconstruction and alteration moved to Kingston early in 1925, when improvements to the road layout at the London Road-Cambridge Road junction necessitated alterations to the track and the provision of a new junction. The work was approved on 3 February at costs of £4,595 towards which Surrey County Council made a contribution of £1,295. At the July directors' meeting, a suggestion was put forward to defer expenditure on track maintenance. Spencer spoke strongly against this, saying that the board should be warned that trouble would come from the local authorities. Spencer conceded that the financial position was acute, but current maintenance costs were quite low. No definite outcome is recorded, but it is evident that the lessons of earlier years of neglect of maintenance had been learned and that Spencer's advice was taken.

The pace of reconstruction had slowed during 1925 and for the time being the company's efforts were directed towards rehabilitation of the car fleet. Evidence of

By 3 July 1902 track laying had reached the crossover at the terminus at Staines Road, Hounslow, close to 'The Hussar' public house. The traction poles are already in place, but without the wires. (Courtesy: Bristol Record Office)

this is seen in a board minute dated 1 April 1926 when authorisation for welding fishplates and rail joints between Kingston and Merton and reconstruction of the track in Twickenham Road between Busch Corner and Ivy Bridge and between Southall and Hanwell, involving expenditure of £59,725 was rescinded, work on these projects not having commenced, although it was sanctioned on 30 June 1922.

As stated in an earlier paragraph the work in Twickenham Road was completed later in 1926 but other work was postponed for several more years. There were originally twenty-four loops in Uxbridge Road between Uxbridge and Southall, two of them a quarter of a mile in length. All these loops were still in position at the end of the war in 1918 and the first reference to the disconnection of any of them is contained in a board minute dated 27 January 1927 which authorised the abandonment of nine of them to take account of increased rolling stock speeds. This arose from the fitting of 80 cars from 1923 with new Metropolitan-Vickers high speed motors and magnetic track brakes. The Engineer's official track plan dated 1 January 1929 shows seventeen loops still in position, and two more had been removed by 1933 leaving fifteen which remained until the end of tramway operation. The removal of these loops and the installation of colour-light signals enabled the company to make the best use of the re-motored cars and the new high-speed "Feltham" type cars which went into service in January 1931.

Work on the Uxbridge Road continued on a "care and maintenance" basis during discussions between the LUT the Middlesex County Council and other interested parties on the reconstruction of the road by the MCC as a dual-carriageway between Hanwell and Uxbridge and the provision of a sleeper-track reservation along the route. At the same time the MCC was undertaking some widenings and re-alignment of the road to the east of Uxbridge. This work was carried out piecemeal and some of the many bends straightened but the trams continued to run on the old carriageway. As described elsewhere in this book proposals for a double line sleeper track tramway on a central reservation between Hanwell and Uxbridge came to nothing owing to financial difficulties.

Meanwhile, the Uxbridge Road track in Acton. which had been reconstructed in 1907-8 between the Askew Arms and Acton Depot, some 1.5 miles, had become the subject of complaints from Acton Borough Council and the MCC early in 1928. The LUT directors, upon learning that the track was "practically worn out" and was costing up to £10,000 annually to maintain, sanctioned its complete reconstruction in 110lb/yard rail with welded joints at the cost of £38,000, covering the whole of the track in the borough from the Askew Arms to the Ealing boundary at Birch Grove. The rails used were short BS No. 8 (slightly shorter in the web than standard BS No. 8), a type of rail recently introduced for use on reserved sleeper tracks and possibly ordered by the LUT with this use in mind. The decision to carry out this work was taken on 3 May 1928, immediately prior to which the directors approved the purchase of two more sets of electrically driven compressors with drills for £500 the pair, for use on reconstruction work.

On 7 June 1928 the LUT board was told of a serious cash crisis, when the Secretary said that £71.000 of capital and authorised extraordinary expenditure remained undischarged and work was coming to a standstill. Meanwhile, the track in Lower Boston Road, Hanwell which formed the westward connection of Boston Road with Uxbridge Road had been out of use for many years. The rails had been taken up in 1916 for use elsewhere during the war, but the section was not abandoned and the rails were later relaid. The directors now decided to abandon this 0.315 miles section and sanction for this was given, the costs of which. after credit for sale of the old rails, amounted to £600.

The "Foden" steam wagon purchased new in 1910 had been fitted with a hydraulic crane in 1922 in place of the original hand-worked jib crane. This new crane was of the swivelling type with extending jib and was able to carry rails, eight at a time, and place them in position for final adjustment and fixing, saving much time and manual labour. Despite the difficult financial position the directors felt able to sanction £450 to procure another second-hand five-ton wagon, of a later type on 6 December 1928. It was made clear that the expenditure was the minimum necessary to keep essential repair and maintenance work going.

From mid-1928 the financial position of the company continued to deteriorate and was causing grave concern to the senior management of the UERL and their bankers. Proposals for an overall traffic Board for London had been discussed from time to time since the Royal Commission on London traffic reported in 1905. By 1929 Bills to give effect to such a scheme were under consideration. Meanwhile, the physical state of the LUT undertaking had reached a point at which important decisions on its future as a transport undertaking were necessary. C.J. Spencer was asked to prepare a scheme for complete rehabilitation of the system. His outline proposals for this, as far as the track was concerned, involved the modernisation of the tramways north of Fulwell Depot together with the line from Stanley Road Junction through Hampton to Kingston via Hampton Court, some reconstruction of the track in Merton with 126 new trams to replace the existing fleet. This scheme covered the long-deferred complete reconstruction of the Hanwell-Uxbridge route as a high-speed tramway, and the total cost was estimated at £554,590. of which £191,200 was accounted for by track reconstruction. The other major part of the proposed scheme was the replacement of trams on the Twickenham-Wimbledon route with trolleybuses and relaying the track in Merton. Spencer envisaged completion of this scheme, if approved, by the autumn of 1930.

The company was not in a position to carry out this scheme without financial assistance. The Development (Loan Guarantees and Grants) Act, passed in 1929 was seen as a source of help to finance the scheme. An application to the Treasury for a loan under this Act was prepared, using the criteria that it was necessary to accelerate the commencement and completion of a scheme which could not

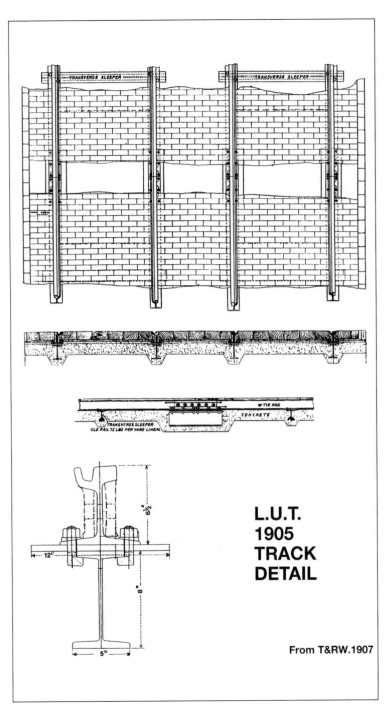

TRANSVERSE SLEEPER

TRANSVERSE SLEEPER

TIE ROD

CONCRETE

TRANSVERSE SLEEPER
OLD RAIL 75 LBS PER YARD LINEAL

6½"

12"

8"

5"

**L.U.T.
1905
TRACK
DETAIL**

From T&RW.1907

otherwise proceed. Leeds City Council were at this time considering the purchase of 150 new trams. They made an application to the Treasury for a grant under the Act, which was refused on the grounds that the work would not assist employment locally and that the industries involved were not in a depressed state. The City Council went ahead with their order for new trams but it was reduced from 150 to 100. The LUT scheme was revised a number of times and finally did not proceed, but the trolleybus scheme and some other works were carried out as described in Volume 2. The Uxbridge Road high-speed tramway did not materialise, but some improvements were carried out for forty-six new trams which were acquired in 1931, the truncated scheme being financed largely by loans from the London & Suburban Traction Company.

A number of minor alterations were made to the track layout in the late 1920s and early 1930s. In January 1920 the junction curve from Eden Street to Clarence Street in Kingston was disconnected. An additional crossover was laid in Uxbridge Road at Southall Park and another was laid in Hampton Court Road near Hampton Court Palace Gates. Earlier, in 1923, the two double line stubs branching from the line in Hampton Court Road towards Hampton Court Bridge were reduced to single lines. The two stubs were laid when the Hampton Court lines were constructed in anticipation of completion of the authorised line across the bridge to the Moleseys and The Dittons, which was never done. A crossover on the quarter-mile loop in Hillingdon Village was removed and the base of the triangle in Victoria Road, Surbiton at the Claremont Road-Victoria Road-St. Mark's Hill junction in Surbiton, which had been out of use for many years, was also removed at an unknown date.

In 1930 the westbound curve into Acton Depot was removed, in Southall a new crossover was laid in near Hambrough Terrace and the single line curve into Hillingdon (Hayes) Depot was taken out. The crossover in High Street, Acton near Church Road was moved a little further east and the facing crossover in Twickenham Road at Busch Corner, Isleworth was replaced by a trailing one. The crossover at the triangular junction at the Middlesex side of Kingston Bridge was removed on 23 May 1930. The LUT still owned 82 yards of double track in the County of London, in High Street. Tooting and in this short section were two crossovers, one trailing, the other facing. The latter, at the London end of the section was removed in the spring of 1930, and at the same time authorisation was given, on 1 May 1930, for reconstruction of the three-quarter mile section between the London county boundary in High Street. Tooting at Longley Road through High Street, Colliers Wood and High Street, Merton to Haydon's Road Junction, all double track, at the cost of £20,000. In the early summer of 1931 a crossover was installed in Broad Street, Teddington near Church Road and an 85-yard length of interlaced track in Heath Road, Twickenham was converted to double line.

The bridge carrying Uxbridge Road across the Grand Union (formerly Junction) Canal at the west end of Southall was only wide enough for a single line and there was no space for a footpath on either side of the bridge. There had been a number of attempts by Clifton Robinson and his successors to agree on a widening scheme for the bridge but the various parties were unable to reach an agreement. Finally, in late 1930, an accord was reached between the Middlesex County Council, the canal company and the LUT for the bridge to be reconstructed, the road widened to 50ft and the curvature in the track slightly eased. The track over the bridge was rebuilt as double line which was continued for a short distance across the bridge over the Yeading Brook and a further short distance west along Uxbridge Road. The Yeading Brook bridge was rebuilt by the MCC. The work was completed early in 1932, the LUT directors having sanctioned £6,000 for the tramway part of the scheme on 1 October 1931.

The LUT lines in the Thames Valley were converted for trolleybus operation, the first stage opening on 16 April 1931 when the Twickenham-Teddington-Kingston route lost its trams. The scheme continued in stages until the St. George's Road loop in Wimbledon was reached on 2 September. This, apart from the abandonment of some track, involved some alterations to the LUT track in Wimbledon because London County Council tram services operated into the town, although the LUT track continued in LUT ownership after LUT trams ceased to run there. At the Summerstown terminus at the end of Plough Lane the track was extended by two yards to meet the LCC boundary to allow LCC cars on the Hop Exchange-Wandsworth service to link with the LUT line, and thereafter LUT trams on the LUT Summerstown-Merton service ceased to run, the LCC trams commencing to run to Wimbledon Hill on 16 April 1931. A conduit/overhead change-pit was installed at the boundary, one of its first operators being the father of the late Charles S. Dunbar, a leading tramway historian. On 6 October 1932 the LUT directors approved the construction of a new terminus for trams and trolleybuses at Wimbledon Town Hall, where the track was re-aligned and a scissors crossover installed. This also involved laying a return feeder to the Wimbledon LUT sub-station to replace the rails removed, the total expenditure for these works amounting to £3,543, towards which Wimbledon Corporation contributed £1,000. This new terminus went into operation on 15 December 1932 when trams operating from Summerstown and Tooting were curtailed from the old Wimbledon Hill terminus and the trolleybuses were extended to the new turning circle at the Town Hall. The LUT trolleybus conversions will be described in Volume 2 of this work.

The Overhead.

The whole of the LUT system was worked on the overhead trolley system, the greater part on the side-pole and span-wire principle, with one notable example of the traction poles being placed in the centre of the road, between the tracks. In addition there were two short lengths of side-pole construction with bracket arms supporting the trolley wire. One of these was on a short length of single track in Beadon Road, Hammersmith, outside the Metropolitan Railway station, which was a one-way section, where two poles sufficed, and a longer section was that between the Brent Bridge at the Hanwell-Southall boundary and the Iron Bridge, a little under half a mile in extent, where poles could be placed on only one side of the road on account of mains below the surface on the opposite side. It was initially proposed to use centre poles in Goldhawk Road, Shepherds Bush, but by agreement between the LUT and Hammersmith Vestry side poles and span-wire construction was adopted.

Traction poles were made in varying sizes and graded by number, starting from No. 1, the lightest in weight, On the LUT system Nos. 3 and 4 were in general use, with a small number of No. 5 at complex junctions or curves where a considerable increase in the weight of the overhead necessarily existed as compared with ordinary straight track. The heavier grade of pole was also used along Uxbridge Road, Ealing where the poles, set in the centre of the road between the two tracks carried both trolley wires. The heavier poles were also used on the Hammersmith section in Beadon Road and the half-mile in Uxbridge Road between the Brent Bridge and the Iron Bridge. Of the three grades of pole used on the LUT system the lightest was capable of with standing strains of 700lb at 30in from the top with a temporary deflection of not more than 6in, the strains being 1,000lb and 1,500lb in the case of Nos. 4 and 5. The poles were set 6ft deep in the ground, the bottom resting on a cast-iron plate and the holes were large enough to allow eight inches thickness of concrete to surround the pole up to ground level.

The design of traction poles was the subject of much discussion, sometimes of a heated nature, between the LUT and the various local authorities, many of whom were opposed to the idea of overhead electric traction on principle, the reasoning being that the poles and overhead wires would detract from the visual amenities of their localities. On one oft-quoted occasion a municipal worthy, objecting to the proposed use of overhead traction, declaimed: "...these monopolists, these company monopolists, are going to obscure the blue vault of heaven!" Clifton Robinson sought to reassure the critics. He had won over Hammersmith Vestry at an early stage and submitted to them drawings of the poles and overhead

Tram Junction, London Road, Kingston

The double junction at London Road, Kingston, showing standard LUT fittings used on the overhead wiring. The pole on the right, however, has decorative ironwork fitted to it. Car No. 235 carries the destination Kingston Hill. (Commercial view. Courtesy: J.H. Price)

equipment adopted for the recently-electrified Bristol tramways. The Vestry readily accepted this design and thereafter the same pattern was accepted by the other authorities, the standard design varying little over the whole system.

In common with many tramways in the opening years of the electric era the LUT poles were elegantly ornate. They were made from three sections of steel tube, which assembled under pressure gave a tapered, or stepped, pole 25ft 6in above ground level. The pole was surmounted by a particularly ornate finial, in the form of a slender baluster which terminated in a "spear-head" some 18in long, below which a cast-iron laurel wreath, some 9in in diameter was affixed. Wrought-iron scroll brackets, again of ornate pattern supported the span-wires, and at the two points where the three tubes had been pressed together, forming a step, a studded cast-iron collar was placed, these being slipped over the top of the pole to rest on the step. The pole base was an octagonal casting, 4ft 6in high and 16in across, formed to a classical pattern and made in one piece, being slipped over the pole at the time the poles were planted. The poles and their fittings, together with section feeder pillars were painted mid-green, each pole bearing a stencilled, white-painted number, There were one or two minor deviations from the standard design. In the Raynes Park area some of the finials consisted of a cap with a short spike, the cap fitting over the top of the pole and secured in place by a set-screw, while in West Ealing a few of the standard finials lacked the wreath, Otherwise all the finials fitted inside the top of the pole, being, slightly tapered to give a wedging action.

The one example of centre-pole construction was in Uxbridge Road, Ealing, and here there were two separate sections, the most easterly being between the boundary with Acton at Birch Grove and The Mall. From the Mall and through the Broadway there was a half-mile section of side-pole and span-wire construction and beyond The Broadway to the Hanwell boundary near Eccleston Road the centre-poles resumed. These centre-poles were similar in most respects to the side-poles on the rest of the system, except that the method of wire suspension was the "bow-string" type and the bases of the poles were taller, having the addition of a "Grecian urn" surmounting, the octagonal base. Each pole was surrounded by a small "refuge", eight-sided and conforming with the shape of the base. The tracks

240

were spaced 6 ft apart on the centre-pole sections. The route length of the track in Ealing was 2 miles, of which a little over one and a half miles was centre-pole construction, involving, 70 poles, 23 between Birch Grove and The Mall and 47 between The Broadway and the Hanwell boundary.

The short stretch of line between Brent Bridge, Hanwell and the Iron Bridge was a little over half a mile (0.430 miles) and here bracket-arm suspension was used, with poles on the north side of the road carrying bracket arms varying between 6ft and 8ft in length, there being some twenty such poles on this section. Outside the Metropolitan and GWR station in Hammersmith there was single track and here were two heavy poles carrying exceptionally long bracket-arms some 15ft long which bore the single trolley-wire on this one-way section.

On the rural sections between Hanwell and Southall and beyond Southall to the outskirts of Uxbridge the poles, while fitted with the standard finials were at many places devoid of the bases and collars. Later, following advice from consulting engineers these were provided with short concrete plinths to prevent surface water on the unpaved footpaths from lying around the bottom of the poles and causing corrosion. Associated with the poles were the section and feeder pillar boxes, the line being divided into half-mile sections to meet the requirements of the Board of Trade regulations. At each half-mile section two section boxes were installed, each trolley wire having its own feeder and distributor, each of which could be disconnected at the respective section box. This arrangement guarded against breakdowns in the underground cables or the overhead. The feeders were connected to the distribution system at intervals of one and a half miles, the maximum voltage drop being 10% and the average 7½%. The trolley-wire, of hard-drawn copper was at first of No. 0 B & S gauge and with a conductivity of 98% of Matthiessen's standard of pure copper. The wires were suspended at a height of not less than 21ft above the ground except beneath bridges, where it was splayed outward from the centre of the "line of pursuit" and run in troughing on the underside of the bridge. The weight of the span-wires, trolley-wire, insulators and other fittings was compensated for by setting the poles with a slight negative rake, preventing them from being pulled from a vertical position.

The original installation on the 1901 lines from Hammersmith to Kew Bridge and Shepherds Bush to Acton was wired with No. 0 B & S gauge conductors, and it was found that this gauge was insufficient for the strains imposed upon the wire. On 11 November 1902, 17 months after the electric trams had started running, a wire parted and fell to the ground at Turnham Green Church, killing two horses. On 13 November W.R. Cottrell, Overhead Superintendent, wrote a memorandum to Clifton Robinson reporting this incident and advising him that the overhead between Young's Corner and Kew Bridge should be re-strung at the cost of £361, less £99.10s 0d for the old materials. Cottrell said that the wire was showing signs of considerable wear and that No. 0 gauge was too light. He recommended the use of heavier material and on 14 November Robinson instructed him to "commence the work gently" and to report on progress. The wire over the existing system was gradually replaced with No. 00 B & S gauge which was used on all future construction. This wire was five-sixteenths of an inch in diameter. At a later date some of the system was wired using "figure 8" section wire with clinch ears.

An innovation first used on the Bristol tramways was the automatic trolley reverser. These were installed at Shepherds Bush, Hounslow and Richmond Bridge termini. Robinson was enthusiastic about their advantages, and on 24 February 1903 he instructed Cottrell to hasten the installation of the reversers at all existing and new termini "to save expense and delay occasioned by manual operation at present being performed". The senior electrical engineer, William Nairn, took a different view, and at an engineering meeting on 5 November 1904 he commented that they were "not much good" and their only advantage lay in car lights being retained during reversals. Robinson was present at this meeting and it was agreed that the Hounslow and Richmond Bridge examples would be dismantled and the one at Shepherds Bush retained.

The poles were supplied by John Spencer & Co. Ltd., of Wednesbury and British Mannesmann Tube Co. and cost £6 10s, £8 10s and £10 for the Nos. 3,4 and 5 sizes respectively, the bases £2, £2 2s and £3, with sets of collars 5s, 7s and 8s per set, with finials for all sizes 7s 9d each. No. 3 span scrolls were 17s each, Nos. 4 and 5, 18s. Cast-iron pole fittings, i.e., sets of collars, 5s 6d per set and Nos. 4 and 5, 7s per set. These fittings were supplied by James Allan Senior & Sons and the wrought-iron span and scroll brackets supplied by Strachan & Henshaw Ltd. The No. 00 B & S trolley wire was priced at £71 per mile and span wire £13 per mile. The span wire was supplied by Dixon, Corbett & Co. Ltd., and section and feeder pillars by the Electrical Transmission Co. Ltd., at the cost of £29 each. Lever frogs were £2 5s and trailing frogs, 19s each. The average cost for one mile of overhead for double line on the span wire system was £1,896, taking the costs of the Boston Road line as an example, and on a mileage basis this figure varied only very slightly over the system as a whole. When the Surrey lines and the Boston Road tramway were built from 1906 some of the suppliers were changed, the section and feeder pillars for these contracts being supplied by W.T. Henley's Telegraph Works Co. Ltd., and on the facing sides of each junction point controllers manufactured by Kitsell & Co., were installed, worked by a hand lever on a roadside pillar which was surmounted by a lamp on a spindle which white or green aspect for up cars, green for Shepherds Bush and white for Hammersmith. The overhead frop was moved by mechanical linkage with the track points. At some places drop lever frogs were installed.

The traction poles bore coloured markings which served to warn motormen of such requirements as compulsory stops. The indication for a compulsory, or "Board of Trade stop was a white spot, some six inches in diameter with a red spot in the centre, placed at the motorman's eye-level. Section insulators were indicated by a white band about 18in deep half-way up the pole on each side of the road and feeder cables by a similar white band with a central red band, again on each side of the road. In addition to stop signs, these reading "Electric Cars Stop Here" in black lettering on a white ground "Electric Cars Stop Here If Required" in white letters on a green background, and at sharp curves signs read "Electric Cars Must Not Pass Each Other On This Curve". At many points on the system were signs reading "Electric Cars Stop Here On Sundays During The Hours Of Divine Service", outside churches and chapels. From 1 January 1923 the fares system was revised, with numbered stages, and the fare stage number was displayed on the pole at a stage point, in the form of a white disc some eighteen inches in diameter bearing the stage number in black, about sixteen feet above ground level.

The LUT overhead was in marked contrast to the trackwork, J.G. White & Co.'s 1909 report to the LUT Chairman spoke favourably of the overhead, saying that the poles were amply strong and only two had had to be removed since the commencement of operations, and signs of deterioration were slight. Painting, however, had been delayed too long and the poles on the Middlesex lines required immediate repainting, with those in Surrey following in 1910, and one-third of the poles being repainted each year at the estimated cost of £350 annually. The report also said that the overhead system in general was in good order, the trolley-wire in use at the time of the inspection was No. 00 B & S hard-drawn copper wire, of both round and grooved sections. Renewals being carried out at the time were in round wire with clip ears without the use of solder. Some of the poles on outlying parts of the system did not have bases and there was no surrounding paving. To prevent corrosion the report recommended the placing of a concrete plinth around the pole to shed water. This recommendation was carried out with satisfactory results.

The poles on the whole system were given a new lease of life in the 1920s when the wrought-iron scrollwork was removed and replaced by plain pole-straps, the ornamental collars removed and the heavy cast-iron finials replaced by a a lighter "ball and spike" pattern, turned from wood. The cast-iron bases remained as protection from corrosion at ground level. At the same time as these operations were carried out the poles were reinforced by lowering steel rods into them from the top and filling them with concrete, this operation being carried out by two men,

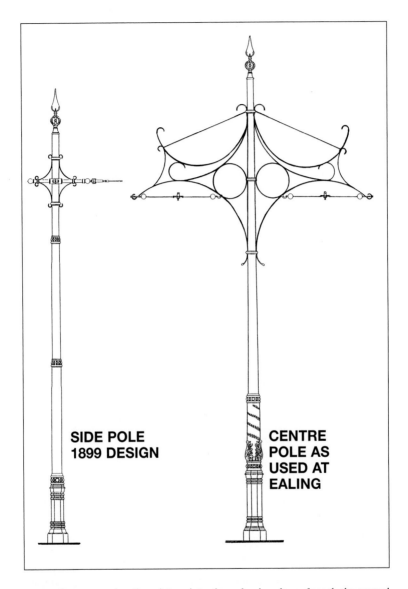

SIDE POLE 1899 DESIGN

CENTRE POLE AS USED AT EALING

one at the top pouring the mixture into the pole via a large funnel, the second keeping the supply of cement mixed. By this means the poles survived until the end of tramway operation, and many were retained and re-strung with double wires when trolleybuses were introduced on the Surrey routes in 1931.

The centre poles in Ealing were the subject of complaints from both Ealing Borough Council and the Automobile Association and other road users from an early date. In 1908 the council asked the LUT to replace them with side poles but were not prepared to bear the cost. Robinson prepared an estimate, dated 25 February 1908 for replacing the 70 centre poles with 140 side poles and span-wires detailing every item involved in the work, which amounted to £2,165 less credit for sale of scrap copper, £125. Robinson submitted this estimate to the council, pointing out that they had requested the use of centre poles in the first place, and the LUT was not prepared to bear the cost of their replacement. The matter rested until 20 March 1913 when Stenson Cooke, Secretary of the Automobile Association wrote to the Board of Trade, asking them to consider taking steps to have the poles removed as they were a danger to traffic. The Board of Trade officers discussed the matter on 22 March and decided they could take no direct action. On 28 March, Sir Arthur Yorke, the Chief Inspecting Officer told the Board of Trade officers that the centre poles had been used at the express wish of Ealing Borough Council, who were now "repentant" and wanted the poles removed. He thought the Board could not intervene, but if a proposal to remove the poles was placed before the Board they could support it. On 3 April E.W. Rowntree, a senior adviser at the Board said they were in no position to initiate any proposals.

On 15 June 1913 the borough council discussed the poles, when a majority agreed that the poles should go and the tracks be respaced, but after further discussion the matter was referred back to the Highways Committee. At this meeting the council had considered a proposal to postpone their purchase of the line by 14 years subject to the LUT agreeing to reconstruct the track in 100lb/yard rails with anchor joints and transverse sleepers every five feet and renew the wood paving for which they were responsible. The centre poles were to be replaced with side-poles but the 6ft space between the tracks retained and maintained at the company's expense, with the council to have power to erect refuges between the tracks. Nineteen of the centre poles were fitted with the council's arc lamps, and they wanted these poles retained and the company to maintain them for the whole period of the term. The £500 annual wayleave was to continue and all work was to be done at the company's expense, and the council required halfpenny fares in the borough. The LUT refused flatly to entertain such proposals and the matter dragged on until 1 October 1914 when the Board of Trade wrote to the LUT saying that in the interests of public safety the centre poles should be removed and none retained. On 23 September A.H. Pott, now Engineer and Manager of the LUT, had sent the Board a plan of the council's proposals for the retention of the centre poles with lamps and showing semicircular refuges with bollards "fore and aft" of each pole. The council had told Pott that they wanted the 19 poles with lamps retained, the remaining 51 replaced with side-poles and the refuges added. On 28 September Col. P.G.Von Donop said the proposed refuges could not be objected to but it was "very desirable that the centre poles should be removed". The refuges would leave only 12in between the kerbs of the refuges and passing cars, whereas Board of Trade requirements were for a minimum of 15in between car and kerb.

The matter was bound up with the reconstruction of the Ealing track, wartime conditions intervened to postpone this indefinitely and with it the question of the poles also had to be shelved. The council was insistent that they would not bear the cost of removing the poles but wanted the track reconstructed which was by this time in a very bad condition. On 13 January 1915 the LUT Managing Director, James Devonshire and the Middlesex County Council surveyor inspected the track and were agreed that reconstruction was required at a very early date. By 27 July it had become clear that the work would have to be postponed, but by 8 December it was re-opened, a quotation having been received from Dick, Kerr & Co. Ltd., to reconstruct the Ealing track. James Devonshire re-opened discussions with the council once more on the poles. Nearly a year later, on 12 October 1916 Devonshire again met the Ealing councillors, and despite much essential repair work being necessary the council agreed not to press the LUT on the matter immediately after the end of the war. The fate of the Ealing centre poles was sealed on 16 May 1919 when the council agreed to replacement of all the centre poles with side-poles and span-wires, the LUT to carry out the work and bear one-third of the cost up to a maximum of £1,500. The work was to be carried out at the same time as the track and paving were reconstructed commencing later in 1919.

The introduction of one-man trams on the Brentford - Hanwell route along Boston Road brought trolley reversers back to the LUT system. Following the introduction of three additional one-man cars in 1924 reversers were installed at the ends of the route, eliminating the necessity for the drivers to leave their cars at each end of the short journey.

Automatic Frog and Point Controllers.

Up to 1909 points and frogs at junctions were set manually by a points boy using a lever which fitted into a slot at the roadside and, by a system of cranks and push-roads set the points for the required direction. Adjacent to this was a pillar surmounted by a revolving spindle carrying a lantern with white and green lenses, which indicated to an oncoming motorman which direction the road was set. The indication was for the up direction, green for Shepherds Bush and white for Hammersmith. At the same time the overhead frog was set. This equipment was manufactured by Kitsell & Company.

The first use of electrically operated frogs and points on the LUT was at the Uxbridge Road-Askew Road junction at the Acton-Hammersmith boundary. The equipment was installed on 2 May 1909 and as a result of an accident which took place there on 29 July the presence of the equipment was reported to the Metropolitan Police. There were two types of such equipment, the "Turner" and the "Collins" The "Collins" type operated on the overhead frog and points when a car passed under the skate in the overhead, irrespective of whether the car was taking power or not. The frog and points were left for the direction taken by the previous car, the next car setting them by passing slowly under the skate to operate the mechanism. The "Turner" type mechanism was always set for one direction only, and motormen operated it by partially applying the handbrake and passing under the skate with one or two notches on the car's controller. After the car had passed the mechanism was automatically reset. The normal practice was for cars making a turn to take power, those passing straight on coasting through without power. A defect in the "Collins" mechanism was overcome by the use of the point iron, and in the case of the "Turner" type the points could be operated by turning a handle on the front of the accompanying roadside pillar.

The Metropolitan Police Commissioner wrote to the Board of Trade on 8 September 1909 asking if sanction had been given the LUT to install the Askew Road controller. The Board of Trade had not, and on 27 September the Board asked the LUT for a report on the accident. A car en route for Shepherds Bush took the right-hand turn into Askew Road and collided with a cab on the opposite side of Uxbridge Road. Robinson wrote to the Board of Trade on 1 October, explaining that the motorman on the tram had not operated his controller correctly for the straight-on road and had not checked the position of his points. The Commissioner asked the Board of Trade to inform him when alterations were made to working tramways already sanctioned by the Board. The Board had not been aware of the existence of the Askew Road mechanism and Col. Yorke said that the Board should not give the Police such an undertaking, neither was it obligatory for the LUT to inform the Board of such alterations. The Board of Trade wrote to the Commissioner on these lines on 1 November 1909.

Evidently the Metropolitan Police Commissioner accepted the Board of Trade's response, and the automatic controllers were installed at the places listed below.

"Turner" Point Controllers

Young's Corner, set for Hammersmith, operated for Shepherds Bush.
Askew Arms, set for Shepherds Bush, operated for Hammersmith.
Kew Bridge, set for Brentford, operated for terminus.
Busch Corner, set for Hounslow, operated for Twickenham.
Stanley Road Junction, set for Hampton Court, operated for Teddington.
Kingston Bridge, set for Hampton Court, operated for Hampton Wick.
London Road, Kingston, set for Kingston Bridge, operated for Eden Street.

London Road, Kingston, set for Richmond Road, operated for Norbiton.
Liverpool Arms, Norbiton, set for Kingston Hill, operated for Malden.
Uxbridge Road, Hanwell, set for Uxbridge, operated for Boston Road.

"Collins" Point Controllers.
King Street, Hammersmith to Chiswick or Acton.
Goldhawk Road to Shepherds Bush or Hammersmith.
Goldhawk Road to Chiswick or Acton.
Hill Road, Wimbledon to Merton or Raynes Park.

Signal Lights
At a number of points in Uxbridge Road between Southall and Uxbridge and in Worple Road, Wimbledon electric light signals were fixed on poles on the left hand side approaching each end of a single track. The lights were in wooden boxes showing three aspects. No light showing indicated that the track ahead was clear, a green light indicated that a car was already on the single line and proceeding ahead. A red light indicated that a car was on the single track and approaching and in the event of a green or red light showing indicated that the car should stop before reaching the actuating switch in the overhead and wait until no light was showing before proceeding, ensuring that after passing beneath the switch the green light appeared to indicate that the signal had operated and the corresponding red light had appeared at the other end. If both red and green lights appeared at once this indicated that two cars had passed under the switches at one and the same time, in which event the down car stopped and allowed the up London bound car to proceed.

A portable air compressor, built by Reavell & Co., used from c1923 for track maintenance purposes by the MET, SMET or LUT, as required. (Photo: LUT)

CHAPTER FIFTEEN

POWER SUPPLY

The LUT was preparing plans for the extension and electrification of the horse tramways almost immediately after acquisition of the West Metropolitan Tramways undertaking in 1894, At this time the concept of a central generating station producing current at high voltages for transmission to outlying parts of an extensive system by way of a number of sub-stations was in its infancy, and early electrification schemes were based upon the establishment of a number of small generating stations producing direct current at the required tramway voltage, between 500 and 600V. Initial legislation for LUT electrification was based on such a scheme but did not proceed, due mainly to objections by local interests on amenity grounds. Immediately prior to the turn of the century development of power transmission systems was sufficiently advanced to enable the provision of large central power stations generating current at high voltages for distribution to sub-stations on outlying sections. At these sub-stations rotary converters and other equipment transformed high-voltage ac current to voltages between 500 and 600 volts for transmission to the tramway overhead or conduit lines.

The various attempts by the LUT to obtain powers to build power stations at some of the existing and intended depots resulted ultimately in sanction to build stations at the Acton and Chiswick depots. The powers in respect of Acton were not exercised and it was resolved to build a central station on a site adjacent to the depot in High Road, Chiswick. This site lay to the east of the car sheds and south of the workshops, all of which are described in Volume 2. The site was sufficiently spacious to allow the construction of such a large building as a power station mainly because a large proportion of the land adjacent to the car sheds had necessarily been devoted to stabling and paddocks for the accommodation of the many horses required to work the tramways before electrification.

The power station building was designed by William Curtis Green, an architect then comparatively unknown but later responsible for the design of a number of highly acclaimed buildings. Rectangular in shape and of single storey construction the building occupied an area of 1,818 square yards, being 154ft by 106ft in extent. It was unusual for a building of this nature in being designed on classical lines and built in high quality Leicestershire red brick, with quoins and facings in Portland stone. Above the lofty main entrance to the building a large stone panel bore female figures in relief representing the spirits of Electricity and Locomotion, with which were incorporated a representation of an electric tramcar together with the initials LUET-London United Electric Tramways.

Construction of the building commenced in March 1899 with clearance of the site and excavation for the deep foundations and the basement. The LUT at first carried out all construction of buildings and the new electric tramways without the use of outside contractors, such help having only been resorted to at the time the old West Metropolitan Tramways were reconstructed from 1894 and when Acton Depot was built in 1895-6. A set of photographs taken at the time the power station and some of the lines were under construction illustrates the methods of construction of the period, making use of large numbers of men and horse-drawn carts with virtually no mechanical or other labour-saving facilities. The building had been largely completed by October 1900 and a photograph taken on 7 March 1901 shows the building completed, the site tidied up and ornamental shrubs planted along the front and side elevations.

Work on preparing the foundations for Chiswick power station had reached this stage in April 1899. Under construction also were the new car sheds, seen in the background.

(Courtesy: Bristol Record Office)

The main building housed the engine and boiler rooms, which measured 154ft by 64ft and 154ft by 42ft respectively. The interior walls of both were faced with glazed white bricks and the engine room floor was laid with mosaic tiles. There were at first eight Babcock & Wilcox boilers in the boiler room, each of which was able to evaporate 11,000lb of water per hour. The boilers were arranged in four batteries of two, and were fired by Vicars' mechanical stokers, which were driven by a 10hp 500 volt dc motor. A Hunt coal and ash conveyor, worked by a 10hp 500 volt dc motor delivered coal to the boilers at a maximum rate of 40 tons per hour, the drive gear for this being situated above bunkers holding 500 tons of coal. The conveyor was also arranged to remove ash by buckets in front of the ash-pits in the basement into an ash-bin, and from there into a receiver outside the building. It was originally intended to take coal direct to the store from the depot of the North and South Western Junction Railway, some 700ft distant from the boiler room, by means of a gravity operated conveyor, direct from the railway wagons to the coal stores and thence to the stoker hoppers. These arrangements failed to materialise and coal supplies were carted this short distance, adding considerably to the cost of power generation.

Water was taken from the public supply and three artesian wells, each 20ft apart and consisting of 6in diameter tubes driven to a depth of 30ft and inter-connected by a 4in diameter pipe which was connected to a 6in diameter main. The wells were each capable of yielding 3,600 gallons per hour, delivered into the water softening tank from whence, after being softened, it was discharged into a reservoir below the cooling towers. Three Barnard-Wheeler cooling towers were placed to the north of the building and arranged in three sections, covering a space of 40ft by 15ft and 38ft in height. They were able to deal with circulating water for 6,000hp and with the feed heaters in the basement were supplied by the Wheeler Condenser & Engineering Company. The water-softening plant was outside the building, consisting of a cast-iron tank 19ft 6in by 19ft 6in by 10ft with its associated carbonating apparatus. At the north end of the boiler room two vertical compound duplex pumps were placed, each able to supply the feed-water for 4,000hp at 15lb of steam per hp per hour. These pumps were supplied by Clarke, Chapman & Co. and Blake & Knowles. Two feed water tanks, each holding 6,000 gallons occupied the space above the boilers between the floor and the coal bunkers. In the flue above the boilers a Green's economiser was placed, containing 360 tubes with electrically driven scraping gear.

The smoke stack, 260ft in height and 10ft in diameter inside the brick lining at the top became a major landmark in the west London suburbs. The upper 200ft was built of steel plates lap-jointed and riveted together and the top was surmounted by a heavy ornamental cap of galvanised steel. The chimney base below the steel stack was of the same red brick and Portland stone as the main building. The foundations

Steeplejacks on the "summit" of the newly-completed Chiswick power station smoke stack, together with those in the cradle of the hoist on the side of the stack, pose especially for the camera on 18 September 1900.   (Courtesy: Bristol Record Office)

for the stack presented the company with a major engineering problem. Test borings at several points revealed that water was present at depths varying between 8 and 10ft. The most suitable location for the stack was at the north end of the boiler room, close to the granary building then in use as a store. A solid mass of concrete put down at this point was expected to endanger this building and the power station foundations. The soil was found to consist of sand and ballast with blue clay at 28ft from the surface. It was necessary to carry the stack foundations down to the clay, and on the advice of the consulting engineer for the scheme, Horace F. Parshall, a scheme involving the laying of a solid concrete base was abandoned. The method adopted involved the construction of a hollow rectangular "box" from pitch pine timbers, which was built up at ground level and heavily strengthened with steel straps and bolts and fitted with a cast-iron cutting edge. The box was filled with cement concrete and when this was set the ground inside was removed and with the aid of heavy pumping operations the whole assembly gradually sunk into the ground. As further layers of concrete were laid the operation was repeated until the whole of the lower portion was filled with concrete, equally distributing the weight of the superstructure.

Chiswick power station generated both alternating and direct current. The dc plant, which supplied the lines in Acton and Chiswick eastward to Shepherds Bush and Hammersmith, was commissioned first, powered by two 700hp vertical cross-compound condensing engines with Corliss valve gear and running at 94rpm. They were built by the Allis-Chalmers Company in the USA. The engines were fitted with re-heaters between the high and low pressure cylinders in the receiver, and each engine was directly coupled to two 250Kw 550 volt dc generators, one on either side of the 36-ton flywheel. The generators were supplied by the British Thomson-Houston Co. Ltd. A third dc set, consisting of a 100hp Belliss & Morcom vertical cross-compound engine direct-coupled to a 75Kw 550 volt dc generator, built by BTH was used for lighting and power in the Chiswick car sheds, workshops and offices when the other plant was shut down.

The ac plant, supplying three-phase alternating current at 5,000 volts to the sub-stations geographically remote from Chiswick consisted initially of another Allis-Chalmers engine of the same type and horse-power as the first two, but direct-coupled to a 500Kw 5,000 volt three-phase 25c/s alternator, built by the British Thomson-Houston Co. Ltd. and installed initially for the Brentford-Hounslow and Acton-Southall lines, A much more powerful engine, manufactured by the Allis-Chalmers Company developing 1,400hp at 90rpm was direct-coupled to a BTH 1,000Kw 5,000 volt three-phase 25 c/s alternator, and this completed the original generating plant at the power station.

The plant in both the boiler and engine rooms was increased at the time the extensions to Hampton Court were built. On 26 February 1902 the LUT directors approved the purchase of two boilers from Babcock & Wilcox Ltd., and on 27 June a further Allis-Chalmers 1,400hp engine, directly-coupled to a BTH 1,000Kw 5,000 volt three-phase 25 c/s alternator were approved, the cost of these being £6,800 and £4,250 respectively. Later in the same year, on 11 November the directors sanctioned £1,370 for purchase of a further Babcock & Wilcox boiler, and these completed the power station. These arrangements remained largely unchanged throughout the life of the station as a generating plant. Other plant at the station included a 500Kw rotary converter and transformers manufactured by the British Westinghouse Electric & Manufacturing Co., which served a double purpose. It could be worked either to transform alternating current to direct to assist the supply of power to the lines nearest to the station or to help the three-phase generators, i.e., it could be driven as a dc motor generating ac stepped up to 5,000 volts for transmission to the distant sub-stations to be transformed there to dc traction current. To assist the earth return two 15hp negative boosters were installed, and the plant at the station now had sufficient capacity to provide for extensions then proposed.

The switchboard, of major importance to the operation of the system, was also an object of considerable interest to contemporary electrical engineers. It occupied

Chiswick power station main hall under construction as at 18 August 1900. The first of the traction poles are also in place to carry the overhead wires above the already-laid depot track layout. (Courtesy: Bristol Record Office)

a prominent position on the south wall of the engine room, placed on a gallery reached by twin staircases. Along the length of the gallery an ornate wrought-iron balustrade was matched by similar balustrading on the staircases, at the feet of which a pair of ornamental lamps were placed. The top of the switchboard itself was surmounted by matching wrought-ironwork in the centre of which was a large clock set in an ornamental wrought-iron frame. The gallery and staircases were supported by four decorative cast-iron columns.

The main switchboard consisted of twenty-seven white marble panels on angle-iron frames and was arranged in three groups. To the left and right respectively were the high and low tension switches and in the centre the machine output was controlled. The dc board consisted of four tramway generator panels, two booster panels, eight feeder panels, one Board of Trade panel and an instrument panel. Switches and bus-bars for the high-tension current were supported by joists in a closed chamber below the switchboard floor, the switches being of the oil-break type and operated by levers placed on the switchboard. The instruments included voltmeters, ammeters and recording meters, all made by the Weston Instrument Company. The lighting switchboard was situated beneath the main gallery and consisted of two lighting panels, two power circuit panels and two panels controlling the rotary converter. The whole of the equipment of the power station, Hanwell and Hounslow sub-stations, feeder cables and the first 100 electric trams was supplied under the terms of a contract with the British Thomson-Houston Co. Ltd., and the work of construction and installation was carried out by the LUT workforce under the supervision of Horace F. Parshall, James Clifton Robinson and his assistant, J.R. Salter.

Current for the lines between the inner London termini at Shepherds Bush and Hammersmith and the first outer termini at Acton and Kew Bridge was supplied directly from Chiswick power station. As the system developed additional sub-

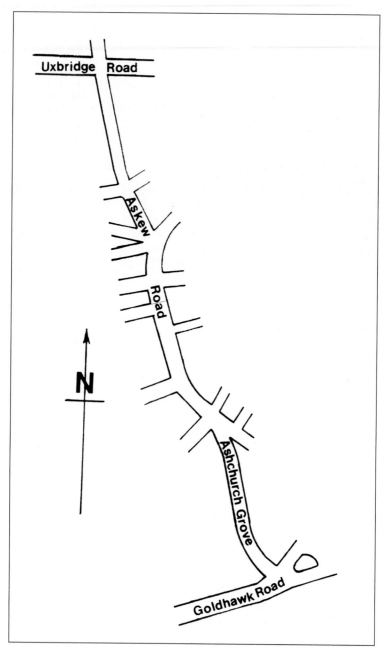

The feeder power cable from Chiswick power station to the Uxbridge Road tramway was taken from Goldhawk Road, through Ashchurch Grove and Askew Road to the Uxbridge Road line at the 'Askew Arms'.   (Courtesy: Bristol Record Office)

stations were commissioned, the first two being on the Uxbridge Road route at Hanwell Depot and at Hounslow Depot on the Brentford-Hounslow route. At the greatest extent of the LUT system in Middlesex forty-two cableways radiated from Chiswick power station; the cabling was supplied by W.T. Henley's Telegraph Works Co. Ltd., and was paper-insulated and lead-covered. The cables were laid in wrought-iron cement-covered ducts laid under the footpaths or between the tracks according to local conditions. The ducts were laid on a bed of concrete not less than 3in thick, this concrete being mixed and laid to stringent quality specifications. The ducting pipes were carefully jointed with Portland cement and each layer of pipes was covered and completely surrounded with concrete extending to 3in all round and laid to a minimum depth of 18in from the road surface to the concrete. On much of the outer part of the system the cables were laid on the solid system in earthenware ducts run in with pitch. On some sections there were as many as five layers of five ducts, and many of the ducts exist in situ to this day, some at least in use for communications services.

The whole of the feeding arrangements were duplicated, and to meet Board of Trade requirements the system was divided into half-mile sections, and at each half-mile two section boxes were provided. This feature allowed each conductor wire to have its own feeder and distribution cable, each of which could be disconnected at the section boxes. This provided against breakdowns in the cables or the overhead installation. In addition, the feeders were tapped to the distribution points at every one and a half miles, and earth return cables of half-inch sectional area were connected to the tracks. These returns were connected to the boosters at the power station and the sub-stations and the lead covering of all the cables was bonded to the manholes and to the rails througout the system.

Following the opening of the first extensions from Kew Bridge and Acton to Hounslow and Southall respectively, which brought into use the Hounslow and Hanwell sub-stations further extensions to Hounslow Heath, Hampton Court and Uxbridge saw the commissioning of further sub-stations at Fulwell and Hillingdon depots. The buildings of these sub-stations are described in Volume 2. Hanwell sub-station, adjacent to the depot, served the Uxbridge Road route between Acton and Southall and contained four 260Kw three-phase rotary converters supplied by the British Westinghouse Electric & Manufacturing Co. Ltd. Three of these were fitted with a negative booster and there were thirteen 100Kw oil-cooled Westinghouse transformers. The switchboard consisted of twenty-eight panels, 16 of which were for direct current and the remainder for alternating current. The switchgear provided for three high-tension feeders from Chiswick power station and two out-going feeders from the sub-station to supply the sub-station at Hillingdon.

The Hounslow sub-station contained two 250Kw three-phase rotary converters of Westinghouse manufacture, each with a negative booster on the same shaft and seven 100Kw oil-cooled Westinghouse transformers, together with a motor-driven air compressor. The switchboard consisted of five ac and fourteen dc panels.

The sub-station at Fulwell Depot was the largest on the LUT system, serving the Thames Valley routes branching from Isleworth through Twickenham and the Hampton Court Loop to the Surrey border at Kingston Bridge. The equipment there was three 500Kw six-phase rotary converters, manufactured and supplied by the British Thomson-Houston Co. Ltd., together with ten 200Kw BTH oil-cooled transformers and two 30Kw motor-driven negative boosters. Three 200Kw BTH oil-cooled transformers were also installed for lighting in the depot and sub-station, an air compressor and a motordriven pump completed the machinery in this sub-station and there was a switchboard consisting of twenty-four panels.

The sub-station built in 1904 to serve the extension of the Uxbridge Road route from Southall to Uxbridge was the smallest of the original sub-stations. For its equipment the LUT reverted to Westinghouse, who supplied two 250Kw three-phase rotary converters with negative boosters and seven 100Kw oil-cooled transformers, of which one was a stand-by. The switchboard consisted of sixteen panels. This sub-station was at Hillingdon, but was later described by the Company as Hayes and was adjacent to the small depot.

As recorded elsewhere in this book not all the authorised lines in Middlesex were built, although if they had been the equipment at Chiswick and the sub-stations had capacity to supply some part of them. However, the lengthy light railway extensions, especially the ambitious proposal for a cross-country light railway to reach Reading, would have made necessary large increases to the generating plant, which could scarcely have been practical at Chiswick, the existing site having little, if any space to extend the power station building. Following the opening of the Uxbridge extension and the Hammersmith-Uxbridge Road link in the summer of 1904 the LUT management discussed future strategy and conferred with the senior management of the UERL and their financiers, Speyer Brothers. By 1904 a decision had been made by the UERL directors to extend their new Lots Road power station at Chelsea with a view to making current available to the LUT at least for the soon-to-be-built Surrey lines.

In the autumn of 1904 discussions between the LUT and UERL directors centred around the completion of the Hampton Court network via Hampton Court Bridge and the extension from Hampton Wick across Kingston Bridge into Kingston through Malden to Wimbledon. The Hampton Court Bridge scheme did not proceed owing to the necessity to rebuild the bridge and as related in Chapter 9 it was decided to concentrate the LUT's resources on the Surrey lines via Kingston Bridge. At this time much attention was being given to power costs and possible alternatives to existing arrangements The General Manager of the UERL, J.R. Chapman, had in 1902 expressed the view that Chiswick power station was not in an ideal situation, remarking that water had to be purchased and coal carted; although three artesian wells existed there they had been formed for stand-by purposes, and probably on their own could not meet the full demands of the station.

The completed power station building, photographed on 7 March 1901. The first of the cars were also to hand with which to commence operations, No. 14 is seen standing outside the depot.
(Courtesy: Bristol Record Office)

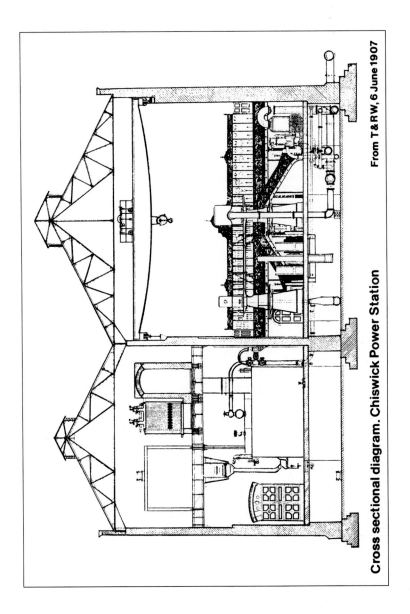

Cross sectional diagram. Chiswick Power Station

From T & R W, 6 June 1907

Power costs at Chiswick were investigated during late 1903 and on 7 January 1904 generating costs for the week just ended were reported. These amounted to £373 for 229,311Kw, or 307,385hp. Later, in August, a detailed statement was produced listing all the men, their duties, wages and working hours at Chiswick and in the sub-stations.

At the same time as the LUT and UERL directors were discussing plans for constructing the Surrey lines and the Boston Road route the question of power supplies for the whole LUT system was considered. The UERL directors thought that economies could be achieved by closing down the Chiswick generating plant and taking power for the whole LUT system, in Middlesex, London and, when built, the Surrey lines, from Lots Road, especially in view of the fact that the cables could be economically run from Fulham to Chiswick alongside the District Railway. Initially, however, concrete proposals were confined to the Surrey lines and a proposal by the UERL was submitted to the LUT directors for a contract to supply the Surrey lines, when constructed, from Lots Road to run for nine years from 18 October 1904. Terms were not agreed, however, and much further discussion took place on the subject during which time construction of the Surrey lines had commenced. A confidential report on the Surrey proposals dated 21 January 1906 was produced, the contents of which have remained undisclosed, and following this an agreement was reached, details of which were treated as strictly confidential. This followed practice in the UERL companies respecting contracts for bulk supplies of fuel and other commodities, whereby agreements and contracts were kept in sealed envelopes to which only the company secretaries had access.

Plans for taking power for the Middlesex and London lines from Lots Road had meanwhile been shelved pending resolution of financial proposals by the UERL affecting the LUT, and during this period the Surrey lines were completed, as detailed in Chapter 9. The supply for these lines was taken from Lots Road via a 10.5 miles 11,000 volt extra high-tension line from Lots Road which was taken to the sub-stations at Wimbledon and Kingston, crossing the Thames by way of Wandsworth Bridge and passing close to the London County Council Tramways depot at Jew's Row. The sub-station at Wimbledon contained three 500Kw rotary converters, ten 200Kw oil-cooled transformers and two 15Kw negative boosters, together with one 20Kw single-phase lighting transformer. The switchboard contained 12 ac and 13 dc panels At Kingston substation there were three rotary converters and ten oil-cooled transformers of the same capacity as those at Wimbledon, with two 15Kw negative boosters and the switchboard consisted of eight ac and 13 dc panels. The equipment at both sub-stations was manufactured and supplied by the British Westinghouse Electric & Manufacturing Co. Ltd,

Discussion of proposals to take power for the whole LUT system from Lots Road resumed at a LUT directors' meeting on 31 July 1906 when the terms of a proposed agreement were discussed and consideration deferred for a further three months. There is no further mention of the subject in the Minute Books and it is evident that whatever decisions were finally taken were regarded as highly confidential and not recorded. Meanwhile the first portion of the Surrey lines had opened on 1 March 1906, using Lots Road power, and matters rested until March 1909 when the LUT Chairman, C.J. Cater Scott expressed doubts about costs and asked J.R. Chapman, who had become a director of the LUT in 1908 and was the General Manager of the UERL, for a report on the comparative costs of power as between Chiswick and Lots Road.

Chapman's report, dated 22 March indicated that the Chiswick output in 1908 was 13.5 million units at a cost of £25,000 or 0.441d per unit. The same from Lots Road would cost £15,750, or 0.280d per unit. Chiswick generated 550 volts for direct transmission to the overhead for short distances and 6,000 volts three-phase 25 c/s to supply the sub-stations. The maximum Bank holiday demand at Chiswick was 1,300Kw direct current and 3,150Kw three-phase ac. Additional plant required at Chiswick would consist of two 600Kw rotary converters with transformers for dc and two 1,500Kw frequency changers for three-phase ac. The capital cost would amount to £15,900 and annual costs £3,124. Chapman estimated that the annual

The stone bas relief above the main entrance to Chiswick power station. Two female figures representing the spirits of electricity and locomotion on either side of a carved shield bearing the letters LUET in relief, are standing upon a ball representing the earth and a tramcar.
(Courtesy: London Transport Museum)

savings by taking current from Lots Road would be £4,000. He did not propose to change the existing plant at Chiswick, saying that the station and its equipment "could be turned over to the Middlesex County Council in 1920, ready to work". This was a reference to the anticipated purchase of the LUT lines by the MCC. The suggestion that the MCC might take over the LUT system at this date does not appear to have been taken seriously at the time. Chapman said that Lots Road would need only to work one extra turbine at Bank holidays and would be able to supply the LUT at 0.250d per unit if the coal price remained at 11s 6d per ton. Chapman's estimate of savings by taking Lots Road power was based upon ten years' output, and he proposed that the UERL should provide the capital and install the new plant on the basis of annual payments by the LUT, removing it in 1920. 5,500,000 dc units at Chiswick would require 6,500,000 dc units from Lots Road at £0.250d per unit or £9,589. An annual charge of £750 would be payable to the Metropolitan District Railway Company for maintenance of cables. Chapman quoted figures from early 1909 of 0.474d per Kw for Chiswick power and 0.820d per Kw for Lots Road power purchased for Kingston and Wimbledon sub-stations.

Chapman concluded his report to Cater Scott by saying that the proposed scheme could not be completed before 31 December 1909, even if orders were placed at once. There is no further reference to this subject until 12 October 1916 when the LUT directors discussed a proposal to close down Chiswick as a generating station and take the supply from Lots Road. On this occasion it was resolved that no further action be taken, probably because negotiations with the London County Council on the Council's intended purchase of the LUT lines in Hammersmith had arrived at a critical stage and wartime conditions were making themselves felt.

At the same time as Chapman's report on power costs was being prepared Cater Scott had asked W.C. Burton, of J.G. White & Co. Ltd., for a comprehensive report on the state of the LUT track, resulting from the many complaints being received from the various road authorities. W.C. Burton, as well as a director of Whites, was also a director of the UERL. When Whites' report arrived it was highly critical of much of the track mileage, and made recommendations for reconstruction of most of it at varying times, some from as early as 1910. Doubtless alarmed by this, Cater Scott wrote to Burton again on 9 September 1909 requesting a supplementary report dealing with the power generation and transmission, rolling stock, overhead and the condition of the car sheds and workshops. Burton produced his report on 11 October, which revealed that the generation and transmission plant, the overhead and rolling stock were generally in good condition, especially the overhead. The rolling stock, however, while kept well painted and of good appearance, required much attention to the trucks, which it recommended should be replaced by new ones of a heavier pattern, while the motors also required replacement by more powerful units. The report indicated that the whole of the plant at Chiswick and in the sub-stations appeared to be in good order and well maintained, with no extensive renewals likely to be required during the company's tenure of the system.

It is evident that all this activity had a bearing upon the intended purchase by the London County Council of the LUT Hammersmith lines, and it is possible that the favourable report on the power equipment caused the LUT and UERL to hold back on the proposal to close down Chiswick power station and take all power from Lots Road, at least for the time being. At this time the future of Robinson as Engineer and Managing Director of the company was about to be decided, and his resignation at the beginning of 1910 placed the LUT more directly in the hands of the UERL, with his replacement as Managing Director by Albert Stanley and as Engineer by Zac Ellis Knapp, both senior members of the UERL staff. On 27 October 1910 Stanley told the LUT directors that some alterations were necessary at Chiswick power station and this and other work on the rolling stock would cost some £25,000. On 17 February 1911 Stanley told the directors that new chain grate stokers had been installed at Chiswick, an additional artesian well was being sunk there and new piston rings were being obtained for the engines, the cost of these

The power station boiler house at 29 March 1902, with additional plant recently installed to cope with increased loads.　　　　　　　　　　　　　　　　　(Courtesy: Bristol Record Office)

items amounting to £5,000. It is possible that the new well was sunk to reduce the company's dependence upon the public water supply.

Maintenance at Chiswick and the sub-stations was now under the close supervision of A.H. Pott, and in June 1915 he became concerned at the continued safety of the 260ft stack at the power station. He called in Horace F. Parshall, consulting engineer to the company to inspect the stack, and following Parshall's report the directors decided on 16 June to arrange for the removal of the heavy cap and to shorten the stack as necessary. It appears that some deterioration of the Chiswick plant had gone unnoticed by J.G. White & Co.; at a time of great financial stress the directors voted £120 to carry out repairs to the coal conveyor, "to avoid breakdown of services". A year later the directors were advised that the price of current supplied from Lots Road to the Surrey lines had been reduced from 0.50d to 0.45d per unit and that a further portion of the Chiswick stack had been removed for safety reasons. At this meeting, on 12 October 1916, the directors expressed concern about conditions at Chiswick and the question of closing down the station and taking all supplies from Lots Road was again raised, and after a lengthy discussion it was resolved to take no action "for the present".

It had probably been felt that resolution of problems at Chiswick might come about in the near future if long drawn-out negotiations on the London County Council's purchase of the Hammersmith lines resulted in a settlement, taking the question of the power station out of the company's hands. At this time an early settlement was expected. Meanwhile, the Managing Director told his colleagues that J.G. White & Co. Ltd., had been commissioned to produce a further report on the state of the system and the commercial prospects of the LUT. This report is mentioned on later occasions, when its consideration was deferred, but no record of its content or any action arising from it has come to light. Meanwhile, on 26 May

1916 the LUT entered into an agreement with the London Electric Railway Co., and the Metropolitan District Railway Company to cover all LUT power requirements, conditional upon the completion of the sale to the London County Council of the Hammersmith lines. The two railway companies had been empowered to enter into agreements to supply power to other parties in Acts of 1911. These agreements had been previously made with the UERL.

An agreement between the LUT and the London County Council was signed on 6 December 1917, covering details of the transfer of the Hammersmith lines to the County Council. This agreement provided, *inter alia,* for the resolution of points of difference between the parties arising from the award of the arbitrator on 4 February 1912 on the dispute between the company and the LCC. The agreement clarified procedural points respecting facilities for the LUT at Chiswick power station, mainly the use of part of the station as a sub-station feeding the lines in Chiswick and Acton after the LCC purchase. In effect the agreement granted the LUT a tenancy of part of the station in which the necessary transforming equipment would be installed. The agreement also permitted the LUT to make use of the rotary converter, step down transformer, switchboard and other plant in the station by agreement between the managers of the undertakings, together with reasonable use by the LUT from time to time of the overhead travelling crane.

The end of Chiswick as a generating station came nearer on 15 January 1918 when the directors were given estimates for equipment to convert it to a sub-station. On 12 February Z.E. Knapp was appointed to advise on the scheme and details would be agreed jointly with A.H. Pott, who had meanwhile succeeded Knapp as Engineer and Manager of the LUT. Because of the financial position of the company details were to be submitted to a committee of the debenture holders before commitments were entered into. By 12 March, Knapp had finalised the scheme, the estimated cost of which was £21,000, after allowing for the sale of the three rotary converters, which were expected to fetch £3,000. The directors approved these arrangements and the Managing Director and the Engineer were instructed to consult their colleague, George Balfour, MP regarding the legality of the scheme and apply for the necessary wartime priority certificates. On 15 May George Balfour gave his approval of the scheme and the purchase of the plant, including rotary converters, transformers and switchgear at an estimated cost of £15,000 and orders for these were placed without further delay.

The cessation of hostilities on 11 November 1918 saw industry in an exhausted state, with shortages of materials and wartime controls delaying all but the most important civilian schemes, and the immediate post war period continued on this path. Late delivery of the equipment for the Chiswick conversion delayed the completion of the scheme and further delays arose from a national railway strike. Consequently, Chiswick power station was kept in commission pending the end of the strike and final completion of the necessary work. At last, on 17 October 1919 the work was almost finished and on 14 November the directors were told that all power had been taken from Lots Road from 31 October and no current was being generated at Chiswick. Chiswick power station, now a sub-station, supplied transformed current for the lines radiating from Hammersmith and Shepherds Bush westward and fresh switching arrangements were made to supply the sections covered from the Hanwell, Hayes, Hounslow and Fulwell sub-stations.

The award by R. Elliott Cooper in the dispute between the LUT and the London County Council over the Hammersmith lines involved the purchase by the LCC of the Chiswick depot and power station property, together with plant and equipment in the station, equipment in the shops and forty-five trams. Elliott Cooper excepted a number of items from the inventory of equipment the LUT claimed the LCC should purchase. These included the two 1,400hp 1,000Kw ac generating sets and their associated panels on the main switchboard, i.e., the Kew booster panel, the Kew Bridge, Gunnersbury and "Packhorse" dc feeder panels and the Hanwell, Hounslow and Fulwell high-tension three-phase feeder panels. Seven Babcock boilers and three-fifths of the coal bunkers, with seven Vicars'

A view of the incomplete generator hall at Chiswick power station in December 1900, showing the wrought-iron tracery on the balustrade of the staircase in the foreground.
(Courtesy: Bristol Record Office)

mechanical stokers were also excluded and no account was taken of the steam piping, valves, tanks and other works connecting with boilers and generating sets.

These arrangements were varied slightly by agreement between the parties and the position of the LUT system in Middlesex was changed by the passing of the company's 1918 Act on 21 November. J.R. Chapman's report to Cater Scott of March 1909 envisaged that the Middlesex lines would fall into the hands of the Middlesex County Council in 1920. The 1918 Act contained measures designed to alleviate the severe financial difficulties besetting the company, including a scheme for restructuring the capital. The Act also postponed the local authorities' power to purchase any part of the system until after 1 January 1950 and it confirmed the agreement between the LUT and the LCC of 6 December 1917, one of the provisions of which was for the LUT to provide free of cost up to 1,800,000 units for the cars running on the Hammersmith lines after the LCC purchase. The agreement also provided that the LUT should not pay rent for the use of the transforming station but would maintain the equipment there, and the LCC was at liberty to sell any equipment there it had bought under the arbitration award but did not require for the purpose of working the tramways. The Act also confirmed arrangements for the supply of current to the LUT system by the Metropolitan District Railway Company and the London Electric Railway Company which were empowered by the two railway companies' Acts of 1911.

With all power now being taken from Lots Road temporary arrangements respecting power supplies were formalised, and a new agreement with the London Electric Railway Company and the Metropolitan District Railway Company was approved by the LUT directors on 29 October 1920. In accord with the practice of the Underground group of companies details of these arrangements were treated as confidential, and as a result do not appear in the minute books or other records. Owing to some last-minute differences between the LUT and the LCC over the use of certain cables, ducts and man-holes in the Hammersmith area the conveyance of the Hammersmith lines and their equipment was delayed for several months. Wth final resolution of the points at issue a special meeting of the LUT directors resolved on 12 October 1922 that the conveyance be sealed, although the properties had effectively changed hands on 2 May.

The company was still in the throes of an acute financial crisis, and moreover was under an obligation to utilise the money paid by the LCC for the Hammersmith lines for rehabilitation of the system, mainly of the track. Under the terms of the LUT 1918 Act a minimum of £400,000 had to be spent within a limited time on such work. As a result of this the requirements of the power supply department were held to a bare minimum. It was found necessary to install an additional rotary converter at Hanwell sub-station and expenditure of £1,250 was approved by the directors on 4 April 1924. However, breakdowns were few, and this was doubtless a reflection of the high standards adopted in the original installation. Replacements and additions were becoming necessary by 1928, and on 28 February £650 was approved for the purchase of a second-hand rotary converter for Chiswick sub-station and later, on 5 April, a further £200 was approved in connection with this.

New 50hp motors were installed in eighty cars commencing in 1923, and in 1928 yet more powerful motors were fitted in a further fifty cars. The increased power requirements of these motors necessitated the installation of an automatic substation at Acton Depot to cater for these re-motored cars, which were concentrated on the Uxbridge Road services. These services had been greatly speeded up to counter fierce omnibus competition. The contract with the Hewittic Electric Company for the supply of a 300Kw mercury arc rectifier sub-station equipment was approved on 4 October 1928 at the cost of £4,200, as was an agreement with the Metropolitan District Railway Company and the London Electric Railway Company for the supply of current to the new sub-station.

The sub-station building at Fulwell under construction and with it the depot entrance tracks being laid July 1902. It would appear that the lamp post in the foreground would soon have to be removed. (Courtesy: Bristol Record Office)

Despite a time of financial stringency the LUT continued with a modified programme of modernisation, the major element of which was the provision of forty-six new high-speed trams as replacements for cars of the original fleet which were then being scrapped in large numbers. The purchase of these new vehicles was sanctioned on 13 February 1929 at the same time as £5,000 was approved for the provision of a new sub-station at Southall, this figure including the acquisition of the site, erection of the building, provision of equipment and mains from the sub-station at Hanwell. This additional capacity was required to provide for the demands of the 70hp motors in the new "Feltham" type trams then under construction.

Experience with operation of the new trams, which had commenced operation on the Shepherds Bush-Uxbridge route on 15 January 1931 had shown that their power requirements called for further capacity at the outer end of the Uxbridge route, and on 2 July the LUT directors approved expenditure of £2,425 for a Cooper-Hewittic mercury vapour rectifier at Hayes (hitherto referred to as Hillingdon) sub-station. On 1 October £250 was voted for the purchase from the North Metropolitan Electric Power Supply Company of a secondhand booster with new coils and switchgear and a secondhand rotary converter, of which details of their ultimate use are not recorded. They may have been added to one of the tramway sub-stations but it is possible that they were intended for use at a new sub-station on the recently-opened trolleybus route in Burlington Road, New Malden, land for which was bought following a decision by the directors on 5 November. No details of the price of the land or of equipment in the station were recorded. Details of the conversion of the tram routes in the Twickenham, Kingston and Wimbledon areas are given in Volume 2.

A short extension to the trolleybus route at Tolworth made a new sub-station necessary there, and on 7 April 1932 £517 expenditure was approved to supply and lay mains to connect the new facility, which was provided by the London & Home Counties Joint Electricity Authority, the work having commenced prior to this and the substation gone into operation on 4 April. On 1 December £2,483 was sanctioned for the short extension of 1,500 yards at Tolworth, covering both cables and overhead construction. The existence of the LUT as a separate entity was at this time about to come to an end, and the purchase, approved on 1 June 1933 of a redundant 800Kw rotary converter from the Sudbury sub-station of the London Electric Railway Company was the last such transaction in the LUT minute books prior to the formal transfer of the undertaking to the new London Passenger Transport Board on 1 July. This equipment was installed at Fulwell sub-station, the costs incurred amounting to £737.

Following the absorption of the London United Tramways into the newly formed London Passenger Transport Board on 1 July 1933 tramway and trolleybus operation continued until electric traction finally ceased on the former LUT system on 20 May 1962 as related in the final Chapter of Volume 2. The power station building at Chiswick remained in use for various purposes connected with transport but for a time was used as a film studio. The building still stands, having been made the subject of a preservation order and was ultimately sold.

Appendix 1
The Horse Tram Fleets
The Southall, Ealing & Shepherds Bush Co. Cars

These were four in number, having been purchased two in 1874, one in 1877 and one in 1878. No photographs, drawings or contracts are known, but the capital expenditure and the allowance of two horses per car indicates that they were double-decked, as does the fact that the SE & SB had a two-class fare structure until 1882 (presumably first class inside, second class outside). The total of 4 cars and 41 horses remained unchanged until 1881. It is likely that all four were built by Britain's pioneer tramcar builder, George Starbuck of Birkenhead, and that the first two resembled the 1874 Starbuck cars for Sheffield, with a primitive iron step-ladder at each end. The 1877/8 cars would have been similar, but with proper stairs, these two cars could possibly have been secondhand purchases from the North Metropolitan Tramways. The SE & SB cars were presumably numbered from 1 to 4, and were probably withdrawn, two in 1888 and two in 1891, though not scrapped until 1894.

The One-Horse Cars

On its formation in 1881, the West Metropolitan company aimed to reduce costs by using light one-man single-deck horse cars on the new Goldhawk Road route. These were one-class only, but a works photograph shows one with a roof-mounted fareboard "Fare any distance, 1d weekdays, 2d Sundays". These small

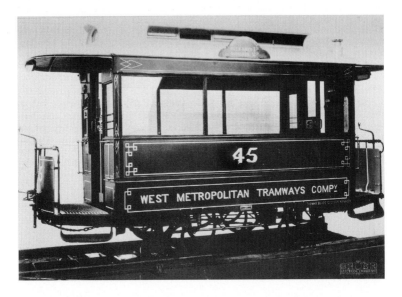

From 1882 to 1894 the Goldhawk Road service was worked by these small one-horse cars. They were apparently in various coloured liveries, one of these being brown and yellow.
(Falcon Engine & Car Works)

cars were built by the Falcon Engine and Car Works, Loughborough, probably nine in 1882 and four more later. The design was based on that of a sample car built by Falcon for Holland, where, after taking part in an exhibition at Arnhem from 31 July to 6 August 1882, it was sold to Amsterdam as their No. 121. The seating was reckoned in Holland as 18 in summer but only 16 in winter, when passengers wore their winter coats. On the Goldhawk Road service the fares were originally placed by passengers in a glass box, but a well-known photograph of No. 10 in Goldhawk Road early in 1890, shows the car with both driver and conductor.

These cars may have been responsible in part for the West Metropolitan's poor public image. They were too lightly built to stand up to the wear and tear, and deteriorated to an extent that in 1892 the police refused to re-licence all but four of them, and these four were only licensed for two months. Their total number was 13 cars, including at least one (No. 45) acquired new in 1887, the builder's photograph showing it bearing the name of Thomas Boyce Goodyer, who was manager for less than a year. Their fleet numbers were re-used for new cars in 1894/5.

The Stephenson Cars

The rapid expansion of London's horse tramways in the 1870s took place at a time when the few British tramcar builders could not cope with the demand. The John Stephenson Company of New York, represented in London by Charles J. Pusey & Co. of 35, Queen Victoria Street, seized this opportunity and sold several hundred Stephenson horse cars to the North Metropolitan Tramways Company and the London Tramways Company. Most of the NMT cars were 46-seaters (22 inside, 24 outside) with seven windows per side, but ten NMT cars bought in 1875 had eight windows per side and seated 52. A Stephenson advertisement shows a similar car built for the London Tramways Co. as their No. 125.

The 52-seaters may have proved to be too large (or heavy) for the NMT and/or the LTC, and had been taken out of use by 1878. Ten of them turned up on the West Metropolitan in 1882 to work the new line from Hammersmith to Kew Bridge. A photograph exists of No. 26 awaiting attention in 1894 with a caption stating that they would be rebuilt to match the newest cars, but the rebuilding (at Chiswick in 1896) was so extensive that the results were equivalent to ten new cars, whose numbers included 22 and 27. The 1896 cars are described later.

Old Style—West Metropolitan Tramways.

No. 26, one of the John Stephenson-type cars withdrawn by the West Metropolitan Tramways after working on the Hammersmith – Kew Bridge service since 1882.   (The Railway World)

The Kew-Richmond Cars

For the opening of the Kew Road line in April 1883, the WMT bought six seven-window knifeboard-seat cars, bringing the fleet total to 30. The builder is not known, but they were British in style and probably new (not second-hand) as they remained in use to 1901. They were well reported in the press, which mentioned their red velvet curtains and smooth riding. They were replaced in 1901 by newer cars displaced from the first electrified routes.

The Falcon Garden-seat Cars

Part of the new WMT capital raised in 1886 was used to buy new cars for the Uxbridge Road line, four in 1886 and possibly more later. These were double-deckers built by Falcon of Loughborough, and were the first WMT cars to have top deck reversible garden seats. A builder's photograph of No. 41 bears the name of the manager Frederick John Farrell in his last year of office (1886). The class was transferred to Goldhawk Road in 1895 when new cars were bought for Uxbridge Road, and lasted until electrification in 1901, latterly with a banner advertising the Central London Electric Railway. They had what was then known as double-approach platforms, permitting access from either side of the road.

The number of cars in this class is not known, but the total WMT stock rose from 31 in 1885 to 35 in 1886 and 50 in 1887. This figure of 50 is not explained, and would have exceeded the combined capacity of the WMT depots, which in 1894 was given as Chiswick 20, Richmond 6 and Shepherds Bush 7, a total of 33. The stock total is given as 48 cars in 1888, 1889 and 1890 and 46 in 1891, then drops suddenly to a more realistic figure of 28 in 1892, rising to 33 in 1894.

Hired Cars, 1892/94

As already mentioned, the police in 1892/4 refused to re-license some of the WMT cars, possibly as many as 16, and eventually including all the one-man single-deckers. A photograph taken at Kew Bridge terminus shows that the WMT hired some cars from another London tramway company; it shows a garden-seat seven-

An 1886 garden-seat car, No. 41 was built at Falcon Works, Loughborough for the Uxbridge Road service of the West Metropolitan Tramways. From 1895 until 1901 it worked on the Goldhawk Road line.   (Falcon Engine & Car Works)

The former Lineff electric car of 1890 as rebuilt in 1894 by the LUT as a horse car for use on the Kew – Richmond line. The passengers were always assured of plenty of fresh air.

(The Railway World)

window double-decker of the type built by the North Metropolitan Tramways at Union Road works, Leytonstone both for its own use and for sale to other operators such as Glasgow Corporation. On the West Metropolitan they would probably have been needed for at least six months.

The 1894 Milnes Cars

George White's appointment as WMT manager and receiver coincided with an urgent need to replace those cars which had been hired or condemned. To obtain quick delivery, an order was placed with G.F. Milnes for 15 garden-seat double-deck seven-window cars to a design recently built for Bristol, seating 20 inside and 26 outside. Some of them took the numbers of the cars the police had condemned (e.g. 1,7 & 11) and others took the next highest vacant numbers (46 to 49).

Four of these cars were allocated to the Richmond–Kew service and others to Hammersmith-Kew Bridge. They were displaced in 1901 by newer horse cars (Richmond) and electric cars (Hammersmith) and were offered for sale. The buyer may have been the North Metropolitan Tramways, whose name was borne by one such car when secured for preservation. It is now displayed at the Caister Castle Motor Museum in Norfolk.

The Lineff Car

In 1894 the newly-formed LUT took over the car used in Lineff's experiments at Chiswick and rebuilt it as an open cross-bench one-horse single-decker for summer use on the Kew–Richmond line, with fleet number 19. *The Railway World* described it as the first open car in London.

The 1895 Milnes Cars

As soon as it was clear that electrification would be deferred, the LUT Board ordered new horse cars for Uxbridge Road. Designed by James Clifton Robinson and built by G.F. Milnes, they had four large Tudor-arch windows per side and resembled Milnes cars supplied to Leeds and Sheffield. They replaced the 1886 Falcon cars on the Shepherds Bush–Acton service in September 1895 and were

267

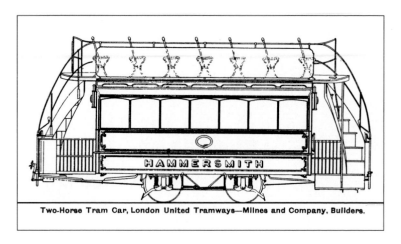

Two-Horse Tram Car, London United Tramways—Milnes and Company, Builders.

One of 15 cars built by G.F. Milnes in 1894 in response to an order from the West Metropolitan Tramways Company, but taken over by the LUT.   (The Railway World)

A number of four-window cars of this type were built by Milnes to the design of Sir Clifton Robinson to work on the extended Acton – Shepherds Bush line. This car is standing outside Acton depot and is decorated for the Diamond Jubilee celebrations held in honour of Queen Victoria in 1897.   (Courtesy: National Tramway Museum)

probably eight or ten in number, based from March 1896 at the new Acton dept. They were retained in stock after the 1901 electrification and some were later used on the Kew Road line, of which a hand-coloured postcard shows No. 45 in a brown and yellow livery.

The Chiswick-built Cars

After the LUT's Chiswick workshop had caught up with arrears of other work, construction began in 1896 of some larger horse cars, again designed by J.C. Robinson. These cars are thought to have re-used the underframes and running gear of the Stephenson cars. They had five windows per side, with curved tops resembling those of Imperial Tramways' electric cars at Middlesbrough. Known fleet numbers are 22, 27, 50, 54 and 57. A rise of ten in the LUT stock from 1896 (49 cars) to 1899 (59 cars) implies a total build of ten cars. Nos. 50 and 54 were photographed on the Hammersmith–Kew Bridge service, the others on the Kew–Richmond service, which they worked until closure in May 1912, when three cars were sold to Oxford. These well-built cars would have been suitable for use as trailers, but although the LUT obtained trailer powers, they were never exercised.

Conclusion

A problem for the historian is that the LUT quoted two different sets of horse car stock totals (cars licensed for service and total stock on hand), without any clear differentiation. The author and the publisher will therefore be interested to hear from any readers who can add to the information shown in this Appendix.

LUT car No. 50, one of ten built at the Chiswick workshop of the company in 1896. These may have been nominal rebuilds of the Stephenson cars, but with considerable alterations made to the structure.   (Courtesy: Lens of Sutton)

Appendix 2

Reckenzaun and Lineff.

One of the earliest trials of an electric traction system for tramways took place on the new West Metropolitan Tramways Company's system in the spring of 1883. In February the Electric Power Storage Company Ltd., asked the WMT for permission to carry out a trial with a battery-driven car. The WMT agreed to their request and asked the Board of Trade to approve the trial on 23 February, saying that it was proposed to undertake the trial on 3 March. On 26 February the WMT solicitors, Walter Webb & Co., told the Board of Trade that the trial might take place on the Shepherds Bush–Acton line. Both Acton and Fulham Local Boards had agreed to the trial. Fulham Local Board was at the time the road authority for Hammersmith and the Shepherds Bush district.

The car used was an eight-window horse tram which had seen several years' service on the tramways in South London, with spiral ladder-type stairs and knifeboard upper-deck seating. It was fitted with an independent four-wheel truck, the necessary work being carried out at the Millwall works of Stephens, Smith & Company who were working in conjunction with Anthony Reckenzaun and the Electric Power Storage Company. The battery consisted of fifty Fauré-Sellon-Volckmar cells, each 13in by 11in by 7in and weighing 80lb, a total of 1¾ tons. A Siemens 100 volts 60-amp motor, mounted in the truck, drove one axle through belting and a countershaft and the car could work for seven hours at one charge with a full load of 46 passengers. The car was lighted with Swan electric lamps and electric bells were fitted.

The car underwent two trials, one on the Shepherds Bush to Acton line, on 3 March 1883 and the second on the Hammersmith and Shepherds Bush to Kew Bridge line, on 10 March. The Acton trial is reported to have been successful, and Maj-Gen. Hutchinson, the Board of Trade inspector, said that the car ran well at 6 mile/h carrying five tons. The trial on the Kew Bridge line took place on 10 March, and a number of distinguished electrical engineers were present, including Dr. Werner Siemens, Sir F. Bramwell and Stephen Sellon. The car ran well but on this occasion the driving belt had stretched and the car had to he hauled up an incline by four horses. Gen. Hutchinson said in his report on the car that the trial

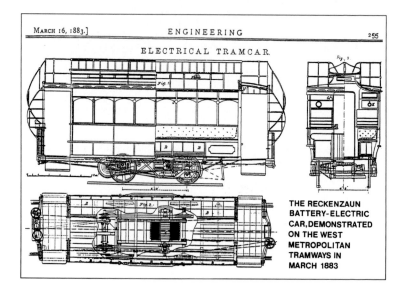

THE RECKENZAUN BATTERY-ELECTRIC CAR, DEMONSTRATED ON THE WEST METROPOLITAN TRAMWAYS IN MARCH 1883

was "more or less successful" and that it might be necessary to alter one or two details but he did not expect that the Board of Trade would make any difficulty in licensing the car. Stephen Sellon said an average of 5 hp would suffice for a car with 40 passengers and traction costs would be 6s 3d per day.

At a luncheon given on the day of the Kew trial at the Star and Garter Hotel, Kew Bridge much optimism was expressed for the future success of the battery system. It was stated that the reason for the failure of the car to ascend the gradient during the Kew Bridge trial was a three-eighth's of an inch difference between the track gauge of the Acton and Kew Bridge lines. One of Gen. Hutchinson's requirements for future operation of the car was the necessity for a speed governor and control and brake equipment at both ends of the car. Anthony Reckenzaun continued his experiments at Millwall with a bogie car (and developing electric braking and worm drive) but these did not involve the West Metropolitan Tramways. In his 1892 book, *Electric Traction on Railways and Tramways* Reckenzaun reluctantly concluded that the weight, cost and short life of batteries made battery traction more expensive than the alternatives and likely to remain so unless the life of batteries could be substantially improved.

The West Metropolitan Tramways Company was more directly involved in a second series of trials, those of the Lineff conduit and surface contact systems the first of which was registered by Alexander Lineff under British Patent 10092 of May 1888. The aim of these trials was to reduce working costs as compared with horse traction, and the trials continued over the next two years as the patentees tried to perfect their inventions and to meet the objections of Hammersmith Vestry to an open conduit system. The open conduit system at first tried consisted of a shallow conduit in which the conduit slot was formed from two Z rails, with a fixed conductor resting in the bottom of the conduit. Inside the conduit contact plugs were fitted at intervals of four feet. Between the fixed conductor and the bottom of the Z rails was a flexible conductor of strip steel which was raised by the collector

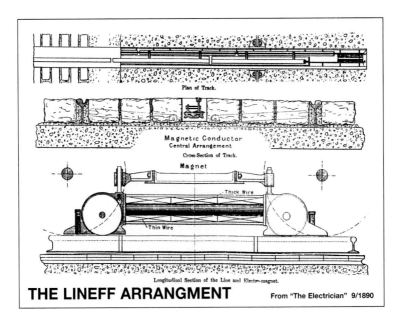

Plan of Track.

Magnetic Conductor
Central Arrangement
Cross-Section of Track.

Magnet

Thick Wire

Thin Wire

Longitudinal Section of the Line and Electro-magnet.

THE LINEFF ARRANGMENT From "The Electrician" 9/1890

271

on the car, consisting of a magnet suspended from beneath the car by a rope. The magnet on the car raised the flexible strip, making contact with the bottom of the Z rails, which became dead as the car passed over each four-foot section.

A short length of track was laid at Chiswick Depot and a small 20-seater car was fitted up for the trials. The car was fitted with a 4hp Immisch motor running at 1,000 rpm and the drive was taken to the axles via two Renold roller chains, the current being taken at 220 volts and 10 amp. A buffer board was fitted at each end of the car and if the board encountered an obstruction the board was pushed back and the power supply to the motor cut off and an electric brake was operated. It was stated that the general arrangement of the line was similar to the Blackpool tramway.

The scheme was submitted to Hammersmith Vestry, who objected to the open conduit and the inventors set about perfecting a "closed conduit" system which it was hoped would be acceptable to the Vestry. The result was a variation on the surface-contact principle, and was registered under British patents 1644 and 13619 of August 1890. Again, a sub-surface conduit was used, and above this, flush with the road surface a third rail was laid. in three feet lengths, a half-inch gap between each length being filled with asphalt, each length thus being insulated from its neighbour. The copper conductor was laid inside the conduit and the collector fixed to the car consisted of a magnet 4ft 6in long. The magnet had a pole-piece consisting of a roller running on the centre rail and two blocks just clearing the rail. The rail, 6in deep, was laid on an earthenware longitudinal sleeper embedded in asphalt extending below the sleepers. The conductor lay in a groove in the sleeper and in a second groove a strip of galvanised hoop iron was laid, one end connected to the conductor, the other end being free. The magnet lifted the loose end and current passed from the conductor through the strip to the rail. After the magnet passed the strip fell and the rail became dead. A second rail. alongside the contact rail underground and embedded in the asphalt, also in short lengths, was arranged to break joint with the first rail to reduce the resistance of the magnetic circuit, allowing, the use of a much less powerful magnet. The earth return was via the running rails.

The car used in the first trial was again used, and in *The Electrician* of 12 September 1890 Gisbert Kapp, MIEE reported favourably on the system, both electrically and mechanically. He ran a steam roller over the line in several directions and the installation was quite undamaged. On the strength of Gisbert Kapp's favourable report to the company on the system the WMT asked Hammersmith Vestry on 25 July 1890 for sanction to use electric traction on the Shepherds Bush–Young's Corner section. The Vestry engaged Professor Henry Robinson, MICE, MIEE to advise them and he visited Chiswick depot in October 1890 and reported to the Vestry on 7 November. His report was favourable noting that the insulation was good and the mechanical properties of the installation were sufficiently strong to withstand heavy traffic. Alexander Lineff demonstrated a model of points and crossings, and Robinson was sufficiently impressed to advise the Vestry to approve its use on the WMT.

A meeting of the Vestry Joint Works and Law Committee held on 13 November 1890 resolved to consent to the use of the Lineff system for two years subject to a deposit to cover the cost of reinstatement of the road if necessary. A further meeting took place on 26 November with Alexander Lineff in attendance and two WMT directors, E.H. Bayley and Alfred Love. A draft agreement was drawn up between the Vestry and the Lineff Electric Traction and Lighting Syndicate Ltd and further meetings took place on 1 and 12 December 1890. It was found that the WMT had no powers to double the track in Goldhawk Road, and the WMT asked the Vestry for consent to electrify the line in Uxbridge Road between Shepherds Bush terminus and Wilton Road (now St. Elmo Road) the boundary between Hammersmith and Acton. On 4 February 1891 this request was approved by the Vestry and negotiations on matters of detail commenced.

A meeting of the Hammersmith Joint Works and Law Committee took place on 6 March 1891. The negotiations had broken down and Bayley and Lineff, who were present at the meeting with Walter Webb, the WMT solicitor asked for the negotiations to be re-opened. The Vestry wanted a two-year trial agreement but Lineff wanted a seven-year term. The WMT offered to limit a proposed extension of time to reconstruct the Uxbridge Road line to one year. The Committee resolved that if under the terms of the draft agreement the Vestry decided that the trial proved unsuccessful and the WMT objected the matter should go to arbitration, two arbitrators, one to be appointed by each of the parties and an umpire appointed by the arbitrators should make a ruling. This clause was embodied in the draft agreement.

At a meeting of the Vestry on 15 April 1891 the Vestry was informed that the reconstruction of the Uxbridge Road track had proved to be an obstacle to further progress; there were other differences which could not be resolved and the matter did not proceed further. The car was later taken over by the LUT, as described in Appendix 1.

Appendix 3

Garrick's Villa

The celebrated actor, David Garrick (1716-1779) rented a riverside estate at Hampton in 1745 and bought it in 1754. He extended the house, adding a Corinthian portico, and improved the extensive grounds. On the riverside lawn (linked to the house by a tunnel under the road) he built an octagonal summerhouse in the form of a small temple with an Ionic portico, containing a life-size marble figure of Shakespeare by Roubillac, which cost 500 guineas. Garrick bequeathed the figure to the British Museum and provided a stone replica for the temple. His widow lived at the house until her death in 1822, but neglected it and it was sold at auction to a Mr. Carr who restored it and resold it to a Mr. Phillips. Its owner from 1864 was Edward Grove, a Lambeth clothier, who made further improvements.

THE TEMPLE AND DAVID GARRICK'S HOUSE AT HAMPTON

An early engraving of David Garrick's Villa by the Thames.
(Courtesy: "Middlesex" by Sir C.W. Radcliffe)

The LUT bought the property from Grove's widow in November 1902 to enable the road to be widened, and set back the frontage by about 20ft. Part of the grounds were added to Bushy Park, in return for which the Office of Works, which managed the Crown estates, allowed a long strip of Crown land in Bushy Park and Hampton Court Green to be taken for road widening. This allowed the LUT to lay double track instead of the single line originally authorised in Hampton Court Road, and to avoid buying expensive property from several owners on the river side of the road. The ornamental railings, paid for by the LUT and replacing a wooden fence, are still in place along Hampton Court Road, and at the time they were installed they were commented upon favourably by HM King Edward VII.

The LUT made the property available to Clifton Robinson as a private residence and he revived a tradition, established by David Garrick, of opening the house and grounds to the public on fete days, and made it available at other times for private functions, including the annual Molesey Regatta and picnic parties on the small island in the river known as Garrick's Ait. The Robinsons entertained many notable personages at the Villa, sometimes on a very lavish scale.

When re-aligning the frontage of the Villa to Church Street and Hampton Court Road, the LUT made provision for a short tram siding into the grounds to allow the stabling of special cars hired to private parties. This was laid without specific authorisation, and was objected to by Middlesex County Council on traffic safety grounds. Robinson pointed out that the Board of Trade inspecting officer (Col. Yorke) had raised no objection to its being used to run in occasional private cars, and that the company had widened the road at the turnout. The siding was probably used for the first time during the opening ceremony for the Twickenham – Hampton Court route on 2 April 1903, and later for the annual garden parties for the wives and children of LUT staff held in the grounds up to 1908. The 1906 event required 35 special cars, and that of 1907 34 cars, one of which brought the LUT band from Hanwell Depot.

Contrary to popular belief, the siding was never used by the LUT's single-deck private saloon tram, as this vehicle was not placed in service until 1911. Sir Clifton and Lady Robinson bought a town house, Keith House, Porchester Gate in Bayswater in the latter part of 1907. It is not known when they gave up the occupancy of the Villa, but Robinson was listed as the occupier in the Hampton electoral roll up to 1909. On 29 April 1910 the LUT directors resolved to place the Villa on the market following the resignation of Robinson as Managing Director and Engineer in February. The price asked was £9,500 plus £550 for the Ait. The tram siding was removed by the date of the 1912 Ordnance Survey but the property remained on the market until 7 May 1913, when it was conveyed to a Mrs. Hutchinson for £5,400. The Ait was sold separately for £550 on 15 October 1913. The LUT had taken possession of the property on 28 November 1902 and Robinson's tenure was in lieu of his £2,000 annual salary as Managing Director. During the 1960s the tall curved brick wall along the frontage was resited to close off the entrance to the former siding. The rails in the grounds were visible from the tops of buses for many years but were later concreted over. The house was converted into expensive flats at this time, together with the adjacent Garrick's Cottage, and Garrick's Lawn on the riverside, with the floodlit temple, is now a public park.

Appendix 4

Board of Trade Inspections and Opening Dates

Section	Inspection	Certificate	Formal Opening	Public Opening
Reconstructed lines in King Street, Hammersmith and Uxbridge Road between Shepherds Bush and Birkbeck Grove, Acton; new relief line in The Grove between Beadon Road and King Street and the new line between Birkbeck Grove and Acton Depot.	30 Aug. 1895	6 Sep. 1895	–	* 31 Aug. 1895
Kew Bridge – Hounslow (The Bell)	+11 Aug. 1900	11 Aug. 1900	10 Jul. 1901	6 Jul. 1901
Hammersmith – Kew Bridge	+30 Mar. 1901	3 Apr. 1901	10 Jul. 1901	4 Apr. 1901
Shepherds Bush – Young's Corner	+30 Mar. 1901	3 Apr. 1901	10 Jul. 1901	4 Apr. 1901
Shepherds Bush – Acton (Birkbeck Grove)	+30 Mar. 1901	3 Apr. 1901	10 Jul. 1901	4 Apr. 1901
Birkbeck Grove – High Street - Acton Depot	+30 Mar. 1901	3 Apr. 1901	10 Jul. 1901	4 Apr. 1901
Acton Depot – Southall	**2 Jul. 1901	13 Aug. 1901	10 Jul. 1901	10 Jul. 1901
Hounslow (The Bell) – Barrack Road	ø20 Jun. 1902	12 Sep. 1902	–	13 Aug. 1902
Busch Corner – Twickenham (Cole's Bridge)	ø20 Jun. 1902	12 Sep. 1902	–	13 Aug. 1902
Cole's Bridge – Cross Deep	ø12 Sep. 1902	29 Sep. 1902	–	13 Sep. 1902
King Street – Richmond Bridge	ø12 Sep. 1902	29 Sep. 1902	–	13 Sep. 1902
Cross Deep – Stanley Road Junction	ø7 Nov. 1902	22 Nov. 1902	–	8 Nov. 1902
Stanley Road – Hampton Wick – Hampton Court	ø28 Mar. 1903	30 Apr. 1903	2 Apr. 1903	2 Apr. 1903
Stanley Road – Hampton Hill – Hampton Court				

Board of Trade Inspections and Opening Dates (cont.)

Studland Street – Askew Arms	ø31 May 1904	7 Jun. 1904	31 May 1904	1 Jun. 1904
Southall – Uxbridge	ø31 May 1904	7 Jun. 1904	31 May 1904	1 Jun. 1904
Hampton Wick – Thames Ditton	21 Feb.1906	1 Mar. 1906	1 Mar. 1906	1 Mar. 1906
Clarence Street – Kingston Hill	21 Feb. 1906	1 Mar. 1906	1 Mar. 1906	1 Mar. 1906
Surbiton – Tolworth	21 Feb. 1906	1 Mar. 1906	1 Mar. 1906	1 Mar. 1906
Brentford – Hanwell	23 May 1906	26 May 1906	–	26 May 1906
Kingston – Ham Boundary	23 May 1906	26 May 1906	–	26 May 1906
Richmond Park Gates branch	23 May 1906	26 May 1906	–	26 May 1906
Norbiton Church – Malden Fountain	23 May 1906	26 May 1906	–	26 May 1906
Malden Fountain – Raynes Park	23 May 1906	26 May 1906	–	27 Apr. 1907
Raynes Park – Wimbledon (Worple Road)	9 Aug. 1906	13 Aug. 1906	2 May 1907	2 May 1907
Wimbledon Hill – Tooting (Longley Road)				
St. George's Road – Francis Grove Loop	ø25 Jun. 1907	29 Jun. 1907	–	27 Jun.1907
Merton – Summerstown				

* Refers to new line in The Grove and from Birkbeck Grove to Acton Hill only. The line in Acton from Askew Arms westward was closed for four months for reconstruction and extension but the line from Shepherds Bush to Askew Arms and the lines in Hammersmith continued to operate during reconstruction.

+ Electrified lines inspected on 15 March 1901 by A.P. Trotter, the BOT electrical adviser.

ø Opened in anticipation of certificate with verbal sanction of Inspecting Officer.

** Electrical inspection by A.P. Trotter on 4 July 1901.

Appendix 5

Immisch Electric Launches

From 1903, following the opening of the LUT routes to Hampton Court the company made arrangements for private parties travelling by tram to Hampton Court to hire battery-powered pleasure boats on the river Thames from the Immisch Electric Launch Company Ltd., of Hampton and Maidenhead. This company was formed in 1894 to acquire the undertaking of the Thames Launch Department of the G.E. Power & Traction Co., and the first directors were Moritz A. Immisch, Emil Garcke and F. Pears. Garcke was Chairman and also Chairman of the British Electric Traction Company Ltd. Immisch, a clockmaker, had set up in business manufacturing electric motors in Perren Street, Kentish Town, London in 1884 and moved to larger premises nearby at Malden Works, Prince of Wales Road by 1889. Immisch was an early experimenter with electric rail traction, and built a battery-operated mine locomotive for Silkstone Colliery in 1889.

The launch company was reconstructed in 1897, with new directors, J.S. Critchley, H.S. Day and C.L. Robertson (Chairman) and was reformed again in 1904 as the Immisch Launch and Boat Co. Ltd., with Critchley replaced by S. Sudworth, Robertson remaining as Chairman together with H.S. Day. The company's premises were at Platt's Eyot, an island in the Thames off Hampton Village, and an article on it appeared in the BET Gazette for December 1905. Its customers included the Prince of Wales in 1899, the King and Queen of Sweden in 1900 and various Indian princes. Moritz Immisch died on 20 September 1903, but the company continued to trade, mainly as boatbuilders until it was sold to John I. Thornycroft & Co. Ltd., in 1914.

The Immisch fleet included three steam-powered floating generating stations for charging the launches' batteries, *Volt, Ohm* and *Ampere,* of which *Volt* later burst its boiler and sank. At one time there were as many as 26 launches operating on the river.

The arrangements between the LUT and the Immisch company for hiring launches are not known, but were still in operation in 1906. Tram passengers joined the launches at a landing stage near Clifton Robinson's residence, Garrick's Villa. It is not known if combined tram and launch tickets were issued, but it seems likely that party bookings from the London termini included the charge for the boat trip and tram fare.

The Wimbledon Common Tramway

In the later part of the nineteenth century, the National Rifle Association's ranges were set up every year on Wimbledon Common, until in 1890 the Association transferred the event to Bisley Camp. During the annual prize meeting, the NRA Camp was served by a tramway which was laid along the rear of the firing points. At the conclusion of the meeting the track was removed and put away in the NRA stores until the following year.

The original NRA venue had been the Woolwich Trial Ranges on Erith Marshes, where a three-mile tramway had been laid from Plumstead station past the firing points and ending at Cross Ness Pier on the river Thames. It was in use by 22 November 1864, the first day of some firing trials held to determine the best type of firearm for the Wimbledon meetings. It was probably worked by the open four-wheel cars later used at Wimbledon and Bisley, each towed by a horse ridden by a soldier.

The NRA's enclosure on Wimbledon Common, of which a map appeared in the *Illustrated London News* for 17 July 1886, was in the south-east part of the common with its main entrance approximately opposite the junction of the present Parkside Avenue and Parkside. The standard gauge tramway, laid in light 14lb/yard rail on sleepers, ran from the entrance gate along the rear of the range to White Houses Gate, where it turned sharply westward past the officials' camp to terminate at the clock tower near the windmill. It is possible that the course of the

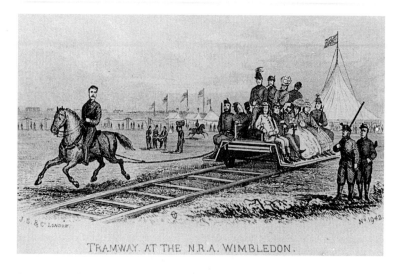

TRAMWAY AT THE N.R.A. WIMBLEDON.

An engraving of the horse-drawn tramway car of the N.R.A. at Wimbledon Common.
(Courtesy: A.A. Jackson)

line varied with the years. The horses ran beside the track and not between the rails.

In 1877 a steam tramway locomotive was loaned to the NRA by Merryweather & Sons of Greenwich, and given the name *Alexandra* in readiness for a visit by the Prince and Princess of Wales. The inauguration of steam working on 9 July 1877 was marked with some ceremony, when the Prince of Wales drove the locomotive for some distance. By 1878 the Council of the NRA had purchased the engine, and used it each year thereafter, renaming it *Wharncliffe* after Lord Wharncliffe, the Association's chairman. It was shorter than most Merryweather tram engines, and may have been the one tried in September 1876 on the Ryde Pier tramway. A testimonial supplied by the NRA Secretary to Merryweathers in 1882 confirmed that it was in use and giving satisfactory service. There were now six cars, the longitudinal seats of which had been turned to face inwards (with a centre entrance), and the locomotive sometimes hauled or propelled all six cars at once.

In the summer of 1883, the tramway was experimentally electrified. Two flat one-inch copper strips were laid between the running rails in grooved channels carried on wooden blocks. They were fed with current from a Weston dynamo driven by a 12hp Robey steam engine. One car was motorised, collecting and returning its current by trailing chains within the conductor channels. It had been hoped to work the line electrically during the annual NRA meeting, but in the event electric working did not commence until 27 July and was intermittent. It was not repeated in later years, one reason being the uneven track with sleepers working loose in the sandy soil.

The last day of firing at Wimbledon Common was 8 July 1889, after which the NRA moved the track, engine and cars and all its other equipment to Bisley Camp. The new ranges and tramway at Bisley came into use on 12 July 1890 and the tramway was still in use with the same engine and cars up to the Summer 1914 meeting.

The foregoing is based, with permission, on articles by Alan A. Jackson in issues 3 and 8 (1951/2) of *The Tramway Review*. A more detailed account of the NRA tramways by the same author was published in *Railway World* for July 1960.

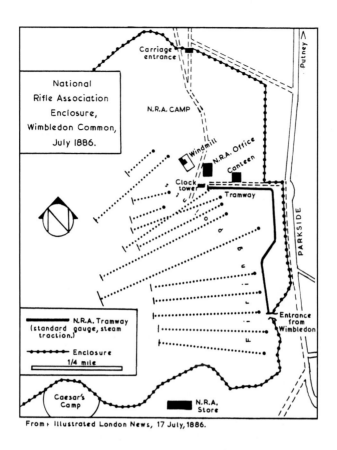

National Rifle Association Enclosure, Wimbledon Common, July 1886.

Carriage entrance

N.R.A. CAMP

Windmill

N.R.A. Office

Canteen

Clock tower

Tramway

Putney

PARKSIDE

Entrance from Wimbledon

N.R.A. Tramway (standard gauge, steam traction.)

Enclosure

1/4 mile

Caesar's Camp

N.R.A. Store

From Illustrated London News, 17 July, 1886.

The steam tram engine 'Wharncliffe' and train at Bisley in 1896, watched by a Trooper of the Royal Scots Greys. (Capt. A. Daniel)

Appendix 6
Early Trolleybus Proposals

Chiswick Urban District Council

To the south of the main LUT line along High Road, Chiswick lay the residential district of Grove Park, contained within a loop of the river Thames. Proposals for tramways (including one by the LUT) did not materialise and on 17 November 1910 Chiswick UDC promoted a Parliamentary Bill for a U-shaped trolleybus route from Turnham Green via Chiswick Lane and Burlington Lane to Chiswick LSWR station, continuing back to the High Road via Fauconberg Road, Sutton Lane and Heathfield Gardens, a little over two miles. The council obtained its Act in 1911, and early in 1912 reached an agreement with the LUT to operate it on lease from the UDC. The Bill included provision for a separate depot , but the LUT would probably have worked the route from their existing Chiswick premises. However, no further steps were taken and the district was served instead by a predecessor of the No. 55 motor 'bus.

Heston & Isleworth UDC

Among the LUT's unrealised proposals of 1901 was a light railway from High Street, Southall via Norwood Green, Heston and Lampton to Hounslow (The Bell). This was never built, and in 1911 Heston and Isleworth UDC promoted a Bill for a trolleybus service along the same route, continuing beyond Hounslow to Whitton, to be operated by a proposed Southall, Hounslow and Twickenham Railless Traction Company with six single-deck vehicles. The Bill was opposed by the LUT and the railway companies and was rejected.

Ealing and Northfields

In October 1911, Ealing Chamber of Commerce launched a scheme for a trolleybus route between Ealing Broadway and Northfields, to be operated by the borough council. A more ambitious variant provided for two lines between the same points, thus forming a circular route. The council were not very interested, and nor were the LUT, who had no depot in the area. The problem was resolved in August 1912 when the LGOC introduced a motor 'bus service.

Haydons Road (Summerstown)

During 1922 and 1923, part of the Haydons Road tramway was used to test an AEC single-deck trolleybus, an additional (negative) overhead wire being strung for the purpose. No mention of this has been found in LUT records, and the costs were presumably borne by the AEC Company.

This Appendix is based, with acknowledgement, on John C. Gillham's article *London Trolleybuses before 1930* which appeared in *Modern Transport* for 12 November 1960.

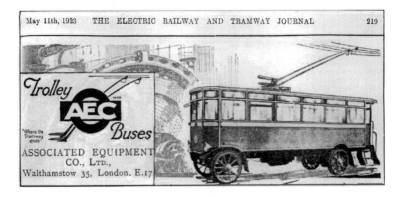

Appendix 7

Biographies

Sir George White Bt., LLD., J.P.

George White was born on 28 March 1854 at No. 2 St. Michael's Buildings, Paul Street, Bristol. His father was a painter and decorator, his mother a lady's maid. He was educated at St. Michael's Boys' School, but left at the age of 14 to become a junior clerk in the office of John Stanley of Stanley & Wasbrough, well-known commercial lawyers in the city. There he was put in charge of the Law Society Library, which he read.

At 16 he took charge of the bankruptcy side of the business and was said to have been capable of superintending as many as 12 liquidations at any one time. At 18 years, on John Stanley's behalf, he formed the syndicate which became the Bristol Tramway & Carriage Company, to which he was appointed part-time Company Secretary. His ability in this respect soon brought him the secretaryship of the Bath and Gloucester Tramways, and according to *Zig-Zag Magazine* he was consulted "in nearly every town in the West and Midlands where trams had been projected". Through the Bristol Tramway Company, he met his lifelong friend and business associate James Clifton Robinson, who joined the company as Manager in 1875.

George White left Stanley & Wasbrough in 1875, turning down the articles offered him, to set himself up in business as *George White, Stockbroker & Public Accountant*. His entrepreneurial and stockbroking skills led him to involvement in audacious financial coups, of a kind which had previously only been associated with the City of London. The local press revelled in his triumphs.

After two early attempts to break the monopoly of the Great Western Railway on Bristol, which failed but did much to enhance his reputation and his bank balance, he startled the transport world by buying up and then selling the Severn and Wye and Severn Bridge Railway, entirely without the knowledge of the Company's directors. While carrying out a number of similarly spectacular coups, he took over York Tramways as liquidator and ran the Company successfully from Bristol for ten years.

In 1892 he acquired a majority holding in the Imperial Tramways Company, which gave him control of networks in Reading, Dublin and Middlesbrough, together with the Corris Railway in North Wales, while in 1893 he undertook the liquidation of the West Metropolitan Tramways in London, took it over and reformed it as the London United Tramways. In both projects he appointed James Clifton Robinson as Managing Director and Engineer.

It was in 1895 that the two men opened electric tramway services in Bristol. They had also devised a scheme for an electric underground railway to be built beneath the streets of London, but this foundered through, it was said, a clash of personalities with J. Pierpont Morgan, the American railway magnate. However, White emerged financially triumphant, and was said to have been the only man ever to have beaten Morgan in a business deal.

As early as 1890, the *Bristol Magpie* said of him "as it was said of Cimon of Greece, that he gets his riches to use them, and so uses them as to be honoured on their account", noting his contributions to the Lord Mayor's Relief Fund and his rescue of the Bristol Benevolent Institution. George White's philanthropy began in earnest however, with a free pension scheme set up in 1899 for his Bristol Tramway employees. This was followed by the presentation of a Stock Exchange "worthy of the City of Bristol to its members", which still stands in St. Nicholas Street.

When on a trip abroad for his health in 1904, he learned that the projected Queen Victoria Memorial Hospital at Nice had become derelict through lack of funds. He financed the work of completing the hospital and served as its President until his death. At home, as President and Treasurer of the Bristol Royal Infirmary, he reversed its heavy debts and raised or gave sufficient funds for the building of the King Edward VII Memorial Wing, opened by King George V in 1912.

His ability to judge new technology, and to be the first to exploit it, led to his introduction of the first motor buses and motor taxis in Bristol in the early years of the century. In 1912 he went into industry himself and set up a factory at Filton to build buses.

Having observed man's attempts at flight from 1904 onwards, he decided, late in 1909 to enter aviation, and in February 1910 founded the first major aircraft factory in Great Britain at Filton. By 1911 the British and Colonial Aeroplane Company (later known as the Bristol Aeroplane Company) carried sufficient stock to construct up to 500 aeroplanes, claiming to be the largest aircraft works in the world.

Most celebrated of the early products of the Company were the Boxkite (1910), the Scout (1914) and the Bristol Fighter (1916). By the outbreak of the Great War, his flying schools had trained 308 of the 664 pilots available to fly. The life-saving 'Paravane', which protected ships from enemy mines, was developed at the expense of the British & Colonial Company, to the design of Lieut. (later Admiral Sir) Denniston Burney.

Sir George (who had received his Baronetcy in June 1904), died suddenly of heart failure in November 1916, aged 62. He was buried at St. Mary's Church, Stoke Bishop, Bristol.

Most of his companies still exist, though in merged form and still provide employment for thousands. The British Aeroplane Company (now British Aerospace) is probably the most notable example, followed by a number of bus companies throughout England. He and Clifton Robinson were largely responsible for a social revolution in the cities which his electric tramways served, allowing inner city dwellers to move out to the suburbs. His hospitals continue to prosper; the Paravane (or its merchant naval equivalent the Otter), is still used in minesweeping.

"When the great aeronautical history of the World comes to be written", stated an article in "The Aeroplane" in 1916, "his name will hold a foremost place among those who have made Britain's command of the air a possibility. As a pioneer of locomotion . . . his name will live for ever".

(The above biography of the late Sir George White Bt., LLD., J.P., has kindly been provided by his great-grandson Sir George S.J. White Bt., F.S.A.)

Sir James Clifton Robinson

James Clifton Robinson was born on 1 January 1848 in Birkenhead. It was also at Birkenhead that the flamboyant American, George Francis Train, established the first street tramway in the British Isles in 1860. It was this that made a lasting impression upon young Robinson, who, at the age of 12, obtained a junior post with Train, and so commenced a lifelong connection with tramways, their construction and management.

Robinson went to America with Train in 1866, where he gained wider experience in a country where horse tramways had been established some thirty years earlier. On his return to England in 1871 he joined the American firm of Fisher & Parrish which was then involved in the construction of tramways in London, Liverpool and Dublin. By 1873 he had gained his first senior post as General Manager of the tramway system in Cork, Ireland. He moved to Bristol in 1875 as General Manager of the newly established horse tramways there, which was to begin a fruitful association with the person who was destined to become one of Bristol's great men, George White. However, this association was interrupted between 1882 and 1891. During this time Robinson was appointed General Manager of the Edinburgh Street Tramways Company, where he built extensions to the system, while in 1884 he joined the Steep Grade Tramways & Works Co. Ltd., as Manager of the Highgate Hill cable tramway in north London.

He later returned to America where he became General Manager of the Los Angeles Cable Railway Company, an extensive system of some sixty miles which opened between June and December 1889. Here, Robinson was noted as a flamboyant character, and it was here that he suffered a setback in his career. In the evening of 24 December 1889 a severe storm caused the flooding of the cable ways, filling them with grit and other detritus, with the cable winding stations suffering from the same problem. Robinson at once set about reinstating the services, a mammoth task, during which he unwisely bet a business associate a cigar that he would have the trams running by 1 p.m. on Christmas Day. With much work still to be done he nevertheless had the engines started, with the result that grit still remaining in the slots ground its way through the cable ways and machinery, causing heavy damage. The outcome is not clear, but it is known that Robinson next set up as a railway consultant in San Francisco. It was at this time that he became convinced of the merits of electric traction.

On his return to England in 1891 he was appointed Managing Director of the Imperial Tramways Company Ltd., which owned tramways in Gloucester, Middlesbrough, Dublin and Reading, together with the Corris Railway in North Wales. George White had acquired control of the Imperial Company by this time and the Bristol Tramways had become part of the Imperial Tramways group. Robinson reported to White upon the feasibility of electrifying the Bristol system; this favourable report encouraged the Bristol directors to seek powers for the extension and electrification of the line from Old Market Street to St. George's and on to Kingswood. A Provisional Order was obtained and the work was pressed ahead, the electrified lines opening on 14 December 1895. At the same time, Robinson was carrying out the electrification of the Dublin Southern system, the first electric services commencing on 16 May 1896.

The part played by Robinson in the acquisition of the West Metropolitan Tramways and the formation of the London United Tramways in 1894 is described in Chapters 3 and 4 of this volume. With George White he was instrumental in defeating the opposition by the Kew Observatory authorities and, to a lesser extent the London County Council, to the LUT electrification schemes.

On 16 July 1898 the Middlesbrough, Stockton & Thornaby Electric Tramways system opened, these being an amalgamation of the horse tramways which came into the Imperial Tramways group of companies in 1896. The reconstruction and electrification of these was carried out by Robinson.

The inauguration of electric street tramways services in London on 4 April 1901 was Robinson's crowning achievement; thereafter, extensions in Middlesex and into Surrey absorbed his energies. Nevertheless he suffered many disappointments resulting from the opposition to tramway development shown by some local authorities in those counties and beyond. With regard to the concern shown over proposals made by Robinson to build lines into central London, the London County Council had become the tramway authority for the county area, and was averse to other undertakings attempting to build lines within its boundaries.

The acquisition of the majority holding in the LUT by the Underground Electric Railways Company of London Ltd. in 1902 broke up the partnership between Robinson and George White, but both remained firm friends. Robinson was appointed to the board of the UERL's associated company, the Metropolitan District Railway Company on 10 December 1902 and of the UERL on 10 January 1905, both of these appointments being proposed by Edgar Speyer, who, from the late summer of 1902 controlled the finances of the LUT.

Robinson was at the height of his powers at the time these events were taking place; he gave evidence to the 1905 Royal Commission on London Passenger Transport, where he spoke strongly in favour of a unified system for the capital. In the same year he received a knighthood as recognition for his services to transport.

From 1907 both the UERL and the LUT were experiencing financial difficulties and proposed expansion schemes were being scaled down. By 1909 differences over policy had arisen between the senior management of the UERL and Robinson, and the UERL directors and Speyer decided that the management of the LUT should be brought into closer co-operation. A meeting took place on 14 January 1910 at 37 Courtfield Road, South Kensington, the residence of C.J. Cater Scott, Chairman of the LUT, at which Robinson and Speyer were present. After discussion, agreement was reached that Robinson should resign his position as Managing Director and Engineer. Following this, the other LUT directors joined the meeting, at which Robinson's letter of resignation was read and accepted. The members present then expressed appreciation of the work done by him over the years on behalf of the company. His place as Managing Director was taken by Albert Stanley by prior arrangement, while Stanley later appointed Zac Ellis Knapp as Engineer and General Manager.

Robinson took a commission shortly afterwards on behalf of Sir Edgar Speyer to assess the prospects for development of traction systems in the Phillipines. On his return, he received other commissions of a like nature, resulting in his sailing to Canada, then proceeding to New York. On 6 November 1910, he and Lady Robinson attended a dinner party in that city and travelled by a Lexington Avenue tramcar back to their hotel. On the way, Robinson became ill and was taken to a chemist, where he died a few minutes later. He was brought back to England, and was buried in Kensal Green Cemetery on 18 November 1910 following a Requiem Mass at the Church of the Immaculate Conception, Farm Street, Mayfair. A large congregation was present, including many distinguished personalities of the day.

Sir James Clifton Robinson was, like Sir George White, a supporter of numerous charitable causes. He was also a member of the Institutions of Electrical and Civil Engineers. He had married Mary Martin of Blackrock, Co. Cork in 1874. They had one son, Clifton, who was born in Bristol in 1880, and who was appointed LUT Traffic Manager at an early age, but who resigned from the position in 1907.

Charles James Cater Scott

Charles James Cater Scott was Chairman of the London and India Docks Company and had various interests in shipping and overseas trade, operating from offices in Leadenhall Street, London E.C. He was also one of the original directors of the Underground Electric Railways Company of London Ltd. He then replaced Charles Tyson Yerkes as Chairman of the LUT on 2 August 1905, Yerkes having resigned in order to devote his energies to the development of the underground railways he was then promoting in the capital.

Cater Scott took office at a difficult time in the history of the LUT; financial problems were beginning to arise, resulting in him overseeing a reduction in the scale of new LUT tramway development. Later, in 1910, he had the difficult task of implementing the replacement of Robinson as Managing Director and Engineer by Albert Stanley and Zac Ellis Knapp respectively. He resigned from his position as Chairman and also that of Director on 24 April 1912, being replaced on 26 April by William Mitchell Acworth, a railway statistician.

Charles Courtney Cramp

Charles Courtney Cramp was an engineer who entered the tramway service at an early date, and became the first Rolling Stock Superintendent of the North Metropolitan Tramways at the start of that company's operations in 1870. He was a member of the Society of Engineers and delivered a lecture to the Society on tramway rolling stock on 2 November 1874. In 1876 he took a lease on the Southall, Ealing & Shepherds Bush Tramway from its owners, retaining this until 1880. Between 1881 and 1892 he was associated with Henry Osborne O'Hagan and the City of London Contract Corporation in promoting and constructing the Croydon & Norwood Tramways, the Accrington Corporation Steam Tramways and the Blackburn Corporation Tramways. He was also a director of the Rossendale Valley Tramways Company, the Contract Construction Company and, between 1889 and 1891 the Harrow Road & Paddington Tramway Company of which he was Chairman.

In 1881 he became a member of the Hammersmith Vestry, and from 1900 of the Hammersmith Metropolitan Borough Council. He also sought powers for the construction of tramways in the district, but these did not succeed. In 1894 he became a supporter of the proposals of the LUT to electrify the West Metropolitan Tramways in Hammersmith, while in 1899 he became Chairman of a sub-committee appointed to advise Hammersmith Vestry on electrification. In their report, the sub-committee stressed the importance of having a unified overhead trolley system, and strongly recommended the Vestry to press the London County Council to withdraw its insistence upon the use of the conduit system in Hammersmith. This came about shortly afterwards, being confirmed in the LUT Act for 1900. Cramp was an original alderman of the Hammersmith Metropolitan Borough Council, from which office he retired by rotation in 1906.

Richard Robert Fairbairn

Richard Robert Fairbairn was born in London on 27 May 1867. He joined the West Metropolitan Tramways Company in 1888 as assistant to the Manager, J.H. Gaynor. Gaynor died during 1890 and Richard Fairbairn was appointed Manager in his place. Following the collapse of the West Metropolitan Tramways Company in 1893 he continued in office under the WMT Receiver, George White, until the assets of the company were bought on behalf of the newly-formed London United Tramways Ltd. on 20 August 1894. The new company appointed an entirely new staff and Richard Fairbairn moved on to become Manager of the Worcester Tramways in October 1894, from which he retired on 30 June 1908. He was elected to Worcester City Council in 1899 as a Councillor for St. John's Ward, and remained on the Council, becoming an Alderman in 1937. He also represented Worcester in Parliament as a Liberal in 1922-23. He passed away in 1941 aged 75. His son, Richard C.H. Fairbairn, was one of the earliest members of the Tramway Museum Society, and was active on behalf of the Society almost up to his death at the age of 90 in August 1985.

Zac Ellis Knapp

Zac Ellis Knapp was born in 1867 at Chowan County, North Carolina, USA and trained as an electrical engineer, going on to construct power stations in Chicago. He came to England in 1901 as assistant to J.R. Chapman, General Manager and Engineer of the newly-incorporated Underground Electric Railways of London, and worked on the schemes planned by Charles Tyson Yerkes, who was Director of Construction.

When Albert Stanley became Managing Director of the LUT in sucession to Sir James Clifton Robinson in 1910, he appointed Knapp as his assistant, and later, in 1911 as General Manager. Knapp organised working methods in the workshops and the traffic department, and introduced annual leave for the tram crews and maintenance staff. Following the merger of the three London company tramways in 1913, Knapp was succeeded in the post of Engineer and Manager by A. H. Pott of the Metropolitan Electric Tramways, being then appointed Chief Engineer of the UERL where he oversaw the continued expansion of the railway network.

He was appointed to the post of General Manager of the Associated Equipment Company in 1918. After this he again became involved in carrying out extensions to the Underground system between Golders Green and Edgware and from Charing Cross to Kennington and Morden. He was a member of the Institute of Transport. He passed away on 1 October 1926 at the age of 59 years.

John Ruffell Salter

John Ruffell Salter was born in London in 1875, and after an education which he completed under the guidance of Prof. E. Wilson at King's College, London, he became, in 1893, an assistant to Prof. John Hopkinson in the latter's consultancy practice, working on tramway and electric lighting installations at Leeds, Liverpool, Stafford and Crewe. Following the death of Prof. Hopkinson in 1898, Salter was appointed as Chief Assistant Engineer to James Clifton Robinson, with responsibility for the initial electrical construction and equipment of the London United Tramways. He was also responsible for much of the electrification of the Bristol Tramways, and was one of the first to demonstrate on a practical scale the use of rotary converters for the conversion of alternating to direct current.

After completion of the electrification of the LUT horse tramways and the construction of extensions to Hounslow and Southall in 1901, Salter was appointed Engineer to the South Lancashire Tramways Company, with responsibility for the construction of the company's systems connecting Liverpool and Manchester, later becoming General Manager of the unified Lancashire United Tramways Company, and Managing Director of the St. Helen's Tramways Company. He also acted as consulting engineer to a number of electrical undertakings in north-west England. His place as Assistant Engineer to Robinson was taken by C.R. Holmes.

Salter was a member of the Institutions of Electrical and Mechanical Engineers, and of the Council of the Tramways and Light Railways Association. In 1909 he gave evidence before a House of Lords Select Committee in support of the 1909 LUT Bill, which sought *inter alia* a postponement of the London County Council's power to purchase the LUT lines in Hammersmith, which were to fall due in July. Unfortunately, after a short illness, he passed away in December 1910 at the early age of 35 years.

Sir Edgar Speyer

Edgar Speyer was born of German parentage in New York on 7 September 1862. His father was Gustavus Speyer, head of the Frankfurt banking house of Lazard Speyer Ellissen, which had two main branches, trading in New York as Speyer & Company, and in London as Speyer Brothers. Edgar Speyer was resident partner at the Frankfurt head office until 1887, when he came to England as the senior partner at the London Office at Lothbury, E.C. He acquired British nationality, and in 1902 he assisted Charles Tyson Yerkes with the financing and development of the Underground Electric Railways Company of London Ltd. Speyer advanced £100,000 to Yerkes to finance his purchase of the Metropolitan District Railway Company, and thereafter financed Yerkes' London electric railway schemes. A partner in the New York branch of the firm, Charles A. Spofford became a director of the LUT in 1902, following the acquisition of George White's controlling interest in the company by the UERL, and henceforth Speyers, through the UERL, controlled the policy and the finances of the LUT.

The unexpected death of Charles Tyson Yerkes on 29 December 1905 resulted in the appointment on 3 January 1906 of Edgar Speyer as Chairman of the UERL board. From this date, Speyer became more directly concerned in the affairs of the LUT, becoming responsible for placing a restraining hand on many of the expansion schemes of Clifton Robinson. One instance of this change came in 1906 when the remuneration of Robinson as Engineer was reviewed. This had been based upon a percentage commission on all expenditure incurred in the promotion, construction and equipment of the tramways, which involved considerable sums. The LUT directors proposed changes which would lead to a fixed salary being paid, covering his twin posts as Managing Director and Engineer, and would result in a considerable reduction in what he received. Both sides took the opinion of Counsel, the resulting settlement giving Robinson a cash payment in respect of recently completed work and a future fixed salary of £2,000 per annum.

Edgar Speyer continued as Chairman of the UERL throughout the period prior to the Great War, which included the acquisition of the Central London and the City & South London Railway companies on 1 January 1913. The formation of the London & Suburban Traction Company Ltd. at the end of 1912, brought together the three company-owned London tramway systems in a holding company, in which the UERL maintained a controlling interest, but in which the Electric Tramways Traction Co. shared through their holdings in the Metropolitan Electric Tramways and the South Metropolitan Electric Tramways & Lighting companies.

The outbreak of war in 1914 had an adverse effect on the positon of Speyer.

Despite his high standing in the banking world and in official cirlces, his German origin attracted criticism. In May 1915 he resigned his chairmanship of the UERL and was replaced by Lord George Hamilton. He had been awarded a baronetcy in 1906 and became a Privy Councillor, but asked the Prime Minister, H.H. Asquith for permission to relinquish both. Asquith told him that King George V declined to agree to this and dismissed allegations against him as unfounded and malicious. However, sections of the press resumed their attacks later in the year, and Sir Edgar Speyer left the country to join his brother in New York.

Speyer was a supporter of many philanthropic causes; he was President of Poplar Hospital and a member of the King Edward Hospital Fund, as well as being a co-founder of the Whitechapel Art Gallery. He died in Berlin on 16 February 1932.

Albert Henry Stanley, Lord Ashfield

Albert Henry Stanley was born on 8 August 1874 at Normanton, Derbyshire, the son of Henry and Elizabeth Knattries. When Albert was still a child, the family emigrated to Detroit, U.S.A., where his father was to take up an appointment with the Pullman car works, and it was then that the family name was changed to Stanley.

After an education at Detroit High School, he decided to find work in the transport industry, and got a job as stable lad with the Detroit City Street Railways, gradually rising through the ranks of the company to eventually become its General Superintendent. He left Detroit in 1903 to take up a post as Assistant General Manager of the Street Railway Department of the Public Service Corporation of New Jersey. By January 1907 he was the Corporation General Manager.

Stanley moved back to England in 1907 to assist in protecting the considerable American financial interests held in a number of the London electric railways, including an involvement in the Underground Electric Railways Company of London Ltd., in which undertaking he was soon to become a Director and, in 1910, Managing Director.

Subsequent to the resignation of James Clifton Robinson, he was to become deeply involved in the affairs of the London United Tramways, becoming its Managing Director, a post he held in addition to his other responsibilities until 1912. Between 1911 and 1913 Stanley, together with Edgar Speyer, brought about the merger between the UERL, LGOC (and with it the Associated Equipment Company), MET, LUT and SMET.

The year 1914 was to see Albert Stanley receive a knighthood "in recognition of his services to London's passenger transport". This was followed in December 1916 by his movement into politics, when he became the M.P. for Ashton-under-Lyne and also President of the Board of Trade.

He relinquished his political duties in 1919, and immediately once again became involved in the affairs of London's public transport by accepting the position of Chairman and Managing Director of most of the "combine" companies. He was raised to the peerage in 1920 with the title The Right Hon. Sir Albert Henry Stanley, Baron Ashfield of Southwell in Nottinghamshire.

During the nineteen-twenties he was publicly stating his beliefs that a unified public transport plan for London was desirable. This came about on 1 July 1933, when the London Passenger Transport Board was formed. Ashfield became its Chairman, remaining in that post until his retirement on 1 October 1947. With the replacement of the Board by the London Transport Executive at the end of that year, he was appointed a founder member of the British Transport Commission which followed, but only remained in office for a short time. Lord Ashfield, Baron of Southwell in Nottinghamshire, passed away on 4 November 1948, aged 74 years.

Charles Tyson Yerkes

Charles Tyson Yerkes was born in Philadelphia on 25 June 1837. He was employed at first in the grain commission trade and later entered the field of banking, a venture which failed in 1871. Later he started street tramways in Philadelphia and Chicago, where he made a fortune, out of which he presented what was then described as the finest astronomical telescope in the world to the observatory at Lake Geneva, Wisconsin, which was named the Yerkes Observatory in his honour.

Yerkes perceived the need for improved passenger transport facilities in London, and visited the capital in 1895 to assess the scope for a network of underground electric railways. In March 1901 he gained control of the Metropolitan District Railway Company, and in July formed the Metropolitan District Electric Traction Company, and acquired a number of companies which had secured powers to build and operate this type of railway. He was present at the ceremonial inauguration of the London United Tramways system on 10 July 1901.

On 9 April 1902, Yerkes formed the Underground Electric Railways Company of London Ltd., which had an authorised capital of £5 million, and of which he became Chairman. Speyer Brothers agreed to raise this sum on behalf of the new company, which in turn was to acquire the recently-formed Metropolitan District Electric Traction Co. Ltd., together with other companies, and also to construct power stations and supply current to electric railways. The purpose for which the MDET Co. had been formed was to electrify the Metropolitan District Railway.

The rash of tube railway promotions in 1901 and 1902 included the joint LUT and J.P. Morgan & Co. scheme for such a railway between Hammersmith, the City of London and north-east London suburbs. This did not succeed, causing a rift between the two partners, resulting in the eventual election of Yerkes as a Director of the LUT on 19 March 1903. On the same day he was also appointed Chairman of the Company. Just over two years later, on 2 August 1905, he resigned his position as Chairman, explaining that he wished to devote his energies to the development of the tube railways. However, his health was failing and, during a visit to New York in November 1905 he fell ill and died there on 29 December 1905. His place as Chairman of the UERL was taken, on 3 January 1906 by Sir Edgar Speyer.